42
51
65
71
73
86

g/t disorder
hallucin

#5 pg 48

LIFE HISTORY RESEARCH IN *Psychopathology*

Life History Research in Psychopathology

MERRILL ROFF AND DAVID F. RICKS, EDITORS

The University of Minnesota Press, Minneapolis

Printed in the United States of America at the Lund Press, Minneapolis. Published in Great Britain, India, and Pakistan by the Oxford University Press, London, Bombay, and Karachi, and in Canada by the Copp Clark Publishing Co. Limited, Toronto

Library of Congress Catalog Card Number: 77-98098

Preface

LIFE histories fascinate everyone, from the most trivial village gossip to the most profound novelist or historian. To the student of psychopathology, whose task is to understand warped or distorted lives, no kind of information is so important as that contained in personal histories. Every human life is influenced by a complex of genetic, familial, and community factors. Awareness of all of these creates in students of human lives an open attitude toward all sources of information, and a healthy awareness of the limits of all specialized perspectives. And since every person is characterized not just by the influences that impinge on him, but by how he integrates them in his own thoughts, feelings, and behavior, the study of lives also creates respect for the ingenuity people show in maintenance of their life styles and integrity.

The lives focused on in this book included some period of psychopathology varying in different people from short periods of disturbance to chronic existence in the back wards of mental hospitals. Since adult patterns of disturbance differ enough to lead to some useful diagnostic terms, some of the following studies group together sets of people who have adult diagnoses in common and study how they developed those life patterns. Other studies begin with groups who have a high risk for one or another type of disorder and follow that group into adult life to see if the factors leading to disturbance can be teased out by contrast of those who break down with those who do not. A persistent theme running through the book is comparison of life patterns – between schizophrenic patients and their genetically identical twins who are not schizophrenic; between adolescents who "break down" into mental illness and carefully matched adolescents who do not; between the early IQ and school achievement patterns of schizophrenics, their brothers and sisters, and their neighborhood peers; and so on. Such comparisons sharpen observational and diagnostic skill, showing which types of early disturbance are relatively benign, which are general precursors of several kinds of psychopathology, and which are related to particular disorders.

The book is an outgrowth of two invitational conferences on life histories leading to psychopathology, and the reader we had in mind when preparing it is the kind of person who attended the conferences. Life history research is scientifically ecumenical—such a reader might be a biologist, a sociologist, a geneticist, a psychiatrist, a psychologist, a statistician, or a research administrator. We had all of these at our conferences, since all offered useful perspectives on life histories, and all had data that the others could ignore only at the peril of scotomic vision. The papers are written as broad overviews of the major current studies of psychopathological development, with technical detail and in-house jargon kept to a minimum. They can be understood by advanced undergraduates in psychology and related disciplines, by medical students, and by graduate students in all of the fields mentioned above. Each writer knew that he was reporting his work to people outside his field as well as to specialists within it, so that the book offers an overview of several approaches to psychopathology in language that does not require specialized training in each field in order to be understood. Edited and shortened versions of the discussions following each paper are included, so that the reader can compare his own questions with those of other investigators, and perhaps get some answers to them. In a sense, as he reads the papers and then the discussions, he becomes a participant in the conferences, and in the general quest to understand warped or underdeveloped lives.

Since the papers were oriented to generalizations about sets of people, they contain little of the basic stuff, the raw data, of life history research. The student interested in further investigation of the materials on which these reports are based should consider reading both autobiographical reports of mental illness, several of which are available, and case materials gathered at various times in the lives of disturbed persons. One book that may prove helpful is already available (Roff, Mink, & Hinrichs, 1966). The reader interested in the more technical details of individual studies can find numerous guides to further work in the chapter bibliographies.

The many clinics, child guidance centers, schools, and hospitals that provided data for these studies deserve special thanks for allowing curious researchers to intrude into their busy days. Without their help, and without the facilities of modern computer centers, these large, complex studies could not have been done. We hope that we have been able to feed back to people entrusted with the lives of children enough new information to show them that their patience can be rewarded.

Almost all the chapters come from research programs, and are not isolated studies. These have received support from various agencies, and detailed acknowledgments are made in the individual chapters. However, it may be noted here that almost every research program discussed in this book received at least part of its support from the National Institute of Mental Health, for at least part of its duration.

We are indebted to Teachers College, Columbia University, and to the Institute of Child Development, University of Minnesota, for sponsoring and supporting the two conferences on which the book is based. The University of Minnesota Press edited the papers with tact and intelligence. Of the many people who labored to help with the original papers, we would like to mention especially Miss Catherine Day, Mrs. Mary Golden, Miss Roberta Plybon, and Miss Barbara Thompson.

M. R.
D. F. R.

Table of Contents

LIFE HISTORY RESEARCH IN *Psychopathology*

MERRILL ROFF

Introduction

PERSONALITY theory in general, and theory concerning personality deviations in particular, have always recognized the importance of childhood as a formative period for subsequent personality development. It is much easier to theorize about the impact of events occurring at various age periods on subsequent personality than it is to obtain firm, factual information in this area.

One kind of attempt to get information here consists in asking the person himself or his family about the earlier events in his life. This method has been used particularly with individuals who are under treatment for one kind of adult maladjustment or another. This provides retrospective information which may be relatively accurate on some points and highly inaccurate, biased, or distorted on others. Until we get follow-up information which makes use of information about behavior recorded at the time it was occurring rather than twenty or thirty years later, it is not possible even to assess the amount of inaccuracy and distortion contained in retrospective information.

With the passage of time it has become possible to obtain follow-up information at the adult level for persons who were studied intensively in child guidance clinics and schools many years ago. This means that we can gradually supplant the inferior retrospective studies of childhoods of adults with known outcomes with more adequate information obtained and recorded during childhood *when the behavior was occurring* and *before the adult outcome was known*. This gives life histories which are more soundly based than the retrospective accounts on which so much dependence has been placed, for want of better. The present book attempts to give an up-to-the-minute picture of the status of these life history studies of adult psychopathology.

The first of all large-scale follow-up studies from childhood into adult life was the Terman follow-up of gifted children in California. Using the then relatively new intelligence tests as measuring devices, Terman was able to select a large sample of highly intelligent children from a larger population in the schools. He made follow-up studies from time to time at intervals of several years until his subjects reached full maturity. This research program is one of the classical landmarks of psychology.

In spite of efforts starting as much as fifty years ago, no one has succeeded in developing any psychometric measure in the so-called personality field which has had the effectiveness and public acceptance of intelligence tests. In many places the IQ has become embedded in the laws of the state in defining degrees of mental retardation and the disposition and treatment of individuals so classified. To the best of our knowledge, no psychometric instrument in the personality field has received such acceptance. Although the Minnesota Multiphasic Personality Inventory, to take one of the most successful instruments in this field, can give much valuable information, it has not yet reached a point where the law says that a person with such and such score or set of scores or profiles shall be disposed of in this way or that on the basis of this information alone.

This has suggested to some of us that we should be willing to depart from the conventional psychometric frame of reference in order to see what use can be made of qualitative case history information on a long-time, predictive basis. The use of case histories which were obtained, let us say, thirty years ago, permits a study of the antecedents of adult maladjustment. Those for whom case histories are made were, in general, those with childhood problems, commonly with family situations somewhat more adverse than the average. Normal, ordinary, non-problem children have never had childhood case histories of a clinical sort prepared for them, as have problem children. In addition to reasons of cost, the ordinary family is not motivated to undergo an investigation of itself simply for the sake of scientific investigation. There have been, however, childhood case histories carefully constructed on thousands and thousands of children with problems, in all parts of the country. Some of these have been — and are being — studied to get information about the childhood of subjects who are later psychotic or neurotic or have adult personality disorders, or who turn out all right. By using information recorded at the time the childhood behavior was taking place, and while the family, school personnel, and so forth were willing and able to give the best descriptions they could of what the child was like at that time, and what his general life situation seemed to be, it is possible to get prospective information about any type of adult maladjustment which occurs with sufficient frequency to generate a sample. As a result of the efforts of a number of persons, many of whom are among the contributors to this book, it is beginning to be possible to get factual information about the childhood characteristics of individuals with various adult maladjustments, which will, in time, take the place of less dependable retrospective information. The present book consists primarily of papers presented at two conferences on life history research in psychopathology.

The original nucleus of the conferences consisted of the editors, who had become acquainted because of the similarity of our lines of research. Following an initial suggestion that we put on a program at the American Psychological Association it was decided that it would be preferable to have a conference, including other interested persons, at a time and place calmer and less crowded than an APA convention. A one-day conference was held at Columbia University in May 1967. This seemed very stimulating to those involved, and plans were made then for a second, two-day conference at the University of Minnesota in April 1968. *

It was decided that the conference papers would be published as a book. There is a powerful advantage in having these materials published under one cover rather than having them dispersed throughout the psychological and psychiatric literature. This permits a comparison of the findings of different investigators working sometimes in markedly different situations. Besides the papers presented, the discussions which followed them are also included. Those give a picture of the reaction of other competent persons, both contributors and others attending, to the paper which had just been presented. When you are reading an article in your own immediate field of specialization, it is not difficult to evaluate it as to the competence with which it has been done, whether or not it had any new ideas, and whether it is a distinctive as opposed to a routine contribution. Once you get even a short distance away from your own area of knowledge, it becomes increasingly difficult to tell even whether an article contains anything that is not already generally known to other similar workers. The discussions included here sometimes contain expressions of vigorous differences of opinion, and we think that these are very healthy. They also give some indication to those not working in this particular field of the reactions of an informed audience to the information presented in a given paper.

Occasionally, members of a conference may share certain presuppo-

* These conferences were made possible through the assistance of Teachers College, Columbia University, and the Institute of Child Development at the University of Minnesota, respectively.

sitions which others might challenge. One example of this is the use of the concept of "minimal brain damage," which was implicitly accepted by several of those conferring. A subsequent reader of the manuscript has questioned the consensus apparent on this point by arguing that there are other competent persons who would dissent vigorously. Discussions such as these obviously cannot give complete representation to all points of view.

We attempted to get papers from all the main workers in life history research in psychopathology with whom we were familiar, and were almost completely successful. In addition, we wanted to include representatives of several major trends in psychopathology research which are relevant to the problems of life history research. Among these are psychopharmacological work, the computerization of case history materials, and the statistical (often factor analytic) study of the classification of symptoms and disorders.

Some comments about the participants and their work will give more information about present authors than is contained in the listing of their institutional affiliations. These will be described in the order in which their chapters appear in the book.

MERRILL ROFF has, for the past fifteen years, been studying the relations between childhood and adolescent histories of child guidance clinic patients and juvenile delinquents, and adult outcomes as indicated by records of the same individuals in the military services and related organizations. He has studied factors operating during childhood for adult groups of various kinds. He has given particular attention to childhood peer adjustments, which have been proved to be predictive of adult maladjustments of various kinds. In partnership with Dr. S. B. Sells, he has recently carried out a large-scale study of peer relations in relation to adjustment, during the grade school and immediately subsequent periods. He has also been working on the family characteristics of different adult outcome groups. Outcome groups for which studies of childhood information have been reported up to this time include neurotics, psychotics, character disorders with severe bad conduct, homosexuals, and schizoid personalities.

DAVID RICKS has been working for a number of years on a follow-up study of childhood and adolescent cases from the Judge Baker Guidance Center, using information from Massachusetts state records as adult criteria. He and other members of that project have been oriented primarily, but not exclusively, toward pre-schizophrenic personality and family characteristics. Starting with an initial sample of around 15,000 individuals who had been seen at the Judge Baker Guidance Center since it opened in 1917, they found about 200 who had been hospitalized and diagnosed schizophrenic. A little more than half of these had been released and were back in the community, and a little less than half were still hospitalized. A comparison of 15,000 with 200 gives a vivid picture of the initial sample size necessary to obtain samples of adequate size among the low-incidence maladjustments in which we are interested. JOHN BERRY worked on this project for several years and recently received his doctor's degree based partly on work done there.

SARNOFF MEDNICK and FINI SCHULSINGER are deeply engaged in a major study of "factors related to breakdown in children at high risk for schizophrenia – that is, children whose mothers had been diagnosed as schizophrenic." Because the record-keeping system in Denmark is markedly superior to anything available in this country and is probably as good as that of any country in the world, it is centered there.

JAMES STABENAU and WILLIAM POLLIN have made very intensive studies of identical twins who are discordant for schizophrenia at the Section on Twin and Sibling Studies of the National Institute of Mental Health. They have been able to study in addition to the index case, the father, mother, and non-schizophrenic individual twin for fourteen pairs of monozygotic twins up to this time. The fact that the twins have been carefully diagnosed as identical, and that this has been, of course, a lifelong condition, gives a mixture of prospective and retrospective information in their study which promises to produce most interesting results.

BERNICE EIDUSON and DIANE RAMSEY of the Reiss-Davis Child Guidance Clinic in Los Angeles have developed what is perhaps the most advanced system available yet for the computer analysis of case history information. Their procedure is called the Psychiatric Case History Events System (PsyCHES). The effective use of computers will have a marked and increasing influence on future life history research, and it was considered very important to include an explicit discussion of this problem.

MAURICE LORR of Catholic University was for many years with the Veterans Administration (VA), and his co-author, JAMES KLETT, is still there. Over a number of years they have described syndromes of psychotic behavior, and developed the Inpatient Multidimensional Psychiatric Scale (IMPS), using VA samples. The present paper presents results from a large-scale, cross-cultural study of acute psychotics in six countries (England, France, Germany, Italy, Japan, and Sweden) and is concerned primarily with the life history characteristics of this cross-cultural sample. As the world becomes increasingly international in character, cross-cultural research in psychopathology will become increasingly important, and may change some of our fundamental ideas. They are concerned primarily with the life history characteristics of their cross-cultural sample.

SOLOMON GOLDBERG is engaged in psychopharmacology, an area we very much wanted to have represented. We were happy to find that Dr. Goldberg was interested not only in psychopharmacology, but also in life history research, since the reaction of psychiatric patients to drug treatment varied enough from one patient to another to lead to a study of the relationship between life history factors and differences in responses to drugs among different schizophrenics. Some results along this line are presented in his chapter.

STARKE HATHAWAY, the senior author of the very widely used MMPI, administered this instrument to over 15,000 Minnesota ninth-graders over the period 1947–1954. The years since then have afforded unique opportunities for follow-up studies of various kinds. One important set of studies concerns individuals who became delinquents. The present paper deals with a recent follow-up of individuals who were high on Scale 8 (schizophrenia) at the time of the original testing. Throughout these studies, ELIO MONACHESI has been co-investigator and co-author of the studies that have evolved. He has been particularly interested in the studies of delinquency. SUSAN SALASIN has been a research fellow on the work described here.

ELLEN LANE and GEORGE ALBEE have collaborated in a series of studies of the relations between IQ's obtained during childhood and schizophrenia in the adult period. Intelligence tests given to individuals after schizophrenia has been diagnosed do not tell what their IQ's might have been at earlier times in their lives. It is impossible with contemporary test data alone to decide whether the onset of schizophrenia brings a decline in IQ or whether, on the other hand, a lower IQ in childhood is associated with adult schizophrenia without a marked decline following the onset of the disease. The availability of a large number of stored tests and test scores in Cleveland made possible their set of studies of the relationship between childhood IQ and adult schizophrenia.

MAX POLLACK and his associates for several years have been studying the earlier life of adult schizophrenics and of other patients with non-schizophrenic diagnoses. The patients have been compared with the closest-in-age siblings, making as much use as possible of information such as birth and school records which are recorded at the time of the event and thus are free of retrospective distortion. Information obtained in this way included childhood personality and behavior ratings, attendance records, special problems, school achievement, and intelligence test results. The paper gives an explicit comparison of some of their findings on childhood IQ with those of Lane and Albee.

LEE ROBINS has already described in her book, *Deviant Children Grown Up* (1966), a follow-up study of persons under nineteen years of age at first referral who had been patients at the St. Louis Municipal Psychiatric Clinic between 1924 and 1929. Follow-up was made by interviewing the subjects some thirty years later. In her present paper she describes a subsequent study of a sample of Negro boys, the earlier information for which was obtained from school records. These boys were born between 1930 and 1934 and were also followed up about thirty years later. These were not clinic cases, but were studied as a group with more problems than would be found in a random sample of the entire population.

PATRICIA FLEMING was also associated with David Ricks in the Judge Baker Schizophrenia Research Project. Her present paper with Ricks is based, in part, on her doctoral thesis and in part on other work. In contrast to the more "objective" demographic variables and test scores which have been discussed in some of the other chapters, she has examined intensively the feelings and emotional experiences of pre-schizophrenic youngsters as reported by the guidance center therapy workers and has related these to later psychiatric outcome.

Since most of these papers were originally presented at a conference, there was some opportunity for discussion following different papers. These discussions, included with the papers, involved not only the contributors, but also others attending the conference. It may be noted that in addition to occasional challenge and dissent, there are also expressions of interest, and sometimes surprise, as one worker learned that a second worker had obtained results similar to his own, often under quite different circumstances. The opportunity to compare both the agreements and disagreements between different research programs is given by the presentation of these papers, with discussion, in one book in a way that would be completely impossible if the papers could only be found by a total search of the research literature.

MERRILL ROFF

Some Problems in Life History Research

WHY is it necessary to have life history research in psychopathology, which places emphasis on *prospective* rather than *retrospective* information? Retrospective information is widely used, and interpreted with cheerful dogmatism by persons attached to a variety of different dogmas. Prospective research, which involves getting information recorded during childhood and following the same people forward, is difficult and not without its own methodological problems. It has enough built-in safeguards, however, to avoid some of the excesses committed in the name of retrospective information, and particularly that obtained under psychoanalytic influences.

In a recent textbook, a case was described in which a man of forty or so was under analysis for a variety of symptoms. In the course of the treatment, it was discovered that when he was an infant, his mother had made the most unfortunate mistake of giving him candy while he was sitting on his potty in the course of toilet training, thus confusing the oral and the anal, and leaving the poor boy mixed up for life. In the last several years, I have read a very large number of child guidance clinic cases, and in none of these that I can remember did the clinician *ever* try to find out from either the child or his mother whether or not this particular mistake in upbringing had been committed. Our data thus do not contain the information necessary to test this hypothesis — but as you may have gathered by this time, I do not think it is a very good hypothesis to begin with. Some of my research assistants who are ex-babysitters assure me that this administration of candy is a common practice; it tends to keep the infant quiet. An unscientifically selected sample of mothers with whom I am acquainted has confirmed this.

If this is indeed a widespread practice, it would not seem likely to be the critical factor in cases such as that just described. Too many other persons have had the same treatment without being psychologically crippled by it.

If it be objected that this is a secondary source, and perhaps a misuse of the Freudian theoretical apparatus, let us take a look at a retrospective study reported by Freud (1919) himself in "The History of an Infantile Neurosis," which was written between 1914 and 1918. The patient was first seen as an adult, when he was a hospitalized psychotic "classified in the most authoritative quarters as a case of 'manic depressive insanity.'" The case shows a severe neurotic disturbance which began before his fourth birthday as an anxiety hysteria, then changed into an obsessional neurosis with a religious content which lasted into his tenth year. This was analyzed not while it actually existed, but fifteen years after its termination.

"His parents had been married young but his father had already suffered from his first attacks of depression which led to his absence from home. His mother began to suffer from abdominal disorders. As a consequence, she had relatively little to do with the children." (p. 13)

"He had a sister about two years his elder. . . . In her early twenties, she began to be depressed, complained that she was not good looking enough, and withdrew from all society. . . . While on a journey she poisoned herself and died while away from home. Her disorder is probably to be regarded as the beginning of a dementia praecox." (p. 21)

In the beginning, "he was looked after by a nurse, an uneducated old woman of peasant birth with an untiring affection for him." (p. 14)

"Then an English governess was engaged who became responsible for the children. . . . She turned out to be an eccentric and quarrelsome person, and, moreover, to be addicted to drink." (p. 15) This English governess quarreled repeatedly and bitterly with the earlier nurse. The little boy had openly taken the side of his beloved nurse.

In spite of what may seem a somewhat adverse home and family situation, he was, according to the retrospective report, getting along fine at least until he was three years old. Then when his parents came back from their summer holiday, "he had become discontented, irritable, and violent, he took offense at every possible occasion, and then flew into a rage and screamed like a savage" (p. 15). It seemed to the parents that the quarrelsome governess who drank might have something to do with this, so she was sent on her way. This did not help things. Only in the course of the analysis (when he was a hospitalized adult) did the true explanation come to light; on two occasions, before he was four years old, his sister (two years older) had seduced him into sexual practices. On the first occasion, they had shown each other their bottoms. On a second occasion, his sister had taken hold of his member and played with it. Following this episode before his fourth birthday, his life was affected by a variety of maladjustments lasting throughout his adult life.

I would like to suggest that anyone who is accustomed to working with childhood case histories would give more weight to the total set of home and family characteristics than to the two childish episodes, in predicting the development of later severe behavior disturbances. In other words, if the other circumstances in the history were all favorable, we would tend to dismiss such episodes as being unlikely to have any lasting effect.

Clearly, prospective studies are needed in which information, recorded at the time the events were taking place, is compared with criterion information at some later period. In practice, what this means is that most of us here are working with earlier information which was obtained by someone else, and that our diagnoses at the later period are also normally, though not always, obtained from records made by someone else. This is a disadvantage since both the earlier and the later information may lack items which we would like very much to have. On the other hand, the cost of obtaining completely ideal information (assuming that we could agree on what this would be) for the sample sizes with which we commonly work would be clearly prohibitive purely as a research venture. Let us consider possible alternatives.

In the classical longitudinal studies, the samples have commonly been small. Three of the best known of these are the California Adolescent Growth Study, the Fels Research Institute's Longitudinal Study, and the Berkeley Guidance Study initiated by Jean Macfarlane (1938). Mary Cover Jones (1957) has described the later careers of boys from the California Adolescent Study who were early- or late-maturing. When this sample was at an average age of thirty-three years, the total group numbered 43 men. Kagan and Moss (1962) have presented information concerning the Fels group when the subjects for whom childhood information was available were between 19 and 29 years of age. Of 89 subjects for whom childhood information was available, 71 (about equally divided between males and females) participated in an adult assessment. Wanda Bronson (1969) has studied as adults persons who had participated in the Berkeley Guidance Study. From an originally larger group of predominantly middle-class backgrounds, those cases were selected for whom information was relatively complete from the ages of 21 months through 16 years. This gave an adult group of 45 males and 40 females. Insofar as any of these studies had a sample that was at all representative of the general population of its area, there would be difficulty in finding more than a single psychotic, or psychoneurotic, or penitentiary inmate, or homosexual, or other severe behavior disturbance.

A LARGE-SCALE LONGITUDINAL STUDY

Some of the problems which would be encountered if an attempt were made to start at the beginning of life, with a sample large enough to promise groups of adequate size for various behavior disturbances at the adult level, can be indicated by considering one current project of this general nature. A very large-scale project, the Collaborative Perinatal Research Project, which started with expectant mothers and is explicitly prospective, has dealt with some 50,000 infants in about fourteen collaborating institutions in various parts of the country. The information presented here has been obtained from a project report (National Institute of Neurological Diseases and Blindness, 1963) and from project personnel in Minnesota. "The purpose of the Collaborative Project is to investigate the relationships between pregnancy and pregnancy outcome." Many facets of pregnancy and birth were studied in great detail, and I am not competent to evaluate the medical significance of the results obtained.

The plan of the behavioral study included periodic examinations (pediatric, psychological, neurological, and speech and hearing) through the age of four years with "a final detailed examination at seven years by members of the disciplines of neurology, pediatrics, psychology, speech pathology and audiology." To one who is interested in life history research, the age of seven seems a little early to end a longitudinal study, and I believe that some further follow-up is being made.

In general, this study has limited itself to intelligence and motor and sensory performance. Considerations of personality development seem to have been largely disregarded, with the possible exception of the later effects of minimal brain damage "which may be expressed in school performance and as reading and writing disorders."

One point which should be emphasized is the kind of sampling involved in getting the 50,000 infants in collaborating institutions. In Minnesota, these consisted of expectant mothers who were seen at the University Hospital. These are in no sense anything approaching a census sample. Any bias resulting from this method of selection may not have been of particular obstetric importance, but it means that this sample may not be much more psychologically representative of the general population than some of our child guidance clinic samples.

This study originated under obstetric auspices, and it may have been completely successful in getting the information sought by those planning it. From a psychological point of view, it seems unfortunate that so little attention was paid to the psychological characteristics of the mother or to mother-child interactions following birth. We do not, of course, have methods of describing the personality of a mother and her interactions with a child which are as well standardized as the Stanford-Binet. It is possible that our life history research may contribute to development in this area by giving more and better information than is now available concerning the relative importance, on a lifetime basis, of different aspects of maternal personality and of mother-child interaction. This whole project indicates some of the administrative and other difficulties which might be expected to occur in any project operating on such a scale from the time of pregnancy onward. It is relatively easy to conceptualize a vast project which would begin at, or before, birth and would follow the entire group throughout their lives. In view of the practical difficulties involved in such a program, it is imperative that we get all the life history information that we can, in ways that can actually be done.

CASE HISTORIES AS PSYCHOLOGICAL DATA

All of us who have worked with case history materials are aware of their inadequacies – the facts that sometimes the father is not seen, so that our only picture of him is that which is filtered through the mother; that any of our information of an interpretive sort was potentially biased by the interpreter; and so forth. It is not necessary to list all the ways in which we could wish that our early data were better than they are.

In reply, I would like to refer to the *Handbook of Projective Techniques*, a book of readings edited by B. I. Murstein (1965). The areas covered are projective tests in general, and the Rorschach, Thematic Apperception Test, Draw-a-Person Test, Bender-Gestalt, and the Sentence Completion Test in particular. In general, there is very commendable concern about the validity of projective tests on a concurrent basis; almost no attention is given to longitudinal studies. Some of the comments in the articles are quite critical. K. B. Little observes that "After this preamble, it is somewhat embarrassing to have to say that the published evidence on projective techniques indicates that they have either zero or, at best, very low positive effective validity indexes."

To those who are familiar with the logic of multivariate work, particularly with multiple correlation procedures, the question immediately arises as to the contribution any of these variables would make in addition to other available information. A study which bears directly on this point is one by H. Peskin, "Unity of Science Begins at Home: A Study of Regional Factionalism in Clinical Psychology," which appeared originally in the *American Psychologist* (1963, 18, 96–100). The editor's abstract (Murstein, 1965) may be used to indicate the content and some of the implications of this article.

This unusual article consists largely of a replication of an earlier study by Kostlan. In the present study, the relative validity of several sources of psychodiagnostic information (case history, Rorschach, MMPI, SCT) was tested using psychiatric out-patients, the basis of validation consisting of statements taken from psychology reports. The method was to pool all information obtained, with the exception of the particular source to be validated. Therapists' reports of the patient served as a criterion.

In Kostlan's study, the case history was the most potent source of accurate prediction. The MMPI, but neither the Rorschach nor SCT, improved prediction significantly when added to the case history. In Peskin's study, similar results were found, except that any *two* tests added to the case history improved prediction over the case history alone.

The article had as a main purpose the comparison of psychologists trained on the East coast and on the Pacific coast. For our purposes the important finding is that "Clinicians so reared apart reveal a common bond in what they require as a necessary condition for valid diagnosis: the availability of the historical and actuarial information that comprise the standard case history." As the editor points out, "Another problem that needs to be considered was the relatively small reduction in errors when the tests were added to the case history as compared with the use of the case history alone." It is of interest to point to the central position of the "standard case history" when combined with some of the best-known and most widely used sources of "psychodiagnostic" information. Such studies would seem to indicate clearly that we are working with the basic data in this area when we use case histories, and that the projective devices so dear to many clinicians can quite properly be disregarded for the time being.

The predictions based on case histories which were just described were global, based on the entire case history. It is highly desirable to work more analytically, in order to evaluate the long-time predictive significance of different variables and combinations of variables. It seems increasingly possible that valuable assistance can be obtained here from computer procedures. However, the problem of coding information still requires the psychological insight of a trained worker, if we are to manipulate more than such already codified data as age, birth order, and IQ. This is a frontier area at the present time.

HYPOTHETICO-DEDUCTIVE ACTIVITY AND LIFE HISTORY RESEARCH

Life history research is able to obtain childhood information, prospective with respect to adult adjustment status, on a scale that has not been reached before. Obtaining the basic data, and observing the complex interrelationships between sets of earlier and later information, is a process for which we do not have the kind of detailed theories that are common in short-time studies, particularly experimental ones, in areas which have been pushed beyond the point of diminishing returns as far as the production of significantly new information is concerned. The use of elaborate hypothetico-deductive procedures in areas which were long ago explored for the first time may have various advantages. Not the least of these is that by a slight change in terminology or in method it becomes permissible to ignore earlier work on the same problem. This practice permits a continuing generation of apparently novel ideas by a mere shift of labels.

Occasionally, persons who are accustomed to the complexities inevitable in life history studies apologize because they have merely obtained new (and interesting) information, without going through the supposedly essential steps of formal hypothesis-formation and hypothesis-testing. On the other hand, sometimes clinicians with a little learning, but not much relevant research experience, may criticize life history work because it does not have elaborate theories which are accepted or rejected at the .05 level. We do obtain new information, and we have an opportunity, given time, to replace fanciful and speculative theories with carefully observed and replicated data which can grow into an organized body of knowledge, without being prematurely forced into some arbitrary kind of theory which someone would like to impose from outside.

It would be presumptuous to attempt to say how all psychological research *should* be carried out. However, there is in the literature a description of the actual process of research which was prepared a few years ago by a committee of the American Psychological Association and published in the *American Psychologist*. This was contained in the article "Education for Research in Psychology" (Garner, Hunt, Taylor, et al., 1959); it indicates quite clearly that the methods of studying data which we use in our work are ones which are really used in productive research throughout psychology. Since this description seems to be generally unknown to psychologists, although it was prepared by some very able research people, I would like to quote from it rather extensively. I think it is a very important statement.

How Research Gets Done

Over the years a stereotype has developed in the scientific as well as in the public mind as to what constitutes serious psychological research and scientific proof. Crucial experiments growing out of previous findings, elaborated by self-conscious and prescient genius, are performed with great precision. The results are subjected to the closest scrutiny, with all alternative interpretations judiciously considered and accepted or rejected in accordance with the most explicit canons of scientific rigor. Finally, the now confirmed discovery is inserted in a systematized lattice of already available knowledge to complete for posterity a forward step, however small, toward man's mastery of the unknown. Commonly, these developments are seen as accomplished only with the aid of extensive intellectual paraphernalia of confirmation that include logic, theory, broad and scholarly knowledge, technical proficiency in mathematics and statistics, and a self-conscious awareness of one's place and role in the larger scheme of things, as given by the history and philosophy of science.

Make no mistake about it, however, this stereotype in name is a stereotype in fact, with all the oversimplification, misemphasis, and error which stereotypes involve. . . .

Our discussions have led to the conclusion that the confirmatory activities described by the stereotype constitute but a small part of the process of active research, and that mostly in the terminal phases. While indeed this model may be reasonably accurate in describing such terminal phases and also useful in communicating clearly the results of research to others, it does not represent well the activities of the individual scientist. The task of the research psychologist is not mainly that of designing a study, collecting data, analyzing the results, and drawing conclusions. This, perhaps, is the formal picture which many people have of the research process; but, if there was general agreement about anything in the group, there was agreement that this is not the essence of doing research — this is not what makes the difference between run-of-the-mill and significant work.

Actually, the process of doing research — that is, of creating and building a science of psychology — is a rather informal, often illogical and sometimes messy-looking affair. It includes a great deal of floundering around in the empirical world, sometimes dignified by names like "pilot studies" and "exploratory research." Somewhere and somehow in the process of floundering, the research worker will get an idea. In fact, he will get many ideas. On largely intuitive grounds he will reject most of his ideas and will accept others as the basis of extended work. To make the picture even less amenable to rational understanding, the ideas he accepts and cherishes and in which he invests his time and resources will sometimes even fly in the face of "known facts."

If an idea he chooses to accept happens to be a poor one, the researcher will perhaps waste a lot of time. But there is no way of knowing this beforehand. If the idea happens to be a good one, he may make a significant positive contribution to his science – may, because between the idea and the contribution lies a lot of persistence, originality, intuition, and hard work. It is in this sort of activity, rather far removed from the public, more orderly and systematic phases of scientific work, that the productive researcher spends much of his time and effort. Moreover, these activities must come first in time, else there is little new or worthwhile to process with the paraphernalia of confirmation. And, of course, the job is rarely, if ever, finished by doing one experiment and finding a significant difference. Making a contribution to knowledge is a process of continuous work during which ideas change and develop.

CROSS-POPULATION ROBUSTNESS AND SAMPLING PROBLEMS

I would like to bring in at this time the concept of robustness, which was originally developed in analysis of variance work, where rather restrictive assumptions about normality were in force. Since such assumptions are sometimes inconveniently restrictive, studies have been made to find how much it would disturb the whole situation if various amounts and kinds of departure from normality were permitted. There seems to be no single answer to this question; it appears that in some circumstances quite wide departures from the initial assumptions will not disturb things very much, whereas in other circumstances violation of assumptions may introduce more disturbances than can be tolerated.

I would like to extend the concept of robustness from this narrower statistical sense to the broader meaning of "cross-population robustness." This refers to the extent to which we get similar findings on different *populations*, and not merely with random samples drawn from a single population. In our life history work, and for that matter in almost all psychological research, we inevitably work with samples that are not exactly random samples of any predefined universe. Although the textbooks are quite clear on this matter, in practice there is widespread disregard of the fact that the ordinary procedures of statistical inference *permit us to go from a random sample to the population from which the sample was randomly selected.* (Adherence to intellectually proper procedures would be particularly crippling in experimental psychology.) That is, sampling error figures are essentially meaningless as applied to a population quite different from the original one. On the other hand, as a matter of demonstrable fact, we can often corroborate our own findings with samples from drastically different populations. What we need most is not more elaborate techniques of statistical inference, but the replication of findings on a variety of different kinds of populations.

As a concrete example of this, in my own work the number of individuals in the total personality disorder category is much larger than the total number of psychoneurotics. This is in a young adult male group and could conceivably be a reflection of the particular psychiatrists involved. It was thus very interesting to find similar results reported from a very different kind of sample by Koegler, Brill, Epstein, and Jordan (1964). They suggest that with an expansion of adult outpatient treatment facilities, there will be a shift in the type of patients dealt with from a largely psychoneurotic group to a group with character disorders. "In the past . . . there was a tendency to select out from a large group of applicants for psychotherapy those patients who had psychoneurosis, who were psychologically minded and who were interested in receiving insight-producing psychotherapy. The extent of this selection has not been generally known." Working through several clinics in the Los Angeles area, they attempted to increase their research sample of psychoneurotic women. They found that many of the psychoneurotic women were already being seen, and that broadening their sample of women in civilian life increased the number with character disorders without much gain in the number of psychoneurotics. This gives a cross-validation of our experience with military personnel, on a civilian population of the opposite sex. This is an instance of *cross-population robustness,* and it is valuable to know that our results are not limited to samples from a single population, although they may still not generalize to all possible populations.

Other instances can be given of cross-population as distinct from cross-sample validation. Robins (1966) found that what she called "antisocial behavior" in her cases may precede a wide variety of types of deviant behavior in adulthood, and is not specifically predictive of a single kind of adult maladjustment. Our own work indicates that childhood behavior which is antagonizing to peers precedes various types of adult maladjustment; there is thus some agreement that there is less specificity than is sometimes assumed in the relationship between childhood disturbances and particular types of adult outcome. Similarly, the finding by several investigators that the childhood intelligence level of schizophrenic patients may average somewhat below that of siblings corresponds rather roughly with the frequent finding in our own childhood cases of a statement by the mother that the pre-schizophrenic child being seen at the clinic at the age of eight or nine had always been more of a problem than his siblings. This finding, incidentally, is not specific to pre-schizophrenics, but also applies to individuals with other types of adult difficulty. Informal conversation with personnel from Ricks's project in Massachusetts indicated that although there had been some history of homosexuality among their schizophrenics, they found no one whom they would call a career homosexual. It is as if the homosexuality were a part of a general social inadequacy, rather than a primary personality trend leading to schizophrenia. This checks with our experience (Roff, 1963; 1966; Roff, Mink, & Hinrichs, 1966) and gives both parties a little stronger belief that we are on the right track.

On the other hand, it may be that there are real differences in something like symptom patterns, in different cultural groups. Lorr is finding some very interesting examples of this in his cross-cultural study described on pages 147–157. Where differences in population do produce real differences in outcome, it is very stimulating to attempt to find a meaningful explanation of these differences.

PROSPECTIVE AND RETROSPECTIVE RESULTS

Although we emphasize the advantages of prospective over retrospective methods of study, there are differences in the adequacy with which different kinds of information can be obtained retrospectively and in the methods used to obtain it. Two examples of this are Gebhard, Gagnon, Pomeroy, and Christenson (1965) and Bieber et al. (1965). In the study by Gebhard and his associates, adult homosexuals were asked what their peer relations had been like at the ages of ten and eleven. The replies indicated that they seemed to have been all right. Bieber and his associates, who worked more intensively with a group that was not so large, found indications that 60 of 106 homosexuals had been "lone wolves" in childhood as contrasted with 27 of 100 controls who were so characterized. They also report the retrospective finding that 33 of 106 homosexuals as compared to 10 of 100 controls had "play activity before puberty predominantly with girls." These results are closer to our findings in a recent *prospective* study than those of the Gebhard group. Only as we do prospective studies can we evaluate the adequacy of retrospective information.

If we can compare different types of retrospective information, or various methods of getting it, with more accurate prospective information, this could contribute methodological information of considerable usefulness.

A related, but somewhat different, problem is that which arises when a group which is already known to have some disorder is being studied. Thus it may be found that cancer patients are more frequently depressed than are persons not so affected. It is difficult to get an accurate picture of the attitudes held before cancer was present at all, either from the patient or from his family.

A somewhat similar pattern prevails in a well-known set of studies of the families of schizophrenics. The Lidz et al. study *Schizophrenia and the Family* (1965) used as a sample 17 families described as follows: "Only families of unmarried patients between the ages of 15 and 30 were included in the study as the patients and other members of the family had to be available. The diagnosis had to be clear-cut and beyond reasonable dispute." One of the things that they now consider established is "that schizophrenic patients virtually always grow up in seriously disturbed families – as is now apparent to any careful observer." We might add, "to any careful observer of families known to have a schizophrenic member, age 15 or above." To get information about the families of pre-schizophrenic children of grade school age would seem to be methodologically sounder than observing families of older persons for whom clear-cut diagnoses had already been made.

A striking illustration of the difference between "before" and "after" scores is described by Hathaway and Monachesi (1963). A number of persons had reported that the MMPI profiles of unwed mothers differed from appropriate control groups. These were made, of course, after the beginning of pregnancy with its accompanying concerns. Hathaway and Monachesi found that when the ninth-grade scores of a substantial sample of girls who *subsequently* had illegitimate children were examined, they did not differ appreciably from those of their total sample of ninth-grade girls. These results are in no sense contradictory; before and after testing simply produced different results.

REGRESSION LINES OVER TIME

The considerations above are concerned primarily with whether or not the information about childhood with which we are concerned was recorded at the time or was obtained retrospectively. Even if we confine ourselves to information which was recorded during childhood, the question is raised, in several chapters of this book, sometimes casually and sometimes more intensively, whether or not our life history work is properly "longitudinal" or differs from longitudinal work in important respects. The essential problem here is whether we start with a childhood sample of some kind and get all the follow-up information we can about them or whether we start with an adult outcome group and look for information concerning their childhood characteristics.

This situation was analyzed and described definitively by the late John E. Anderson (1946, p. 6) in his chapter "Methods of Child Psychology" in the *Manual of Child Psychology*. Since this was written more than twenty years ago, it is, of course, unknown to more recent generations of psychologists.

> Many generalizations on the effect of home discipline and management upon children are derived from working backward from problem and normal children to descriptions of the home and neighborhoods from which they come. If, however, homes of contrasting disciplinary programs equivalent in other respects were observed for some time and the children's behavior measured, more significant results would be obtained. The fundamental scientific question is not "From what home environments do children who show behavior problems or who are well adjusted come?" but "What types of home environments produce behavior problems or good adjustment?" There are two regression lines, which are not identical. Scientific information is obtained from both, and, lacking the second, we can use the first. It is much more difficult to interpret, however, and, from the point of view of experimental design, less effective, since it goes from an end result in behavior to context rather than from context to behavior.

For those who are not accustomed to thinking in terms of regression (which, incidentally, is currently on a rising trend as psychological fashions shift) the accompanying diagram can be used to illustrate the situation. We can let the vertical axis represent a variable (such as height or intelligence) for which childhood information is available and more or less normally distributed. The same comments would apply if the vertical axis were compressed to two entries, the presence or absence of some trait or behavior. We can let the horizontal axis represent some imagined tendency toward or proneness to schizophrenia at the adult level with the extreme right-hand end of the scale containing those who are formally diagnosed, and the left-hand end representing those with the least possible proneness to schizophrenia (if such a group can be imagined). In the absence of any actual information about the distribution of such a variable, let us assume that it is also more or less normal (this assumption is not

	1	2	3	4	5	6	7	8	9	10
10	5	4	24	41	45	49	19	8	2	0
9	4	20	50	69	80	78	44	32	11	1
8	8	22	47	108	117	35	102	63	29	7
7	6	31	73	108	196	222	200	162	81	31
6	8	29	69	170	252	317	292	269	77	64
5	8	18	88	175	270	367	374	352	204	87
4	6	6	49	120	225	290	269	308	151	65
3	2	5	21	61	127	197	200	182	90	37
2	2	0	7	46	75	110	93	75	39	9
1	1	0	4	10	17	30	21	120	11	6
	1	2	3	4	5	6	7	8	9	10

Scatter diagram with regression lines showing a correlation of approximately −.20 (modified from unpublished values from Roff & Sells, 1967).

necessary for the purpose of the present argument, but is a convenient one for the purpose of making a diagram). Let us further assume that the correlation between the childhood variable and tendency toward schizophrenia is around −.20, which is low, but is high enough to permit a significant difference between the means of an extreme group and the remainder of the population. We would then have something like the accompanying diagram.

In this situation, the two regression lines are quite different. These, of course, run near the means of the rows and the means of columns. If we examine the extreme right-hand column of the diagram, we see that the mean for the column is below that of the rest of the table. This would be significantly different from the mean score on the childhood variable for the rest of the columns, and thus would fit the situation where the childhood measures of future schizophrenics are significantly lower than that of a control sample. On the other hand, if we look at the number of cases with childhood variable scores in rows 1–4 across all the rest of the table, it is obvious that there are large numbers of individuals who were below average who were not diagnosed schizophrenic. Thus, in this particular situation, the answer to the question, "From what childhood levels do adult schizophrenics come?" does not give us the answer to the question, "What childhood levels are followed by adult schizophrenia?"

If we turn the diagram 90°, we get the regression of the childhood variable on our imagined tendency toward schizophrenia. The answer to the question "What childhood score levels are followed by adult schizophrenia?" would then be given by the bottom row of the regression table, when it has been turned on its side (this is, of course, the same set of numbers whose mean was found to be below that of the rest of the table). The answer to the question is, then, "almost all childhood score levels can precede adult schizophrenia, with the greatest number coming from score levels near and just below the mean in the childhood variable." With a correlation of this size, those with lowest childhood scores are schizophrenic a good deal more frequently than those with the highest. But the numbers in this row are much greater near its center than at its extremes. We can thus see from the diagram that the two questions, "From what childhood score levels do adult schizophrenics come?" and "What childhood score levels are followed by adult schizophrenia?" have different answers. This fact must be considered in attempting to assign causal status to childhood measures in relation to schizophrenia.

THE TIME FACTOR IN RESEARCH ON THE EFFECTS OF PSYCHOTHERAPY

Apart from considerations of the age of the sample with which a particular life history study starts, there is a second time problem which should be mentioned. This is the amount of time which elapses between the administration of some kind of psychological treatment and the final evaluation of the effects of such treatment, at any age.

There has been a great deal of discussion about whether or not the "medical model" is the best possible model for use with human maladjustments of various kinds. Without getting into that controversy, it may be pointed out that one important procedure seems to be more commonly practiced by sophisticated medical research workers than by psychologists. This is the habit of asking not only whether a group of patients show improvement immediately after treatment, but also how many of them are still alive, or still symptom-free, or still improved in some way after a substantial interval, such as five years. There are various medical situations in which an immediate improvement may be obtained, but where the results are not necessarily permanent, or where recurrence is not uncommon. The practice of waiting five years to see how something has worked is probably too much for most psychologists, with our strong tradition of short-time studies and instantaneous publication. It would be unfortunate if the controversy over the medical model in general should inhibit the growth of the research habit of wondering whether or not a given "improvement" is lasting or not. In other words, an important part of the evaluation of the effects of psychotherapy falls in the area of life history research. This is recognized by some people making validity studies, but not by enough.

GENETIC INFLUENCES

There seems to have been an increase recently in interest in genetics in relation to personality development and psychopathology. Most of the resulting work along these lines has yet to reach the level of sophistication achieved in studies of heredity and intelligence forty years ago. One result of the development of the area of "human behavior genetics" is that it is to some extent forced to come up with answers before the appropriate problems have been adequately studied.

It has been generally recognized for the last forty years that results obtained with either identical twins or ordinary siblings who had been reared together give an impure picture of the operation of heredity. This led to the conclusion that it was necessary to study children who had been separated from their true parents, if a serious attempt was to be made to separate genetic from environmental influences. For intelligence, where an IQ or comparable measure could be obtained for whole populations, this was much easier to do than for a relatively rare disorder like schizophrenia. If, however, the further restriction be made that the children separated from their true parents should also be identical twins, it became almost impossible to get an adequate number of cases, as Newman, Freeman, and Holzinger (1937) found in their classic study of nineteen pairs of identical twins who had been reared apart, and the results of this and other studies of heredity and intelligence remain equivocal. That this is still true is recognized by a careful pronouncement of the National Academy of Sciences (1967), which was prepared in response to a proposal for a crash program to settle once and for all the problem of genetic differences in intelligence between racial or ethnic groups. This points out that "the detailed understanding of the molecular basis of heredity is one of the intellectual triumphs of the 20th century." When the problems of *molar* behavior are considered, however, the situation remains essentially unchanged by the developments in molecular genetics:

> With complex traits like intelligence the generalities are understood, but the specifics are not. There is general agreement that both hereditary and environmental factors are influential; but there are strong disagreements as to their relative magnitudes – which is another way of saying that the evidence is not conclusive. Furthermore, it is not obvious that really substantial increases in this knowledge will come soon, even if the amount of research were greatly increased. The problem of disentangling hereditary and environmental factors for complex intellectual and emotional traits where many genes may participate, where measurements are often not reproducible, where it is not certain what is being measured, and where subtle environmental factors are involved is extremely difficult. It is unrealistic to expect much progress unless new methods appear.
>
> Even greater difficulties are encountered in any attempt to assess the relative role of heredity and environment in determining racial differences in intellectual and emotional traits. Despite the great number of tests that have been performed on Negro and white populations, it is still not clear whether any differences found are primarily genetic or environmental. For example, there is no scientific basis for a statement that there are or that there are not substantial hereditary differences in intelligence between Negro and white populations. In the absence of some now-unforeseen way of equalizing all aspects of the environment, answers to this question can hardly be more than reasonable guesses. Such guesses can easily be biased, consciously or unconsciously, by political and social views.

As is pointed out in more detail in a later chapter (p. 282), this problem of "equalizing all aspects of the environment" is hard to solve in the situation where the children of schizophrenic mothers are raised by "normal" foster-parents, and care must be taken in drawing conclusions based on such histories.

BRIEF CONSIDERATIONS

I would like to mention briefly a few general problems, and to indicate by reference to specific kinds of studies how they relate to research in our area.

A persisting and widespread problem is that of getting the greatest possible precision in the use of terms. One of the most important of these is the term *children.* If there is one terminological usage that is well established, not only in the child development field, but also in the older and more general usage reflected in Webster's Second Unabridged Dictionary, it is that there is a clear difference between children and adolescents or youths. (Dictionary definitions are not, of course, binding on scientific persons, but in the interests of precision, departures from established usage should be intentional rather than inadvertent.) Thus, the dictionary defines *youth* as "the part of life that succeeds childhood; the period preceding maturity, usually that from puberty to maturity; adolescence." The same source defines a *child* as "a young person of either sex, especially one between infancy and youth." In our own work we have found clear differences between the behavior patterns of, for example, prepsychotics at the age of eight or nine as compared with those of fourteen or fifteen. Adolescents tend to be crystalizing or structuring in the direction of their adult outcome much more definitely than are children. Although it is possible to predict good and poor adult outcome from the grade school period, it is more difficult to predict the specific adult outcome from the age of eight or nine than it is from the age of fourteen or fifteen.

This distinction between childhood and adolescence, which is clearly established in the child development field, is not always recognized in life history research. The term *children* is sometimes applied to individuals as old as eighteen years. It is thus wise for the reader to note the precise ages of the "children" under discussion.

Frequently, careful analysis may indicate that two types of phenomena, one malignant and one benign, are referred to by the same word or phrase. When this occurs, we need further information which will permit a sharpening of our terminology. For example, the relation between stress and psychotic breakdown is sometimes discussed. Here we have to be careful how *stress* is defined. If it is defined as purely subjective stress, unrelated to happenings in the outside world, the following remarks do not apply. If *stress* is defined in terms of the situation, such as one where the possibility of loss of life is much greater than usual, wartime experience indicated clearly for both military and civilian personnel that the incidence of psychosis did not increase in stress situations. This included heavy and effective bombing of civilians in cities or intense fighting with accompanying heavy loss of life among combat personnel. This was found to be the case in various countries, and one student of this situation observes (Kalinowsky, 1950), "The importance of this uniform experience for the etiological problem of the major psychoses is obvious."

Another example is the term *dominant* as used in describing mothers. For several types of maladjustments, it has been suggested that a dominant mother and a passive father seem to be part of the etiological picture. However, we know from our own work that a "dominant" mother may be successful in raising a child (or children), in spite of a passive or absent father. What we need, then, are new terms which distinguish between dominant (malignant) mothers and dominant (benign) mothers. This is a researchable problem.

A related problem is that emphasis on labels gives an impression of greater difference between two or more things than really exists. It is possible that the distinction between reactive and process schizophrenia is an example of this. Bleuler (1950), in his original treatise on schizophrenia, expressed the opinion that early character anomalies can be demonstrated by careful retrospective study in more than half of the individuals who later were schizophrenics. On the other hand, often "not even the most searching examination by an expert succeeds in demonstrating the presence of specific symptoms in those early years." A distinction can obviously be made between those who showed early symptoms and those who did not; it is possible that the differences between these two groups are exaggerated by the use of the terms *reactive* and *process*. In a recent follow-up study (Vaillant, 1964) of a prognostic scale for the course of schizophrenia, it was found that "the presence of all three of the most highly correlated items (acute onset, non-schizoid premorbid adjustment, and precipitating cause) accurately delineate the so-called reactive schizophrenic; but, in fact, such patients comprised less than one half the schizophrenics in the study who actually remitted. Nonreactive schizophrenics got well too."

CONCLUSION

Even with the best data available, the results of longitudinal studies of personality are, in general, apt to be somewhat disappointing to anyone who is eager for simple and final answers. When we have carefully worked out some of the antecedent conditions for a variety of adult maladjustments, it becomes inescapably apparent that the most careful possible specification of early life-history factors does not yield anything approaching a one-to-one correspondence between early conditions and later outcomes. To some extent this may be due to the inadequacies of our present data, but we are beginning to get enough cross-validation in the area to lead to a realization that probabilistic results are what we get, and that the set of conditions which may be antecedent to adult psychosis will also lead, in more than a chance number of cases, to other types of adult difficulty instead.

A study of an increasing variety of different populations indicates clearly that there is simply a greater complexity in personality history than our rather primitive theories can account for. We have a relatively new area of study which we are really just beginning to explore. If the results of our explorations were merely illustrations of already existing theory, this would be a much less fascinating line of work.

REFERENCES

Anderson, J. E. Methods of child psychology. In Leonard Carmichael (Ed.), *Manual of child psychology*. New York: Wiley, 1946.

Bieber, I., et al. *Homosexuality: A psychoanalytic study*. New York: Vintage Books, Random House, 1965.

Bleuler, E. *Dementia praecox or the group of schizophrenias*. New York: International Universities Press, 1950.

Bronson, W. C. Stable patterns of behavior: The significance of enduring orientations for personality development. In J. P. Hill (Ed.), *Minnesota symposia on child psychology*. Vol. 2. Minneapolis: University of Minnesota Press, 1969.

Freud, S. *The complete psychological works of Sigmund Freud*. Vol. 17. (1917-1919) *An infantile neurosis and other works*. Toronto: Clarke, Irwin, 1955.

Garner, W. R., H. F. Hunt, D. W. Taylor, et al. Education for research in psychology. *American Psychologist*, 1959, 14, 167–179.

Gebhard, P. H., J. H. Gagnon, W. B. Pomeroy, & C. V. Christenson. *Sex offenders: An analysis of types*. New York: Harper & Paul B. Hoeber, 1965.

Hathaway, S. R., & E. D. Monachesi. *Adolescent personality and behavior: MMPI patterns of normal, delinquent, dropout, and other outcomes*. Minneapolis: University of Minnesota Press, 1963.

Jones, M. C. The later careers of boys who were early- or late-maturing. *Child Development*, 1957, 28, 113–128.

Kagan, J., & H. S. Moss. *Birth to maturity: A study in psychological development*. New York: Wiley, 1962.

Kalinowsky, L. F. Problems of war neuroses in the light of experiences in other countries. *American Journal of Psychiatry*, 1950, 107, 340–346.

Koegler, R. R., N. Q. Brill, L. J. Epstein, & S. J. Jordan. The vanishing American. *International Journal of Social Psychiatry*, 1964, 10 (No. 1), 14–18.

Lidz, T., S. Fleck, & A. Cornelison. *Schizophrenia and the family*. New York: International Universities Press, 1965.

Macfarlane, J. W. Studies in child guidance: I. Methodology of data collection and organization. *Monographs of the Society for Research in Child Development*, 1938, 3 (6, Serial No. 19).

Murstein, B. I. (Ed.) *The handbook of projective techniques*. New York: Basic Books, 1965.

National Academy of Sciences Council. Academy Statement. Racial studies: Academy states position on call for new search. *Science*, November 17, 1967, 158, 892–893.

National Institute of Neurological Diseases and Blindness. The collaborative perinatal research project: Five years of progress. *Collaborative Project Reporter*, Special Issue, Autumn 1963.

Newman, H. H., F. N. Freeman, & K. J. Holzinger. *Twins: A study of heredity and environment*. Chicago: University of Chicago Press, 1937.

Robins, L. N. *Deviant children grown up: A sociological and psychiatric study of sociopathic personality*. Baltimore: Williams & Wilkins, 1966.

Roff, M. Childhood social interaction and young adult psychosis. *Journal of Clinical Psychology*, 1963, 19, 152–157.

———. Some childhood and adolescent characteristics of adult homosexuals. Report No. 66-5, U.S. Army Medical Research and Development Command, May, 1966.

———, W. Mink, & G. Hinrichs. *Developmental abnormal psychology*. New York: Holt, 1966.

Roff, M., & S. B. Sells. The relations between the status of chooser and chosen in a sociometric situation at the grade school level. *Psychology in the Schools*, 1967, 4, 101–111.

Vaillant, G. E. Prospective prediction of schizophrenic remission. *Archives of General Psychiatry*, 1964, 11, 509–518.

DAVID F. RICKS
JOHN C. BERRY

Family and Symptom Patterns That Precede Schizophrenia

FOR the past seven years, the Judge Baker Schizophrenia Research Project has been collecting information about the life histories of young people seen at a child guidance center, with various adult outcomes, ranging from chronic schizophrenia to well-adjusted lives. Using data gathered by the guidance center in childhood or adolescence, several years before hospitalization and diagnosis, we have tried to discover symptom patterns, feelings, and ways of life predictive of schizophrenia, other disorders, or eventual social adjustment. Currently we are trying to develop some general models for patterns of psychopathological development.

Our perspective on schizophrenia, and on other types of warped or arrested lives, is developmental. In looking at each disturbed person, or at any set of persons whose adult characteristics are similar enough to fit them together under the common umbrella of a diagnostic label, we have asked four main questions: How did this person develop, in relation to what specific environment? How did the symptoms start? Were there precursors to the symptoms? Might the disorder have been recognized early, and if so, might early intervention have changed the course of this person's life? A developmental perspective is evolutionary, studies patterns of change, and recognizes that disorders may have overlapping characteristics. It contrasts with a static diagnostic scheme in the same way Darwinian evolutionary biology contrasts with the older biological doctrine of specially created, discrete, unchanging types.

In taking an approach that classifies people by adult diagnosis and asks how each person with a particular diagnosis "got that way," we are of

NOTE: This research was supported by Grant MH 10,466 from the National Institute of Mental Health, and by grants from the Scottish Rite Committee for Research in Schizophrenia.

course assuming some reliability and validity in the diagnoses hospitals mete out to their inmates. The scepticism about diagnosis that dominated psychology through the 1950's has freed us from the idea that a psychiatric diagnosis is a completely solid criterion on which to validate our attempts at prediction. The earlier corrosive cynicism of some of our academic colleagues has recently been tempered, however, by the results of Kreitman (1961), Beck (1962; Beck, Ward, Mendelson, Mock, & Erbaugh, 1962), and the sophisticated work of Spitzer and Endicott (1968a; 1968b), which indicate that psychotic and neurotic disorders are diagnosed with good reliability, so long as one does not get too detailed about subdivisions. Lorr (pp. 147–157) shows how to put diagnostic work on a sounder, more systematic basis. For the time being, adult diagnoses can be regarded as a good basis from which to start research, which can then improve the diagnostic process through systematic feedback of research findings.

Our data, like the data in Roff's studies and those of Robins (pp. 226–238), Eiduson (pp. 127–143), and several others, are found in the dusty files of child guidance clinics and mental hospitals. The aim of our group has been to do clinical research, drawing our main ideas from clinical experience and theory, as well as using clinical materials. Our methods, and most of our research standards, have come from the university. There are stresses built into this cooperation, but we believe that the synthesis between clinical experience and research sophistication has values that make the tensions bearable. Our university researchers show evidence of becoming better diagnosticians and therapists as a result of studying large numbers of children from their early lives to adult outcomes. Clinical practitioners working with us have learned about research design, come to respect research results, systematized ways of keeping records, and sometimes reported changes in their ways of working with patients.

The richness of available guidance center records is only beginning to be appreciated by people interested in clinical research. These files contain half a century of accumulated information about the early environments, behaviors, and experiences of children — information that is not retrospective, not falsified by memory, not too tailored to fit theory. Everything in the files is based on direct observation, often long-term, by serious adults whom the children and their parents had good reason to trust. As Healy and others noted long ago, if the childhood and adolescent antecedents of adult disorder can be found and methods of intervention studied, it might be possible to identify factors that can modify the course of emotional development, for some vulnerable children, into relatively competent adjustment.

The characteristics of our sample and the methods we have developed for the study of clinical records are described briefly below. We shall then describe some family patterns and the main symptom syndromes our project has been able to isolate in groups of boys who were later schizophrenic, as contrasted with those who were later impulsive characters, alcoholic, or normal. We shall end by proposing a schematic model of the determinants of schizophrenic breakdown and of social recovery from schizophrenia, a model that argues for different main determinants of these two phases in the schizophrenic life trajectory.

METHOD

Subjects. Almost 18,000 children have been seen at the Judge Baker Guidance Center since it opened in 1917, and by 1965, over 15,000 had reached adulthood. Checking the data that identified these children—names, birth dates, and so forth—against the mental health department files of the state of Massachusetts during 1965 disclosed the following sets of people who had been hospitalized and given reasonably definite diagnoses:

Schizophrenic	
Chronic, still hospitalized	84
Released, back in the community	112
Alcoholic	68
Impulsive Characters	87

Smaller groups had been given psychotic and neurotic depressive diagnoses, no diagnosis at all, or mixed diagnoses.

Although there was considerable reliability about the diagnoses of the sets selected for study, it must be recognized that "schizophrenic," "alcoholic," and especially "impulsive character" are rough categories covering non-homogeneous groups. We accepted the hospital diagnoses as a starting point, but we found it necessary to distinguish between those schizophrenics whose disorders appeared chronic, as evidenced by being still in hospitals at the time we started our study and remaining in during its progress, and those whose hospitalizations had been terminated by return to some degree of participation in community life. A check on the validity of this distinction is provided by the percentage of each person's life spent in mental hospitals in the two groups: the median for the chronic group was 45 per cent, for the released 6 per cent. The descriptive title "impulsive characters" is used, rather than the mental hospital diagnoses of psychopathic personality, sociopathic personality, character disorder, or pathological sexual deviation, because it has fewer "sick" connotations and implies fewer etiological assumptions.

Except for these hospital-diagnosed groups and 100 children in a socially adequate comparison sample, we do not have data on adult adjustments of the Guidance Center patients. A complete follow-up of such a large child guidance population can be done, but it is a huge task.

A few things should be pointed out about this sample. First, it is selective rather than exhaustive. It includes only those patients who were hospitalized in one state, Massachusetts, and for whom there was substantial agreement from hospitalization to hospitalization upon diagnosis. It does not include the unknown number of patients who were hospitalized in other states, whose disorders led to many different diagnoses, or who lived eccentric, schizoid lives but still escaped hospitalization. The alcoholics and impulsive characters were located through mental hospital diagnoses, and not through AA, corner bars, or jails. This undoubtedly lends a special character to the groups. When we can make comparisons with other groups, as we can on the Phillips Scale with schizophrenics studied by Garmezy and Rodnick (1959), our schizophrenics appear to be more disturbed.

Our comparison group was picked from among children also seen at the Guidance Center, matched to the pre-schizophrenics on age, IQ, period when seen at the Center, and so forth. They were contacted and interviewed, or a relative was interviewed, and if they met criteria for responsible social participation, they were considered to be socially adequate. The comparisons that follow will be between pre-schizophrenics and a group that by adult life was meeting reasonable work and social participation criteria for adult adjustment.

RESULTS

Following a model established in our first work on family patterns (Waring & Ricks, 1965), this report will look in order at the mother, the father, the relationship between the two, and finally the environment that is created for the child. Nameche (1965) used both Guidance Center and hospital records in a replication study of Waring and Ricks, with judgments done in full awareness of which children were later schizophrenic and which were not. Since his methods were the same as those used with the earlier sample, we shall report here on the combined sample, 100 schizophrenics and 100 controls. Field (1967; 1969) and Berry (1967), working only on the basis of Guidance Center records and blind as to adult outcomes, have provided a test of the initial results and some suggestive new ideas. We shall concentrate here on a few points where all the investigations agree.

Mothers. The mothers were grouped into seven categories: clearly psychotic, schizoid, depressed, compulsive, character disordered, or normal. The character disorders were further divided into dependent, impulsive, and borderline psychotic types. These categories, and those for marital relationships and the environments provided for the child, are fully described in Waring and Ricks (1965, pp. 353–360).

Three types of women, the psychotic, schizoid, and borderline psychotic character disorders, accounted for 48 per cent of the mothers whose children became chronic schizophrenics, but the three types combined accounted for only 13 per cent of the mothers of released schizophrenics and 16 per cent of the controls. Two types of mothers were much more frequent for the controls — those with impulsive character disorders, and mothers who were normal or only mildly neurotic.

The classic "schizophrenogenic" compulsive mother appeared in all of our groups, but most frequently as a parent of either a released schizophrenic or one of the less adequate controls, least often as a mother of a chronic schizophrenic. It seems time to lay this stereotype to rest.

Two main conclusions seem warranted by the whole set of data. The mothers of all groups spread over the whole set of categories, so that if there is only one type of mother who is conducive to schizophrenia, we didn't find her. However, the mothers do pile up in certain areas. If you want to predict chronic schizophrenia, it seems best to look among the children of schizophrenic, schizoid, or borderline psychotic women, more or less as Mednick has been doing (see pp. 51–89). If you want to predict episodes of schizophrenia, or what Vaillant (1964) calls schizo-affective psychoses, the best place to look might be among the children of depressed, compulsive, and dependent women. And children who mature into normal adult life seem, more than other groups, to have impulsive or normal mothers.

When Berry (1967) and Field (1967) replicated this set of observations, with partly overlapping sets of cases, but with the crucial difference of purity as to knowledge of adult outcome, the main finding was clearly confirmed. Compared with mothers of boys in all other groups, mothers of future chronic schizophrenics were the most frequently seriously disturbed.

Fathers. Fathers are unlikely to be well known to most guidance clinics. Nameche (1965) found little to differentiate the fathers of the different groups from each other, with the one clear finding of greater frequency of healthy fathers in the control group. Berry and Field also found little to differentiate the fathers of released and chronic schizophrenics. When we lack data, as we do for fathers of children seen in conventional child guidance work, we are not likely to generate new knowledge or what Roff calls "robust" results. Newer forms of treatment such as family therapy may remedy this gap as the children treated in these ways grow up.

The Marital Relationship. Here we have an abundance of data, since most mothers, given a sympathetic woman listener, appeared to enjoy dissecting their marital situation. Of the many types of relationships that lie about in the literature, waiting to be tested, one came through our data unscathed: "emotional divorce," Bowen's (1961) category to cover those marriages that retain a shell of relatedness with no content inside it. This typified 27 per cent of the marriages that produced children who became chronic schizophrenics, 13 per cent of the marriages that produced released schizophrenics, and only 2 per cent of the families that produced normals. Other types of marriages that have been indicted at one time or another — "pseudo-mutual masking marriages" with a facade of perfection, "skewed marriages" in which one parent was overly dominant, marriages split by conflict, and one-parent families — did not produce more than their share of schizophrenics. It may be worthwhile to quote the definition of emotional divorce in the manual Waring and Ricks developed for categorizing marital patterns: "Mutual withdrawal and schismatic isolation. Interaction is minimal, husband and wife sleeping in different rooms, or at different times, with infrequent or no sexual or other contact. In spite of covert hostility, estrangement, and distrust between the couple they do not seek an actual divorce."

Environment Provided for the Child. The most productive of our typologies was the classification of families in terms of the environment they provided for the child (see figure on p. 37). Symbiotic union between a parent and the pre-schizophrenic child, forming an inseparable unit prolonged far beyond the usual termination of symbiosis, was present in 38 per cent of the chronic cases, 20 per cent of the released, and 11 per cent of the controls. Over half of the symbiotic unions between parent and child occurred in families in which the parents were in a state of emotional divorce. The most frequent symbiotic patterns united mother and daughter in a small island apart from the world, but there were also many symbiotic mother-son combinations, and even two bizarre father-son unities, one of which persisted through the son's many hospitalizations into his middle age and the father's old age. Released schizophrenics tended to come from families typified by a depressed atmosphere and rejection of the child, a rejection which had often begun by the time they came to the clinic, but which deepened and became more extreme during the years between clinic contact and hospitalization. A detailed comparison of symbiotic and rejecting family atmospheres is provided in Ricks and Nameche (1966). It should be noted that symbiosis is normal in infancy, not too unusual in early childhood, and increasingly striking in later childhood, adolescence, and early adult life. Observers classifying families with only childhood data available sometimes found few apparent problems in families that were clearly providing a symbiotic environment by adolescence. For adequate classification of symbiosis — as compared with mere overprotection, compulsive Momism, and so forth — both adolescent and young adult data, such as that found in hospital records, may be necessary.

The crucial questions are, first, how long does a symbiotic tie to a parent last, and second, what does it mean to its participants? For example, one mother-son symbiosis began to end when the 16-year-old son's

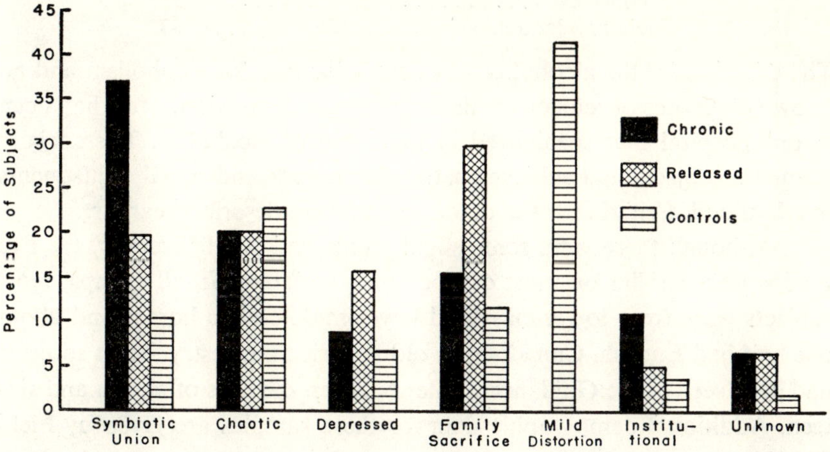

Environment provided for the child data combined from Waring and Ricks (1965) and Nameche (1965). Waring and Ricks provide a detailed description of the categories. Percentages are based on a total sample of 45 chronic schizophrenics, 55 released schizophrenics, and 100 controls. No released schizophrenics or controls fell into the category Mild Distortion.

therapist asked if he had an erection when his mother bathed him. He said that he did, thought it over, and began bathing himself. Since clinic involvement with these families usually began in adolescence, it was not possible to decide with any assurance whether symbiosis more often reflected a vulnerable child's need for protection or a parent's need to protect. Often the two were combined—one little girl was born with defective hearing, often had high temperatures as a child, and so on, and she was quite literally wrapped in cotton batting by a mother who seemed to find much more satisfaction in this "sick" child than in her healthy one.

The homes of impulsive characters also provided a unique environment for the child, one that encouraged and approved socially deviant activity. The homes of prealcoholics ranged from normal to moderately disorganized, with the more disorganized families generally split by conflict among family members.

DIAGNOSTIC GROUP COMPARISONS

Judge Baker Guidance Center records of 191 males for whom our best childhood or adolescent data were available were classified according to adult mental status:

Chronic schizophrenics	30
Released schizophrenics	38
Impulsive characters	31
Alcoholics	55
Socially adequate subjects	37

The criterion for the alcoholics was hospitalization for alcoholism and no known diagnoses of schizophrenia or psychotic depression. Most had been in one hospital that specialized in treatment of alcoholics. The socially adequate subjects had achieved satisfactory work and social adjustments in adulthood. Criteria for the other groups were described earlier.

Although there were some slight ethnic and IQ differences, the five groups were similar on most demographic variables. In all groups, most subjects were from lower-class and lower-middle-class homes and about one half had English, Canadian, or old American ancestry. Most subjects had been seen at the Guidance Center between the ages of eleven and sixteen. Additional demographic data for these samples are given by Field (1969).

Chronic and Released Schizophrenics. Boys who later became chronic schizophrenics were of two distinct types which we shall label for later reference as: C1 "withdrawn" and C2 "delinquent." C1 boys who later became chronic schizophrenics accounted for half of all chronic patients. These boys showed withdrawal from school and community in conjunction with many other serious symptoms, including psychotic-like behavior, low self-esteem, obsessive thinking, and symptoms often associated with neurological impairment. These latter symptoms included hypoactivity, rigidity, abnormalities of speech output, abnormal gait, poor coordination, and impaired attention span. As *withdrawal* implies, social adjustment was very poor, and capacity for empathic ties to peers was low. Relatively uncontrolled acting-out behavior in the home — such as defiance of parents, tantrums, and disorganized destructive activity — was frequent. Acting out in the community, except for truancy, was rare.

C2 boys who later became chronic schizophrenics accounted for a third of the total. These boys acted out extensively in the community and, in addition, showed many other symptoms, particularly low self-esteem and a second set of symptoms suggesting neurological impairment: hyperactivity, incorrigibility, short attention span, overreaction to frustration, and enuresis. (We recognize that no one of these symptoms, by itself, implies neurological damage. In combination they do raise this issue.) Their acting out in the community consisted largely of stealing, lying, truancy, and destructive activity. Rarely, however, did they physically molest others. Unlike later impulsive characters, and some released schizophrenics, they generally were not aggressive or sadistic toward peers. Their home behavior was similar to the defiance and tantrums found among withdrawn chronics. Peer relationships of C2 boys, unlike those of C1 boys, were characterized by an apparent capacity for peer identification and empathic ties, and a passive kind of sociability. These boys, however, usually appeared peculiar and eccentric to peers, and consequently they had few friends.

Two unique types, which we shall label R1 and R2, composed slightly more than half of the boys who were later released schizophrenics. R1 boys accounted for a third of the released sample. In many respects, these withdrawn boys resembled C1 youngsters. However, they less frequently showed obsessive characteristics, psychotic-like symptoms, and symptoms associated with neurological impairment.

R2 schizophrenics accounted for a fifth of the released sample. These were non-withdrawn boys in whom extreme symptoms of low self-esteem and/or psychotic-like symptoms were associated with extensive acting out, including deviant sexual behavior and sadistic, aggressive behavior toward peers. Social adjustment was generally poor and capacity for empathic ties to peers nearly always absent. Symptoms associated with neurological impairment were infrequent.

An additional one fourth of the later released schizophrenics presented sets of serious symptoms that were rare in non-schizophrenic boys, but did not form distinctive homogeneous patterns. The remaining boys appeared to have no unusual difficulties during the time they were being seen at the center, as compared with children who turned out well.

Several conclusions were drawn. First, a large proportion of preschizophrenics showed characteristics that differentiated them from other boys. Withdrawn boys (C1 and R1) and released schizophrenics who had both serious acting-out features and extremely low self-esteem (R2) showed symptom patterns that were almost nonexistent among other sets of boys. The general pattern of characteristics shown by the (C2) delinquent boys who later became chronics, although less amenable to concise definition, was also unique to the chronic group. Thus, most of the pre-schizophrenic boys in the two groups showed distinctive patterns that differentiated them from nearly all boys in the other three groups. The magnitude of these differences, if replicated in later studies, will have clear implications for early identification of boys who have an especially high risk for later becoming schizophrenic.

Symptom patterns also differentiated between the chronic and the released schizophrenics and, therefore, seemed to be potentially useful in predicting chronicity among boys who became schizophrenic. Withdrawal, apathy, and passivity, particularly in conjunction with many symptoms associated with neurological impairment, were particularly frequent among later chronics.

Since our interpretation of these data is not in keeping with the traditional distinction between organic and functional disorders, in which schizophrenia is considered to be functional, we should like to discuss in more detail the question of neurological abnormality in these boys. In order to assess this area, two approaches were used. First, twenty-five specific behavioral symptoms often associated with neurological impairment were investigated. Although these twenty-five symptoms are often related to neurological dysfunction, most also may be psychogenic. The symptoms that differentiated the groups were described above, in connection with the C1 and C2 syndromes. A second estimate of neurological impairment, the investigator's global judgment regarding brain damage, was used as a more rigid criterion of neurological impairment. This judgment was based not only on the presence of the symptoms associated with neurological impairment, but also on physical and neurological examination conclusions and other professional opinions of qualified personnel at the Guidance Center. A global judgment of brain damage was made only when the evidence for brain damage was obvious and consistent; subtle or controversial evidence was given little weight.

Later chronics tended to have more judgments of actual brain damage, as well as having more specific symptoms associated with neurological impairment, than boys in all other groups. Even when the clearly brain-damaged chronics were excluded, the remaining later chronics had more symptoms associated with neurological impairment. These symptoms, in fact, had more potential value for predicting chronicity among pre-schizophrenics than any other single category of symptoms.

These data raise several questions about the possible relations between neurological impairment and later development of schizophrenia. If all of these children had come from matched homes, or even comparable ones, the issue would be simpler. In fact, however, the homes differed a great deal. In general, children who grew up to chronic schizophrenia came from homes with disturbed mothers, many of them psychotic — but very few of the mothers of children who showed clear brain damage, and were later chronic schizophrenic, were psychotic. Apparently, a component of early brain damage shifted the psychiatric careers of several children whose home environments were much like those of released schizophrenics over toward chronic hospitalization. These findings echo Stabenau and Pollin's (pp. 94–122) finding that early biological deficit leads to low competence, which in turn leads to schizophrenia. They suggest that if the deficit is extreme enough to be clearly apparent early in life, schizophrenia is likely to be chronic.

Although it is possible that the chaotic home environments and everyday anxieties typical in the histories of pre-schizophrenic children could have produced some of the neurological symptoms on a psychogenic basis alone, or even have had a part in producing actual neurological disorder, this seems far less likely than the alternative sequence. Mednick (pp. 51–89) and Stabenau and Pollin have offered evidence that the biological deficits in pre-schizophrenic children can be evident before the home has much chance to influence the child.

In sum, it seems likely that brain damage, though not essential to the *genesis* of schizophrenia, is related to its *chronicity*. This conclusion awaits confirmation with more adequate neurological data than that provided by records gathered with unsystematic coverage of neurological factors.

Despite the variety of premorbid patterns, most boys resembled pre-schizophrenics previously described in the literature. Arieti's (1955) "stormy personality" corresponded in a rough way to R2 delinquent boys with extremely low self-esteem who later became released schizophrenics, and Bender's (1959) "pseudopsychopathic schizophrenic" bears a resemblance to the C2 later chronics who were delinquent in childhood. Withdrawn pre-schizophrenics, such as those found in the C1 and R1 groups, are commonly referred to in the literature.

Impulsive Characters. The antisocial behavior and deviant peer relationships of later impulsive characters differentiated them from boys in other groups. Acting-out behavior in both the home and the community were more characteristic of these boys than of boys in any other group. Moreover, their patterns of acting-out behavior were specific to the group: one syndrome consisting of sexual deviance, stealing in the home, flagrant disobedience of both parents, and running away from home was characteristic only of future impulsive characters. They also tended to be defiant of community authorities and frequently engaged in destructive behavior in the community. Regarding social adjustment, capacity for empathic ties to peers was usually absent, and a high proportion had sadistic or sadomasochistic peer relationships.

This syndrome can be interpreted in terms of inadequate superego development, related to home environments that stimulated and approved impulsive behavior, and manifest in the nature and extent of their acting out, their inability to form empathic bonds with peers, and their callous treatment of others. To a surprising degree, these boys also had neurotic problems. Hysterical symptoms, fears, phobias, and diffuse anxiety were particularly frequent. A few symptoms sometimes associated with neurological impairment were also common: hyperactivity, incorrigibility, short attention span, overreaction to frustration, and abnormalities of speech output. In this group, such symptoms usually occurred together with hysterical symptoms and seemed more psychogenic than biogenic.

These findings had two main implications. Early identification of later impulsive characters appears to be feasible. The pattern of characteristics presented by these boys was almost as differentiating as the sets exhibited by pre-schizophrenics. Even compared with aggressive boys in other groups, those moving into character disorder showed many distinctive features. The second implication concerned the nature of the disorder.

The neurotic symptoms in many of these boys indicated a surprising amount of early internal stress in these cool, callous boys. The finding of hysterical features is of particular interest. Possibly some of the boys who later carried psychopathic diagnoses actually were misdiagnosed acting-out hysterics.

Prealcoholics. In contrast to pre-schizophrenics and future impulsive characters, whose symptoms pointed to grave difficulties in later life, most prealcoholics had relatively good early adjustments. A substantial majority, two thirds, had no significant neurotic symptoms. In addition, peer relationships were generally quite adequate. In their capacity for empathic ties to peers, the prealcoholics were comparable to boys who were later socially adequate adults. Even more than these boys, however, they showed a capacity for intense, mutually dependent relationships with peers, frequently peers of both sexes. Such relationships often appeared to be their primary source of support and self-esteem. The comparison group boys, although often well integrated into peer-group life, seemed more involved in parents and family.

A second major characteristic of prealcoholic boys was extensive acting out in the community. Like later impulsive characters, prealcoholics were often court-referred juvenile delinquents. Boys developing impulsive characters often acted out in ways destructive to others, but prealcoholics were rarely malicious. Instead, these often dependent and suggestible boys acted out within the context of peer-group loyalties and close empathic ties. Their delinquent behavior seemed to be only an exaggeration of the kind of acting out occasionally engaged in by non-delinquent boys.

Many of these characteristics of prealcoholic boys have been mentioned in the literature. Good peer-group relationships in the context of socially deviant behavior and freedom from neurotic symptoms have been reported previously (McCord & McCord, 1960; Wellman, 1955). Moreover, the kind of close involvement that these boys had with peers, their dependency and group-mindedness, are qualities often observed in adult alcoholics.

Also of interest is the similarity between the characteristics of prealcoholic boys and a constellation of personality traits suggested by several authors (Lisansky, 1960; Zwerling & Rosenbaum, 1959) as antecedents of alcoholism. This constellation of traits consists of passive-dependent longings, dependent-hostile relationships, and a low degree of frustration tolerance with impulsivity in response to frustration. Although passive-dependent longings and low frustration tolerance were not observable in all prealcoholics, they were much more conspicuous in this group than in any other, a finding that supports the proposition that there is at least one pattern of motivational variables that renders an individual particularly vulnerable to dependence on alcohol.

The pattern of social adjustment in prealcoholic boys also supported Schilder's (1941) hypothesis that alcoholism is a product of "social tension." Most gave evidence of strong needs to be accepted and appreciated by peers, and may have been especially vulnerable to rejection or loss. Anxiety, tension, or depression in response to losses might have stimulated excessive drinking in later life.

Although most prealcoholic boys showed little neurotic behavior, one third of the sample did show neurotic symptoms, particularly depression. Although little data on characteristics of these boys in adulthood were available, it may be speculated that many of them later became depressive alcoholics. These neurotic prealcoholics had the longest hospitalizations in adulthood, usually three months or longer, as compared with brief hospitalizations for non-neurotic alcoholics.

The findings regarding the early personality characteristics of prealcoholics seem to have implications for theories of alcoholism. In most cases, a major premorbid characteristic was extensive acting out in the community in the absence of neurotic conflict. In addition, the homes of prealcoholics frequently included parents who sanctioned social deviancy. Such findings suggested that alcoholism in males does not, as many assume, invariably have its origins in neurotic conflict. On the contrary, it would seem to originate as socially patterned group behavior, strikingly free from conflict. When neurotic characteristics were present, they suggested depressive syndromes in the making.

Socially Adequate Subjects. Relative to the four pathology groups, the symptoms presented by boys who were later socially adequate were generally mild. The current difficulties these boys were having, however, were usually substantial and occasionally quite serious. This group was not free of psychopathology. Even when specific symptoms were serious, however, they usually appeared in the context of an otherwise relatively adequate adjustment; rarely did serious symptoms appear in combinations. Relationships with peers were usually adequate, and disturbances in this area were rarely accompanied by other serious symptoms. Signs of neurological impairment were infrequent in this group. Thus, at least in the majority of cases, the more adequate adult adjustment of these boys was foreshadowed by better adjustment in childhood and adolescence.

CONCLUSION: TOWARD A LIFE HISTORY MODEL FOR SCHIZOPHRENIA

From a developmental perspective it is possible to argue, as Goethe did, that "the history of the individual is the individual" and so to believe that everything in a person's history is relevant. But some periods are particularly important, and for schizophrenia we have come to believe that adolescence is such a period. In the next stages of our research (Ross, 1969), we have begun to concentrate on adolescent tasks, and the emotional reactions to success or failure in those tasks, as especially relevant to the development of schizophrenia.

Taking into account the research just reported, we can begin to sketch out some routes into a schizophrenic life history. The child headed toward schizophrenia, particularly the child headed toward a chronic disorder, is one whose biological and social equipment offers small margin for error in development. Lacking some of the components of integrated, competent adjustment, or having these elements seriously underdeveloped, the child is vulnerable to disorder. He often, perhaps usually, knows that he is vulnerable, and he makes various efforts to defend himself. If these succeed he may move into a low stimulation pattern of living (Hathaway, Monachesi, & Salasin, pp. 171–185), stabilize at some intermediate stage of breakdown, or recover. If they fail, and fail progressively over a long period of time (the typical adolescent we have studied came to treatment at 14, and was not hospitalized and diagnosed schizophrenic until he was about 21), then the ultimate outcome may be schizophrenia.

The stages of retreat into schizophrenia resemble those extensively studied in younger children by Robertson (1962), by Bowlby (1960), and in a different context, by Mahler (1959). In the first stage, *protest*, the person who has experienced long continued or unmanageable failure, loss, or rejection attempts to deal with his world by angry confrontation, demands for special attention and privilege, and temper tantrums or provocativeness that test the limits to which he can arbitrarily violate expectations and norms and still be loved, or at least tolerated (Goffman, 1963). This behavior seems to be the type that predominates in the acting out C2 and R2 groups of pre-schizophrenics. In general, these children seem more troublesome, but less "sick" than those whose regression goes further. If protests are both ineffectual and uncontrolled, with a quality of disorganization and low competence suggesting poor functioning of the higher integrative brain centers (C1), protest rapidly deteriorates into despair. If the adolescent has the resources to be successful in his protest, or if he finds some route into a low-pressure life style, then stabilization as a schizoid or impulsive character, or even recovery to normality may proceed.

The second stage, *despair*, is characterized by increasing hopelessness, withdrawal, and decreasing efforts to make contact with others. Episodes of protest may still occur, but they are preceded and followed by longer periods of depression. The person who temporarily stabilizes at this point may be diagnosed as depressed, schizo-affective, or an acute schizophrenic, but regardless of the diagnosis his prognosis for getting out of the hospital eventually is relatively good. Patients whose adult syndromes were dominated by despair were characterized early by extremely low self-esteem, and by a more or less total sense of rejection and worthlessness (the R2 pattern of this study). Our project (Ricks & Nameche, 1966), and others (Lu, 1960) in reports dealing with the family, have described some of the roots of this sense of rejection. Both the adolescents at the first stage of schizophrenic retreat and those at this stage seem to have the feelings described in Fleming's (pp. 240–260) research: anxiety, vulnerability, isolated alienation, and feelings of unreality. Geller's (1969) research on schizophrenic rather than pre-schizophrenic groups indicates that those who are already schizophrenic during this period may also have mystical or cosmic experiences, shown by Fleming to be rare before the appearance of overt schizophrenic symptoms. When despair fails to evoke a helping response from others, or provokes only rejection, hopelessness becomes chronic.

In the third stage of withdrawal, *detachment and apathy*, protest no longer occurs, depressive feelings and self-blame give way to apathetic unconcern, and the environment ceases to matter. Restitutional efforts, which in the two earlier stages of withdrawal could lead back to some form of adjustment to societal expectations, seem now to be directed toward the creation of an imaginary world. Most of the patients who reach this third stage seem resigned to remaining chronic.

What pushes people toward protest, despair, and apathy? Feelings before schizophrenia (Fleming & Ricks, pp. 240–260) suggest an answer. It seems reasonable to propose that the immediate impetus to psychotic retreat is some set of intolerable feelings — feelings so painful that psychotic rebellion against the world, or a psychotic reinterpretation of its meanings, can promise to be less painful than a continued life within the outward boundaries of normality. This seems to hold regardless of whether the long-term pressures toward breakdown are familial, neurological, or simply accumulating failures in significant areas of life. It is striking that the extreme feelings we have studied distinguish pre-schizophrenics from other groups, but, with the possible exception of depressive affects and apathy, do not distinguish the chronic schizophrenics from those who are eventually released. Intolerable feelings seem to characterize all pre-schizophrenics, and to push them all into some form of protest or despair.

Whether the process moves on from protest or despair to apathy does not seem to depend so much on intolerable feelings as it does on neurological integration and the set of social and vocational capacities that White (1959) sums up in the concept of competence. If one can be active, effective, and successful, protest can work. If one can extrapolate from past solutions to future solutions, so that hope is not lost, then despair need not develop even after extreme losses or disappointments. On the other hand, if one has a long history of failure, then even a minor disappointment can have a subjective meaning of disaster (e.g., one boy became overtly psychotic when a co-worker refused to accept a box of candy, another when a schoolmate told him he couldn't become a pilot because he wore glasses). Our results here are consistent with those of Hathaway, Monachesi, and Salasin (pp. 171–185), Lane and Albee (pp. 189–201), and Pollack, Woerner, and Klein (pp. 208–222) in indicating that the determinants of regression or recovery, staying in the hospital or getting out, are not such ephemeral things as feelings, but the clear, hard data of IQ, social and vocational success, and a reasonably receptive environment. When we ask, in turn, what determines competence, then the characteristics of the parents, the home environment, and the presence or absence of biological handicap all are relevant.

This model would imply a differential weighting of information regarding competence and information regarding feelings. If one wants to predict schizophrenic retreat, the most powerful measures available may be measures of intolerable feelings during late childhood and adolescence. If one wants to predict recovery, it seems clear that the best predictors are measures of competence and integration, including neurological integration.

This conception of schizophrenic withdrawal, the intolerable emotions that precede withdrawal, and the determinants of recovery has several implications for research and for practice.

With regard to research, it serves as a general framework on which to hang the specific syndromes and sets of emotions we have been studying.

With regard to therapy, it suggests that the good "schizophrenia preventing" parent, therapist, or teacher would be one who could help his adolescent children, patients, or students to confront painful feelings in an atmosphere, and at a pace, that could keep these feelings from becoming overwhelming—and who could, at the same time, help them to develop enough competence to deal with the world in a relatively satisfying way. We have some evidence that poor therapists (by the criterion of adult outcome of their case load) tend to elicit more anxiety and despair than the patient or the therapist can cope with, and that they then join the patient in losing hope. The best therapists, in spite of large differences in style and personality, seem to proceed in roughly the way we have described.

COMMENTARY

QUESTION. Was your study based entirely on boys? Were there any girls in your sample?

RICKS. We have a fairly large number of girls, but more boys are brought to a child guidance clinic than girls. Dr. Berry's results are strictly on boys because we didn't want to confuse some of the issues by having both groups. We do have one large study by Gail Gardner comparing boys and girls which has been published in a couple of articles,* and we do find differences. Symbiosis, for instance, is more typical with the girls and their mothers. There's a closer relation between the amount of disturbance in the mother and the amount of disturbance in the daughter than there is between mother and son. Some symptoms, such as obsessiveness, which are predictive of later psychopathology in boys, are not so predictive for girls. Dr. Gardner makes a convincing argument that this has to do with social norms.

QUESTION. For any of the cases that you followed, did you also attempt to get data on possible siblings within these home set-ups, in terms of whether or not these siblings themselves might have been ill, whether or not the siblings might have had any kind of effect on the development of the disorder? We know from regular developmental studies that siblings can have effects on sex identification and so forth.

RICKS. Well, I think you hit upon one of the limitations of child guidance data. Typically, there is an index child who is brought to the clinic, and we know a great deal about him because he's been observed by many people, tested, and so on. For siblings, we generally have only anec-

* G. Gardner, The relationship between childhood neurotic symptomatology and later schizophrenia in males and females, *Journal of Nervous and Mental Disease*, 1967, 144 (No. 2), 97–100; and Role of maternal psychopathology in male and female schizophrenics, *Journal of Consulting Psychology*, 1967, 31 (No. 4), 411–413.

dotal information. We haven't systematically gone after sibling data the way Merrill Roff has in some of his studies, and the way you can if you have school data, so that I don't think we have much to say about siblings. We were a little surprised to see how many of the schizophrenic children turned out, when we investigated the family, to have very disturbed siblings, but certainly there's nothing systematic or patterned that we can report.

GARMEZY. The questions and answers raised in this discussion pose an interesting problem. Suppose we could reconstitute some of the traditional intake procedures of child guidance clinics in the hope of improving research in developmental psychopathology – Would it not be possible to request of parents that they bring not only the disturbed child to the clinic for evaluation but the siblings as well? This is frequently done in family therapy, but I am focusing on the task of assessment primarily. I believe that parents would understand our request for an intensive appraisal of the entire family. Imagine the comparative data that would have been available to Dr. Ricks had this been the practice of the Judge Baker Guidance Center in decades past.

REFERENCES

Arieti, S. *Interpretation of schizophrenia.* New York: Brunner, 1955.

Beck, A. T. Reliability of psychiatric diagnoses: 1. A critique of systematic studies. *American Journal of Psychiatry*, 1962, 119, 210–216.

———, C. H. Ward, M. Mendelson, J. E. Mock, & J. K. Erbaugh. Reliability of psychiatric diagnoses: 2. A study of consistency of clinical judgments and ratings. *American Journal of Psychiatry*, 1962, 119, 351–357.

Bender, L. The concept of pseudopsychopathic schizophrenia in adolescents. *American Journal of Orthopsychiatry*, 1959, 29, 491–508.

Berry, J. C. Antecedents of schizophrenia, impulsive character, and alcoholism in males. Unpublished Ph.D. thesis, Teachers College, Columbia University, 1967.

Bowen, M. A family concept of schizophrenia. In D. Jackson (Ed.), *The etiology of schizophrenia.* New York: Basic Books, 1961. Pp. 346–372.

Bowlby, J. Grief and mourning in infancy and early childhood. In R. S. Eissler et al. (Eds.), *Psychoanalytic study of the child*, Vol. 15. New York: International Universities Press, 1960.

Field, H. Early life patterns of male schizophrenics, delinquent character disorders, and socially adequate subjects. Unpublished Ph.D. thesis, Teachers College, Columbia University, 1967.

———. Early symptoms and behavior of male schizophrenics, delinquent character-disordered individuals, and socially adequate subjects. *Journal of Nervous and Mental Disease*, 1969, 148, 134–146.

Garmezy, N., & E. Rodnick. Premorbid adjustment and performance in schizophrenia: Implications for interpreting heterogeneity in schizophrenia. *Journal of Nervous and Mental Disease*, 1959, 129, 450–466.

Geller, R. Subjective experience of schizophrenia: Reported emotional experiences of schizophrenic children. Ph.D. thesis, Teachers College, Columbia University, 1969.

Goffman, E. Mental symptoms and public order. *Research publication of the Association for Research in Nervous and Mental Disease*, 1963, 42, 262–269.

Kreitman, N. The reliability of psychiatric diagnosis. *Journal of Mental Science*, 1961, 107, 876–886.

Lisansky, E. S. The etiology of alcoholism: The role of psychological predisposition. *Quarterly Journal of Studies on Alcohol*, 1960, 21, 314–343.

Lu, Y. C. Contradictory parental expectations in schizophrenia. In D. Jackson (Ed.), *The etiology of schizophrenia*. New York: Basic Books, 1960.

McCord, W. F., & J. McCord, with J. Gudeman. *Origins of alcoholism*. Stanford, Calif.: Stanford University Press, 1960.

Mahler, M. S., M. Furer, & C. F. Settlage. Severe emotional disturbances in childhood: Psychosis. In S. Arieti (Ed.), *American handbook of psychiatry*, Vol. 1. New York: Basic Books, 1959.

Nameche, G. Life patterns of children who became adult schizophrenics. Unpublished Ph.D. thesis, Brandeis University, 1965.

Ricks, D. F., & G. Nameche. Symbiosis, sacrifice, and schizophrenia. *Mental Hygiene*, 1966, 50, 541–551.

Robertson, J. Mothering as an influence on early development. In R. S. Eissler et al. (Eds.), *Psychoanalytic study of the child*, Vol. 17. New York: International Universities Press, 1962.

Ross, S. Reported emotional experiences of disturbed & non-disturbed adolescents. Unpublished Ph.D. thesis, Teachers College, Columbia University, 1969.

Schilder, P. The psychogenesis of alcoholism. *Quarterly Journal of Studies on Alcohol*, 1941, 2, 277.

Spitzer, R. L., & J. Endicott. DIAGNO: A computer program for psychiatric diagnosis utilizing the differential diagnostic procedure. *Archives of General Psychiatry*, 1968, 18, 746–756.

———. DIAGNO II: Further developments in a computer program for psychiatric diagnosis. *American Journal of Psychiatry*, 1969, 125, 12–21.

Vaillant, C. An historical review of the remitting schizophrenias. *Journal of Nervous and Mental Disease*, 1964, 138, 48–56.

Waring, M., & D. F. Ricks. Family patterns of children who became adult schizophrenics. *Journal of Nervous and Mental Disease*, 1965, 140, 351–364.

Wellman, M. Towards an etiology of alcoholism: Why young men drink too much. *Canadian Medical Associations Journal*, 1955, 73, 717–725.

White, R. W. Motivation reconsidered: The concept of competence. *Psychological Review*, 1959, 66, 297–333.

Zwerling, I., & M. Rosenbaum. Alcoholic addiction and personality (nonpsychotic conditions). In S. Arieti (Ed.), *American handbook of psychiatry*, Vol. 1. New York: Basic Books, 1959.

SARNOFF A. MEDNICK
FINI SCHULSINGER

Factors Related to Breakdown in Children at High Risk for Schizophrenia

SCHIZOPHRENICS excite a good deal of behavioral research, the goal of much of which is to produce information concerning the etiology of schizophrenia. It may be difficult, however, to isolate etiological factors in studies carried out with individuals who have lived through the process of becoming and being schizophrenic. The behavior of these individuals may be markedly altered in response to correlates of the illness such as educational, economic, and social failure, pre-hospital, hospital, and post-hospital drug regimens, bachelorhood, long-term institutionalization, chronic illness, and sheer misery. In research with non-schizophrenics, these same factors have been shown measurably to affect behavioral research results. If researchers used control groups which were equated with their schizophrenic groups for all of these correlates of schizophrenia, then any observed differences could reasonably be ascribed to the variable of schizophrenia. But such control groups are apparently not readily available. Consequently, in comparisons of normals and schizophrenics, it is often difficult to judge what portion of the reported differences have unique relevance to schizophrenia. If, for example, comparisons of non-psychiatric prisoners and normals produced differences identical to those found for schizophrenics and normals, we might tend to attribute the schizophrenic-normal differences to the effects of institutionalization rather than to some intrinsic quality of the schizophrenic.

Variables such as institutionalization and drug effects may be considered epiphenomenal in relation to the basic pathological process of schizophrenia. When these epiphenomenal correlates of schizophrenia are studied for their own sake, we find that they, by themselves, have important effects on perception (Silverman, Berg, & Kantor, 1966), psychological adjustment (Knupfer, Clark, & Room, 1966), family harmony

(Crain, Sussman, & Weil, 1966a, 1966b), personality tests (Braginsky, Grosse, & Ring, 1966), and interview data (Pokorny, 1962). Yet almost *no* research on the schizophrenic takes these consequences into account when planning for a control group. Because of this, most research ascribes research results to the variable of schizophrenia when actually some part of the differences observed may be due to one or more of this myriad of consequences.

For example, in discussing a study in stimulus generalization, Mednick and Freedman (1960) state, "Using the dimension of space [he] found that schizophrenics generalized more than normals." Mednick, implying that generalization is important in etiology, neglects to consider the fact that his schizophrenics had been hospitalized, on the average, 119.05 months, whereas his normal control group had been hospitalized only 2.18 months. In this manner, while attempting to study some aspect of schizophrenia, Mednick could have been, unwittingly, chiefly investigating the effects of long-term institutionalization.

Three Research Methods

Most psychological and psychiatric research on the etiology of schizophrenia takes one of three forms: (a) observation of individuals already schizophrenic, (b) observation of the families of schizophrenics, or (c) inspection of earlier records reporting on childhood behavior of adult schizophrenics. We shall discuss the methodological problems of each of these approaches.

OBSERVATION OF INDIVIDUALS ALREADY SCHIZOPHRENIC

This method is the most common one. Typically, the subjects are patients in mental hospitals, as in Mednick and Freedman (1960). Since institutionalization is the most common and easily defined offender, it is well to begin by examining evidence that differences ascribed to diagnosis might be at least partly attributable to institutionalization effects.

Almost all schizophrenics whose behavior is summarized in the journals were originally found in hospitals. A survey of five recent volumes of the *Journal of Nervous and Mental Disease*, the *Journal of Abnormal Psychology*, and the *American Journal of Psychiatry* showed that 63 per cent of 115 empirical studies which compared schizophrenic with schizophrenic or schizophrenic with normal, did *not* provide information which might reveal the length of hospitalization of the subjects. The other 37 per cent noted that their chronic or process schizophrenics had been hospitalized for an average of 7.1 years; the acute or reactive subjects had been hospitalized for an average of 2.3 years. In almost all cases, the normals were not hospitalized, so that this factor was not controlled at all.

Despite the existence of great differences in length of hospitalization, the authors of these studies typically attributed their results exclusively to diagnostic group. In many cases, at least some part of the results could as easily have been ascribed to hospitalization. Two cases will demonstrate this point.

Silverman (1964), using the Titchener and Pettigrew apparatuses, demonstrated that compared with normals, acute schizophrenics and chronic schizophrenics, in that order, tend to evidence more severely restricted perceptual scanning and narrow concept width. As might be expected, his three groups differed substantially in duration of hospital stay. Concerned, and wishing to evaluate the effects of institutionalization, Silverman et al. (1966) took the unique step of repeating the same two tests used on the schizophrenic subjects on 50 long-term and 50 short-term non-psychiatric prisoners, all felons. (They roughly equated the prisoners and schizophrenics for length of institutionalization.) They found that the differences observed on these conceptual and perceptual measures among the normals and "acute" and "chronic" San Quentin inmates were almost precisely the same as those among the normals and acute and chronic schizophrenics. The mean scores for the imprisoned and the hospitalized were highly similar. "The failure to observe noteworthy differences between them [referring to the schizophrenic vs. the prisoner groups] on the Titchener Illusion and on the Pettigrew Category Width Test indicated that exaggerated performances on these procedures are not pathognomic of particular subtypes of schizophrenia . . . comparable response patterns may be found among nonschizophrenics who live in a similar environment" (p. 656). Thus, the results of the first Silverman study, originally ascribed to the effects of schizophrenia, could conceivably be completely attributed to the fact that the groups had resided in hospitals for different numbers of years.

In addition to the *effects* of being hospitalized, there seems to be some selection among those who frequent particular hospitals, in this case VA hospitals. Gladis and Wishner (1962), noting a series of studies "suggesting that schizophrenics are peculiarly sensitive to aversive content," conducted a verbal learning study employing aversive and neutral learning materials. As they had hypothesized, the VA-hospitalized schizophrenics showed much more relative sensitivity to aversive material than did the control subjects (evening college students). However, Gladis and Wishner also took the precaution of including a control group of VA surgical and medical patients. The results for the schizophrenic and the nonpsychotic surgical and medical VA groups were virtually identical. "It is worth emphasizing that if only schizophrenic (hospitalized) subjects had been employed one might have been willing to conclude that the results obtained support a hypothesis previously mentioned, namely, that schizophrenics are uniquely sensitive to aversive stimulus characteristics in the environment. The markedly similar performance of the nonpsychotic subjects strongly suggests that Veterans Administration hospital status and not diagnostic label was the relevant factor in this study" (p. 254).

The Silverman et al. and Gladis and Wishner studies suggest that testing schizophrenic patients can bias learning, perception, and thinking measures independently of diagnostic group. In their studies, hospitalization could be interpreted as an important basis for differences they observed between schizophrenics and non-schizophrenics. The effectiveness of mental hospital life in influencing the behavior of inmates has been documented by Goffman (1961) and Belknap (1956). There are at least two ways that hospitalization might affect research results: (a) it may alter the patient's attitude and personality and, in turn, produce changes in test measures, or (b) the patient may simply bias his responses to the tests in terms of some personal motive related to his hospital career.

With respect to personality alteration effects, Sommer and Hall (1958) have given evidence relating to the personality changes engendered by an institutional setting. A scale of alienation was administered to admission ward, active treatment, and continued treatment (chronic) patients as well as to hospital physicians. The chronic patients were significantly more alienated than either the admission ward or active treatment patients. Most surprising was the finding that the hospital *physicians* were significantly *more* alienated than were the admission ward patients. One possible interpretation of these data is that institutionalization influences scores on this psychological research instrument more than does schizophrenia.

The hospital patient facing an investigator may slant his responses in a direction favoring a specific goal such as discharge. This would be an example of the second way hospitalization can affect research results. Dunham and Weinberg (1960) have observed that "Since discharge is the highest value among patients, especially in the hopeful wards, certain general practices emerge. These behavioral acquisitions, as peculiar hospital products, take the form not only of external conformity, but of concealment of delusions and even hallucinations, provided the patient can control them. Many patients even consider improvement as subsidiary to discharge from the hospital" (pp. 89–90). Furthermore, Dunham and Weinberg indicate that patients seeking discharge see all of their behavior as being related to this goal. As one patient states, "I try to do my best around here. I run errands and do anything to help the hospital. I figure that it may get back to the doctor and it may help me to get out of here" (p. 104). Braginsky et al. (1966) have empirically demonstrated the decided effect hope or fear of discharge can have on questionnaire and paper-and-pencil research. Chronic and acute patients (mostly schizophrenic) shifted their scores on a group of MMPI test items in accordance with whether they thought their performance would help them get out of the hospital or remain in it. The chronic patients slanted their responses so as to appear sick, whereas the acute patients faked in the direction of greater health. Had the experiment been studying not response biases but rather differences between the chronic and acute groups on the MMPI items, the differences which were found would have typically been attributed to some less superficial cause. Gordon and Groth (1961) have shown the influence of this same variable on the semantic differential. They found differences on semantic differential ratings between patients who wanted to remain in the hospital and those who wished for an early discharge. Again we must ask, To what extent does response slanting produce differences reported between acute and chronic schizophrenics and normals? On the other hand, how often have such pervasive attitudes produced response biases that have contributed only extreme variance to research results?

Zarlock (1966) observed a related phenomenon with patients in recreational, occupational, social, and medical situations. Each of these situations was set up with the same research personnel except that in the medical situation the personnel wore white coats and nurses wore uniforms. Zarlock tape-recorded conversations and observed physical behavior. Instances of pathological verbal behavior were judged from typescripts of the tapes; bizarre physical behavior was rated in the actual situations. The bizarre and pathological behavior was at least ten times more frequent in the medical situation than in the other three situations and ranged up to one hundred times more frequent. Zarlock (whose study would be improved by the inclusion of normal control groups) suggests that the white coats *demand* deviant behavior in the schizophrenic patient.

In any case, this study raises serious questions regarding the reliability and the inter-experimenter generality of the behavior we observe and report. To what degree do differences between schizophrenics and normal controls depend on whether the investigator wore a white coat?

Shakow (1946) and his Worcester co-workers have long recognized the need to understand the response of the patient to the experimental situation. Indeed, a member of this group, Rickers-Ovsiankina (1937), carefully chose as controls "institutionalized individuals such as inmates of state infirmaries, who in general, live according to a routine similar to that of our patients. Twenty-five of them were destitute and the rest were suffering from some form of chronic illness, such as arthritis, cardiac conditions, neuritis, etc." Differences she reports between her control and experimental samples are less likely to be ascribable to hospitalization effects.

OBSERVATIONS OF FAMILIES OF SCHIZOPHRENICS

Fontana (1966) has carefully evaluated the methodology of research dealing with the "familial etiology of schizophrenia." He divides the studies into three groups: (a) clinical observations from treatment situations, (b) retrospective accounts from interviews, and (c) current family interaction recorded directly by the investigator. He dismisses the clinical approach — although it is of value for insights and hypotheses, "intrinsic difficulties make it unsuitable as a firm basis for a scientific methodology." With respect to retrospective studies, it seems clear that parental recollection data are too unreliable to serve as scientific evidence. The evidence cited by Fontana for distrusting the validity of historical parental reportage is decisive. Further confirming evidence is found in Mednick and Schaffer (1963), Hefner (1962), and Hefner and Mednick (in press).

Fontana raises the problem of the "etiological assumption," which forms the basis of family studies of schizophrenia. This assumption states that disturbed family processes had a role in the development of schizophrenia. It is just as reasonable to assert the obverse of this assumption: the serious illness of the schizophrenic as a child or adolescent had a role in the development of family disturbance. Fontana does not present evidence which might help us choose between the alternative assumptions. However, there is some indirect evidence. In general, it suggests that "patterns of parent-child relations similar to those we find in schizophrenia have been described for several other types of illnesses, manic-depressive psychosis, ulcers, and anorexia nervosa as well as for juvenile delinquency and drug addiction" (Kohn & Clausen, 1956, p. 312). Indeed, maternal overprotection and elevated family conflict have also been reported for the parents of diabetics (Crain et al., 1966a, 1966b), hemophiliacs (Mattson & Gross, 1966), infantile paralytics (Rosenbaum, 1943), and children with scoliosis and osteomyelitis (Kammerer, 1940). In these cases it seems likely that the overprotection and marital conflict was a result rather than a cause of the disease. This suggests the use of control groups consisting of families with a chronically ill child. Illustrating the importance of this, Pokorny (1962) studied the family background of schizophrenics but used tubercular patients as controls. He found no evidence of differences between these groups in "completeness of family life" or "security of childhood." (He did note some differences in other areas.) Klebanoff (1957) compared the mothers of childhood schizophrenics with the mothers of normal children on the Parental Attitude Research Instrument and found the usual tendency for the mothers of schizophrenics to have more pathological attitudes than mothers of normal children. There was no difference, however, between the mothers of the schizophrenic children and a control group consisting of mothers of hospitalized brain-injured and retarded children. Klebanoff states that his results support the hypothesis "that pathological attitudes observed in the mother arise as a result of the stress of trying to deal with the disordered child." Nameche has presented evidence that the family with a to-be-schizophrenic child suffers progressive deterioration before the onset of the illness (Ricks, 1967). Studying families of individuals already schizophrenic may generate new methodology and hypotheses; however, because of the apparent heavy influence of the illness on the families' responses, extreme caution must be employed in asserting relationships of cause and effect. As is stated by Fontana, "The greatest value of current studies of family interaction seems to lie in the guidelines the findings might provide for longitudinal research."

These arguments are not presented to discredit the hypothesis that family structure and interactional patterns may be etiologically important in schizophrenia. They instead suggest that in studying the family of an individual already schizophrenic, we may be hard pressed to separate etiological factors from reactions to the illness.

But institutionalization and families' reaction to their children's severe illnesses are not the only factors that influence research in an uncontrolled manner. We must face the fact that we are studying individuals who, in comparison to their controls, have had less sexual experience and less marriage, lack occupational success, have been exposed to pre-hospital, hospital, and post-hospital drug regimens, are educationally disadvantaged, and often have suffered lives of chronic illness, misery, and loneliness. Although some of these factors could be considered contributory causes, they are certainly also *consequents* of the schizophrenic condition. These consequents of the schizophrenic condition heavily shade and quite often completely overshadow attempts to examine the origins of schizophrenia.

If we are to continue to study the etiology of schizophrenia through individuals already schizophrenic, we have only two choices: First, we can obtain adequate controls. These controls must match the schizophrenic subjects for the usual factors plus extent of institutionalization, presence of severe and chronic illness, educational level and achievement, sexual and marital history, occupational success, past and present drug regimens, and misery and loneliness. Second, we can eliminate the contaminating variables from consideration by establishing the effects of these variables on the specific measures to be used in a given investigation. After Silverman et al.'s findings, anyone who would study some aspect of the perceptual behavior of hospitalized schizophrenics who did not first evaluate the effects of institutionalization on his measures would be laying himself wide open to the danger of spending his time unproductively. Research measures that survive this kind of evaluation can be said to have a much higher likelihood of being related to the etiology of schizophrenia. Either of these alternatives may prove difficult to effect. A way of overcoming the difficulties inherent in studying individuals already schizophrenic may be to study them *before* they become schizophrenic. Two methods for this may be found in the literature, the childhood-records method and the high-risk sample method.

CHILDHOOD-RECORDS METHOD

The childhood-records method studies school, child guidance clinic, or birth records of individuals now schizophrenic. This method has been used quite successfully by many investigators (Albee, Lane, & Reuter, 1964; Birren, 1944; Nameche, Waring, & Ricks, 1964; O'Neal & Robins, 1958; and many others). It has the great advantage of evaluating records produced by individuals ignorant of the eventual schizophrenic condition of their charges. The information, at the time it was inscribed, was relatively current, not retrospective. The subjects on which the study focuses are all schizophrenic. (For a more complete discussion of this method see Ricks, 1967; Roff, pp. 10–29). Along with these advantages come some problems. The records are produced by different individuals with differing vocabularies. If one therapist calls a patient *nervous* is this equivalent to what another terms *tense*? The information is not complete and systematic. If a child is not explicitly called *nervous*, does this mean he was not nervous or that the therapist saw no point in mentioning this factor in his case report? When working with twenty- to thirty-year-old case records, one must take what he finds. One must be very lucky to find, in these data, information which tests hypotheses of interest to the researcher.

Perhaps the most serious shortcoming of the childhood-records method is the danger of disabling sampling biases. Since this problem is difficult to explain in the abstract, we shall discuss it in relation to a study by Albee et al. (1964) which is part of a series; we chose it as an example because of the methodological sophistication of the authors. This study selected schizophrenics hospitalized "in the Cleveland area" who in childhood had attended second grade in Cleveland. The elementary school IQ scores for the schizophrenics were then compared with the IQ scores of their elementary school classmates and found to be lower. It is important to note that the schizophrenics were apparently lifelong residents of Cleveland; the only direct information on the mobility history of the control group is that they resided in Cleveland when they attended elementary school. Approximately 4 per cent of the Cleveland population migrates out of that area each year. From figures available, it could be conservatively estimated that over the period of time covered by the study, 50 per cent of the original control group had moved from the Cleveland area (Lansing & Mueller, 1967) whereas none of the schizophrenics had moved out of the area. Thus, the two groups differ markedly not only in diagnosis but also in mobility. Mobility has been shown to be directly related to IQ (Gist & Clark, 1938; Maxwell, 1954) and educational and social class level (Lansing & Mueller, 1967). In view of the finding that disturbed individuals evidence greater mobility than non-disturbed (Robins & O'Neal, 1958), it seems clear that Albee et al.'s study has selected a very special subgroup of nonmobile schizophrenics. The more mobile schizophrenics who have left the Cleveland area (and are consequently included in the "control" group) are very likely to have scored higher on IQ tests in second grade. This sampling bias might explain at least part of the reported eleven-point IQ score differences between the controls and hospitalized schizophrenics. It seems possible that any selection from the second-grade population of a nonmigrant subgroup (i.e., still living in the metropolitan statistical area of Cleveland) would have been biased toward a lower IQ test score. In view of the large population turnover in the United States and the very special characteristics of this migratory group, the results of much of the childhood-records research must be evaluated with caution. To avoid this sampling bias, one must begin with a large school population and trace *all* the pupils to find which had become schizophrenic. Without a national psychiatric register, this is a difficult undertaking. Another approach might be to compare the nonmobile schizophrenics with a nonmobile local control. Robins (p. 226 below) has also studied antecedents of character disorder in this manner. This would inform us of the pre-schizophrenic condition of the nonmobile schizophrenic. In view of the relatively high schizophrenic rate among migrants and the high migrant rate among the disturbed (Robins & O'Neal, 1958), generalization from such a nonmobile population could only be done with caution. Thus, although the childhood-records method avoids the problems encountered in studying the schizophrenic, this method also has some potentially serious drawbacks.

We have made three points: (a) Schizophrenics may be too "contaminated" by the consequents of their illness to be suitable subjects for research on the etiology of schizophrenia. (b) The family with a child schizophrenic has been changed by the experience, so it is difficult to assess the original role of this family in the development of the illness. (c) The childhood-records method has many important advantages but often suffers from serious sampling problems as well as data insufficiencies at the source.

THE HIGH-RISK SAMPLE METHOD

These points emphasize the difficulty of developing etiological findings from studies based on individuals already schizophrenic. In our own research (Mednick, 1965, 1966, 1967; Mednick & Schulsinger, 1964, 1965a, 1968), we have turned almost completely from the study of the patient to the longitudinal study of young children at high risk for schizophrenia, children who have chronically and severely schizophrenic mothers. When some appreciable number of subjects become seriously deviant (including schizophrenic), we shall be able to look back at the 1962 examination and determine early premorbid characteristics which distinguish those that succumb, investigate the interaction of these premorbid characteristics with life circumstances, and plot these factors as they change from the time of the first examination to breakdown.

ADVANTAGES OF THE HIGH-RISK METHOD

There are certain methodological advantages in the longitudinal study of high-risk samples.

a. The subjects are not yet schizophrenic; they have not experienced the epiphenomena of the illness. Thus, their reactions on our tests are not heavily colored by these epiphenomena.

b. The researchers, relatives, and the subject himself do not know that he will become schizophrenic. This relieves the data of a certain part of the burden of bias. The bias is certainly no greater for the future schizophrenic than for other high-risk subjects who do not succumb to schizophrenia.

c. The information gathered is current, not retrospective. That part of the investigation which is retrospective is less so than it would be if the subjects were adults.

d. The data are uniformly and systematically obtained. This is in contrast with retrospective studies which make use of childhood and school records concerning adult schizophrenics.

e. One advantage of the high-risk method which may not be immediately apparent is the fact that *the ideal controls for the high-risk subjects who become schizophrenic are the high-risk subjects who develop other deviancies and the high-risk subjects who do not become deviant.* Such controls are an integral part of the design (see Fig. 1).

f. There are other samples at high risk for schizophrenia but none

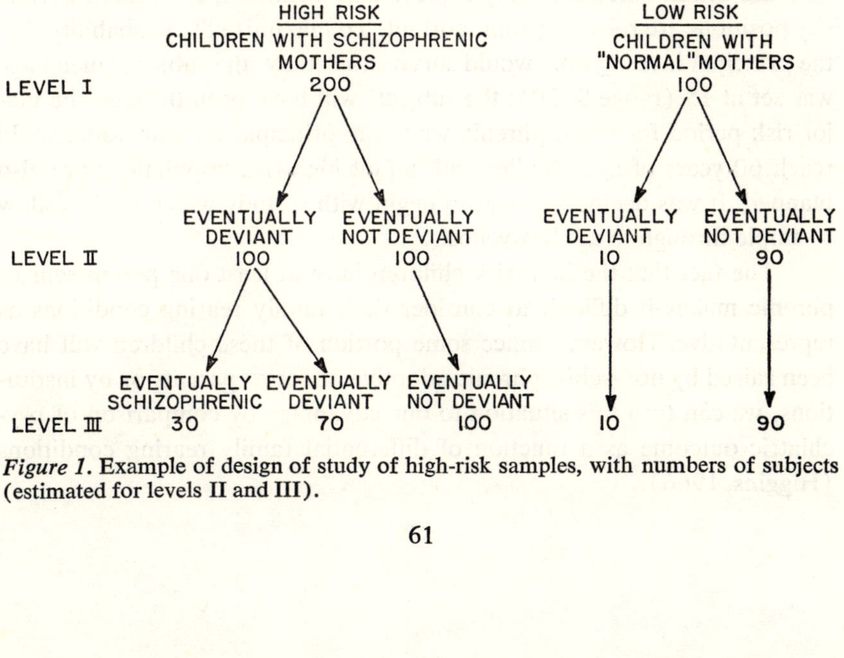

Figure 1. Example of design of study of high-risk samples, with numbers of subjects (estimated for levels II and III).

of these fulfill the research requirements as well as the children of schizophrenics. Identical twins of adult schizophrenics are too old, as are siblings and parents of adult schizophrenics.

g. Of the masses of research on the already schizophrenic there is doubtless much which does relate to etiology. Information on premorbid characteristics may be of value in culling these etiologically relevant findings. In this manner, the two methods may be mutually supportive. For example, Zahn (1964) has reported poor habituation on the part of chronic schizophrenics. It is of great interest that this was an important distinguishing premorbid characteristic of a group of the high-risk sample which has suffered serious psychiatric breakdown (further discussed below).

A long-term longitudinal study of a relatively large sample faces certain problems, the chief one being successfully following the subjects. After an abortive attempt to conduct this study in Michigan, a study conducted in Denmark by Fremming (1951) was brought to the attention of the senior author. Fremming achieved 92 per cent success in locating 5,500 individuals in a sixty-year follow-up. He was aided immeasurably in this task by the Danish Folkeregisters, which have on file the current address of every resident of Denmark. Subsequent experience has made it clear that because of these bureaus a highly successful follow-up can be anticipated in this research.

An additional problem of such a long-term study is the potential loss of key personnel. Two major causes of loss are shift in university affiliation and death. Since the study is located in Denmark, changes in university positions are relatively unimportant. To maximize the probability that the principal investigators would survive the study, the subjects' mean age was set at 15 (range 9–20); the subjects will have been through the major risk period for schizophrenia when the principal investigators should reach 60 years of age. Studies with infant high-risk populations are also planned. It was deemed crucial to begin with a study which could follow a sample through to adult psychosis.

The fact that the high-risk children have at least one parent schizophrenic makes it difficult to consider their family rearing conditions as representative. However, since some portion of these children will have been raised by non-schizophrenic adoptive or foster parents or by institutions, we can turn this situation to our advantage by comparison of psychiatric outcome as a function of differential family rearing conditions (Higgins, 1966).

SARNOFF A. MEDNICK · FINI SCHULSINGER

The Copenhagen Study

In 1962 we began to gather a sample of 207 children who have a high risk of becoming schizophrenic (they have schizophrenic mothers). We estimate that approximately 30 of these children will become schizophrenic and approximately 100 will become seriously mentally ill or deviant (Heston, 1966; Kallmann, 1946; Reisby, 1967). We intend to follow these subjects until 1982, when most of those fated to succumb will have done so.

AIMS OF THE RESEARCH

The study had three aims:

Aim I. An immediate aim was to compare the high- and low-risk subjects on a broad range of measures. Since about 50 per cent of the high-risk group seems to be heading for some serious deviancy (Heston, 1966), differences between these two groups may relate to factors predisposing to deviance. Since the schizophrenics will represent a large subgroup of the deviants, some of these differentiating characteristics may relate to schizophrenia.

Aim II. We intend to follow both high- and low-risk samples and periodically retest them. Changes in personal characteristics and/or life conditions or their interactions which instigate or signal developing illness may make themselves evident through such procedures.

Aim III. As mentioned above, 50 per cent of the high-risk group may be expected to become seriously deviant. At some future time it will be possible to look back at our initial assessment and discover which (if any) of our test variables could have differentiated this deviant group from the high-risk subjects that develop more normally. Of the 50 per cent of the high-risk group expected to become seriously deviant (approximately 100 subjects), about 30 per cent may be expected to develop some form of schizophrenia. It will be of great interest to see which (if any) premorbid characteristics and life circumstances differentiate the schizophrenics from the other varieties of deviance, from the "non-deviant" high-risk subjects, and from the low-risk controls. We shall give special attention to the interaction of premorbid personal characteristics and life circumstances as possible factors contributing to mental illness.

The aims relating to premorbid differentiating characteristics assume that measures relating to factors predisposing to schizophrenia will be present in our test battery. The test battery was designed to be broad-ranging, tapping areas of function shown by empirical research to be aberrant in the schizophrenic. It also related to a theory of schizophrenia (Mednick 1958, 1962) which will be referred to below in connection with the discussion of results. Despite our best efforts, the test battery represents a limited realm of variables. It is only too possible that the factors differentiating the pre-schizophrenic are not directly present in this limited realm. However, even if some of the variables are only indirectly related to variables crucial to the development of schizophrenia, our findings may serve to orient future research efforts toward fruitful areas of study.

METHOD OF PROCEDURE

The project was first attempted in the state of Michigan in the summer of 1961. It soon became clear that the necessary records in the state were inadequate for our purposes and that following the subject for twenty years would result in an unacceptable rate of loss of subjects (Lansing & Mueller, 1967; U.S. Bureau of the Census, 1956). In contrast to this, Fremming (1951) had 92 per cent success in locating 5,500 individuals in Denmark in a sixty-year follow-up. When this work came to our attention, it became clear that our study was possible in Denmark. Denmark also has the advantage of small size and great population concentration in the Copenhagen area.

The excellent follow-up record of the Fremming study is easier to understand in the context of the Danish Folkeregister. These municipal bureaus maintain a lifelong up-to-date register of the address of every resident of Denmark. Another Danish institution which proved to be of great value to this project is the National Psychiatric Register, which maintains a central file on every psychiatric hospitalization in Denmark. The use of these institutions will be described below.

Our first aim was to check, in Denmark, the frequency of schizophrenia among individuals with schizophrenic mothers. In view of apparent disparities between psychiatric genetics investigations in Scandinavia and other countries over the years, which have recently come to light, it is of special value now to have this independent check. In connection with this project, Reisby (1967) investigated the risk of hospitalization for schizophrenia among children of a relatively small, resident-hospital, female schizophrenic, *Danish* population. This risk proved to be 10.4 per cent, which falls in the lower range of other estimates, such as Kallmann (1946).

SUBJECTS

We chose to take children whose *mothers* are *process* schizophrenic for a number of reasons. (a) Allegations of paternity are not always free of challenge. It might be difficult to be quite sure of our major independent variable with alleged fathers, especially if they were schizophrenic. (b) Schizophrenic women have more children than schizophrenic men (Goldfarb & Erlenmeyer-Kimling, 1961). In a study of all schizophrenic patients in a Danish state hospital, we found schizophrenic women to be five times as fertile as schizophrenic men. (c) Psychodevelopmentally, mothers presumably play a greater role in shaping children. Using mothers has permitted us to carry out research on the effects of being reared by a schizophrenic mother (Higgins, 1966). (d) The offspring of process (typical) schizophrenic mothers yield a higher rate of schizophrenia than offspring of reactive schizophrenics (Lewis, 1957; Schulz, 1940).

Diagnosis of Mother. Two experienced Danish psychiatrists trained together and then independently tested their reliability in making judgments from hospital records. Their agreement as to diagnosis on twenty test cases was found to be 100 per cent. They merely had to judge whether the mothers were typical schizophrenics. They were instructed to discard *any* questionable cases. Following this reliability check, only one psychiatrist checked each record. For each mother a precoded form was filled out which listed her symptoms, provided information concerning her dates of hospitalization, and summarized her clinical status.

The intent in the selection of the mothers was to choose only cases that would be readily agreed upon in Europe or the United States as being severe and typical schizophrenics. We required at least five years of hospitalization, or at least three separate periods of hospitalization, each of at least three months duration, with no sign of improvement during discharge, or an extended hospitalization plus a certified State Invalid Pension for schizophrenic symptoms.

Matching of High-Risk and Low-Risk Subjects. Pairs of high-risk (H) subjects were matched on sex, age, father's occupation (the best measure of social class in Denmark [Svalastoga, 1959]), rural-urban residence, years of education, and institutional upbringing versus family life. Next, a single low-risk (L) subject was selected who was matched on these same variables person for person with each H pair.

When an H child was in a children's home, he was paired with another H child in a children's home; the matching L child was also from a children's home. In most of these L cases the parents had divorced, died, suffered from serious somatic illnesses, or were alcoholics or criminals. They afford the opportunity of some degree of control for the broken-home aspects of being the child of a schizophrenic mother.

Table 1 presents the mean values for the H and L groups for the matching variables used in this study. As may be seen, the average age of the sample was 15.1 years. There would have been some advantage in testing a younger group; however, it will take twenty years for the present sample to pass through a major part of the risk period for schizophrenia. As indicated above, the subjects' mean age was selected so as to maximize the probability that the investigators would still be alive at the conclusion of this risk period.

Alarm Network. As the subjects of the long-term follow-up begin to break down, it will be crucial to be on the spot as soon as possible in order to gain a picture of the circumstances precipitating the breakdown. An alarm network was instituted to deal with this problem. Through the health insurance system, each of the subjects has a family physician. These physicians know that their patients are under study and provide information concerning contacts they may have with the subjects.

All hospitals on Zealand and all psychiatric hospitals in Denmark have submitted blank hospital registration cards to us. A registration card has been prepared for each of the 311 subjects on the particular form for

Table 1. Characteristics of the Experimental and Control Samples

Characteristics	Control	Experimental
Number of cases	104	207
Number of boys	59	121
Number of girls	45	86
Mean age [a]	15.1	15.1
Mean social class [b]	2.3	2.2
Mean years of education	7.3	7.0
Percentage of group in children's homes [c]	14%	16%
Mean number of years in children's homes [c]	8.5	9.4
Percentage of group with rural residence [d]	22%	26%

[a] Defined as age to the nearest whole year.

[b] The scale runs from 0 (low) to 6 (high) and was adapted from Svalastoga (1959).

[c] We considered only experience in children's homes of five years or greater duration. Many of the Experimental children had been in children's homes for brief periods while their mother was hospitalized. These experiences were seen as quite different from the experience of children who had to make a children's home their home until they could earn their own living.

[d] A rural residence was defined as living in a town with a population of 2,500 persons or fewer.

each and every hospital. Stamped on each card is a message requesting that the project be informed immediately if the subject presents himself for hospitalization. The secretaries responsible for informing us receive small financial incentives for every notification. The network has been operative for two years and seems effective.

TESTING PROCEDURE

Until testing was complete, none of the examiners was informed whether the children tested were H or L subjects. All visits were scheduled by the social worker. The procedures were identical for all subjects.

Subjects arrived at 8 A.M., and height and weight were measured. They were then escorted to the psychophysiology laboratory, where they underwent mild stress, conditioning, and generalization procedures. They were then tested with a full Wechsler Intelligence Scale for Children (WISC) and a selection of items translated from the Minnesota Multiphasic Personality Inventory (MMPI). Then came lunch. After lunch they took the Word Association Test (WAT, single word response) and the Continuous Association Test (CAT) and completed the Adjective Check List (ACL) describing themselves. They then returned for a second psychophysiology session where they underwent mild stress, semantic conditioning, and mediated generalization procedures. Finally, they were interviewed by a psychiatrist and given an honorarium.

Psychophysiological Procedures. Psychophysiological measures relate to states of cortical activation and emotional arousal. Researchers in the area of schizophrenia have very frequently included these measures in their research designs. Psychophysiological techniques, particularly electrodermal measures, have revealed significant aberrancies in the schizophrenic (Venables, 1966). In addition, these measures are crucial to aspects of a theory of the etiology of schizophrenia proposed by the senior author (Mednick, 1962). Inclusion of these measures in a conditioning paradigm affords the opportunity to record measures related to the learning and generalization of fear responses. We also wished to observe the psychophysiological response to mild stress.

An Offner-Beckman Type R Dynograph was used to record the physiological variables. After washing and alcohol sponging at points of electrode placement, the subject reclined and was asked to relax. Respiration, heart rate, galvanic skin response (GSR), and electromyography (EMG) electrodes were attached: To measure *respiration*, an Offner respiration transducer was fastened just above the waistline and below the diaphragm. To measure *heart rate*, electrodes were attached with rubber straps to the ankles and to the left arm just below the elbow. To measure EMG, electrodes were fastened with elastic tape 2 cm. above the eyebrows and 5 cm. on either side of the nose line. And to measure GSR, a special Wheatstone skin resistance bridge was constructed for the project (Ax & Zacharopolous, 1961). The bridge reversed the polarity of the 1.5 volt reference current every 1.2 sec. The input was processed from the bridge to the preamplifier via a straight-through coupler. Recording was through high-sensitivity ink penwriters.

When the transducers were attached, recording was started and was continuous until the conclusion of generalization testing. *S* was instructed to relax, and earphones were fitted.

Approximately 30 sec. after the tape recorder was started, *S* heard instructions informing him of the procedure, followed by 8 presentations of the conditioned stimulus (CS, 1,000 cps. tone). These 8 presentations were included to desensitize *S* to the CS and provide information concerning *S*'s orienting response. Conditioning trials began 9 sec. after the final "desensitization trial." The unconditioned stimulus (UCS) was an irritating noise of 96 db. presented for 4.5 sec. following .5 sec. after the onset of CS (54 db.). There were 14 partial reinforcement trials (9 CS–UCS pairings, and 5 interspersed presentations of the CS alone). Trials were separated by intervals which varied from 17 to 77 sec.

Following the final conditioning trial, there was an interval of 3 min., following which conditioning and stimulus generalization testing began. Generalization stimuli were tones of 1,311 cps. (GS_1) and 1,967 cps. (GS_2). There were 9 trials, 3 each of CS, GS_1, and GS_2. Duration of CS, GS_1, and GS_2 was 2 sec., and stimuli were separated by intervals which varied from 10 to 18 sec. The order of the CS, GS_1, and GS_2 was counterbalanced.

The final conditioning and stimulus generalization-testing trial marked the end of the morning psychophysiology session, which took approximately 50 min. *S* was then disconnected from the apparatus and escorted from the laboratory.

The afternoon psychophysiology session was identical to the morning except that verbal stimuli and verbal mediation were used for conditioning and generalization (Mednick & Wild, 1962). The verbal materials were taken from Kent-Rosanof word association norms we established on Danish schoolchildren between the ages of 9 and 16 years.

Wechsler Intelligence Scale for Children. There has been a considerable amount of research showing an IQ deficit in the childhood school record of adult schizophrenics (Albee et al., 1964; Lane & Albee, 1963, 1964). Despite limitations in methodology, the great consistency of the findings prompted us to include the WISC. Added to this is the breadth of the perceptual, reasoning, motor, and memory functions, which may be examined in a standard manner. The test also yields examples of reasoning and verbal behavior which may be analyzed by existent clinical techniques. A translation of the WISC commonly used in Denmark was administered in accordance with standard instructions.

Minnesota Multiphasic Personality Inventory. A test of personality characteristics was deemed essential. The size of the sample dictated the use of an objective measure. The MMPI offers the possibility of the establishment of premorbid scales for the schizophrenic and other deviant outcomes. One drawback of this Danish translation is the lack of corresponding Danish norms. The MMPI was shortened to 304 items by removing items deemed inappropriate or offensive to children. The items were printed on cards and individually administered in the standard manner. In cases where children had difficulty in reading, the examiner read the items aloud.

Word Association Test. Considering thought disorders in schizophrenia and using associative techniques to isolate and observe these disturbances have been a frequent and fruitful approach to the study of schizophrenia. The Kent-Rosanof Word List was chosen because of the large body of comparison literature available. Danish word association norms did not exist, so we gathered and tabulated the word associations of 145 Danish schoolchildren between the ages of 9 and 16. These norms enabled us to evaluate the statistical features of the sample's associations. It will be of great interest to observe changes in associative behavior correlated with changes in psychiatric status and other variables. The list was read to the subject with the instruction to respond to each word with the first single word that came to mind. Response latency was recorded.

Continuous Association Test. In addition to the reasons cited above for inclusion of the WAT, we wished to study the flow of the subject's associations to a single word over a period of a minute. Research has indicated that differences between normals and schizophrenics change qualitatively and quantitatively during the minute.

The thirty stimulus words were each printed on a card which was presented to the subject. He was asked to look at the word during the association period and report all of his associations to the word. Responses and latencies were recorded. If the subject gave multi-word responses or responded to his own associations rather than the stimulus he was cautioned two times.

Adjective Check List. Although the interviewing psychiatrist and the WISC examiner wrote brief clinical sketches of the subjects, it was clear that these would be difficult to handle statistically for 311 subjects. Nevertheless, we felt it to be of some importance to be able to summarize the clinical impression the subjects made on the professional personnel. The ACL was chosen because of its objective scoring and because of the large number of scales which have been empirically constructed using this test — the ACL lends itself to the construction of new scales. The ACL also afforded an opportunity for the subject to describe himself in objective terms.

The ACL of 241 adjectives was handed to the subject with instructions to use it to describe himself. The interviewing psychiatrist, and the administrators of the WISC and WAT also used the ACL to describe each subject. Each simply checked all the adjectives that were applicable.

Psychiatric Interview. An important reason for the inclusion of the psychiatric interview was to screen children that were already mentally ill. Four children were excluded from the sample on this basis. The interviewer focused on the subject's mental status, social history, and attitudes. Parts of the interview were precoded; the interviewer also presented his clinical impression of the subject. The 30- to 40-minute interview was conducted by Schulsinger in his office.

Parental Interview. This interview was meant to give us information concerning the current social, familial, and educational status of the subject. The interview also aimed at obtaining information relative to rearing conditions. A social worker interviewed the individual responsible for the child, in a highly structured interview with precoded sections. This usually took place in the home of the interviewee and had a duration of 1½ to 2½ hours.

School Report. Bower, Shellhamer, and Daily (1960) and others have demonstrated the value of school information in delineating characteristics of the pre-schizophrenic. They obtained their information from teachers; this was also our source of data. The teacher is a professional spending many hours with the children. He can make judgments concerning his interactions with them, their peer interactions, and their academic achievement. A questionnaire was mailed to each subject's school with the request that the teacher that knows him best respond. Of 311 forms sent out, 310 were returned.

Midwife's Report. Many investigators have suggested the possibility that schizophrenia may be a product of damage to the brain occurring during pregnancy or birth. Every birth in Denmark (except under extraordinary circumstances) is attended by a trained midwife who completes a detailed form concerning the pre- and post-birth condition of the mother, the birth process, and the condition of the newborn. The forms were located and copied.

Analyses

The project is now in its sixth year. We shall present two data analyses that will serve to illustrate the manner in which this "follow-up high-risk" design may be exploited. The first analysis compares the behavior and characteristics of the high- and low-risk groups. This comparison is relevant to Aim I. Due to limitations of space, and in view of the fact that much of this material has appeared earlier (Mednick, 1966; Mednick & Schulsinger, 1965a; 1965b), this presentation will take the form of a narrative summary of some of the significant findings. Twenty of the high-risk subjects have suffered psychiatric breakdowns since the inception of the study. The second analysis reports on characteristics which differentiate these individuals from comparable high- and low-risk subjects. These results are relevant to Aim III.

HIGH-RISK VERSUS LOW-RISK GROUP COMPARISONS

Birth Data. There is a general trend for the birth of the H subjects to have been attended by more difficulties. This is in conformance with previous reports on pregnancy and delivery in schizophrenic women. Significantly more of the mothers of the H subjects tended to be unwed. The birth process took much longer for the H subjects and was attended by significantly more exploratory examinations. Perhaps most significant is the fact that abnormal placentas were present for 11.3 per cent of the H subjects and only 1.2 per cent of the L subjects. Many of the placental disturbances took the form of infarcts.

Psychophysiologic Findings. Extremely consistent and highly significant differences were observed in the latency of the galvanic skin response (GSR). These differences, however, seem to be rather complex. Unequivocally and without exception, the H group responds with a shorter period of latency to the stress stimuli. In every case, the differences are significant and marked. This short latency period suggests that the H group is characterized by a volatile autonomic nervous system that is easily and quickly aroused by mild stress.

The differences between the two groups in latency of response to more neutral stimuli are not so marked. Although the H group continues to respond more quickly, there are many instances in which this trend becomes reversed.

We predicted differences in amplitude of response, speed of recovery, and generalization responsiveness. The two predictions concerning amplitude of response and generalization were strongly supported. The H group responds with much greater amplitude to the stress and to the generalization stimuli than does the L group.

In complete contradiction to our prediction is the fairly consistent finding that the H group recovered from its response to the stress stimuli at a relatively greater rate of speed. For the past ten years our hypothesis in research in schizophrenia has been that the pre-schizophrenic should show slower recovery from stress. Our data seem definitely to contradict this hypothesis. We shall discuss some possible interpretations of this finding below.

The pre-schizophrenic is an individual quick to react with extremely vigorous autonomic responses. His autonomic responses are not discriminating but overgeneralized. (Perhaps the overgeneralization is in part due to the excessively quick latency of the response system.) This very rapid, highly vigorous responding is balanced by an equally labile rate of recovery from autonomic imbalance.

Cognitive Findings. The single-word association and the intelligence tests yielded few differences between the H and L groups. The H group tended to give more idiosyncratic and fragmented associations. Although the H groups performed a bit more poorly on most of the subtests of the WISC, the differences reached significance only on the Arithmetic and Coding subtests.

In a thesis at the University of Copenhagen, Diderichsen (1967) compared the H and L groups on the CAT. The H group gave a significantly greater number of responses; they also gave a greater percentage of clang associates, chain associations, and repetitions of the response words. These findings suggest that disorders of association are already discernible in the thought processes of some members of the H group. Whether or not these are the individuals slated for schizophrenia remains to be seen. The low magnitude of the single-word association and the intelligence test differences probably reflects the fact that no member of either group was mentally ill at the time of the first examination.

Level of Adjustment. At the conclusion of the psychiatric interview, the psychiatrist rated the state of adjustment of each subject, taking into consideration personal and environmental factors. This resulted in a five-point scale: 1, poor; 2, relatively poor; 3, doubtful; 4, relatively good; 5, good. In the H group 24 per cent were rated 1 or 2; only 1 per cent of the L group fell into these categories.

Social-Developmental Factors. In the brief narrative summary which follows we shall combine many individual findings. The first characteristic that all of the H subjects have in common, of course, is that they have mothers who are schizophrenic. Their home life has not been harmonious, but has been marked by frequent parental quarrels. The mother has apparently been relatively dominant in the home. However, her influence has not been benign; the child sees her as scolding, unreliable, and not worthy of his confidences.

This difficult environment has been imposed upon (or perhaps has been responsible for producing) a child whose autonomic nervous system is highly labile, reacting to threat abnormally quickly and with abnormal amplitude. To make things still more difficult, reactions are not specific, but overgeneralized. This serves to broaden the range of stimuli that are adequate to provoke this sensitive autonomic nervous system.

In school, the child's teachers recognize his tendency to get upset easily. He seems to react to excitement by withdrawing. He handles peer relations and classroom challenges by passivity. Perhaps this mode of reaction is learned, since it is usually followed by the reduction of his anticipatory fear. Despite the use of passivity and withdrawal, the child is still approachable and is performing relatively adequately. He shows his "nervousness" enough for his teacher to remark on it. However, having begun to learn avoidance behavior, the child has a difficult time stopping, since the behavior takes him away from the very social situations in which he might learn more direct means of dealing with his anticipatory anxiety. His autonomic recovery being more rapid, his withdrawal is even more effectively rewarded. Since he withdraws, his peers reject him, and the circle gets tighter and more difficult to break.

Although, in general, the child performs adequately, he has already learned to effect momentary withdrawal responses whenever pressures build up. In tasks that require continuous concentration and effort (Arithmetic and Coding in the WISC), his performance will begin to slip.

The child is a loner much of the time. He does not share associations with his peer group as much as do his schoolmates. In addition, he is beginning to learn to escape from autonomic arousal by drifting off into idiosyncratic thought.

Every statement in the preceding summary is based on a statistically significant finding separating the H and L groups. Two points should be made: First, the groups overlap on all of the measures mentioned. Second, the summary is written as though all of the characteristics were present in a single group of individuals. What is more likely is that different subgroups of the H group were responsible for the significant findings on different items.

TWENTY HIGH-RISK SUBJECTS WHO SUCCUMBED

Since the 1962 assessment, the Alarm Network has identified 20 high-risk subjects who have manifested severely abnormal behavior. We shall call these individuals the Sick Group. Of these, 12 have been admitted to psychiatric facilities or placed under psychiatric care. The remaining 8 are severe schizoids, delinquents, alcoholics, or have manifested bizarre symptomatic behavior. Case summaries are presented below.

Case Summaries of Sick Group

1. *Male*, born March 16, 1953; extremely withdrawn, no close contacts; two months psychiatric admission following theft; currently in institution for boys with behavior difficulties, still performing petty thieveries.

2. *Female*, born January 19, 1943; married, one child; extremely withdrawn, nervous; evidence of delusional thinking, pulls her hair out, has large bald area.

3. *Female*, born March 29, 1946; promiscuous, recent abortion; highly unstable in work; no close contacts; confused and unrealistic; psychiatric admission for diagnostic reasons, some evidence of thought disorder.

4. *Male*, born July 1, 1946; under minor provocation had semipsychotic breakdown in Army; expresses strange distortions of his body image, thought processes vague, immature.

5. *Male*, born May 2, 1944; severe difficulties in concentrating, cannot complete tasks; marked schizoid character; marginally adjusted.

6. *Male*, born June 3, 1947; lonely in the extreme, spends all spare time at home; manages at home only by virtue of extremely compulsive routines; no heterosexual activity; marked schizoid character.

7. *Male*, born October 1, 1953; no close contact with peers; attends class for retarded children; abuses younger children, recently took a little boy out in the forest, undressed him, urinated on him and his clothes, and sent him home.

8. *Male,* born January 17, 1954; has history of convulsions, constantly takes antiseizure drug (Dilanthin), nervous, confabulating, unhappy, sees frightening "nightmares" during the day; afraid of going to sleep because of nightmares and fear that people are watching through the window; feels teacher punishes him unjustly.

9. *Female,* born March 18, 1944; nervous, quick mood changes; body image distortions, passive, resigned; psychiatric admission, paranoid tendencies revealed, vague train of thought.

10. *Male,* born March 14, 1952; arrested for involvement in theft of motorbike; extremely withdrawn, difficulties in concentration; passive, disinterested; father objected to his being institutionalized – consequently, he is now out under psychiatric supervision.

11. *Male,* born October 19, 1947; level of intellectual performance in apprenticeship decreasing; private life extremely disorderly; abreacts through alcoholism.

12. *Male,* born January 20, 1944; severe schizoid character; no heterosexual activity; lives an immature, shy, anhedonic life; thought disturbances revealed in TAT.

13. *Female,* born May 25, 1947; psychiatric admission, abortion, hospital report suspects pseudoneurotic or early schizophrenia; association tests betray thought disturbance; tense, guarded, ambivalent. Current difficulties somewhat precipitated by sudden death of boy friend.

14. *Male,* born August 13, 1950; sensitive, negativistic, unrealistic; recently stopped working and was referred to a youth guidance clinic for evaluation. Is now under regular supervision of a psychologist.

15. *Male,* born May 28, 1947; history of car stealing; unstable, drifting, unemployed, sensitive, easily hurt; one-year institutionalization in a reformatory for the worst delinquents in Denmark.

16. *Female,* born June 1, 1945; psychotic episode, one year of hospitalization; diagnoses from two hospitals: (1) schizophrenia, (2) manic psychosis.

17. *Male,* born September 3, 1946; severe schizoid character; psychotic breakdown in Army, preceded by arrest for car thievery. Now hospitalized.

18. *Male,* born January 28, 1953; perhaps borderline retarded; psychiatric admission for diagnostic reasons; spells of uncontrolled behavior.

19. *Male,* born June 23, 1948; repeatedly apprehended for stealing; severe mood swings, sensitive, restless, unrealistic; fired from job because of financial irregularities.

20. *Female,* born July 5, 1941; highly intelligent girl with mystical interests; very much afflicted by mother's schizophrenia; TAT reveals thought disorder; receiving psychotherapy.

Why did these particular high-risk subjects become ill? How are they different from the other high-risk subjects? The answers could lie in certain personal characteristics (physiological, psychological, or early experiential) which they already possessed at the time of the assessment in

1962; the answers could lie with the experiences they have had since 1962; the answers could lie in the interaction of these factors. We have recently completed a personal examination and home interview of the H and L samples. Two aims of the personal examination were to obtain information on the course of the subject's recent life and observe the subject interacting with his family in his home. This information may help us to evaluate the role of recent experience in contributing to breakdown. These data are not yet available. In this report we limit ourselves to an attempt to fulfill Aim III, to discover which (if any) of our test variables could have differentiated this sick group from the high-risk group that developed more normally.

Selection of Comparison Groups. At an early stage of this research the H subjects were set off in matched pairs. It was hoped that these matched pairs would provide us with a preselected control for subjects who break down. This strategy failed for two reasons. First, though not ill enough to be in the Sick Group, many of the erstwhile controls are likely candidates and could hardly be said to have "developed more normally." Second, the original matching variables did not include any indicant of the subject's psychiatric status at the time of the first examination, such as the interviewing psychiatrist's rating of Level of Adjustment. Many of the otherwise matched pairs were widely discrepant for Level of Adjustment. Any differences in the 1962 assessment data between such pairs of subjects might not be prognostic but might simply reflect already existing differences in Level of Adjustment.

In view of these two considerations, in 1967 we rematched each subject in the Sick Group, person for person, with one high-risk subject and one low-risk subject. The matching variables were: the psychiatrist's rating of Level of Adjustment at the time of the initial assessment, age, sex, and social class. In addition, we imposed the restriction that the H group controls must have either maintained or improved in their Level of Adjustment since the time of the first assessment. This rating was independently obtained by the junior author from the material of the personal follow-up mentioned above. Of the 20 controls from the high-risk group, 11 had shown definite improvement in Level of Adjustment; 9 had maintained their Level. These controls from the high-risk group will be called the Well Group. Comparable follow-up Level of Adjustment ratings are not yet available for the matched low-risk group control subjects.

The mean values for each of the matching variables may be found in Table 2. "Control Group" refers to the low-risk comparison group. The

Table 2. Identifying Characteristics of Sick, Well, and Control Groups[a]

Characteristics	Sick	Well	Control
Mean age	15.1	15.1	15.1
Mean socioeconomic status[b] ..	1.45	1.05	1.85
Mean Level of Adjustment[c] ..	3.0	3.0	3.3
Number of females	5	5	5
Total N	20	20	20

[a] The figures in the table refer to the subjects' status at the time of the initial assessment.

[b] The social class scale was adapted from that developed for Denmark by Svalastoga (1959). The scale runs from 0 (low) to 6 (high).

[c] The Level of Adjustment rating is drawn from the psychiatric interview.

socioeconomic status (SES) of these groups is somewhat lower than that of the parent H and L groups, which had SES scores of 2.2 and 2.3, respectively. This is mainly due to the presence in the Sick Group of a disproportionate number of children raised in children's homes, for whom SES is zero. (This factor was originally matched for both the Well and Control groups.) Notice also that the Control Group could not be perfectly matched with the Sick and Well groups for Level of Adjustment because too few low-risk subjects had low enough Level of Adjustment scores for this purpose. We have, however, selected the worst of the low-risk group for the Control Group.

This matching process yielded three groups. Two of these groups (Sick and Well) are drawn from the high-risk sample – that is, they have schizophrenic mothers. An experienced psychiatrist found these two groups to be equivalent in Level of Adjustment in 1962. Since that time the members of the Sick Group have suffered severe psychiatric breakdown; the members of the Well Group have tended to maintain or improve their Level of Adjustment. The matched Control Group, drawn from the low-risk group, is at the lower end of the "normal" psychiatric spectrum. We shall now turn to a consideration of the variables in the 1962 assessment that differentiate these groups.

Results of Sick, Well, and Control Comparison

This report is a preliminary impression of the important differences that characterize the Sick Group. Not all variables and tests have been analyzed.

Birth Data. The birth factors examined included mother's age, marital status, duration and conditions of the birth process, condition of the newborn, and the postpartum status of mother and infant. Our first analyses compared Sick, Well, and Control groups on incidence of specific complications; because of the small number of instances of any specific complication, these analyses were unproductive. However, when all serious complications were lumped together, it was clear that the Sick Group had the largest relative incidence of serious birth complications: 53 per cent of the Sick Group (we have birth data on 19 of these subjects), 15 per cent of the Well Group (birth data for 13), and 28 per cent of the Control Group (birth data for 14) evidenced serious complications. The *least* serious conditions categorized as "serious" complications were "dry" birth, placental infarcts, unfortunate fetal position, unusually long labor (ordinal position of fetus taken into consideration), and mild prematurity.

It is clear that the Sick Group as a whole had more difficult births. Not only do they evidence more instances of complications, but the complications are of a more serious order. We shall forego further comment on these Sick Group data, because we are currently following some promising leads suggested by these results. It may be worth pointing to the relatively large number of serious complications uncovered in the Control Group. It is interesting to note that these subjects are in the worse-adjusted subgroup of the parent low-risk group.

Parent Interview. Of all the 88 coded items in the Parent Interview, only a few significantly differentiated the groups. Most significant is the fact that the Sick Group tended to lose their mothers to a mental hospital quite early and permanently. These figures are shown in Table 3. It is important to emphasize that the tabulated percentages refer to the *total* absence of the mother from the home during the specified period. Thus, if

Table 3. Percentage of Group with Mother *Completely* Absent from Home during Specified Periods

Child's Age in Years	Sick	Well	Control	χ^2	p
0–1	7	5	0		ns
1–2	11	5	5		ns
3–5	30	10	10		ns
5–10 [a]	65	15	30	20.6	$<.01$
11–13 [a]	81	40	35	15.1	$<.01$
14–17 [a]	85	42	46	11.8	$<.05$

[a] The Sick and Well groups differ significantly for ages 5–10 ($\chi^2 = 6.5$, 1 *df*, $p < .01$), for ages 11–13 ($\chi^2 = 18.63$, 1 *df*, $p < .01$), and for ages 14–17 ($\chi^2 = 4.96$, 1 *df*, $p < .05$).

the mother was in the home for three months during the third to fifth year of the child's life and absent thereafter, this absence was first coded in the 5- to 10-year category. It should be noted that the absence of the mother from the home occurred at about the same time and frequency for the Well and Control groups. In every case where there is overall significance among the three groups, the Sick and the Well groups taken by themselves are also significantly different.

For the Sick and Well groups, the absence of the mother from the home was in every case occasioned by psychiatric hospitalization. On the basis of length of hospitalization, degree of recovery between hospitalizations, and treatment received, the illness of the mother was rated as very severe or moderately severe. Of the Sick Group mothers, 75 per cent were rated as very severe; of the Well Group mothers, 33 per cent were rated as very severe ($\chi^2 = 6.35$, 1 *df*, $p < .05$). The mothers who were very severely ill left the home for the hospital at a time when the child was significantly younger.

In view of the greater severity of illness of the mothers who left the home early, these data concerning the mothers' absence from the home could be interpreted in relatively environmental or relatively genetic terms. It is also of interest that absence of the mother from the home was correlated with signs of disturbed behavior even in the initial assessment.

School Report. The teacher found it characteristic of 67 per cent of the Sick Group that when upset or excited their reaction persisted and they continued to be upset. He reported this for only 22 per cent of the Control Group and 23 per cent of the Well Group. ($\chi^2 = 6.69$, 2 *df*, $p < .01$.)

The Sick Group was also rated by the teacher as being more disturbing to the class. We can identify subjects who were either rated as being class disciplinary problems, domineering, aggressive and creating conflicts, or disturbing the class with chatting; 53 per cent of the Sick Group, 18 per cent of the Well Group, and 11 per cent of the Control Group were listed in one or more of these three categories. The frequencies for the three groups are significantly different, as are the Sick-Well differences taken by themselves.

WISC *and* WAT. There were *no* statistically significant differences on these tests between the Sick and Well groups. On all twelve of the WISC subtests the Well Group achieved a higher mean raw score than did the Sick Group. The three groups differed significantly on the Picture Arrangement subtest; however, the Sick-Well differences were not significant.

Continual Association Test. In this test the subject is asked to give multiple single-word associations to a stimulus word; the Sick Group distinguished itself by frequently rattling off a whole series of words which were interrelated but contextually relatively irrelevant. This series might be given to the stimulus word *afraid* (*opremsning* in Danish) as follows: "Mother is afraid; father is afraid; brother, sister, aunt, uncle, etc." The mean *opremsning* scores (corrected for Total Number of Responses) for the Sick, Well, and Control groups were 1.33, .11, .33, respectively ($F=4.33$, 2/51 *df*, $p<.05$). The Sick versus Well differences were also significant ($t=2.30$, 36 *df*, $p<.05$). (Diderichsen, 1967.)

Another characteristic of the associations of the Sick Group is a tendency to slide away from the original stimulus word, despite cautions by the examiner. This characteristic has been named *Drifting*; each of the Sick and Well groups' sets of associations to each of the thirty stimulus words has been rated on a scale from 1 (no drifting) to 3 (much drifting). The Sick Group had a mean Drifting score of 1.72, the Well Group 1.33 ($t=2.10$, 38 *df*, $p<.05$). (B. R. Mednick, 1968.)

ELECTRODERMAL MEASURES

Basal Level. There were no significant differences among the three groups in basal level at any point. The basal levels all hovered around the mean high-risk group levels. The relatively low basal skin resistance of the Control Group is probably related to their relatively low Level of Adjustment rating.

Responsiveness-Stress Stimuli. Table 4 presents the mean GSR amplitude for the three groups for the stress stimuli (UCS trials). As can be seen, the Sick Group gives the largest responses to the stress stimuli, with the Well Group falling in the middle. On three of the nine trials differences between the Sick and Well groups were significant. On most of the stress trials the variance for the Sick Group proved to be five to seven times that of the Well Group. This suggests that a subgroup of the Sick Group might have given abnormally large responses which were producing the mean differences in response amplitude. This point will be discussed below. A count was made of the number of individuals responding to the stress stimuli. Since almost everyone responded on almost every trial, there were no differences between the groups on this measure.

A comparison of the Sick and Well groups with the total high-risk

Table 4. Comparison of Mean Amplitude of GSR Response to Stress Stimuli, Conditioned Stimuli, and Generalization Stimuli in Sick, Well, and Control Groups

Points of Measurement	Mean GSR Response in Ohms			
	Sick	Well	Control	p[a]
UCS Trials				
CS-UCS 1	25,859 [b]	17,194	9,238	<.01
CS-UCS 2	14,467	10,472	6,583	<.05
CS-UCS 3	11,128	8,167	4,133	<.01
CS-UCS 4	10,823	11,567	5,365	ns
CS-UCS 5	10,759	6,859	4,900	<.05
CS-UCS 6	10,900 [b]	5,494	3,606	<.05
CS-UCS 7	8,778	6,728	2,922	ns
CS-UCS 8	10,983 [b]	5,761	4,241	<.05
CS-UCS 9	9,682	7,217	3,244	<.05
CS Trials				
CS 1	3,744	2,917	3,189	ns
CS 2	5,394 [b]	1,959	4,094	ns
CS 3	6,139 [b]	1,617	2,853	ns
CS 4	5,694	2,067	1,433	ns
CS 5	6,178	3,106	1,711	ns
Generalization Trials				
CS 1	6,611	2,717	1,300	<.05
GS_1 1	6,189 [b]	2,822	422	<.05
GS_2 1	3,739	1,422	233	<.05
CS 2	5,222	2,389	756	<.05
GS_1 2	4,400	2,139	50	ns
GS_2 2	2,088	1,278	0	<.05

[a] Significance of differences was tested in all cases by analysis of covariance. Basal level just preceding response was the covariance control.
[b] Significant *t* test between Sick and Well.

group reveals that on most trials these two groups fall on either side of the total high-risk group. However, reversals occur, and the differences are not large.

Responsiveness-Conditioned Stimuli. There seems to be some evidence that the Sick Group showed more conditioning than the other groups. This may be seen in Figure 2. The Well and Control groups show almost no evidence of conditioning. The mean summated GSR's to the conditioned stimuli for the Sick and Well groups were 5,430 and 2,311 ohms, respectively. This difference was significant ($t=2.15$, 38 *df*, $p<.05$). As may be seen in Table 4, the Sick and Well groups differed significantly on the second and third conditioning trials.

A count was made of the number of CR's per subject. This conditioning score could vary from 0 to 5. The Sick, Well, and Control groups had means of 3.28, 2.00, and 1.28, respectively. These three means were

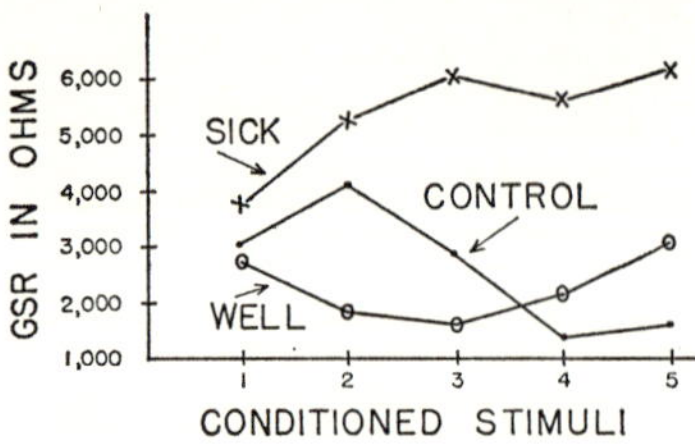

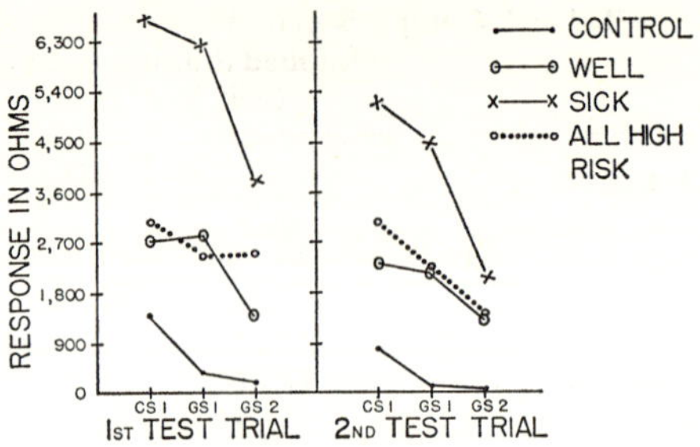

Figure 2. Amplitude of conditioned responses for five test trials with conditioned stimulus (CS) alone for Sick, Well, and Control Groups. *Figure 3.* Generalization gradients for Sick, Well, Control, and entire high-risk groups.

significantly different ($F = 4.72$, $2/53$ *df*, $p < .05$), as were the Sick and Well means ($t = 2.00$, 38 *df*, $p < .05$).

Demonstrating a conditioned response with the GSR as a response measure has always proved difficult because of the relatively rapid adaptation of the GSR. This suggests that rapid adaptation could have been a reason for the poor conditioning shown by the Well and Control groups (see Fig. 2). On the other hand, it could be taken as an indication that the Sick Group is not so much evidencing conditioning as failing to habituate. This argument can be countered by pointing to the fact that from Trials 1 to 5 the CR's of the Sick Group tended to increase in amplitude (unfortunately, this increase was not significant). This increase was taking place while their responses to the UCS (among which the CS trials are mixed) were decreasing.

The weight of the evidence slightly favors the conclusion that the Sick Group evidenced superior GSR conditioning. When the conditioning performance of the Sick and Well groups is compared with that of the total high-risk group, this conclusion is strengthened. The Well Group behaves like a somewhat enfeebled version of the total high-risk group.

Generalization. The CS, GS_1, and GS_2 were presented in extinction test procedures three times each in counterbalanced order at the conclusion of conditioning. Table 4 and Figure 3 present the mean amplitude of the generalization responses for the first two test trials. Data from the third test trial are not presented since very few subjects were responding.

The generalization responsiveness of the Sick Group is well above the level of the Well and Control groups; the differences are significant on five of the six trials. When each subject is given a generalization score by adding together the amplitude of his responses to the first presentations of GS_1 and GS_2, the Sick Group evidences significantly more generalization than the Well Group ($U = 222$, $N = 18$, $p < .04$). As can be seen in Figure 3, the Well Group's level of generalization responsiveness is about the same as that of the total high-risk group. The Sick Group is well above this level.

It should also be pointed out that the shape of the gradients are approximately the same for the Sick, Well, and total high-risk groups (concave downward), whereas the gradients for the Control and total low-risk groups are in the "normal" concave-upward form (Mednick & Freedman, 1960). This is also shown in the fact that the amount of relative generalization (ratio of generalization responsiveness to conditioned responsiveness) is about the same for the Sick and Well groups. Another way of saying this is that the Sick and Well groups' generalization curves are essentially parallel and different from the Control curve. The earlier comparison of the high-risk–low-risk gradients demanded the interpretation of an essential difference between these groups in generalization responsiveness. Both the Sick and the Well groups continue to evidence this heightened generalization responsiveness. The fact that the Sick and Well groups evidence parallel curves could suggest that some additional factor might be acting to increase the overall responsiveness of the Sick Group. This factor could either be a higher level of arousal or a failure of habituation or both.

Latency. A summary of the latency data may be found in Figure 4. The groups differed significantly on all but one of the trials with the UCS (stress stimuli). The mean latencies across all UCS trials were 1.57, 1.77, and 2.47 sec. for the Sick, Well, and Control groups, respectively ($F = 8.63$, $2/52$ *df*, $p < .005$). Of great interest in Figure 4 is the difference in habituation shown on the one hand by the Control and Well groups and on the other by the Sick Group.

The difference is especially marked in response to the stress stimuli. The Control and Well groups' rapid habituation may be seen in the pro-

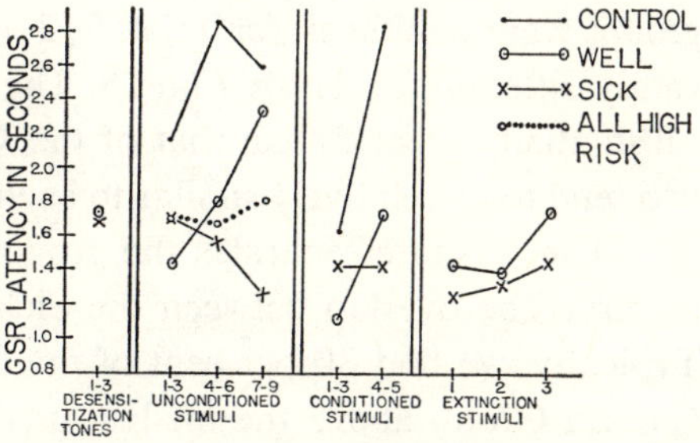

Figure 4. Mean galvanic skin response (GSR) latencies for the three groups for the entire session. Control Group latencies were omitted for the Extinction Stimuli Trials 1–3, since there were very few responses and the latencies were completely off the figure. The mean latencies for the Control Group for Trials 1, 2, and 3 were 2.63, 3.12, and 4.83 seconds, respectively.

gressive increase in their response latencies from the first to the last of the stress trials. The latencies of the Sick Group progressively decrease, suggesting a negative habituation or even increasing irritability. The Sick Group distinguishes itself quite sharply from the Well Group in this regard. Moving from UCS Trials 1 to 9, 69 per cent of the Well Group exhibit a slowing of response latency, whereas 75 per cent of the Sick Group actually *increase* the speed of their response. This difference is significant ($\chi^2 = 6.13$, 1 *df*, $p < .02$). A tendency for the same failure of habituation of latency in the Sick Group is also shown in response to the conditioned stimuli (Fig. 4).

As is also indicated in Figure 4, the Sick and Well groups were substantially quicker than the Control Group in latency of response. This mirrors the differences between the parent high- and low-risk groups.

Recovery. We devised a rather simple score to analyze the recovery results, the number of ohms recovered per second. We have used the time to *half*-recovery as the score for this index since this initial recovery phase is less likely to be contaminated by intruding external stimuli (such as the next stress stimulus) or internal stimuli. If a response were 1,000 ohms and the recovery of half of that response took 10 sec., then the subject's recovery rate was 50 ohms per second.

We have not studied the operating characteristics nor GSR correlates of this measure, and to our knowledge neither has anyone else. However, it is possible to guess that it is related to basal level and the size of the response from which recovery began.

Mean ohms recovered per second is reported in Table 5 for the Sick, Well, and Control groups. Because of our interest in evaluating degree of distribution overlap with this measure, the differences were evaluated by the Mann-Whitney U Test. Significance levels were determined by reference to a set of prepared tables (Auble, 1953). All comparisons of the Sick and Control groups were significant. All comparisons of the Well and Control groups were not significant. Comparisons of the Sick and Well groups were significant for Trials 2, 3, 4, 5, 6, and 9; they were not significantly different for Trials 7 and 8. The recovery rate of the Sick Group is substantially greater than that of the Well or Control Group. The latter two tend to be relatively similar to each other.

The measure separates the groups better than any other in our test battery. The overlap between the Sick and Control groups is not large. Typically, we find 80 per cent of the Sick Group and 20 per cent of the Control Group above the median of the pooled distribution on any one

Table 5. Rate of Recovery of GSR Response to Stress Stimuli [a]

UCS Trial [b]	Mean Ohms Recovered per Second		
	Sick	Well	Control
2	128.5	44.0	32.0
3	103.8	43.2	24.0
4	88.0	44.4	22.7
5	91.7	36.1	32.7
6	74.3	36.2	19.1
7	65.4[c]	49.4	24.4
8	67.8[c]	53.4	25.1
9	83.4	42.0	21.9

[a] The rate of recovery is computed for the first half of the ohms recovered. If a response were 1,000 ohms and recovery of half of that response took 10 sec., then the recovery rate was 50 ohms per second.

[b] UCS Trial 1 was omitted because most *S*s did not succeed in recovering half of their response to this stimulus before the onset of UCS 2.

[c] On UCS Trials 7 and 8 extremely high recovery scores for a Sick subject were omitted since they badly distorted the mean value.

stress stimulus trial. On UCS Trial 6, all but one of the Sick subjects and only two of the Controls are above the median of the pooled distributions. The pooled Sick and Well distributions typically find 70 per cent of the Sick Group and 30 per cent of the Well Group above the median.

Discussion

The outstanding findings in the comparison of the Sick, Well, and Control groups implicate hyperlabile and hypersensitive autonomic functioning, early maternal loss, and disturbed associative behavior as precursors of a variety of psychiatric breakdowns.

The findings of this study relating to autonomic hyperfunctioning are in agreement with certain recent work with both acute and chronic schizophrenics. Zahn (1964) has reported hyperresponsiveness, lower basal skin resistance, and a failure of habituation of the GSR for schizophrenic subjects in selected parts of a relatively nonstressful situation. Other recent and methodologically sophisticated studies in which schizophrenics have been subjected to stress have produced evidence of extremely high autonomic responsiveness in even the chronic schizophrenic (Ax et al., 1962; Malmo, Shagass, & Smith, 1951; Ray, 1963). A review by Venables (1966) of recent research in this area seems to place the general form of the hyperresponsiveness hypothesis on a rather firm empirical footing.

When the senior author first advanced the hypothesis of autonomic hyperresponsiveness, as one of several hypothesized etiological precursors of schizophrenia (Mednick, 1958), there were only a few supportive studies that could be cited. "The majority of these studies reported lowered autonomic responsiveness in chronic schizophrenics" (Zahn, 1964, p. 167). The essence of the more recent empirical work on the schizophrenic and the results of the present study bolster this hypothesis, which is central to the theoretical orientation of this project. Two additional pre-schizophrenic characteristics, which were first hypothesized in 1958, were excessive generalization of autonomic responses and excessively *slower* recovery from stress. The first of these, generalization responsiveness, has found support in the present study. Both the high-risk and the Sick groups evidenced elevated generalization gradients. However, the same cannot be said for the hypothesis of slow recovery. Both high-risk and Sick groups unequivocally showed abnormally *fast* rates of recovery from autonomic imbalance. It seems clear that this hypothesis of slow recovery merits abandonment. It may be of interest to try to reshape the theory to see what role *quick* autonomic recovery could play in the development of schizophrenia.

The theory identifies schizophrenia as a learned disorder of thought and suggests that there are certain physiological and environmental factors that predispose individuals to such learning.

The thought disorder consists of a set of conditioned avoidance responses which help the schizophrenic to control his autonomic hyperresponsivity. The avoidant responses (associations or thoughts) are learned on those occasions when the pre-schizophrenic escapes from some arousal-producing stimulus by switching to a thought which interrupts this arousal stimulus. The intruding association may then enable the individual to avoid (perhaps for just a moment) the arousal stimulus. This will automatically result in a momentary reduction in arousal level (such a reduction in arousal has been shown to have great reinforcement value). This reduction in arousal level will reinforce the association between the arousal stimulus and the avoidant thought. This, in turn, will increase the probability of an avoidant associate response to future arousal stimulation. Each time this "arousal-avoidant thought" pairing occurs, it will be automatically reinforced by a reduction in arousal and will increase in probability. Notice that the "avoidant thought-reinforcement" relationship is completely internal to the subject. It is a truly autistic process requiring no physical or social interaction for successful operation. After many such learning trials, the individual will have built up a single avoidance response or a small repertoire of responses which will have the ability to remove him from arousal stimulation or at least to modulate his arousal stimulation.

This repertoire of avoidant responses will be *automatically* cued whenever the individual senses a stressful stimulus. Perhaps we are observing the beginnings of this process in our Continual Association Test results. This automatic avoidance response will seriously interfere with sustained thought processes and long-term sets. It is at the point when these conditioned avoidant responses begin to dominate the individual's thinking that he may be classified as schizophrenic.

According to the earlier version of the theory, the pre-schizophrenic is especially prone to learning this avoidant pattern because of his extreme hyperresponsivity, excessive generalization, and slow recovery from autonomic imbalance. However, the hypothesis of slow recovery has always caused critics to point out that this would cause the pre-schizophrenic to be reinforced more slowly and meagerly for avoidance than even the normal. The finding of an abnormally fast rate of recovery has forced us to alter the theory. It is now our hypothesis that one of the determining features of the pre-schizophrenic is his abnormally fast recovery; because of this fast rate of recovery, he is more easily, quickly, and thoroughly reinforced for avoidance than the normal. This, taken together with his tendency to chronic hyperarousal, will, in a harsh environment, inexorably push him to learn conditioned avoidant thought mechanisms. The revised theory, then, implicates rapid autonomic recovery from states of autonomic imbalance as a key factor in a complex of factors predisposing individuals to schizophrenia.

As mentioned above, the finding of a failure of habituation has been reported by Zahn (1964). At first glance, this finding may be seen as antagonistic to the findings on quick recovery. However, the recovery finding refers to single instances of states of imbalance, whereas failure of habituation refers to a tendency to continue to respond to stimuli over an entire experimental session as though they had never been experienced before. Failure of habituation may prove to be an independent factor. Before accepting this assertion, however, we shall explore the relationship between this variable and GSR latency, responsiveness, and generalization.

Maternal Loss. Early maternal loss through psychiatric hospitalization was a common precursor of breakdown in the Sick Group. This finding might be compared with research which has found a greater frequency of schizophrenics suffering early maternal loss by death (Hilgard & Newman, 1963). Both of these findings suggest an environmental-stress etiological contribution. However, in our sample we found that the mothers of the Sick Group not only were lost to the family earlier but were also more severely schizophrenic. In view of the findings reported by Kety et al. (1967), we cannot disregard the possibility of a heavier genetic burden in the Sick Group, as evidenced by the greater severity of their mother's illness. Two findings within the Sick Group reflect on this possibility. First, we found that within the Sick Group the very severely schizophrenic mothers were separated from their children when the children had a mean age of 3.75 years; the children of the moderately severe mothers were 8.80 years of age at separation ($t = 2.33$, 18 *df*, $p < .025$). The second finding concerns those members of the Sick Group who have been admitted to a psychiatric hospital or who are under psychiatric care. These subjects tend to be the more overtly ill members of the Sick Group, with promiscuity and criminality as common symptoms. Of these 88 per cent have very severely schizophrenic mothers; of those Sick Group subjects who have not been hospitalized, 50 per cent have very severely schizophrenic mothers ($\chi^2 = 4.40$, 1 *df*, $p < .05$). What is suggested tentatively by these results is that the very severely ill schizophrenic mothers (who had less contact with their children) had children with symptom-rich, acutely disturbed, psychiatric involvement. The Sick subjects who spent more time with their moderately severely schizophrenic mothers tend to be classed as severely schizoid, anhedonic, overconforming, and obsessive. They also tended strongly to manifest more severe associative Drifting ($t = 2.90$, 18 *df*, $p < .005$); these subjects also had significantly poorer Level of Adjustment scores ($\chi^2 = 4.8$, 1 *df*, $p < .05$). They also tended to be in a subgroup of individuals chosen as fast GSR responders, poor in habituation, high in generalization, fast in recovery, and high-amplitude responders ($\chi^2 = 11.22$, 1 *df*, $p < .005$). These results are highly congruent with those of Reisby (1967). He found that schizophrenics who had spent a relatively long time with their schizophrenic mother tended to develop more of a process schizophrenic condition with slow, insidious onset; schizophrenics who had been separated earlier from their schizophrenic mother developed more acute, symptom-rich, reactive schizophrenia.

We present these results on the Sick-Well-Control comparisons with great tentativeness. Although the groups are rather well matched and the Sick Group was carefully selected, there is a total of only sixty cases. Our tentativeness is even greater about the comparisons relating to time spent with the schizophrenic mother—here there are only twenty cases. We hope to increase the interpretability of these results by selection of both "relatively sick" and "well" subgroups of the total low-risk group instead of just a single Control Group. We have one other safeguard built into the research design. As indicated above, we can expect approximately 50 per cent (100 subjects) of the high-risk group to develop some form of manifest psychiatric disturbance. This means that we have observed just the first wave of twenty disturbed subjects, and we can expect four more waves of twenty subjects each. These waves offer opportunities for cross validation. As the number of cases mounts, it will be possible to separate diagnostic groups (such as schizophrenia) for differential data analysis.

COMMENTARY

QUESTION. Have you done any studies of the schizophrenic mothers themselves?

MEDNICK. Not very much. A dissertation under way now in Copenhagen is looking at their influence. We have hospital case files on the mothers, and we can go through them. Many of them are now hospitalized. We do know that the mothers of the individuals who became mentally ill were more severely psychotic. They were hospitalized earlier in the life of the child than were the mothers of those who did not become mentally ill.

QUESTION. Has anyone checked to see whether GSR recovery rate changes when treatment is successful? One of the things that troubles me is that you may not be getting at causes at all. You may be just describing; and as a treatment person, interaction is the thing that is important to me.

MEDNICK. I completely agree with you, and I suddenly realize that I may have given the impression that I'm talking about causes. We don't have the experimental manipulative design that I referred to before. All we have now are correlations. These could relate to any number of things: the effects of early schizophrenia, some peripheral epiphenomenal things that co-vary with schizophrenia, something causing or predisposing schizophrenia, or something completely independent of schizophrenia. I also believe that interactions are crucial. An advantage of our study is that we can look at interactions between characteristics of the individual and the environment. If we look only at environmental variables, we may end up missing important things that are visible only in interaction. The great problem in looking at interactions between physiological and environmental characteristics is that there are an infinite number of possible causes. When we take any subset from this infinity, we have only a portion of the total number of possibilities. What each of us can do is a weak and small thing.

QUESTION. It would be interesting to see whether GSR recovery rate changes after treatment, and to determine whether it is constitutional or really a reaction to something.

MEDNICK. It would be interesting for me to know if anybody knows of *any* way of changing recovery rate.

GARMEZY. Those few studies of schizophrenics that have measured behavior over long periods of time have indicated the patient's capacity to approximate normal responses. For example, in the Houston-Shakow pursuit-meter study, it took schizophrenics almost a month to reach the level that normals were able to achieve within a day. The question that has been raised represents a curious area of neglect over the many decades in which schizophrenia has been studied. We have had many clinical studies of remitted patients aimed at evaluating post-hospital status, but experimental laboratory studies of remitted schizophrenics have been absent from the literature of schizophrenia.

POLLACK. I'd like to mention Valerie Cowie's study which found no difference in school records or in anything else between offspring of schizophrenic parents, both mothers and fathers, and offspring of parents hospitalized for medical reasons. But she did find temporary disturbances in the children at the time of hospitalization which seemed to be associated with a disruption in the home. These were significant, but not necessarily of lasting significance, since she had only cross-sectional data. I don't know how many of these children were shifted elsewhere, but rather than implicating only a chronic parent, it might be better to study this as an interaction with disruption of the home. Perhaps it might be better to give these families a housekeeping substitute so there will be some continuity of care.

GARMEZY. Dr. Pollack's remarks are interesting in the light of ongoing investigations. One can now think of four or five studies of high-risk populations similar to those initiated by Mednick. James Anthony, for example, has a Bowlby orientation and views parental psychopathology plus maternal separation as extremely important. He therefore studies children whose mothers have just entered the hospital; this is one of his criteria for case selection. His controls are children of tubercular mothers who have had long-term institutionalization. His work may shed further light on Mednick's observations.

REFERENCES

Albee, G. W., E. A. Lane, & J. M. Reuter. Childhood intelligence of future schizophrenics and neighborhood peers. *Journal of Psychology*, 1964, 58, 141.

Auble, D. Extended tables for the Mann-Whitney Statistic. *Bulletin Institute Educational Research,* Indiana University, 1953, 1, No. 2.

Ax, A. F., P. G. S. Beckett, B. D. Cohen, C. E. Frohman, G. Tourney, & J. S. Gottleib. Physiologic patterns in chronic schizophrenia. In B. Wortis (Ed.), *Recent Advances in Biological Psychiatry*. Vol. 4. New York: Plenum Press, 1962.

Ax, A. F., & G. Zacharopolous. Psychophysiological data processing. In P. L. Frommer (Ed.), *Fourth International Conference on Medical Electronics. Fourteenth*

Annual Conference on Electrical Techniques in Medicine and Biology. Washington: McGregor & Werner, 1961.

Belknap, I. *Human problems of a state mental hospital*. New York: McGraw-Hill, 1956.

Birren, J. E. Psychological examinations of children who later became psychotic. *Journal of Abnormal and Social Psychology*, 1944, 39, 84–96.

Bower, E. M., T. A. Shellhamer, & J. M. Daily. School characteristics of male adolescents who later became schizophrenic. *American Journal of Orthopsychiatry*, 1960, 30, 712–729.

Braginsky, B. J., M. Grosse, & L. Ring. Controlling outcomes through impression management: An experimental study of the manipulative tactics of the mental patient. *Journal of Consulting Psychology*, 1966, 30, 295–301.

Crain, A. J., M. B. Sussman, & W. B. Weil, Jr. Effects of a diabetic child on marital integration and related measures of family functioning. *Journal of Health and Human Behavior*, 1966, 7, 122–127. (a)

———. Family interaction, diabetes and sibling relationship. *International Journal of Social Psychiatry*, 1966, 12, 35–43. (b)

Diderichsen, B. Formelle Karakteristika ved Associations-forløbet hos en gruppe børn med høj risiko for skizofreni. Cand. Psyk. Speciale, Københavns Universitet, 1967.

Dunham, H. W., & S. K. Weinberg. *The culture of the state mental hospital*. Detroit: Wayne State University Press, 1960.

Fontana, A. F. Familial etiology of schizophrenia: Is a scientific methodology possible? *Psychological Bulletin*, 1966, 66, 214–227.

Fremming, K. H. The expectation of mental infirmity in a sample of the Danish population. *Papers on eugenics*, No. 7. London: Eugenics Society, 1951.

Gist, N. P., & C. D. Clark. Intelligence as a selective factor in rural-urban migration. *American Journal of Sociology*, 1938, 44, 36–58.

Gladis, M., & G. J. Wishner. Schizophrenic and normal response patterns to "aversive" and "neutral" associations in two paired-associate paradigms. *Journal of Abnormal and Social Psychology*, 1962, 64, 249–256.

Goffman, E. *Asylums*. Garden City, N.Y.: Doubleday (Anchor), 1961.

Goldfarb, C., & L. Erlenmeyer-Kimling. Mating and fertility trends in schizophrenia. In F. J. Kallmann (Ed.), *Expanding goals of genetics in psychiatry*. New York: Grune & Stratton, 1962.

Gordon, H. L., & C. Groth. Mental patients wanting to stay in the hospital. *AMA Archives of General Psychiatry*, 1961, 4, 124–130.

Hefner, L. T. Reliability of mothers' reports on child development. Ph.D. thesis, University of Michigan, 1962.

——— & S. A. Mednick. Reliability of developmental histories. *Pediatrics Digest*. In press.

Heston, L. L. Psychiatric disorders in foster home reared children of schizophrenic mothers. *British Journal of Psychiatry*, 1966, 112, 819–825.

Higgins, J. Effect of child rearing by schizophrenic mothers. *Journal of Psychiatric Research*, 1966, 4, 153–167.

Hilgard, J. R., & M. A. Newman. Parental loss by death in childhood as an etiological factor among schizophrenic and alcoholic patients compared with a non-patient community sample. *Journal of Nervous and Mental Disease*, 1963, 137, 14–28.

Kallmann, F. J. The genetic theory of schizophrenia. *American Journal of Psychiatry*, 1946, 103, 309–322.

Kammerer, P. C. An exploratory study of crippled children. *Psychological Record*, 1940, 4, 47–100.

Kety, S., D. Rosenthal, F. Schulsinger, & P. Wender. The types and frequencies of mental illness in the biological and adoptive families of adopted schizophrenics. Paper presented at the Transmission of Schizophrenia Conference, Dorado, Puerto Rico, July 1967.

Klebanoff, L. B. A comparison of parental attitudes of mothers of schizophrenic, brain injured, and normal children. Ph.D. thesis, Boston University, 1957.

Knupfer, G., W. Clark, & R. Room. The mental health of the unmarried. *American Journal of Psychiatry*, 1966, 122, 841–851.

Kohn, M. L., & J. A. Clausen. Parental authority behavior and schizophrenia. *American Journal of Orthopsychiatry*, 1956, 26, 297–313.

Lane, E. A., & G. W. Albee. Childhood intellectual development of adult schizophrenics. *Journal of Abnormal and Social Psychology*, 1963, 67, 186–189.

———. Early childhood intellectual differences between schizophrenic adults and their siblings. *Journal of Abnormal and Social Psychology*, 1964, 68, 193–195.

Lansing, J. B., & E. Mueller. *Geographic mobility of labor*. Ann Arbor, Mich.: Institute of Social Research, 1967.

Lewis, A. J. The offspring of parents both mentally ill. *Acta Genetica*, 1957, 7, 309–322.

Malmo, R. B., C. Shagass, & A. A. Smith. Responsiveness in chronic schizophrenia. *Journal of Personality*, 1951, 19, 359–375.

Mattson, A., & S. Gross. Adaptational and defensive behavior in young hemophiliacs and their parents. *American Journal of Psychiatry*, 1966, 122, 1349–1356.

Maxwell, J. Intelligence, fertility, and the future. *Eugenic Quarterly*, 1954, 1, 244–247.

Mednick, B. R. Continuous associative behavior in high-risk children who broke down. MS., University of Michigan, 1968.

Mednick, S. A. A learning theory approach to research in schizophrenia. *Psychological Bulletin*, 1958, 55, 316–327.

———. Schizophrenia: A learned thought disorder. In G. Nielsen (Ed.), *Clinical psychology, Proceedings of the XIV International Congress of Applied Psychology*. Copenhagen: Munksgaard, 1962.

———. Primary prevention and schizophrenia: Theory and research. In *Public health practice and the prevention of mental illness*. Copenhagen: World Health Organization, 1962.

———. A longitudinal study of children with a high risk for schizophrenia. *Mental Hygiene*, 1966, 50, 522–535.

———. Psychophysiology, thought processes, personality and social development of children with a high risk for schizophrenia. *Sociological Micro-Journal*, 1967, 1, Nos. 1–3, 1–100.

——— & J. Freedman. Stimulus generalization. *Psychological Bulletin*, 1960, 57, 159–200.

Mednick, S. A., & J. Schaffer. Mothers' retrospective reports in child-rearing research. *American Journal of Orthopsychiatry*, 1963, 33, 451–461.

Mednick, S. A., & F. Schulsinger. A preschizophrenic sample. *Acta Psychiatrica Scandinavica*, 1964, 40, Suppl. 180, 135–139.

———. A longitudinal study of children with a high risk for schizophrenia: A preliminary report. In S. Vandenberg (Ed.), *Methods and goals in human behavior genetics*. New York: Academic Press, 1965. Pp. 255–296. (a)

———. Children of schizophrenic mothers. *Bulletin International Association Applied Psychology*, 1965, 14, 11–27. (b)

———. Some premorbid characteristics related to breakdown in children with schizophrenic mothers. In D. Rosenthal & S. Kety (Eds.), *Transmission of schizophrenia*. Oxford: Pergamon Press, 1968. Pp. 267–292.

Mednick, S. A., & C. Wild. Reciprocal augmentation of generalization and anxiety. *Journal of Experimental Psychology*, 1962, 63, 621–626.

Nameche, G., M. Waring, & D. Ricks. Early indicators of outcome in schizophrenia. *Journal of Nervous and Mental Disease*, 1964, 139, 232–240.

O'Neal, P., & L. N. Robins. Childhood patterns predictive of adult schizophrenia. *American Journal of Psychiatry*, 1958, 115, 385–391.

Pokorny, A. D. Background factors in schizophrenia. *Journal of Nervous and Mental Disease*, 1962, 134, 84–87.

Ray, T. S. Electrodermal indications of levels of psychological disturbance in chronic schizophrenia. *American Psychologist*, 1963, 18, 393.

Reisby, N. Psychoses in children of schizophrenic mothers. *Acta Psychiatrica Scandinavica*, 1967, 43, 8–20.

Rickers-Ovsiankina, M. Studies on the personality structure of schizophrenic individuals. II. Reaction to interrupted tasks. *Journal of Genetic Psychology*, 1937, 16, 179–196.

Ricks, D. Discussion: Early differentiation of psychopathological life patterns. Paper presented at the meeting of the American Psychological Association, Washington, D.C., September 1967.

Robins, L. N. *Deviant children grown up: A psychiatric and sociological study of sociopathic personality*. Baltimore: Williams & Wilkins, 1966.

——— & P. O'Neal. Mortality, mobility and crime. *American Sociological Review*, 1958, 23, 162–171.

Rosenbaum, S. Z. Infantile paralysis as a source of emotional problems in children. *Welfare Bulletin*, 1943, 34, 11–13.

Schulz, B. Kinder schizophrenen elternpare. *Zeitschrift für Neurologie und Psychiatrie*, 1940, 168, 332–381.

Shakow, D. The nature of deterioration in schizophrenic conditions. *Nervous and Mental Disease Monographs*, 1946, No. 70.

Silverman, J. Scanning-control mechanism and cognitive filtering in paranoid and nonparanoid schizophrenia. *Journal of Consulting Psychology*, 1964, 28, 385–393.

———, P. S. Berg, & R. Kantor. Some perceptual correlates of institutionalization. *Journal of Nervous and Mental Disease*, 1966, 141, 651–657.

Sommer, R., & R. Hall. Alienation and mental illness. *American Sociological Review*, 1958, 23, 418–420.

Svalastoga, K. *Prestige, class and mobility*. Copenhagen: Gyldendal, 1959.

U.S. Bureau of the Census, U.S. *Census of Population: 1950*. Vol. IV. Special Reports, Pt. 4, Ch. B, Population Mobility — States and State Economic Areas. Washington, D.C.: U.S. Government Printing Office, 1956.

Venables, P. Psychophysiological aspects of schizophrenia. *British Journal of Medical Psychology*, 1966, 39, 289–297.

Zahn, T. P. Autonomic reactivity and behaviour in schizophrenia. *Psychiatric Research Report*, 1964, 19, 156–171.

Zarlock, S. P. Social expectations, language and schizophrenia. *Journal of Humanistic Psychology*, 1966, 6, 68–74.

JAMES R. STABENAU
WILLIAM POLLIN

Experiential Differences for Schizophrenics as Compared with Their Non-Schizophrenic Siblings: Twin and Family Studies

During the past two decades efforts to uncover the nature and role of environmental factors in the etiology of schizophrenia have been directed toward the study of differences in intrafamilial environment in children, with a focus of the efforts on clarifying the issues that may have contributed to the development of schizophrenia in one child and not in the other children within the family (Bowen, 1960; Brodey, 1959; Jackson, 1960; Lidz, Corneilson, Terry, & Fleck, 1958; Lu, 1962; Mishler & Waxler, 1965; Pollin, 1968; Pollin, Stabenau, Mosher, & Tupin, 1966; Pollin, Stabenau, & Tupin, 1965; Stabenau & Pollin, 1967a; 1968b; Stabenau, Tupin, Werner, & Pollin, 1965; Wynne, Ryckoff, Day, & Hirsch, 1958). The two studies discussed in this paper will consider this question.

One part of the paper will present in detail findings in a comparative family study of schizophrenics, delinquents, and "normals," where the focus has been not only on differences between the index child – that is, the schizophrenic or delinquent and his non-schizophrenic or non-delinquent same-sexed co-sibling – but also on experiential differences for the families of index schizophrenics, families of delinquent subjects and for the siblings in the "normal" control families (Stabenau & Pollin, 1968b; Stabenau, Tupin, Werner, & Pollin, 1965). Genetic differences among siblings and the fact that each sibling occupies a special and different chronological position in his family's life course tend to place restrictions on what one could conclude from such studies about the more clearly environmental aspects of schizophrenia.

In an effort to control for genetic and family position differences, a

NOTE: This paper was completed when Dr. Stabenau was still with the Section of Twin and Sibling Studies, National Institute of Mental Health, Bethesda, Maryland.

second study of families of monozygotic twins (MZ), where one has become schizophrenic and the other has not (discordant), has been conducted at the Clinical Center, National Institute of Mental Health (NIMH). The experiential differences and early characteristics of fourteen schizophrenic monozygotic twins and their non-schizophrenic co-twin controls will be presented, along with a review of similarly obtained life history material as reported in the literature for monozygotic twins discordant for schizophrenia.

Although the comparative family study and the twin study represent two separate investigative efforts the similarity of their design and the fact that the same investigative staff interviewed all families in the same clinical setting may allow for a discussion of the data in a single continuous manner.

Methods

The data to be reviewed in this paper derive from three separate sources, which will be described in turn: the NIMH twin study; other relevant twin studies in the world literature; and the NIMH comparative family study.

NIMH TWIN STUDY

Fourteen pairs of monozygotic twins discordant for schizophrenia, along with their parents, were intensively studied at NIMH. Detailed descriptions of the study and the methodology have been reported (Pollin & Stabenau, 1968; Pollin, Stabenau, Mosher, & Tupin, 1966; Pollin, Stabenau, & Tupin, 1965; Stabenau & Pollin, 1967a). Identical blood group types for each member of a twin pair, along with similarity of fingerprints and anthropometric characteristics served as presumptive evidence of monozygosity. A panel of two independent psychiatric consultants interviewed each twin separately. Their diagnostic impressions, coupled with detailed hospital records of the schizophrenic (S) index cases, were employed to decide on the presence of and character of the schizophrenic symptoms for all twins. In this sample each index twin had been hospitalized for schizophrenic symptoms and was felt when seen at NIMH to have evidence for the classification as schizophrenic. In each of the fourteen pairs the co-twin had not been hospitalized for psychiatric problems, and the diagnostic panel did not feel there was evidence indicating a past or current schizophrenic reactive pattern. In order to locate pairs with such

Table 1. Case Reports Monozygotic Twins Discordant for Schizophrenia

Investigator	Year	Country	No. of Cases	Sex: Male	Sex: Female	Sampling Method [a]	Zygosity Blood and/or Fingerprints
Grillmayr	1929	Austria	1		1	CR	No
Burkhardt	1929	Germany	1		1	CR	Yes
Wigers	1934	Norway	1	1		CR	Yes
Kasanin	1934	U.S.A.	1	1		CR	No
Reed	1935	Canada	1		1	CR	No
Kallmann	1948	U.S.A.	1		1	CR	No
Kallmann	1953	U.S.A.	1		1	CR	No
Hobson	1964	U.S.A.	1		1	CR	Yes
Total single-case reports			8	2	6		
Rosanoff	1934	U.S.A.	9	7	2	RH	No
Essen-Möller	1941	Sweden	6	3	3	CA	Yes
Slater	1953	U.K.	15	8	7	RH & CA	Yes
Kurihara	1959	Japan	26	8	18	R	Yes
Tienari	1963	Finland	16	16	0	BR	Yes
Kringlen	1964	Norway	6	6	0	RH & CA	Yes
Pollin, Stabenau	1966	U.S.A.	14	4	10	R	Yes
Total all reports			100	54	46		

[a] Resident hospital population (RH), consecutive hospital admission (CA), birth registry (BR), referral (R), case report (CR).

clear discordance of symptoms, a nonrandom and non-sequential sample of "volunteer" families was necessarily produced.

OTHER TWIN STUDIES

Studies from Sweden, the United Kingdom, Finland, and Norway have provided consecutive and more random samples of discordant monozygotic twin pairs. Studies by Essen-Möller (1941) and Slater (1953) produced relatively satisfactory evidence about diagnosis and zygosity, but early life history material in their case reports is sparse and lacking in detail. Studies by Tienari (1963) and Kringlen (1964), of male subjects only, have case history details which cover the birth and early personality characteristics of the twins, along with clear evidence for the consideration of diagnosis and zygosity. In addition there are single-case reports (Burkhardt, 1929; Grillmayr & Kohlmann, 1929; Hobson, 1964; Kallmann, 1948; 1953; Kasanin, 1934; Reed, 1935; Wigers, 1934) and other studies of twin series (Kurihara, 1959; Pollin, Stabenau, Mosher, & Tupin, 1966; Pollin, Stabenau, & Tupin, 1965; Rosanoff, Handy, Plesset, & Brush, 1934; Stabenau & Pollin, 1967a). A comparison of the hereditary and environmental aspects of twin studies has been reported elsewhere (Stabenau, 1968).

A summary analysis was made of the material covering birth, neonatal, childhood, and pre-illness environmental experience from one hundred pairs of monozygotic twins discordant for schizophrenia from our series and those reported in the world literature (Stabenau & Pollin, 1967a). The cases included were those in which zygosity, diagnosis, and discordance for schizophrenia were reasonably established. Table 1 lists the investigators, their country, the number of cases, sampling method, and whether zygosity was determined by blood and/or fingerprints. The reports for these hundred pairs were reviewed for variables that appeared to distinguish the twins, or which the parents used to differentiate or delineate early differences between the twins, or which the twins used in describing consistent differences between themselves. Twenty-six items were selected as the items which most often were used by the case report authors to differentiate a twin from his co-twin by intrapair comparison. Verbatim quotes from tape-recorded interviews with both twins and their parents while at NIMH were used to designate a trait that distinguished one of a given twin pair from the other. Only where the trait was clearly described as a characteristic for one twin and not the other was the trait considered for the twin pair. Two problems were frequently encountered in reviewing the published case reports: (a) investigators directed attention to certain variables with which others did not concern themselves; and (b) investigators used different words to describe what appeared to have been the same variable. Where possible, the original author's description of the trait was used to judge its presence in the case material of another investigator.

THE NIMH COMPARATIVE FAMILY STUDY

Twenty-four families completed an extensive battery of group and individual psychiatric interviews and psychological tests. These families compose three groups matched on the basis of age, sex, and socioeconomic status (see Table 2). In eleven families the index was schizophrenic (S); in eight the index was delinquent (D); and in five the index was a non-schizophrenic, non-delinquent "normal" (N). Each family unit included an index child, a non-schizophrenic non-delinquent sibling of the same sex, a mother, and a father (Stabenau & Pollin, 1968b; Stabenau, Tupin, Werner, & Pollin, 1965).

Each family was intact, and all children were raised by their biologic parents. Schizophrenic subjects were referred by psychiatric facilities and delinquents by courts. Normal subjects were referred by local schools and were matched to the schizophrenic and delinquent families. The clinical features and selective criteria have been described elsewhere (Stabenau,

Table 2. Matching Variables of Age, Education, and Social Class for Families of Schizophrenic, Delinquent, and Normal *S*s

Variable	Father	Mother	Index	Control
Schizophrenic index ($N = 11$)				
Age [a]	51.9	48.7	21.5	22.4
Education [a]	12.6	12.9	10.1	12.8
Social class [b]	2.8			
Delinquent index ($N = 8$)				
Age [a]	51.1	45.0	16.4 [c]	17.4
Education [a]	10	11.8	9.8	11.4
Social class [b]	3.8 [d]			
Normal index ($N = 5$)				
Age [a]	47.4	45.2	19.0	17.8
Education [a]	13.6	13.2	13.2	10.4
Social class [b]	2.6			

[a] Mean years.
[b] According to the Hollingshead-Redlich Index.
[c] D vs. N and D vs. S, $p < .02$.
[d] D vs. N, $p < .05$.

Tupin, Werner, & Pollin, 1965). All families who were referred and who met the criteria were studied. Both parents and both siblings participated in all phases of the research. The schizophrenic indexes were in-patients, and all other subjects were seen during outpatient visits.

Clinical data in this report were obtained from reviewing typescripts of an open-ended first interview with all four family members and semi-structured individual interviews with each parent and child. Future rating by unbiased judges of blind protocols of the clinical material would be desirable in order to test the reliability of the impressions derived from this material.

On the Interpersonal Checklist (Leary, 1957), each family member rated himself, every other family member, and the "ideal" person immediately after the first group interview (at a time when they might be least biased by the investigation itself); the family members were instructed to rate the index and control children as they were *before* the index child became schizophrenic or delinquent. Scores for 16 descriptive clusters from the 128 items on each checklist were obtained. These clusters essentially describe issues of dominance, submission, love, and hostility. A correlation matrix was derived for each individual in which the view of self, ideal, and the other three family members were compared for the 16 cluster variables.

Results

TWIN STUDIES

In order to obtain perspective on the relative importance of examining discordant monozygotic pairs as a subgroup of schizophrenic subjects, it is important to consider the most recent body of data providing estimates of concordance and discordance for schizophrenia among monozygotic and dizygotic twins. The data in Table 3 represent studies, essentially the same experiment, done in eight different countries (Essen-Möller, 1941; Gottesman & Shields, 1966; Harvald & Hauge, 1965; Inouye, 1961; Kallmann, 1946; Kallmann & Roth, 1956; Kringlen, 1964; 1966; Luxenburger, 1928; Rosanoff et al., 1934; Slater, 1953; Tienari, 1963). There is similarity in that the concordance figures are higher in monozygotic than in dizygotic pairs in all the studies comparing monozygotic and dizygotic twin pairs. However, from the time of Luxenburger's (1928) study in Germany to Gottesman's (1966) study in England, several important study variables became more rigorously controlled. In the early studies of Luxenburger, Rosanoff et al. (1934), Essen-Möller

Table 3. Studies of Schizophrenia in Twins

Investigator	Year	Country	Concordance for Monozygotic Pairs [a]		Concordance for Dizygotic Same-Sex Pairs [a]		Concordance for Dizygotic Opposite-Sex Pairs [a]		Sampling [b]	Diagnosis [c]	Zygosity [d]
			Pairs	%	Pairs	%	Pairs	%			
Luxenburger	1928	Germany	10/14	71 [e]	0/13	0	0/15	0	RH, CA, BR	A	S
Rosanoff	1934	U.S.A.	28/41	68	10/53	19	5/48	10	RH	H	S
Essen-Möller	1941	Sweden	2/7	29	4/27	15			CA, BR	A	S+F
Kallmann	1946	U.S.A.	120/174	69	34/296	11	13/221	6	RH, CA	A	S
Slater	1953	U.K.	24/37	65	11/61	18	2/54	4	RH, CA	A	S+F
Kallmann	1956	U.S.A.	15/17	88	... [f]		... [f]		RH, CA	A	S+F
Inouye	1961	Japan	33/55	60 [e]	2/11	18	0/6	0	RH, CA	A	F+B
Tienari	1963	Finland	1/16	6	1/20	5			BR (1920–1929)	A	F+B
Kringlen	1964	Norway	2/8	25	2/12	17			RH, CA	H	F+B
Harvald & Hauge	1965	Denmark	4/9	44	4/33	12	2/29	7	BR (1870–1910)	H	F+B
Kringlen	1966	Norway	19/50	38	13/94	14			BR (1901–1930)	A	F+B
Gottesman & Shields	1966	U.K.	10/24	42	3/33	9			CA	H	F+B

[a] Uncorrected for period of risk, since pairs were not proband cases.
[b] Resident hospital population (RH), consecutive hospital admission (CA), birth register (BR).
[c] Hospital diagnosis (H), diagnosis established by author (A).
[d] Similarity method (S), fingerprints (F), serologic blood-typing (B).
[e] Includes schizophrenic-like psychoses. When cases listed as "schizophrenic-like" or "probably schizophrenic" are not counted, monozygotic concordance figures are: Luxenburger, 10/17 (59 per cent); Inouye, 20/55 (36 per cent).
[f] Dizygotic same- and opposite-sex pairs not separately reported.

(1941), and Kallmann (1948; 1953), either case reports giving diagnostic data were not available or the criteria for diagnosis were not made clear; zygosity was established by the method of anthropometric similarity, and the sampling was in the main from the residential hospital setting. All three of these conditions raise considerable question about the meaning of the concordance rates so reported. Slater (1953) in England and Inouye (1961) in Japan, though employing more rigorous zygosity measures, were still sampling hospitalized patients. With the advent of the Scandinavian studies of whole demographic populations, made possible through the use of nationwide birth registries, entire subsamples of twins could be studied for the presence or absence of schizophrenia among living twin pairs (Kringlen, 1964; 1966; Tienari, 1963). Thus, estimates of concordance rates for monozygotic twins have dropped from the range of 44–88 per cent as of 1961 to a range of 6–44 per cent for the studies of 1963–1966, a complete reversal from over 50 per cent concordance to clearly under 50 per cent concordance. In these later studies, zygosity was carefully established by serological methods, sampling was from other than hospitalized populations, and definitive diagnostic criteria were strictly adhered to. In the earlier studies, monozygotic twins were considered to have four to six times the risk of schizophrenia in both twins as compared with same-sexed dizygotic twins. Currently, it appears that the risk for concordance in monozygotic twins is only two to four times that for same-sexed dizygotic twins. If one considers evidence from the large-scale demographic studies, it would appear that there are more monozygotic pairs discordant for schizophrenia than concordant for schizophrenia. The importance of assessing the relation between experiential difference and the occurrence of schizophrenia therefore becomes apparent and more critical than it would be if one could assume that the major factor in schizophrenia is an immutable genetic determinism.

The source of monozygotic discordant case report material is presented in Table 1. In all but fourteen of the hundred cases zygosity was established by serologic or fingerprint comparison. There is an essentially equal representation of the sexes — fifty-four males and forty-six females.

Table 4 shows the tabulation of the twenty-six characteristics which were most often used by case report authors in describing the hundred pairs of monozygotic twins discordant for schizophrenia. The number of twins is listed wherever an item clearly differentiated one twin from the other by intrapair comparison. The items for the schizophrenic indexes

Table 4. Monozygotic Twins Discordant for Schizophrenia (100 Pairs): Early Characteristics [a]

Item	Other Studies		NIMH Study		Total		Ratio
	I [b]	C [c]	I [b]	C [c]	I [b]	C [c]	
Neurotic as child	11	1	5	0	16	1	16.0 [d]
Submissive	27	2	10	2	37	4	9.3 [d]
Sensitive	26	3	12	2	38	5	7.6 [d]
Serious-worrier	10	2	12	2	22	4	5.5 [d]
Obedient-gentler	21	2	10	4	31	6	5.2 [d]
Central nervous system illness as child	12	2	5	2	17	4	4.3 [d]
Birth complication (any)	18	5	6	1	24	6	4.0 [d]
Asphyxia at birth	8	3	4	0	12	3	4.0 [d]
Dependent	2	0	10	3	12	3	4.0 [d]
Well behaved	9	0	7	5	16	5	3.2 [d]
Quiet-shy	16	4	9	4	25	8	3.1 [d]
Stubborn	14	4	6	3	20	7	2.9 [d]
Weaker	16	10	11	1	27	11	2.5 [d]
Shorter	27	16	13	1	40	17	2.4 [d]
Lighter at birth	29	18	12	2	41	20	2.1 [d]
Slower development (walking)	3	1	6	4	9	5	1.8 [d]
Somatic illness as child	9	9	9	5	18	14	1.3 [d]
Second born	27	29	10	4	37	33	1.1 [d]
Fiery	9	5	5	9	14	14	1.0 [d]
Athletic	0	4	5	3	5	7	1.4 [e]
Leader	9	21	5	9	14	30	2.1 [e]
Outgoing-lively	8	26	5	9	13	35	2.7 [e]
Spokesman	4	11	3	11	7	22	3.1 [e]
Better at school	6	18	2	11	8	29	3.6 [e]
More intelligent	2	7	2	9	4	16	4.0 [e]
Married, co-twin not married	1	21	0	5	1	26	26.0 [e]

[a] Number of twins where item clearly differentiated one twin by intrapair co-twin comparison.
[b] Schizophrenic index twin (I).
[c] Non-schizophrenic monozygotic co-twin (C).
[d] I/C. [e] C/I.

(I) and non-schizophrenic co-twin controls (C), are ranked according to the decreasing ratio I/C and according to increasing ratio C/I.

Nine behavioral traits — submissive, sensitive, serious-worrier, obedient-gentler, dependent, well behaved, quiet-shy, stubborn, and neurotic as a child — and six physical traits — having had a central nervous system illness as a child, any birth complication, neonatal asphyxia, weaker, shorter, and lighter at birth — were characteristic of the pre-illness index twin. The criterion employed here was that the designated trait was present for the index twins by a ratio of two to one or greater. Conversely, six traits — more intelligent, better at school, the spokesman, outgoing-lively, the leader, and married but co-twin remained unmarried—characterized the controls. Five items—slower in development, somatic illness as a child, second born, fiery disposition, and athletic—did not serve as early characteristics which differentiated schizophrenic monozygotic twins from their non-schizophrenic co-twins to the described degree.

A graphic demonstration of the differential pattern in these early characteristics for the schizophrenic twins as compared with their non-schizophrenic co-twin controls was made by arranging the items according to frequency of description for the indexes and then the controls (see figure on p. 104).

The methodology employed in the NIMH twin study (having family members mutually evaluate and interact with one another's historical account; drawing on family and community sources; and using objective photography and written records) has given us considerable confidence in the data. There does remain, however, a core of irreducible doubt regarding validity of the findings, a doubt which is associated with any retrospective study. The case material from the non-NIMH cases varied with respect to the number of family members seen and the detail of information obtained. Nevertheless, the same trends that appear in the overall sample are found to a degree in each of the subsamples from such culturally different areas as Japan, the Scandinavian countries, the United Kingdom, and the United States of America (Gottesman & Shields, 1966; Harvald & Hauge, 1965; Inouye, 1961; Kringlen, 1964; 1966; Pollin, Stabenau, Mosher, & Tupin, 1966; Tienari, 1963). However, individual items discriminating between schizophrenic and non-schizophrenic co-twins, such as the association of lower weight at birth and subsequent development of schizophrenia, were not found to be present equally in all subsamples. Since the twins studied lived during a time span covering nearly a century, and the reports issued from investigators of clearly hereditary to clearly environmental investigational bias, we feel with some confidence that these data are not primarily artifactual in nature, but do represent underlying early premorbid characteristics for schizophrenic twins.

COMPARATIVE FAMILY STUDY

The above described characteristics differentiated schizophrenic from non-schizophrenic children *within* families. We now shift our attention to the differences in early childhood experience among three diagnostically different groups of families: schizophrenic (S), delinquent (D),

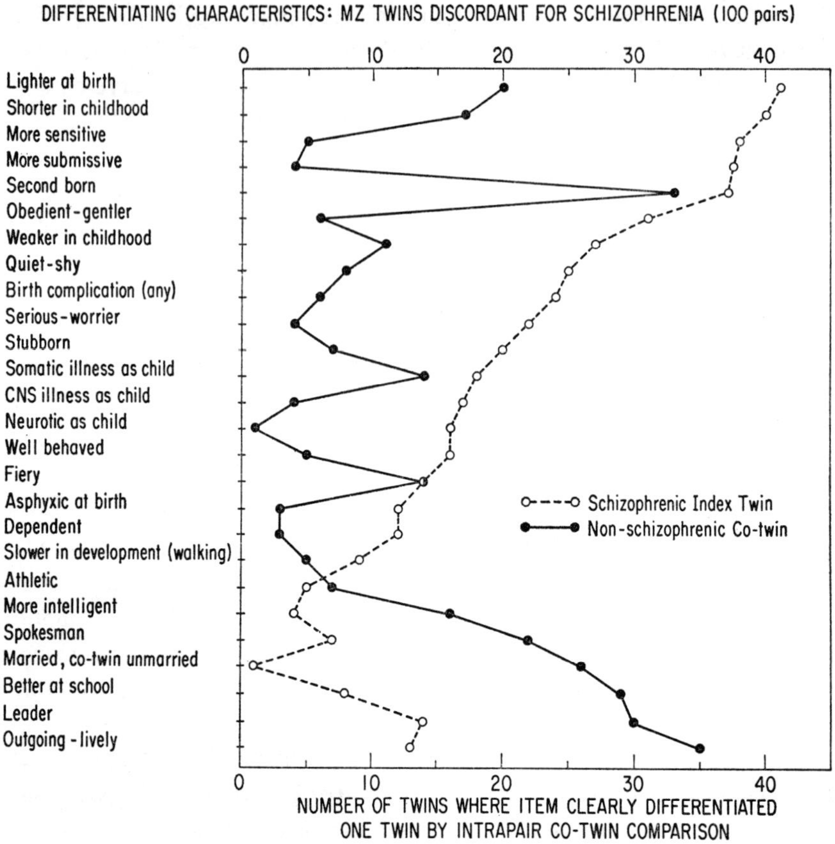

Differentiating characteristics of index and control monozygotic twins for schizophrenia (100 pairs).

and "normal" (N). The following observations come from the life history interview material obtained from family members in the three groups of families.

Family Crisis. For the majority of schizophrenic and delinquent families, periods of major crisis were described as occurring when the index child was from six months to three years old, and they reached a peak when the child was about eighteen months old. A period of crisis was defined as involving an event or series of events which were spontaneously characterized by the family as the "worst time" or the time of most serious family disequilibrium. Some of the early postnatal crisis experiences for the index and control subjects are given in Table 5.

Family crisis appeared during the first three years for nine of the elev-

Table 5. Early Postnatal Experience for Index and Control Siblings in Schizophrenic, Delinquent, and Normal Family Diagnostic Groups

Experience	Schizophrenic (N = 11)	Delinquent (N = 8)	Normal (N = 5)
Family crisis "worst time" (age <3 yrs.)			
Index	9	8	1
Control	1	0	0
Birth of sibling (age <2 yrs.)			
Index	7	7	1
Control	2	3	1
Depression in mother (age <3 yrs.)			
Index	9	6	0
Control	2	1	0
Seen as "damaged" (age <6 yrs.)			
Index	9	2	0
Control	0	0	0

en schizophrenic indexes, all eight delinquent indexes, and one of the five normal indexes. Only one of eleven control siblings in the schizophrenic group, none of the delinquent control siblings, and none of the control siblings in the normal group experienced family crisis during a similar period of life. Not only were there fewer such events in the normal families, but where they did occur, the parents handled them differently. For example, when one N father went into the service, the mother secured the help of an elderly housekeeper who readily became seen as one of the family. The mother then worked in an aircraft plant, feeling that she too was "doing something" during the war, thereby reducing the effect of separation and loss. In contrast, a D mother whose husband went to Europe for a year of employment became lonely, despondent, and symptomatically depressed because the event intensified the remembrance of her barren and lonely childhood. The S and D families described these periods as intensely disruptive and filled with notes of hopelessness, whereas the N families described such events in terms of challenge and mastery. In addition, the degree of external sources of disruption and stress appeared to be greater for the S and D families than for the N families.

Maternal Depression and Guilt. Depression of a subclinical nature was inferred from statements made by the mother as she described these same crisis periods early in the life of the index child. Such statements were: "I was so blue," "sad," "didn't have enough strength," "didn't see how I could keep going." In the schizophrenic group, nine of eleven mothers were considered as depressed during that period, as compared with two instances during the analogous period in the life of the eleven S control siblings. In the delinquent group, six of the eight mothers became depressed during the first two years of the index's life compared with only one episode in these same eight mothers during the first two years in the life of the non-delinquent control siblings. For the normals, there were no equivalent reports of maternal depression associated with either index or control.

In both the S and D groups there were reports of guilt feelings stimulated by the birth of the index. However, the themes varied, centering around hostility in the S group and sexuality in the D group. Four of eleven S mothers reported guilt feelings centered on thoughts of a contemplated or previously accomplished abortion (i.e., guilt related to death), whereas three D mothers related their guilt to previous sexual transgression. Similar guilt feelings were not elicited from mothers of normals nor were they associated with the births of the S and D control siblings.

Birth of a Sibling. The birth of another child in the period two years after the birth of the index child was often subjectively experienced by the parents of the psychopathologic families (S and D) as a source of family pressure, frequently leading to maternal turmoil and depression. For fourteen of the nineteen index siblings from both psychopathology groups, there was a younger sibling born within two years after the birth of the index. For the twenty-nine controls (S and D controls and N siblings) this occurred only seven times ($p<.01$). This difference does not appear to be an effect of sibship size, since the mean sibship size did not differ significantly for the three groups (S, 4.1; D, 5.1; N, 4.0 siblings per family).

In summary, one of the important consequences of this differing incidence of family crisis appeared to be its potential for serving as the origin of a negative identity in a child, partly through identification with a depressed, guilty, and anxious mother. In addition, the disruptiveness of the family life at that time may have further served to reduce the sense of internal security for the index child.

Description of the Children. In describing their children, the parents in the S group more often described or viewed the child who subsequently became schizophrenic as either physically or psychologically "damaged." They most often referred to the changes being noticed before age six, usually shortly after birth or when the infant was beginning to toddle. Nine of the eleven indexes in the S group were so characterized – for example, "his hair stood out; it always reminded me of an animal" or "she had something wrong with her neck and I had to rub it, even as a baby." Only two of the eight D indexes were described in similar terms. None of the S or D controls and none of normal control siblings were considered "defective" in some similar fashion.

Parents' descriptions of early characteristics in the children also differed. For example, the description of the child who subsequently became schizophrenic quite often included, "He is quiet, shy, stubborn, a worrier." These descriptions are similar to those found in the NIMH twin study and in those reported in other studies of the pre-schizophrenic child (Fleming, 1967; Pollack, Woerner, Goodman, & Greenburg, 1966; Stabenau & Pollin, 1967a). Some of the descriptions for the controls in the same families were "rebellious, the sensible one, active, a joker, the worker." The index delinquents quite often were described as "friendly, lovable, hyperactive, nice looking, show off," and their siblings were described as "takes it easy, goes along, calmer, more freedom." The descriptions of the delinquent indexes convey active and lovable qualities, in contrast with the more passive aspects of the individuals who subsequently became schizophrenic.

Projective Identification. Early in the life of the S and D indexes, often at birth, certain attributes such as the shape of the nose, the name given, the color of the skin, or the way the child held its body or walked appeared to have served as a focal point for projection of some parts of the parents' negative self-image onto the child. Data from other portions of the interviews suggest that what is projected appears to be the dissociated, repudiated, negative elements from the parents' personalities or representative portions of repudiated objects from the parents' own lives.* Data from these families suggested, further, that repudiated aspects of the parents' own psyche were constantly drawn to the child's attention – that is, promoted and encouraged as enduring, though negative, qualities belonging to that child. Later, the parents reacted to these characteristics by punishing the child for having such qualities. An example is a mother of a schizophrenic who berated herself for ungainly looks and quiet passiveness as an adolescent, and then unwittingly promoted, through persistent phobic concern over her index daughter, the same qualities of hesitancy,

* Freud and Klein have viewed projective identification in terms of the loved object — that is, "The process implies this loved object is felt to contain the split off loved valued part of the self which in this way continues its existence inside the object. It thereby becomes an extension of the self" (Freud, 1955). Freud stated that "We love it (object) on account of the perfections which we have striven to reach for our own ego" (Klein, 1963). Conversely, one might consider that one may hate the object for the imperfections of the self seen as part of it.

shyness, guardedness, and inability to get along with playmates. When this girl was a teenager, she was constantly compared by the mother unfavorably with her more active, bubbly, involved, younger sister, leaving her with a sense of despair and worthlessness which was followed by withdrawal and a delusional, personal relationship to a mark on her hand which she neologistically called her "wome."

On the other hand, positive aspects of parental personality and positively held early life objects and experiences were more quickly and persistently seen as belonging to (projected onto) the control sibling. Thus, the ambivalent tie and conflict that developed between the parents and the index schizophrenic or index delinquent were much less prominent in their relationship with the control siblings. Subsequently, a clearer differentiation and elaboration of a positive sense of identity was attained by the control sibling. Further, as he achieved successful passage through the age appropriate psychosocial phases, there was enhancement of a sense of personal and social competence not attained by the index sibling in the same family.

Projective-Identification and the Interpersonal Checklist. The clinical material suggested that the parents characterized the index as less like themselves or their ideal, and the control sibling as much more like themselves or their ideal.

In order to test the hypothesis developed from the review of our clinical material, that parental projective identification operates in differentiating the siblings in the psychopathology families, we chose to analyze data which were independent of the interview material. Each family member had rated himself, the three other family members, and the "ideal" person on the Interpersonal Checklist. A correlation matrix between the view of self, ideal, and the other three family members for sixteen checklist variables was derived for each individual. Correlations of prime interest were those between the parent's view of himself and his view of the index sibling just before illness and the parent's view of himself and his view of the control sibling at a similar time. Similarly, correlations between a parent's ideal and his view of the index and of the control sibling were determined.

For eight of eleven S families and seven of eight D families, comparison of the correlations support the hypothesis that the parent's view of the control siblings more closely approximates the parental self-ideal image, and the view of the index was less highly correlated with the parent's own self-ideal image (Table 6). For six of the eleven S families, but only two of eight D families, the parent's self-ideal image was in fact negatively cor-

Table 6. Projective Identification Correlation Coefficients of Interpersonal Checklist Profiles [a]

Family Diagnostic Group and Code Number	Parent View of Self: View of Index [b]	Parent View of Self: View of Control [c]
Schizophrenic ($N = 11$)		
5	−.28	.42
11	−.23	.68
10	−.22	.57
4	−.16	.13
1	−.09	.37
3	−.01	.67
7	−.08	−.03
6	−.05	−.17[d]
9	.07	.35
8	.25	.24
2	.45	−.02
Mean	−.03	.29
Delinquent ($N = 8$)		
1	−.13	.64
7	−.07	.48
5	−.21	−.18
2	.08	.18
4	.08	.13
6	.31	.48
3	.57	.78
8	.25	.04
Mean	.11	.32
Normal ($N = 5$)		
1	.13	.36
5	.14	.43
4	.14	.21
2	.15	.23
3	.42	−.10
Mean	.20	.23

[a] Pearson product-moment method.

[b] Mean correlation coefficient for each family derived from the average of the correlations: father's view of self and view of index sibling; father's ideal and view of index; mother's view of self and view of index; mother's ideal and view of index.

[c] Mean correlation coefficient for each family derived from the average of the correlations; father's view of self and view of control sibling; father's ideal and view of control; mother's view of self and control; mother's ideal and view of control.

[d] Subsequently developed delinquent symptoms.

related with the view of the index child while positively correlated with the view of the control child. This suggests a clearer negative-positive split in the S parents' view of the index and the control sibling. For the five N families all correlations were positive except for one control sibling.

For the twenty-two S parents the mean correlation for parental self-ideal view and the parents' view of the index was negative, though only very slightly so (−0.03). In contrast, the mean correlation for the same parents' self-view and view of control was positive (+0.29). In the D group, the mean correlation for the index was positive (+0.11) but less than the +0.32 for the control. For the normals, correlations were positive and of similar magnitude for both index (+0.20) and control sibling (+0.23).

Correlation between father's and mother's view of a sibling was used as a measure of the reliability of the ratings for the children in each group. The correlation between the view by each father and mother, respectively, were: +0.53 for the schizophrenic index, +0.43 for the non-schizophrenic control; +0.30 for the delinquent index, +0.44 for the non-delinquent control; and +0.37 for the normal index and control.

The Interpersonal Checklist data provide evidence supporting the hypothesis that projective identification may be operative in parents' discriminating between index and control siblings to a greater degree in the S families than in the D families and to a greater degree in both S and D families than in N families. However, this analysis has not yet considered the cluster of characteristics in which there was difference or similarity between the parents' self-image and their view of the sibling. This and similar questions require further investigation.

Discussion

Using the NIMH twin series life history material, which is very detailed and quite consistent with the accumulated world case literature, a representative life-course description can be constructed. From this, we can derive a tentative theoretical formulation for the phase-by-phase difference in personality development and life experience for pairs of monozygotic twins who become discordant for schizophrenia. Since the data from the comparative family study reveal a similar differential view of the index and the control sibling by the parents, extrapolation to non-twins on the basis of this model seems justified. The formulation will be divided into those life periods in which major differences in life experience for the twins seemed most evident.

Fetal Intrauterine Development. Studies have shown that relative differences in intrauterine nutritive environment (i.e., in placental placement, anastomoses between placentas of the fetuses, cord embarrassment, and relatively disadvantageous fetal positioning) may lead to one twin of a monozygotic pair weighing less at birth and being less mature or fully developed than his co-twin (Morison, 1949; Price, 1950; Sydow & Rinne, 1958). Twins who share a common chorion and especially those few sharing in addition a common amnion are most likely to be born with excessive differences in maturity or development.

In sixty-nine of the hundred case report pairs, material was available giving an indication of which twin was lighter at birth or whether the twins' weights were equal. Forty-one of the sixty-one schizophrenic index twins were lighter than their non-schizophrenic co-twins at birth ($p<.01$). Thus, there is an apparent statistically significant relation between relative fetal maturity, as measured by birth weight, and the development of schizophrenia within discordant monozygotic twin pairs. In the following sections, we shall consider the possible intervening stages of development between birth and adulthood for such twins.

The Birth Process. The heavier of the twins is more often born first. The second, lighter one is more likely to experience periods of anoxic cyanosis during delivery or respiratory distress after delivery as a consequence of immaturity. Of the two, the lighter, less mature twin often feeds less well, may display a lag in development, and may be seen as — and in fact often is — the weaker and slower of the two (Pollin & Stabenau, 1968; Stabenau & Pollin, 1967a). In contrast, the heavier twin, even when near or below the premature weight threshold, tends to be seen as the "healthy," "normal" twin and indeed does not require so extensive neonatal care, is less likely to have respiratory embarrassment, and teeters on the very brink of survival less often than his co-twin.

The Early Biologic Differences (First Three Months). The mother often finds early in the first week or two that the heavier twin nurses well and sleeps better. The lighter twin (premature or near premature) is seen as a feeding problem. His natural loss of weight following delivery places him in an even more precarious state. He usually cries more readily and is less easily calmed down or satisfied.

Graham, Matarazzo, and Caldwell (1956), in a study of 81 infants suffering neonatally from transient periods of anoxia and 265 non-anoxic controls, found significant increases in pain threshold, irritability, and tension, and decreases in measures of maturation and visual capacity. The syndrome of the dysmature infant may encompass neonatal anoxia (Clemetson, 1956) and hypoglycemia (Cornblath, Joassin, & Weisskopf, 1966). Recent analysis of the NIMH twin series has shown that the adult protein-bound iodine value appears to be in part determined by the degree of maturity at birth, as measured by the birth weight (Stabenau & Pollin, 1967b; Stabenau & Pollin, 1968a; Stabenau, Pollin, Mosher, Frohman, Friedhoff, & Turner, 1969). Another variable to consider is the relative thyrometabolic state at birth, since it may directly influence the development of the central nervous system and indirectly influence subsequent somatic growth and intellectual development.

It does not seem to be just the biologic differences but the feelings elicited from the parents that begin to shape the parent-child interaction. This excerpt and the following are from verbatim typescripts of the recorded first interview between the parents and both twins, and the two NIMH investigators. The mother from Family 9 stated, "Actually when I think back, it's been all his life, even from the time he [index] was brought home from the hospital — hasn't had quite the placid disposition that [control] has. For a long time [index] was lighter than [control] — not much but 7 or 8 pounds until they were 13 or 14." The mother from Family 4 stated, regarding the period just after birth, "At first [index] was smaller and I think I fed her at first with an eye dropper." The same mother commenting on the period from six to twelve months of age stated, "[Index] was more of a feeding problem than [control] — wouldn't swallow. She would [index] hold it in her mouth — would hold the food in her mouth — and I had that checked and there was nothing organically wrong." "Well, I think [control] always remained the heavier and a little taller — now I imagine they are about equal." The mother from Family 3 stated, "During that spell there she [index] was a really small baby and she wouldn't eat the way you wanted her to — she would fall asleep all the time and you would have to keep waking her up and at certain times it got to be really bad and you really cried tears while you were feeding her." "I was worried about her [index]. I always thought if a child didn't eat they were sick. I was concerned about her health because I felt that if she didn't get this food, that it really would make her ill."

Early Parent-Child Interaction (Three to Six Months). The characteristic differences between monozygotic twins established in utero and during the birth process are present from birth on, but they most characteristically serve in part to differentiate the parental response to each twin during the first six months. Moss (1967), in a study of thirty firstborn children and their mothers by means of direct observation during the first three months of life, concluded that "the state of the infant affects the quantity and quality of maternal behavior and thus in turn would seem to influence the course of future social learning." In a large-scale study of infants and mothers, Knobloch (1962) has shown that the number of mothers called tense increased with the degree of neurologic disturbance in the infant. Many of the low birth weight twins are in actual peril of death. It has been shown that for some parents, reaction to impending loss of a child modified the relation to that child; what followed was infantilization of the child, leading to overdependence on the parents (Green & Solnit, 1964).

The very fact that one twin is slightly more vigorous and responsive and the other less so may lead to an unconscious splitting of ambivalent feelings toward the pregnancy. Of many possible such splits, the one we have seen most consistently leads to greater direction of feelings of warmth and acceptance toward the heavier, more "capable/healthy" infant, and an unevenly repressed hostility toward and rejection of the lighter, "weak" part of the pregnancy.

The mother from Family 18 stated, "I didn't think they'd live. They looked so tiny. . . . People said, 'Oh, you're going to smother them.' They used to whimper just a little weak whimper, not a real lusty cry like most babies, and I wanted them so badly – *one* baby anyway, or the two if it was going to be twins." The mother from Family 10 stated, "One of them [index] was fussy and worried and the other one going around doing everything [control]."

Thomas, Chess, Birch, Hertzig, & Korn (1966), in their studies of behavior, individuality, and early childhood, cite two cases where mothers of twins showed differences in initial and subsequent patterning of reactivity. In each family the mother started with the same general maternal attitude toward the two infants but developed increasingly dissimilar affective bonds and responses to them as they grew older. Bayley and Schaefer (1960) report from the Berkeley Growth Study that although they were unable to show consistent stability of maternal or child behavior over time, several correlations between the two were established. Loving mothers had happier sons (at age three), and controlling hostile mothers had excitable, unhappy sons. In adolescence, girls who are maladjusted (rated as gloomy, unhappy, sullen, and hostile) more often have mothers who are hostilely controlling – that is, punitive, irritable, controlling, isolating, and making excessive contact with their daughters. Although they report no study of twins, they note for two brothers separately studied that maternal behavior was markedly different toward each and that it was never recognized by the blind raters that the mother was the same person.

An additional feature for some families in the NIMH series was that during the early neonatal period the father was either psychologically or physically unavailable to the mother. Where relative intramarital dissatisfaction existed (i.e., father felt mother was not strong enough under the load, or mother felt father was not devoting enough of himself to the family), the mother appeared to have been left with an inner sense of ineffectual rage that was directed away from the husband toward the "weak, ineffective, helpless" twin. Seemingly, the thought "I need you, husband" may have been transformed and directed toward the weak and helpless child as "You need me." This appeared to be a possible influence on the development of a different parent/child relation for each twin.

Emergence of Individual Personality (Second Year). Although in the first six months, early differences between the twins are of a more *biologic* nature, by age twelve to twenty-four months, parents find differences in *behavioral* characteristics of the twins. The lighter at birth often appears the fussier, more troublesome, more fragile and helpless. Studies of prematurity suggest that some of this relates to maturational processes. Shirley (1939) has reported a behavior syndrome which characterizes prematurely born children as showing irascibleness, stubbornness, negativism, shyness, and overdependence on the mother. He states: "Indications are that in family relations prematures differ from their siblings in being more jealous, less good to the siblings, and making more demands for attention, showing off and in being dependent and less self-reliant as they grow older. In general, prematures seem to try to preserve their status as over-protected and over cared-for members of the family group." The parent may feel the need to do something special for the weaker twin and thus have a different set of expectations for that child, which will be perceived by that twin as being different from the expectations for his heavier, stronger, "healthier" co-twin. This may reinforce a feeling that there is something especially hazardous for him in the world about him. The feelings of internal disequilibrium as experienced in the initial physiologic disequilibrium associated with the periods of respiratory distress and difficulty in assimilating food which characterized his first few hours of neonatal existence may be projected onto the outside world to a greater degree during this period. Thus, the environment might take on the appearance of a hostile, threatening, disorganized world at a time that he is developing an inner sense of inadequacy. Characteristically at this age, for the pre-schizophrenic index twin, there has appeared a phase of worriedness and fearfulness. None of the non-schizophrenic co-twins in the NIMH series was described in these terms.

From the study of families of normal monozygotic twins, we know that not all twins with birth weight differences react in the above manner. However, our sample of control families is too small and as yet not optimally matched to the above sample, so it would be premature to discuss this issue at this time.

During the twins' first few years, the parents in this group of discordant twins often described finding little satisfaction in each other. There was often a lack of complementarity and support for each other which did not allow a full degree of communication and expression of affect between them. This is in contrast to the findings for normal families, but is similar to the pattern that Caplan (1960) describes for parents where the crisis of premature birth was disruptive to the developing family. A split between the parents may readily be perceived by the already sensitized, fearful youngster — that is, one good, one bad parent, not too dissimilar from the parents' view of the twins as one good, successful, healthy; one bad, weak, a failure. Incorporation and internalization of this split by the "sensitive" twin may add to the twin's sense of internal confusion and faulty identity formation. Index from Family 14 stated, "I had the fear if my mother should leave father where would it leave me."

Data from the comparative family study suggests that periods of intense disturbance of the family equilibrium occurred predominantly just after the index child was born, and especially during the second year of his or her life. Of critical importance during this stage of development is the mastery of motoric coordination in walking and in fine movement, and the mastery of using language to label objects, to communicate, and to make one's needs known to someone else. Any severe disruption of the mother/child relation during this period could be anticipated to have profound effect on the subsequent development of the child and may in some way determine the child's responsive style to disruptive stress met later in life. Clinical data linking maternal fetal loss and/or depression with subsequent psychosis in a child have been reported by Terris, Lapouse, and Monk (1964), who found a significantly higher incidence of fetal loss (previous stillbirth and abortion) in 182 mothers of childhood schizophrenics as compared with 182 matched controls, and by Reiser (1966), who in a study of 170 families, found a relation between prolonged, subclinical depression in mothers after childbirth and infantile psychosis in those children.

When considering why psychopathology occurs in one child and not in another, one theoretical consideration might be that identification with a depressed mother on the part of the index may serve as a modus for the development of a sense of negative identity. The term *negative identity* is used here to cover what is clinically seen in the adolescent delinquent or schizophrenic as a pervasive sense of inadequacy and depression (Erikson, 1959). The delinquents in our sample, though initially posing with a bravado of lack of concern for others along with notions that "the world owed them a living," quickly revealed their sense of inadequacy, despair, helplessness, and lack of worth. The schizophrenics also spoke of their sense of inadequacy, inability to satisfy anyone, and worthlessness. The grandiose delusions of power and omnipotence displayed by some indexes seem to be reactions to these same feelings of worthlessness.

Individuation versus Dependence (Second to Sixth Year). The heavier, stronger twin often begins to walk first, talks with more facility, and is capable of earlier mastery of complex coordinated tasks. Overall, there is an *expansion of differentiation,* most noted in motoric mastery. On the other hand, the lighter twin, as a result of a relative developmental lag, is seen as less independent, less competent, and less secure, and therefore makes fewer attempts at ego-stretching experiences for fear of failure. A phase of ego restriction may then be seen to begin for him, though he often may have a more advanced verbal capacity than his co-twin (Gifford, Murawski, Brazelton, & Young, 1966).

The details of the mutual interplay between biological competence of the child, the evoked parental response to this, and the child's response to the subsequent parental attitude is exceedingly complex and not within the proper scope of this paper. However, Levy (1943) and Kanner (1957) describe an aspect of this behavior ("maternal" overprotection) as excessive contact, treatment of the child as a baby for an inappropriate length of time (infantilization), and prevention of social maturation (the mother won't let the child grow up). Subsequently, with little encouragement for exploration, the child clings to the mother for dependent support. The maternal reaction may take the form of either overindulgence or maternal domination. Harper (1961), in discussing the special problem of the premature, speculates, "A certain amount of the handling of the prematurely born is not related directly to the physical or physiologic hazards of low birth weight, but rather is an indirect result of the mother's apprehension and of her tendency to insulate him from the normal hazards of life." Sontag, Baker, & Nelson (1958) report from experience at the Fels Institute on mental growth and personality development that "From years 3 to 6 it would appear that the learning of broad patterns of behavior in relation to parents is of primary importance in establishing a foundation for later interaction with the environment. The child who is emotionally dependent upon his parents during these years would appear to be establishing a mode of behavior which is not conducive to the 'learning to learn' during this time. However, if the child is learning to meet some of his needs, through appropriate aggressive behavior, competitiveness or individual problem-solving, it would appear that he is laying groundwork for the kind of motivation characterized in need for achievement which may operate as a motive in learning experiences."

Two additional pairs of monozygotic twins discordant for schizophrenia have been studied since the above data were collated. In each, the heavier birth weight twin was the one who subsequently became schizophrenic. In Family 22 that twin experienced a period of greater asphyxial cyanosis as compared with her co-twin when three months of age, was thought to have a heart murmur in infancy, and had a minor lip deformity suggestive of an early stage of harelip. The co-twin was markedly less cyanotic and had neither of the latter stigmata. In childhood and thereafter, this index twin had a pervasive concern that something was wrong with her that was not wrong with her sister. The heavier *S* twin in pair 23 at age three had a severe bout of Rocky Mountain Spotted Fever, with the subsequent development of fearfulness, guardedness, and sensitivity as compared with his co-twin. These two indexes who were heavier at birth appear to fit the model described for lower birth weight twins in terms of subsequent development of ego restriction. For their co-twins a differential life history course of more normal growth and development was described.

Features of premature children or lighter birth weight twins in most instances do not lead to abnormal psychological development. Gifford et al. (1966), in a longitudinal direct study of a pair of normal premature monozygotic twins, note: "The smaller twin's relative 'immaturity' in birth weight but not in gestational age, followed by a maturational lag in motor coordination, might be interpreted as a constitutional basis for the advantageous ego characteristic of social responsiveness, which has proved to have enduring qualities. In contrast, the larger twin's maturational lead in motor development which might be related to the character traits of perseverance, self-sufficiency, became a disadvantage in the early part of the second year, when she showed some depression and regressive imitation of her twin. But this disadvantage was temporary and she has retained her superiority in motor skill and coordination."

Social Competence and Self-Esteem (Sixth Year to the Teens). The clinical data from the comparative family study have suggested that different parent/child relationships developed for the S or D index as compared with a control sibling within the same family. The majority of S and D families' own Interpersonal Checklist data support the hypothesis that parents tend to characterize the control sibling as more in keeping with their own self or ideal view, and the index, as remembered before illness, as less like the parents' self or ideal view. It has already been noted that early in life there was projection of repudiated negative elements from the parents' personalities or representative portions of repudiated objects from the parents' own lives onto the index child. The data from the twin study that suggest minor differences in biologic competence may serve as a point for differential perception and relationship. An additional aspect of this process may be that many of the repressed hostile wishes originally directed toward early objects in the parent's life were reawakened at the time of family crisis and then were displaced onto the selected index child. These warded-off feelings, while being seen in the child and attributed to the child, appeared to be a source for the beginning of a disturbed, conflictual parent/child relationship. These data may not entirely represent longstanding views of the premorbid child, but may in part be a reflection of an ongoing current disavowal, disattachment, or repudiation of the pathologic child. However, when considered with the discordant twin data in this report, they appear representative of an ongoing life process rather than mainly a retrospective distortion.

The more socially competent, heavier twin turns to peers, and his sense of identity and self-image increase as overt signs of confidence appear in the attainment of better school grades than his co-twin and in significant and continued peer relations. The twin heavier at birth usually is the longer at birth and continues to be slightly taller in adulthood (Tanner, 1962). For normal twins, Shields (1962) has documented a significant positive direct relation between height and IQ. Other studies have shown that in twins of disparate birth weight the low birth weight twins have significantly lower IQ and more impaired performances than their heavier monozygotic co-twins (Babson, Kangas, Young, & Bramhall, 1964; Churchill, 1965; Drillien, 1961; Willerman & Churchill, 1967).

Large-scale longitudinal studies of prematures by Wiener, Rider, Oppel, Fischer, and Harper (1965) have revealed that "premature twins are psychologically impaired" and "the degree of impairment increases with decreasing birth weight." Further, "perceptual motor disturbances, flaws in comprehension and abstract reasoning, perseveration trends, poor gross motor development, immature speech and impaired IQ significantly identified low birth weight children." DeHirsch, Jansky, and Langford (1966) report, "Prematurely born children whose IQ fell within the average range of intelligence did less well than maturely born peers on a large battery of tests administered at kindergarten age, and while they showed some indication of a 'catching up' during the years between kindergarten and end of second grade, significant lags persisted well into the eighth year of life." Lane and Albee (1964), in a study of schizophrenics and their siblings and normals, have shown that schizophrenics during their childhood scored significantly lower in IQ than their own siblings as well as lower than normal non-schizophrenic children. This evidence may demonstrate that the defect in intellectual functioning in schizophrenia (perhaps secondary to disturbances in attention and perception related to faulty object relations, subtle central nervous system dysfunction, or both) occurs in a period before the onset of overt symptomatology of adult schizophrenia. On the other hand, it may indicate that such a reduced function may play a contributory part in the process leading to the subsequent development of schizophrenia.

During this period from six to the teens, the first major separations of twins in school or in summertime activities become an issue, and often point up the dependence of the lighter twin upon the heavier. Following the early period of worry and self-doubt, and the first experience of less efficacy, there is an intensified dependence upon the co-twin which precedes but also overlaps the heavier twin's turning to others. Thus, as the heavier twin turns to peers for expansion of ego by identification with others—that is, leaving the twinship—the lighter clings dependently to the twinship, restricting attempts to relate to others.

Separation (Adulthood). In the late teens and early adulthood there are periods of long separation for the twins. Here there often is a collapse of the dependency of the lighter on the heavier twin as the heavier moves toward individuality (i.e., chooses to dress differently, begins to have friends other than his co-twin, and begins a stable heterosexual relationship). As noted in the case material (Table 4), in twenty-six instances where the schizophrenic index had not married, his co-twin had married.

The lighter twin often responds by withdrawal. Abortive attempts at duplicating the co-twin's success through an inappropriate choice of friends, situations, and so forth often result in failure. This suggests that the lighter twin has begun a life-long repetition compulsion of being in the inferior position. Another psychodynamic view is that a unique co-twin transference is manifest in that all significant figures are heretofore reacted to as being "more successful, more competent"; this leaves the index with an intensified feeling of low self-esteem and reduced efficacy. The index in Family 7 stated: "I was more or less the black sheep or something"; the index in Family 8 said, "I was skinny when I was little, I was the typical 90-lb. weakling." The important role of diminished efficacy in the development of schizophrenia has been poignantly described by White (1963).

Further, the heavier twin's successes and pride in his accomplishments act to reinforce the feeling of inadequacy in the lower birth weight index. In many pairs a move of the family home or the loss of a significant family figure during this period has led to an accentuation of the inadequacy in that the customarily taken-for-granted minor but supportive relationships are in one blow removed from the lighter, less secure twin. The heavier recoups by "leaving" his twin and relating more to peers, accentuating a sense of loneliness and despair in the lighter twin. Often, disorganization, withdrawal, and schizophrenic symptomatology develop in the lighter birth weight twin at just this time when the heavier, more differentiated twin is making a sudden spurt in the development of an individual identity and the establishment of heterosexual and genital level of personality organization. In a retrospective study, Prout and White (1956) have reported personality trait differences similar to those noted in this report between schizophrenic and non-schizophrenic siblings. Independence and rebelliousness characterized the control adolescent sibling, whereas the pre-schizophrenic adolescent was often dependent, scared, quiet, unsociable. Further, though both schizophrenic and non-schizophrenic individuals had personality change in the adolescent period, for the healthy siblings the change was in a "positive direction" toward increased responsibility, but for the pre-schizophrenic there was more self-involvement, sensitization, and seriousness. In a careful review of the character structure of non-schizophrenic monozygotic co-twins as reported in the literature, Planansky (1966) concluded that typical schizophrenia can be paired with all types including schizoid, neurotic, and non-pathologic personality patterns.

Thus, by late adolescence, distinctions between the pre-schizophrenic monozygotic twin and his co-twin have developed through the interplay of early nongenetic biologic, parental attitudinal, interactional, social, and environmental experiential differences. The review of monozygotic twins discordant for schizophrenia has produced an aggregate of descriptive terms describing early characteristics which seem to differentiate the schizophrenic from the non-schizophrenic co-twin. Other studies of retrospective nature provide similar differentiating features which characterize the pre-schizophrenic, but, as in our review, the data must be considered to bear the imprint of the bias of recall at a time when the pathology already exists (Lu, 1961; McGhie, 1961). Pollack et al. (1966) reduced the source of error from investigator bias by blindly analyzing maternal retrospective reports for characteristics of thirty-three schizophrenics and their non-schizophrenic siblings. They found, "The schizophrenic patients were more irritable and more shy than their siblings from as early as the 2 to 5 year period. They were rated higher on chronic worrying or unhappiness; they were more shy and dependent, had more neurotic traits and conduct problems, and they were more often rated as non-affectionate during the 5 to 12 year period. The patients in the group performed less well in school than their siblings and had more difficulty relating to their peers." A study from the Judge Baker Center in Boston suggests that these comparative findings differentiating schizophrenic from non-schizophrenic siblings are duplicated when one looks at individual schizophrenic patients. Child guidance center records for children who later became schizophrenic and records from matched control children who were non-schizophrenic in adulthood were reliably judged and compared blindly. The pre-schizophrenics were found to be preoccupied, self-conscious, embarrassed, insecure, tense, or worried, and more often they related feelings of being overcome with anxiety, vulnerability, defenselessness, isolated, unloved and unable to communicate with others (Fleming & Ricks, pp. 240–260). A prospective investigation by Mednick and Schulsinger (1964) has compared twenty-five children born to schizophrenic mothers and reared by them, with twenty-five children matched in age and sex who at the average age of nineteen months were separated and were reared apart from their psychotic mothers. They found the children raised by their schizophrenic mothers significantly different from the foster children in being more shy, withdrawn, and unengaged, as judged independently by their schoolteachers.

Although the description of the pre-schizophrenic state has been more sharply characterized by the body of work just described, defining the exact nature of specific etiologic factors, and their interplay, is only beginning. It appears from the material in this report that differences in early biologic maturity relate to differences in competence, which, in turn, appear related to the development of schizophrenic symptomatology.

Studies by Bender (1955), Goldfarb (1961), and Vorster (1960) suggest that for childhood schizophrenia, and perhaps a subgroup of adult schizophrenics, subtle impairment of the central nervous system may be of significant etiologic importance.

However, as indicated in this report and in others' work, it is the understanding of the interplay between innate capacities of the child and the environmental, familial, and social forces that may best explain the development of schizophrenia in one child and not another (Bowen, 1960; Jackson, 1960; Laing & Esterson, 1964; Lidz et al., 1958; Searles, 1959; Wynne et al., 1958). Thus, the chief value from these current investigative efforts may be in designating more clearly the variables which describe the population where high risk for schizophrenia exists and where a prospective longitudinal lifetime study of such individuals may lead to the more complete understanding of causal relationships.

COMMENTARY

QUESTION. Tienari's 1963 report that none out of sixteen pairs of identical male twins were concordant was a very shocking finding to everybody in this business. That finding did not accord with any environmental theory or with any genetic theory. I'd be interested in hearing something about Tienari's data since he's come to work with you this year.

STABENAU. He does have one pair concordant for schizophrenia, 6 per cent of his sample. To the best of my knowledge, no more pairs have become concordant.

MEDNICK. I think this kind of design is a marvelous one, and it can be best exploited, perhaps, in looking for the environmental influences that tend to shape people into schizophrenia. That is, what you have in comparisons of twins discordant for schizophrenia is more or less a leveling out of genetic variables. In a sense, what you do then is give the environmental variables a good chance to show themselves. This is a point that Leon Eisenberg has made, and I think it applies very nicely to the kind of work you're doing. I was very interested to hear the kind of environmental situations that you were describing that seem to differentiate the early environment of these children.

QUESTION. Are there a lot of schizophrenics who are not breaking down in the age periods covered by all three of these studies?

STABENAU. We don't at this time have data to answer that question. My view of schizophrenia is that of a spectrum; I think that when we take a more detailed look at this twin material, we're going to be able to line up our index twins along a spectrum according to a number of variables. This step may be related to the issue you raise. What are some of the family, interpersonal, experiential, and developmental differences for one end of the spectrum versus the other end of the spectrum? In other words, are we going to find more of the soft neurologic signs and evidence of prenatal cyanosis in the more severely ill chronic individuals as compared with those who are more reactive, who've been overtly schizophrenic but in a hospital for only a short period of time and then for the rest of their life have not been overtly ill? I think that the whole issue of the premorbid personality is a very important one and indeed needs to be taken into account. All schizophrenics aren't the same.

RICKS. I suggest that an earlier question really raises a further question that we all have to think about and especially the youngest people in the audience have to think about. How could you design a really good study of the development of schizophrenia right away, start it, and survive it? Clearly, you have to begin with the evidence about parents and you have to begin with early childhood data, birth data. You need to know something of the genetic background, need to have the records throughout life, you can't lose the probably three out of five schizophrenics that we lost through movement into other areas. But if you take Stabenau's and Mednick's and our and other studies, you begin to see the possibility of designing a really good study, one better than anything that has been done yet. It might be that we have to move away from the Ph.D. model for research, something you can do in a couple of years by yourself, into designing our research along lines that can only be done in the lifetimes of a lot of people.

REFERENCES

Babson, S., J. Kangas, N. Young, & J. Bramhall. Growth and development of twins of dissimilar size at birth. *Pediatrics*, 1964, 33, 327–333.

Bayley, N., & E. Schaefer. Maternal behavior and personality development, data from the birth and growth study. *Psychiatric research reports of the American Psychiatric Association*, 1960, No. 13.

Bender, L. Twenty years of clinical research on schizophrenic children with special reference to those under six years of age. In G. Capla (Ed.), *Emotional problems of early childhood.* New York: Basic Books, 1955.

Bowen, M. A family concept of schizophrenia. In D. D. Jackson (Ed.), *The etiology of schizophrenia.* New York: Basic Books, 1960.

Brodey, W. Some family operations and schizophrenia. *Archives of General Psychiatry*, 1959, 1, 379–402.

Burkhardt, H. Über ein Diskordantes eineiiges Zwillingspaar. *Zentralblatt für die Gesamte Neurologie und Psychiatrie*, 1929, 121, 277–282.

Caplan, G. Patterns of parental response to the crisis of premature birth. *Psychiatry*, 1960, 23, 365–374.

Churchill, J. The relationship between intelligence and birthweight in twins. *Neurology*, 1965, 15, 341–347.

Clemetson, C. The difference in birthweight of human twins and twin blood studies. I. Oxygen analysis of umbilical cord blood. *Journal of Obstetrics and Gynaecology of the British Commonwealth*, 1956, 63, 1–8.

Cornblath, M., G. Joassin, & B. Weisskopf. Hypoglycemia in the newborn. *Pediatric Clinics of North America*, 1966, 13, 905–920.

DeHirsch, K., J. Jansky, & W. S. Langford. Comparisons between prematurely and maturely born children at three age levels. *American Journal of Orthopsychiatry*, 1966, 36, 616–628.

Drillien, C. The incidence of mental and physical handicaps of school-age children of very low birthweight. *Pediatrics*, 1961, 27, 452–464.

Erikson, E. H. Identity in the life cycle. *Psychological Issues*, 1959, 1 (No. 1).

Essen-Möller, E. Psychiatrische Untersuchungen an einer Serie von Zwillingen. *Acta Psychiatrica Scandinavica*, 1941, 16 (Suppl. 23).

Freud, S. Group psychology and the analysis of the ego. In *The complete psychological works of Sigmund Freud*, Vol. 18. London: Hogarth Press, 1955.

Gifford, S., B. Murawski, B. Brazelton, & G. Young. Differences in individual development within a pair of identical twins. *International Journal of Psycho-Analysis*, 1966, 47, 261–268.

Goldfarb, W. *Childhood schizophrenia*. Cambridge, Mass.: Harvard University Press, 1961.

Gottesman, I., & J. Shields. Schizophrenia in twins: 16 years' consecutive admissions to a psychiatric clinic. *British Journal of Psychiatry*, 1966, 112, 809–818.

Graham, F., R. Matarazzo, & B. Caldwell. Behavioral differences between normal and traumatized new borns. I. The test procedures. II. Standardization, reliability and validity. *Psychological Monographs*, 1956, 70, 20–21.

Green, M., & A. Solnit. Reactions to the threatened loss of a child: A vulnerable child syndrome. *Pediatrics*, 1964, 34, 58–66.

Grillmayr, W., & T. Kohlmann. Diskordante Psychiatrische Bilder bei einem eineiigen Zwillingspaar. *Wiener Zeitschrift für Neruenheilkunde und deren Grenzgebiete*, 1929, 2, 441–460.

Harper, P. Comments on prevention of prematurity. In M. Kowlesser (Ed.), *Fifth conference on physiology of prematurity*. New York: Macy Foundation, 1961.

Harvald, B., & M. Hauge. Hereditary factors elucidated by twin studies. In J. U. Neel, M. W. Shaw, & W. J. Schull (Eds.), *Genetics and the epidemiology of chronic diseases*. Washington, D.C.: U.S. Dept. of Health, Education, and Welfare, 1965. Pp. 61–76.

Hobson, J. A. Identical twins discordant for schizophrenia. *Journal of Nervous and Mental Disease*, 1964, 138, 432–442.

Inouye, E. Similarity and dissimilarity of schizophrenia in twins. In R. Cleghorn, A. Moll, & C. Roberts (Eds.), *Proceedings Third World Congress Psychiatry*. Montreal: University of Toronto Press and McGill University Press, 1961. Vol. 1, pp. 524–530.

Jackson, D. D. A critique of the literature on the genetics of schizophrenia. In D. D. Jackson (Ed.), *The etiology of schizophrenia*. New York: Basic Books, 1960.

Kallmann, F. J. The genetic theory of schizophrenia: An analysis of 691 schizophrenic twin index families. *American Journal of Psychiatry*, 1946, 103, 309–322.

———. Heredity and constitution in relation to the treatment of mental disorders. In P. Hoch (Ed.), *Failures in psychiatric treatment*. New York: Grune & Stratton, 1948.

———. *Heredity in health and mental disorder*. New York: Norton, 1953.

——— & B. Roth. Genetic aspects of preadolescent schizophrenia. *American Journal of Psychiatry*, 1956, 112, 599–606.

Kanner, L. *Child psychiatry*. Springfield, Ill.: Thomas, 1957.

Kasanin, J. A case of schizophrenia in only one of identical twins. *American Journal of Psychiatry*, 1934, 91, 21–28.

Klein, M. *Our adult world and other essays*. New York: Basic Books, 1963.

Knobloch, H. The developmental behavior approach to the neurological examination in infancy. *Child Development*, 1962, 33:181–198.

Kringlen, E. Schizophrenia in male monozygotic twins. *Acta Psychiatrica Scandinavica*, 1964, 40 (Suppl. 178).

———. Schizophrenia in twins, an epidemiological-clinical study. *Psychiatry*, 1966, 29, 172–184.

Kurihara, M. A study of schizophrenia by the twin method. *Psychiatria et Neurologia Japonica*, 1959, 61, 1721–1741.

Laing, R., & A. Esterson. *Sanity, madness and the family*. London: Tavistock, 1964.

Lane, E. A., & G. W. Albee. Early childhood intellectual differences between schizophrenic adults and their siblings. *Journal of Abnormal and Social Psychology*, 1964, 68, 193–195.

Leary, T. *Interpersonal diagnosis of personality*, New York: Ronald Press, 1957.

Levy, D. M. *Maternal overprotection*. New York: Columbia University Press, 1943.

Lidz, T., A. Corneilson, D. Terry, & S. Fleck. Intrafamilial environment of the schizophrenic patient. VI. The transmission of irrationality. *Archives of Neurology and Psychiatry*, 1958, 79, 305–316.

Lu, Y. Mother-child role relations in schizophrenia: A comparison of schizophrenic patients with non-schizophrenic siblings. *Psychiatry*, 1961, 24, 133–142.

———. Contradictory parental expectations in schizophrenia. *Archives of General Psychiatry*, 1962, 6, 219–234.

Luxenburger, H. Vorlaüfiger bericht über Psychiatrische Serion unter Suchungen an Zwillinger. *Zeitschrift für die Gesamte Neurologie und Psychiatrie*, 1928, 116, 297–326.

McGhie, A. A comparative study of the mother-child relationship in schizophrenia. *British Journal of Medical Psychology*, 1961, 34, 199–221.

Mednick, S. A., & F. Schulsinger. A pre-schizophrenic sample. *Acta Psychiatrica Scandinavica*, 1964, 40 (Suppl. 180), 135–146.

Mishler, E., & N. Waxler. Family interaction process and schizophrenia: Review of current theories. *Merrill-Palmer Quarterly*, 1965, 11, 269, 315.

Morison, J. Congenital malformations in one of monozygotic twins. *Archives of Disease in Childhood*, 1949, 24, 214–218.

Moss, H. Sex, age and state as determinants of mother-infant interaction. *Merrill-Palmer Quarterly*, 1967, 13, 19–36.

Planansky, K. Schizoidness in twins. *Acta Geneticae Medicae et Gemellologiae*, 1966, 15, 151–166.

Pollack, M., M. G. Woerner, W. Goodman, & I. M. Greenburg. Childhood development patterns of hospitalized adult schizophrenic and non-schizophrenic patients and their siblings. *American Journal of Orthopsychiatry*, 1966, 36, 510–517.

Pollin, W., & J. Stabenau. Biological, psychological and historical differences in a series of monozygotic twins discordant for schizophrenia. In S. S. Kety & D. Rosenthal (Eds.), *The transmission of schizophrenia*. London: Pergamon Press, 1968.

———, L. Mosher, & J. Tupin. Life history differences in identical twins discordant for schizophrenia. *American Journal of Orthopsychiatry*, 1966, 36, 492–509.

Pollin, W., J. Stabenau, & J. Tupin. Family studies with identical twins discordant for schizophrenia. *Psychiatry*, 1965, 28, 60–78.

Price, D. Primary biases in twin studies: A review of prenatal and natal difference-producing factors in monozygotic pairs. *American Journal of Human Genetics*, 1950, 2, 293.

Prout, C., & M. White. The schizophrenic's sibling. *Journal of Nervous and Mental Disease*, 1956, 123, 162–170.

Reed, G. Uniovular twins: Schizophrenia and tuberculosis. *Canadian Medical Association Journal*, 1935, 32, 180–182.

Reiser, D. Infantile psychosis, overview of studies at the James Jackson Putman Children's Center. *Mental Hygiene*, 1966, 50, 588–589.

Rosanoff, A., L. Handy, I. Plesset, & S. Brush. The etiology of so-called schizophrenic psychoses, with special reference to their occurrence in twins. *American Journal of Psychiatry*, 1934, 91, 247–286.

Searles, H. Integration and differentiation in schizophrenia: An over-all view. *British Journal of Medical Psychology*, 1959, 32, 261–281.

Shields, J. *Monozygotic twins brought up apart and brought up together.* London: Oxford University Press, 1962.

Shirley, M. A behavior syndrome characterizing prematurely born children. *Child Development*, 1939, 10, 115–128.

Slater, E. Psychotic and neurotic illness in twins. *Medical Research Council special report*, Series No. 278. London: H.M.S.O., 1953.

Sontag, L., C. Baker, & V. Nelson. Mental growth and personality development: A longitudinal study. *Monographs of the Society for Research in Child Development*, 1958, 23 (2, Serial No. 68), 1–143.

Stabenau, J. Heredity and environment in schizophrenia: The contribution of twin studies. *Archives of General Psychiatry*, 1968, 18, 458–463.

——— & W. Pollin. Early characteristics of monozygotic twins discordant for schizophrenia. *Archives of General Psychiatry*, 1967, 17, 723–734. (a)

———. Maturity at birth and adult protein bound iodine. *Nature*, 1967, 215, 996–997. (b)

———. Adult protein bound iodine and maturity at birth in monozygotic twins. *Journal of Clinical Endocrinology and Metabolism*, 1968, 28, 693. (a)

———. Comparative life history differences for families of schizophrenics, delinquents, and "normals." *American Journal of Psychiatry*, 1968, 124, 1526–1534. (b)

———, L. Mosher, C. Frohman, A. Friedhoff, & W. Turner. Study of monozygotic twins discordant for schizophrenia: Some biologic variables (Lactate-pyruvic ratio; 3, 4-dimethoxyphenlethylamine; S_{19} macroglobulin; anti-rabbit red cell hemagglutin; protein bound iodine). *Archives of General Psychiatry*, 1969, 20, 145–158.

Stabenau, J. R., J. Tupin, M. Werner, & W. Pollin. A comparative study of families of schizophrenics, delinquents, and normals. *Psychiatry*, 1965, 28, 45–59.

Sydow, G., & A. Rinne. Very unequal "identical" twins. *Acta Paediatrica*, 1958, 47, 163–171.

Tanner, J. *Growth at adolescence.* Oxford: Blackwell, 1962.

Terris, M., R. Lapouse, & M. A. Monk. The relation of prematurity and previous fetal loss to childhood schizophrenia. *American Journal of Psychiatry*, 1964, 121, 476–481.

Thomas, A., S. Chess, H. G. Birch, M. Hertzig, & S. Korn. Behavior individuality in early childhood. In M. Haimowitz & N. Haimowitz (Eds.), *Human development.* New York: Crowell, 1966.

Tienari, P. Psychiatric illnesses in identical twins. *Acta Psychiatrica Scandinavica*, 1963, 39 (Suppl. 171).

Vorster, D. An investigation into the part played by organic factors in childhood schizophrenia. *Journal of Mental Science*, 1960, 106, 494–522.

White, R. Ego and reality in psychoanalytic theory, a proposal regarding independent ego energies. In G. Klein (Ed.), *Psychological Issues*, Vol. 3 (No. 3). New York: International Universities Press, 1963.

Wiener, G., R. Rider, W. Oppel, L. Fischer, & P. Harper. Correlates of low birth weight: Psychological status at six to seven years of age. *Pediatrics*, 1965, 35, 434–444.

Wigers, F. Ein Eineiiges, Bezüglich Schizophrenie Diskordantes Zwillingspaar. *Acta Psychiatrica et Neurologica*, 1934, 9, 541–556.

Willerman, L., & J. Churchill. Intelligence and birthweight in identical twins. *Child Development*, 1967, 38, 623–630.

Wynne, L., I. Ryckoff, J. Day, & S. Hirsch. Pseudo-mutuality in family relations of schizophrenics. *Psychiatry*, 1958, 21, 205–220.

BERNICE T. EIDUSON
DIANE M. RAMSEY-KLEE

A Strategy for Life History Research Using Computer-Based Information Processing Techniques

CONVENTIONAL applications of computers to life history research have primarily involved the automatic scoring and interpretation of questionnaire data and psychological tests, and the application of a wide variety of statistical procedures to the analysis of behavioral data which have been scaled or quantified in some manner. Although these applications of computers have indeed expanded the scope of possible research investigations and have liberated the researcher from much clerical and computational drudgery, they have not exploited the full potential of current computer technology as an adjunct to life history research. The use of the computer as a processor of narrative text opens an additional area of research methodology heretofore confined primarily to limited content analyses or experimental studies in verbal behavior. The capability of transforming a patient's entire case history file into computer-manipulatable form is a relatively recent innovation whose merit is evident on immediate examination. In addition, this capability constitutes the basis for a new research strategy which offers an exciting and productive departure from more traditional research approaches.

At the Reiss-Davis Child Study Center, our attempt to apply computer-based technology to psychiatric data has resulted in the development of a generalized information processing system—the Psychiatric Case History Event System (PsyCHES). PsyCHES permits one (a) to automate the maintenance of the total case history file on a patient as collected by an institution, and (b) to store the case history record in such a manner that it can be retrieved in diverse and flexible ways that optimize

NOTE: This research has been supported by U.S.P.H.S. Grant MH 11306-03 from the National Institute of Mental Health.

research on patients and their psychiatric disorders. This latter capability seemed particularly desirable because, despite their well-known limitations and difficulties, psychiatric case records contain the primary bank of information about the nature and course of psychiatric disorders and the patients who are subject to them.

The latest developments in PsyCHES have evolved primarily during the large-scale implementation of the system in research on clinical decision-making in diagnosis (Eiduson, Brooks, & Motto, 1966; Eiduson, Platz, & Carmichael, 1967). In the course of this and other investigations using the PsyCHES System, it became evident that this general information system embodies a new strategy (Eiduson, Brooks, Motto, Platz, & Carmichael, 1968) which is particularly felicitous to the study of psychiatric, and especially clinical, questions. This paper describes this strategy, contrasting it with traditional scientific approaches (Braithwaite, 1953; Festinger & Katz, 1953; Popper, 1961).

Traditionally, an investigator first defines a research problem and formulates relevant hypotheses. He then collects data that will permit him to test these hypotheses. These data are analyzed and the results they provide become the basis for generating new hypotheses, specifying additional data to be collected, and new analyses to be performed.

This strategy places certain well-recognized constraints on the investigator. All hypotheses to be tested must be posed on an a priori basis, because the hypotheses themselves determine what data are to be collected. Thus, data gathered are relevant only to the single problem under study, except in the infrequent situation where a subset of the data collected is suitable for further analysis. More typically, however, initial results suggest new or related hypotheses to be tested for which the data already collected are not appropriate. Also, if during the course of the investigation data originally thought to be relevant do not actually prove to be so, or if it becomes obvious that certain additional variables should have been included in the analysis to provide meaningful tests of the hypotheses, the research effort to that point must be abandoned in the worst and all too frequent case or, at best, modified to accommodate the new research plan. And a new data collection procedure must be initiated.

These difficulties stem from the emphasis in the classical methods on a priori delineation of the experimental design, predisposing the investigator to set out in advance all the questions he proposes to ask, to collect only data appropriate to answering these questions, and to decide on the ways in which the relevant variables will be quantified or categorized.

Even in studies employing strategies that encourage collection of a broad spectrum of data about a field situation, with subsets of data subsequently singled out for specific study, there is an early focusing of emphasis on delineation of the problem areas to be studied. Within the field study approach, a number of simultaneous and successive problem areas can usually be investigated by examination of a single data base. However, the optimal exploitation of the data base is hampered by the Herculean task of extracting relevant data, ensuring that contextual significance is retained and that the variables of interest are accurately drawn from the comprehensive information pool in which they are embedded.

The research strategy permitted by use of a computer-based generalized information processing system such as the PsyCHES System overcomes such obstacles. It capitalizes on three primary capabilities which enhance the more traditional approaches to behavioral research: (a) a more comprehensive data base is available for the research endeavor; (b) the data base can be examined in an iterative fashion because of the rapid and flexible access that the computer provides; and (c) there is a common format for structuring the information contained in all kinds of reports contributing to the data base. A more detailed discussion of each of these three capabilities follows.

a. The information pool in a computer-based generalized information processing system can be the total body of data or information collected about an individual, about a phenomenon, or about certain behaviors of more than one individual. In clinical problems where therapy notes, case history data, or hospitalization records form the information base, the data pool usually is comprised of the entire body of such material. Often these data have been collected independently of and without regard for the requirements of any particular research investigation. From this data bank, information responsive to answering a wide variety of research questions can be retrieved.

This research strategy also can pertain to an experimental problem where a complex behavioral system is under investigation. A comprehensive data pool encompassing all the relevant aspects of the behavioral system can be collected systematically. Once this data pool exists, information that is pertinent to the specific questions under study can be retrieved. For example, in a study that was undertaken on the behavioral and biochemical development of a neonate during his first 96 hours, information concerning the biochemical and behavioral systems that were likely to be relevant to the experimental issues furnished the total data pool (Eiduson

& Eiduson, 1967; Eiduson & Lubitz, 1966). The notions that had led to the investigation determined what behaviors were relevant for observation and collection in the total data base. Of particular interest were the precursors of ego development. Therefore, data were subsequently gathered and retrieved on the neonate's motor development, perceptual responsiveness, state of arousal, and crying, smiling, and other emotional behaviors. Other information, of course, remained available for further analyses as desired.

b. A second characteristic of a computer-augmented research strategy is its potential for recycling through the data base because of rapid and flexible access to the stored data. There seems to be no question that the laboriousness and tediousness of searching clinical data for variables of interest has hampered the systematic pursuit of many research investigations in psychiatry. Without the computer, the number of variables that could be searched for in case history records was limited. But with the aid of the computer, the entire body of information contained in a record is open to systematic scrutiny.

Many studies in psychiatry have shown that as soon as certain variables are isolated from their context, relevant information may be lost or distorted. Inherent in the nature of some psychiatric variables are complexity and dynamic relationships with other variables. It is difficult to ascertain the nature, magnitude, and importance of these relationships if the variables are isolated for consideration one at a time. Furthermore, isolating such variables from their context might change their original meaning. However, with proper data input and retrieval programs, the computer can preserve these essential relationships and present and summarize them as units, as regression equations, or as predictive probability statements, depending on the nature of the variables.

A comprehensive data pool makes possible an iterative approach to research in which the same data bank can be tapped repeatedly, thus permitting the researcher to formulate some of his research questions on an a posteriori basis. When variables originally thought highly relevant prove to be unimportant, or when an original plan of study warrants redirection, data that may be more profitably studied can be retrieved from the data bank.

A large data base collected without regard for the specific research questions that will be investigated is vulnerable to criticism on two counts: first, that a welter of irrelevant and inconsequential data may be gathered, and second, that data essential to the research investigation may be left out. In answer to the first criticism, it should be recognized that the computer-based iterative approach just described offers the possibility of rapidly sifting through large amounts of data in order to select empirically those data elements that are relevant to a particular research question. One can afford to explore a broader base of data than was possible with manual techniques. The second criticism also is ameliorated by the computer's ability to scan the entire data base rapidly, identifying gaps in the information store and the amount of data actually missing relevant to the variables under study. For example, data may be missing for a patient in a clinical study, either because the event of interest never happened in the patient's life or because it was never reported in the case history record. The proportion of missing data in a data base pertaining to a variable under study is an important finding in itself. It points out the need to clarify the significance of omitted information. Was it absent in the patient's life? Was it not important enough to be recorded? Does its absence signify freedom from a pathological sign? Of course, the researcher's encountering missing data complicates the analysis. However, there are ways to cope with this problem that provide a useful analysis and meaningful results (Cochran & Cox, 1957; Winer, 1962).

The process of recycling investigations so that the most discriminating variables can be retrieved seems to be particularly valuable in life history research. Often the investigator proceeds on the basis of minimal empirical clues about which variables are likely to be the most crucial for elucidating phenomena under study. When he realizes that other variables might be more discriminating than those collected initially, the prospect of beginning anew is usually discouraging enough to cause the investigation to be terminated. The findings of the original study are often published with a mere statement of what other variables might have provided more definitive answers to the problem – in fact, the concluding section of many research reports is entitled "Suggestions for Future Research." However, with the capability for successive iteration through the total data base, promising variables suggested at each stage of the analysis can be subjected to scrutiny and evaluation. Of course, the more brilliant the insights into the key variables, the faster the iterative research process will converge to a satisfactory solution.

It should be emphasized that the iterative research strategy just described is not diametrically opposed to or incompatible with traditional approaches to research. The major difference is that the iterative approach encompasses a two-step procedure. In the first step, a large body of behavioral data relevant to a broad problem area is transformed into computer-manipulatable form. In the second step, research questions are generated, hypotheses are formulated, and pertinent data to test these hypotheses are retrieved from the computer-based data store. This second step essentially employs the classic approaches to scientific inquiry. However, the investigator has the option of specifying simultaneously or sequentially a rich spectrum of hypotheses to test, depending upon his initial hunches or his revised notions as results accumulate at each iteration of the analysis.

c. *The third capability of a computer-based research strategy is that a common basis can be provided for structuring information collected originally in diverse reports or with diverse measuring instruments.* In clinical work, questionnaires, application forms, telephone calls, medical reports, neurological findings, process notes, interviews, and so forth form the corpus of documents from which patient data are derived (Eiduson, 1966b; Eiduson, Brooks, & Motto, 1966; Eiduson, Platz, & Carmichael, 1967). In experimental settings, a variety of measuring instruments can be used, each contributing a special kind of information which can then be interrelated by means of a common data format.

In PsyCHES, the Event serves as the common unit of information into which all data are structured. The Event Concept was thought particularly felicitous to psychiatric data, since it embodies both their temporal or historical and their spatial focus. Since a detailed description of the transcription procedures for formatting report data into PsyCHES has already been reported (Eiduson, 1966a), only a summary of the characteristics of the Event and the Event Statement will be included here in order to show the advantage of having the Event as the common basis for storing, manipulating, and retrieving psychiatric case history material.

THE EVENT MODEL

Events are defined as happenings or occurrences in the life of the patient or relevant persons in his environment. In the case of an experimental situation, events would be behaviors or experiential phenomena of subjects who were monitored during the course of the investigation.

The Event encompasses two kinds of phenomena: first, the factual, objective, "hard" data whose validity can be established by outside criteria; and second, the body of subjective, judgmental, impressionistic, "soft" data whose validity tends to resist easy verification.

Some examples of the kinds of occurrences or happenings that are defined as events are given below in a partial list of event names from the A section of the event name lexicon. It can be seen that some events such as adoption or accident have behavioral referents, have a high degree of objectivity, and can be validated. Others, however, such as anger and anxiety, are inferential and subjective, and may serve as second—or even third—level constructs. Yet the ability to consider them all as events provides a common unit for information processing.

Ability	Alcoholism
Abstract thinking	Allergic reaction
Academic performance	Ambition
Accident	Anger
Activities	Antisocial behavior
Activity level	Anxiety
Addiction	Appearance
Adjustment	Asthma
Adoption	Attendance
Affect	Attention
Affection	Attire
Aggression	

The inclusion of event names of different levels of generality is also encouraged in the PsyCHES event name lexicon because the decision about which data segments are termed events is determined by a number of factors, such as the frequency of occurrence or incidence in the material being transcribed and the tendency of the clinician or experimenter to use content-laden words and phrases in recording observational and impressionistic data. In PsyCHES, the exact working vocabulary of the clinician or investigator is retained wherever possible.

For example, certain general decision rules determine whether associative ideas are classified as a specific event called Fantasy or as a generic event labeled Thought Processes. The details of these decision rules are made explicit in a transcription manual prepared for use with the PsyCHES System (Eiduson, 1966a). No a priori hierarchy or grouping of event names in the lexicon has been imposed as a system constraint. Consequently, events can be retrieved in a flexible manner, depending on the questions under study and the manner in which the investigator feels that event names are related for his particular inquiry.

An event is transcribed as an Event Statement, which consists of a set of standardized fields that define each event. The Event Model below portrays the structure of an event. The Event Statement includes the event name, the date associated with the event (including a beginning and ending date if both are part of the information), and also some indication whether the date is specific or approximate (date-type field). Also provided in the Event Statement are fields for location, subject, object, and reporter (i.e., the person or persons reporting the event to the record). This standard sequence of fields is associated with every event.

EVENT MODEL

Event Data

Name of event	Reporter of event
Date of event	Subject of event
Beginning and ending	Object of event
Date-type	Descriptors of event
Location of event	

Descriptors of Event

Nature	Context
Frequency	Duration
Circumstances	Reasons
Sequelae	

Report of Event

Date of report	Source of report
Location of report	Context of report

The narrative portion of the Event Statement is then formatted into a series of modifier fields called descriptors. Some of the possible descriptors used to organize the narrative material are shown in the Event Model. As can be seen, the information contained in the modifier fields may concern the nature, frequency, or duration of the event; the circumstances under which it occurred; the context in which the event was reported; or reasons for it. The sequelae modifier is used to describe sequential relations within the event.

Events are reported in the experiment or to the record at certain times and under certain conditions. These data about the origin of the report are contained in four fields (see Event Model): the date of the report, where the event originated (location), who was sending it to the record (source), and the type of report, such as medical report or a telephone call (context). In this way, data regarding the origin of the event become an integral part of the event itself.

A single sentence taken from a Reiss-Davis interview will illustrate this process of transcribing data from its original clinical context to computer-listed form: "Mrs. R. died suddenly from a heart attack about three and a half years ago, which produced long-lasting traumatic consequences for mother and Donna" (sentence from Case R-D 8001, interview). This sentence is part of Donna's case history record and comes from an interview with her mother in which the mother is discussing the death of her own sister. The process of transcribing this sentence for input to PsyCHES is a logical one which follows standard conventions. First, two events were identified in the sentence: one deals with the death itself, and the other with the subsequent effect on the patient and her mother. After specifying the content area signified by each event name, the transcriber notes the date, the location, the reporter, the subject, and the object of the event and then identifies the descriptors. Each descriptor has a modifier name and a modifier entry. Then the reporting information which identifies the origin of these events is noted. In the Transcription Format below, the report data are portrayed first since they apply to both events contained in the source material.

It can be seen from the Transcription Format that the source ma-

TRANSCRIPTION FORMAT

Report Data

Event name	Report
Date	September 3, 1963
Date-type	Beginning
Location	Reiss-Davis
Reporter	Social worker
Modifier: context	Interview
Modifier: name	P. S., M. S. W.

Event Data (1)

Event name	Death
Date	1960
Date-type	Approximate
Location	Not pertinent
Reporter	Mother
Subject	Maternal aunt
Modifier: circumstance	Died suddenly
Modifier: reason	From a heart attack
Modifier: date supplement	About 3½ years ago
Modifier: reference	Subsequent event for sequelae

Event Data (2)

Event name	Traumatic situation
Date	1960
Date-type	Approximate
Location	Not pertinent
Reporter	Mother
Subject	Mother + patient
Modifier: nature	Produced traumatic consequences
Modifier: duration	Long-lasting

terial was reported to the case history record on September 3, 1963, in an interview conducted by P. S., a social worker at Reiss-Davis. Next, the structure of the event dealing with the maternal aunt's death is shown. The descriptive information regarding the death is contained in four modifier fields, the last of which is a reference to the succeeding event in the record for sequelae. The reference descriptor functions much as a cross-referencing index in a library system. It permits events which have been related in the text by the clinician or person reporting to the record to be considered together, thus permitting any connecting and causal relationships in the content to be retained. The following event describes the traumatic situation resulting from the maternal aunt's death.

Once these events are entered into the PsyCHES System as part of the patient's case history record, they can be retrieved and listed by the computer. One of a number of optional computer listings of the data, R-D 8001, is given in Figure 1. In the case of the first event, note that the computer lists the report data associated with the event by means of an origin line at the beginning of the computer listing. It is relatively easy to reconstruct the first part of the original sentence from the information contained in the fields of this event. By examining the computer printout of the subsequent event, the reconstruction of the original sentence can be completed. All of the information inherent in the original sentence has been retained. Furthermore, transcription, keypunch, and computer processing have also retained the wording of the clinical text in natural English.

In a series of reliability studies undertaken in the PsyCHES project, it has been shown that under experimental conditions, reconstruction of data from the computer-listed format into the original narrative text proceeds with a high degree of reliability. In a subset of data from one study, for example, six segments of diverse text containing over a thousand words were independently transcribed by three trained and experienced tran-

```
REPORT-NO   4, INTERVIEW BY SOCIAL WORKER AT REISS-DAVIS, SEP 3, 1963

 112 EVENT      DEATH
                   1 CIRCUMSTANCES     DIED SUDDENLY
                   2 REASON            FROM A HEART ATTACK
                   3 DATE SUPPLEMENT   ABOUT 3-1/2 YEARS AGO
                   4 REFERENCE         SUBSEQUENT EVENT
      SUBJECT   MATERNAL AUNT
      REPORTER  MOTHER
      DATE      1960, APPROXIMATE

 113 EVENT      TRAUMATIC SITUATION
                   1 NATURE            PRODUCED TRAUMATIC CONSEQUENCES
                   2 DURATION          LONG-LASTING
      SUBJECT   MOTHER AND PATIENT
      REPORTER  MOTHER
      DATE      1960, APPROXIMATE
```

Figure 1. Computer listing, R-D 8001.

scribers, yielding discrepancies in only 4 per cent of the data. Of this 4 per cent, three out of four discrepancies among transcribers were judged to be semantically equivalent – only one out of four discrepancies represented a loss or distortion of information.

In another study in which reliability was evaluated on the basis of the comprehensiveness and accuracy of retrieval of information relevant to a series of specific research queries, a similar high degree of reliability among transcribers was achieved (Eiduson, 1967, pp. 112–146). In this study, a set of documents transcribed independently by three transcribers upon retrieval yielded virtually the same body of information in response to the research queries posed to the system.

DATA DISPLAYS

Formatting data in fields essentially divides the narrative text into discrete variables. Once the variables are isolated in this manner, they can be automatically selected for retrieval. The data contained within any of the fields specified in the search can be listed for a group of subjects or patients or for a single individual. The sorting and listing of selected variables is done by computer and can be performed according to whatever selection criteria the researcher specifies in his query. For example, a sort can be performed on the event name field, the subject field, the date field, or a nested combination of fields. If one were interested in determining the incidence of asthma in a child clinical population, the data base would be searched for events with asthma as the event name. If one wished to examine developmental data on a patient in chronological sequence rather than in the order in which it was reported to the record, the developmental history events in the patient's record would be sorted into chronological sequence on the date field. If one were interested in studying the marital history of the mothers of child psychiatric patients, the marital history events in the data base would be searched for those with mother as the subject.

From these examples it can be seen that data of interest can be sorted and listed by individual patients, for all patients in the data base, or for a subset of patients. An illustrative partial listing of events pertaining to school behavior of one patient is shown in Figure 2. Here can be seen the behavior problems in the school history of this patient that contributed to his being referred for help. The medical history on another patient contained in his case record is shown in Figure 3. Although this is only a partial listing, it illustrates the manner in which medical events can be re-

```
SCHOOL BEHAVIOR EVENTS                                      PARTIAL LIST/R-D 007
                                                            SUBJECT - PATIENT

067 EVENT     CONDUCT
                 1 NATURE               HAS BEEN A MANAGEMENT PROBLEM
                 2 DATE SUPPLEMENT      SINCE KINDERGARTEN
    SUBJECT   PATIENT
    REPORTER  SCHOOL COUNSELOR
    DATE      1958, APPROXIMATE

093 EVENT     WORK HABITS
                 1 DATE SUPPLEMENT      SINCE LAST SEMESTER
                 2 NATURE               REFUSES TO DO HIS HOMEWORK
    SUBJECT   PATIENT
    REPORTER  MOTHER
    DATE      SEP 1963, APPROXIMATE

108 EVENT     ATTENDANCE
                 1 NATURE               PLAYS HOOKY
                 2 FREQUENCY            OCCASIONALLY
    SUBJECT   PATIENT
    REPORTER  SOCIAL WORKER
    DATE      SEP 30, 1964, CURRENT

154 EVENT     AUTHORITY
                 1 RESPONSE             HE IS DEFIANT
                 2 CONCURRENT           REFUSES TO FOLLOW INSTRUCTIONS
    SUBJECT   PATIENT
    REPORTER  TEACHER
    DATE      1964, APPROXIMATE

201 EVENT     ACADEMIC PERFORMANCE
                 1 NATURE               GRADES HAVE SHOWN STEADY DECLINE
    SUBJECT   PATIENT
    REPORTER  PRINCIPAL
    DATE      1964, APPROXIMATE
```

Figure 2. Sample computer sort: school behavior events.

```
MEDICAL HISTORY EVENTS                                      PARTIAL LIST/R-D 197
                                                            SUBJECT - PATIENT

142 EVENT     DERMATOSES
                 1 NATURE               HE DEVELOPED ECZEMA
                 2 DATE SUPPLEMENT      SHORTLY AFTER BIRTH
    SUBJECT   PATIENT
    REPORTER  MOTHER
    DATE      OCT 1953, APPROXIMATE

083 EVENT     ASTHMA
                 1 NATURE               FIRST DEMONSTRATED SEVERE ASTHMA ATTACKS
                 2 DATE SUPPLEMENT      DURING HIS THIRD YEAR
    SUBJECT   PATIENT
    REPORTER  MOTHER
    DATE      1956, APPROXIMATE

168 EVENT     ACCIDENT
                 1 NATURE               WAS HIT BY A CAR
                 2 CIRCUMSTANCES        WHILE PLAYING IN THE STREET
    SUBJECT   PATIENT
    REPORTER  SOCIAL WORKER
    DATE      1961, APPROXIMATE

024 EVENT     INJURY
                 1 NATURE               HE SUFFERED A BASAL SKULL FRACTURE
    SUBJECT   PATIENT
    REPORTER  MEDICAL DOCTOR
    DATE      1961, APPROXIMATE

041 EVENT     PHYSICAL AND NEUROLOGICAL DATA
                 1 NATURE               BITEMPORAL NON-FOCAL CEREBRAL DYSRHYTHMIA
    SUBJECT   PATIENT
    REPORTER  MEDICAL DOCTOR
    DATE      1964, APPROXIMATE

198 EVENT     MEDICATION
                 1 NATURE               WAS PLACED ON MELLARIL 10 MG. B.I.D.
                 2 STATUS               WITHOUT SUCCESS
    SUBJECT   PATIENT
    REPORTER  MEDICAL DOCTOR
    DATE      1964, APPROXIMATE
```

Figure 3. Sample computer sort: medical history events.

```
EATING EVENTS                                         PARTIAL LIST/R-D 001, 005,
                                                        009, 014
                                                      SUBJECT - PATIENT

058 EVENT      EATING PROBLEMS
                    1 NATURE           HE IS A FINICKY EATER
                    2 EXAMPLE          TRIES TO GET ALL THE FAT OFF THE MEAT
    SUBJECT    PATIENT
    REPORTER   MOTHER
    DATE       JUN 1965, APPROXIMATE

128 EVENT      EATING PROBLEMS
                    1 NATURE           HE DOESN'T KNOW WHEN TO STOP EATING
                    2 CONCURRENT       WILL EAT ANYTHING IN SIGHT
    SUBJECT    PATIENT
    REPORTER   MOTHER
    DATE       SEP 1961, APPROXIMATE

021 EVENT      EATING PROBLEMS
                    1 NATURE           HIS INTAKE IS RESTRICTED TO CARBOHYDRATES
    SUBJECT    PATIENT
    REPORTER   MEDICAL DOCTOR
    DATE       MAY 1968, APPROXIMATE

326 EVENT      EATING ARRANGEMENTS
                    1 NATURE           HE REFUSES TO EAT WITH THE FAMILY
    SUBJECT    PATIENT
    REPORTER   PARENTS
    DATE       FEB 1965, APPROXIMATE

015 EVENT      EATING PROBLEMS
                    1 CONTEXT          AS STATED BY MOTHER ON APPLICATION
                    2 NATURE           THE CHILD OVEREATS
    SUBJECT    PATIENT
    REPORTER   MOTHER
    DATE       JAN 1966, APPROXIMATE

389 EVENT      EATING PROBLEMS
                    1 FREQUENCY        OFTEN
                    2 NATURE           THROWS AWAY HIS LUNCH
                    3 CONCURRENT       BUYS CANDY BARS
    SUBJECT    PATIENT
    REPORTER   SCHOOL NURSE
    DATE       OCT 10, 1967, CURRENT
```

Figure 4. Sample computer sort: eating events.

trieved and listed in the order in which they occurred in the patient's life. Figure 4 shows a listing of eating events for a selected group of patients. Such a listing can help reveal the range of eating problems and arrangements noted in a child psychiatric population.

With the computer's capability for rapidly searching formatted fields, it is possible to automatically generate lists of numerical data and frequency counts for statistical analysis. The data so retrieved can be reformatted as required for input to sort, report generation, and statistical analysis computer programs. The linkage to these programs can also be automatic if the researcher foresees the requirement for frequent use of them.

METHODOLOGICAL CONSIDERATIONS

In the Reiss-Davis study on decision-making during the diagnostic process in child psychiatry, the development of a generalized information processing system was a requisite for studying the complex mechanisms and large body of interrelated variables involved in the diagnostic decision process. In this investigation, decision-making is first viewed as a two-step process. Initially, the clinician must decide on the amount and kind of data he should collect in order to arrive at a reliable, representative, and relevant picture of the patient, his environment, and his disorder. These early decisions about what information to gather are called preliminary decisions. The clinician then derives certain final or summary decisions as a result of his processing the body of data he has collected. It is hypothesized that preliminary decisions may be predictive of summary decisions.

In order to study preliminary decisions, certain structural features of the data base are analyzed. A determination is made of the total amount of data in the record, its distribution into areas of psychiatric significance such as developmental and medical history categories, and the depth into which inquiry is made concerning various events. Also identified are such structural characteristics of records as the amount of redundant data they contain and the areas in which these data occur, as well as unique, infrequent, or invariant events appearing in the record.

The next primary area of interest in this research has been to move to an intensive study of the content of the material so that significant variables that discriminate among various types of patients can be identified. The majority of schema used at present to assign diagnostic labels to child psychiatric patients employ a nomenclature based on symptom formation. The Reiss-Davis data base is being searched for significant variables in such additional areas as background of the disorder, the environmental context in which it evolved, precipitating stresses, present manifestations, the course before intervention, and so forth. It is hoped that a natural taxonomy of children's disorders can be developed by clustering techniques which identify the significant variables in all these areas that differentiate among patient groupings.

An ancillary model of clinical decision-making that provides a useful way to conceptualize the diagnostic process is a series of hypothesis-generating and hypothesis-testing sequences. The clinician initially sets up certain hypotheses about the patient and/or his disorder on the basis of available preliminary information about the patient. His subsequent information gathering then proceeds as a data collection effort to test these hypotheses. His mental processing of these data (or events) in turn leads to the generation of new hypotheses. This process continues until a set of diagnostic considerations is reached – including the assignment of a diagnostic label to the patient, the formulation of a treatment plan for the patient and his parents, the decision whether or not to use adjunctive therapies such as special tutoring or speech therapy, and a judgment concerning prognosis.

Because the reports that make up a case history record are dated, the information contained in each report can be studied sequentially to determine how events collected at various stages of the diagnostic process for a patient are related to each other. This approach promises to provide basic data for modeling how information is collated and evaluated by clinicians in order to arrive at diagnostic decisions. It is anticipated that a variety of information-processing models will emerge as characteristic of clinical styles. In subsequent work, an attempt will be made to identify those variables differentiating various clinical styles of decision-making.

Considering the diagnostic workup as a sequential process permits one to view the procedure along a time continuum. In essence, a moving aperture can be employed that allows one to take a series of "snapshots" of the influx of data to the patient's case history record. The first picture is obtained at the intake interview. In addition to providing identifying data about patient and family, the admitting parent also lists the complaints about the patient that motivated the family to seek help. These complaints take the form of comments such as, "He has frequent nightmares" or "She can't get along with her sister." On the average in the Reiss-Davis data base, there are seven chief complaints per patient, with some patients having as few as three and other patients having as many as fifteen. It was possible to group these narrative complaints into nineteen symptom categories such as eating or sleeping problems, psychosomatic ills, and antisocial behavior. Once this was done, each patient's symptom profile on intake was represented by means of a nineteen-element binary vector of zeros and ones, zero for absence of complaints in a symptom category and one for their presence. This method of scaling patient symptoms was also employed by Achenbach (1966) in his factor-analytic study for classifying children's psychiatric symptoms. The binary vectors for each patient, then, form the data input to cluster analysis programs; in turn, these programs help define the number of patient configurations that can be identified on the basis of their symptomatology on intake alone.

Another picture that might be taken of the patient could contain developmental information obtained in the intake interview. Again these developmental variables could be scaled to allow them to be handled in a vector representation, thus permitting the application of cluster analysis techniques. Further on in the diagnostic workup the patient might be viewed again in terms of his school history data and so on. As one moves along this time continuum in the analysis, slightly different pictures of the sample of patients are obtained, all of them relevant to diagnostic considerations. The question can then be asked, Do the same patients cluster together on the basis of their initial symptom picture, their developmental characteristics, and their school history? It is of interest to find out if stable patterns of patient groupings can be identified as one moves an aperture along the continuum of the diagnostic workup. If stable groupings do emerge, such a finding would lend great credence to the value of using a new taxonomic structure for assigning diagnostic tags, one based on the empirical evidence contained in the patient's case history record.

A cluster analysis approach also permits one to view a sample of patients through the several sides of a prism — for example, through the eyes of the mother, the school, and the clinician. Using data provided by each of these three types of informants, a triad of cluster analyses can be performed on the sample of patients to look for commonality in the patient groupings that result. This method of analysis offers exciting possibilities for identifying stable patient groupings, the key variables that permit such discrimination, and the kinds of data that on an empirical basis contribute substantially to summary diagnostic decisions over the course of the work-up.

The type of scaling used to represent the data under study has implications for the form of cluster analysis that can be used. A useful paradigm for considering such a problem is a schema which first divides clustering techniques into those techniques which are statistically based and those which are heuristic. The statistically based clustering algorithms can further be divided into those which employ agglomeration for building up clusters and those which employ a divisive approach to break down the cluster space into the optimum number of clusters (Gower, 1967). Within the agglomerative and the divisive clustering approaches, the algorithms employed can further be divided on the basis of whether the data to be clustered are discrete (categorical) or continuous. Lingoes (1968) presents an illuminating discussion of three methods for the multidimensional analysis of both qualitative and quantitative data and of both linear and nonlinear relationships based upon a minimum number of assumptions, an approach which is consonant with the usual ignorance regarding the metric and distributional properties of social science data.

Heuristic clustering techniques usually operate on some symbolic representation of the data which may involve its syntax — that is, the way in which it is strung together — or may involve a data reduction operation in which key properties of the data are extracted to form a profile or pattern. This symbolic representation is then used to group the objects or subjects of interest. The heurism implicit in decision tree structures can also be applied to psychiatric data whereby critical incidents in Flanagan's (1954) sense could represent nodes in a decision tree. For example, new studies may show that a series of events such as an early deviation in development in the context of a weak relationship with mother may be the index triggering a series of distortions in reality testing ability, perceptual instabilities, and so forth, such that they then become pathognomonic for childhood schizophrenia. It is unlikely that the events will fall out so simplistically, but it is hoped that heuristic techniques will show the mechanisms by which events are related to one another and are employed by clinicians in differential diagnostic decision-making.

The advent of computer technologies makes it possible to optimize the use of life history data in research. It is anticipated that as greater accessibility to data in its complex naturalistic form becomes available, new insights into the nature of continuity in life processes will be afforded. This, in turn, will provide new perspectives from which to view how human development proceeds and how differences arise which lead to normal and pathological growth processes.

COMMENTARY

MEDNICK. Have you done any studies to compare results of cluster analyses using the agglomerative method, as you call it, and the divisive method?

RAMSEY-KLEE. That is what we are planning to do next. We have done one pilot study, in which we used the agglomerative method to build up clusters. The problem in doing a small pilot study is that, if the vector representation used has a large number of components in it (that is, if the decision space has many dimensions), then a large sample is required for any meaningful groupings to emerge. We did one pilot study using 50 cases from the Reiss-Davis sample, and then we expanded the analysis to include all 150 cases in the Reiss-Davis data base. In the pilot study with 50 patients, we found three primary groupings (Eiduson, 1967, pp. 96–111). One cluster included children with learning problems only. The second cluster included children having problems in one or more of the following areas: developmental, learning, and social adjustment. They were also notable in lacking psychotic tendencies and withdrawal or schizoid features. The third cluster included socially maladjusted patients who exhibited withdrawal, schizoid, anxiety, or psychotic tendencies.

STRAUSS. Dr. Dana, Dr. Wynn, several others, and I are involved in a study of the number of patients who are questionable, actual, or definite schizophrenics. The nature of the project is an international one. We are trying to minimize some of the biases of the different investigators contributing data to the study, and trying to make the data we collect as descriptive as possible. We have millions of items on symptoms and history; however, these cannot be combined for our purposes into larger clusters because of the different academic biases and the different methods of grouping used by the various investigators participating in the study. I gather that what you are offering is a computer method for organizing a large number of minutely defined but descriptively clear variables in order to understand how they might relate to one another in some meaningful way.

RAMSEY-KLEE. That certainly is one way that the computer can help you. However, I view the process as a continual interaction of man with computer. Initially, one might simply take a "stroll" through the data base to determine the range of information it contained. Subsequently, specific areas of information could be retrieved and listed for perusal. At this point, methods for codifying or categorizing the narrative material might be applied, permitting a variety of statistical analyses of the retrieved information. For example, chi-square tests of common distribution could be applied, if one were working with categorical data from two or more groups; or if the data were quantitative, a more sophisticated form of analysis could be employed. One might want to compute straightforward correlations, establishing relations among variables and then later look for the causal factors. I view the computer as a highly complementary partner in doing research.

QUESTION. At Reiss-Davis, with respect to the psychiatric decision-making project, do you have any specification as to the events or data which lead to particular decision-making? Or are you finding that considerable decision-making may be based on data which do not appear in the case history? If that is the case, to what extent are you getting results that might be artifactual?

RAMSEY-KLEE. The decision-making project is not far enough along yet to determine if that is a possibility. This is an unlikely prospect because most people would agree that the case history record exists for some purpose, that the clinician collected these data because he felt they were somehow relevant to the hypothesis he was formulating about the nature of the patient's disorder or relevant to his recommendations. Although the results we have obtained thus far are preliminary, we have already learned that certain patient characteristics influence the direction that the diagnostic inquiry will take. For example, we have established that the age of a patient and the fact that he has had a prior psychiatric contact do influence the amount of data collected and its nature. We can establish how salient such factors are only when many more variables have been studied for their influence on decision-making.

RICKS. I have several practical questions about implementation of a system such as that at Reiss-Davis. Whose computer do you use? How expensive is it to process a case? Who does the coding? How do you establish trustworthiness of clinical judgment?

RAMSEY-KLEE. All of the data processing for the PsyCHES System has been done at the Health Sciences Computing Facility at UCLA. As an NIMH grant recipient, we are eligible to use that computer without having to pay for the computer time.* In addition, we have an Olivetti Underwood Programma 101, which is a desk-top electronic calculator/computer. It operates somewhat in the fashion of a Friden or Monroe calculator, but in addition it can function as a stored-program computer. The program is contained on a magnetic card which is dropped into the machine. The operator simply enters the data on a keyboard, and the computations are performed and printed automatically. We use this device to calculate means, variances, standard deviations, and all the various correlation coefficients. It can compute a product moment correlation matrix as large as five by five, and it can perform a two-way analysis of variance with equal *N*'s. But anything larger than that involving matrix operations is beyond the memory capacity of this small device. Then we use the biomedical computing programs at UCLA.

The second part of your question dealt with how time consuming it is to prepare case history data for input to the computer – it's very time consuming. In our case it took especially long because we were developing a system as we went along. We used three research assistants who were highly trained to transcribe the input. They were very much aware of the psychiatric and psychological significance of the case history material. One of them holds a master's degree in psychology; the other two hold B.A.'s. A fairly high level of competence is required to transcribe the information for input into the system at its present stage of development.

We certainly intend to do time studies of the processing procedure when we consider the system to be close to its final operating form. However, at present we are still evaluating its performance and modifying those aspects of the system that can be improved.

REFERENCES

Achenbach, T. M. The classification of children's psychiatric symptoms: A factor-analytic study. *Psychological Monographs*, 1966, 80 (7, Whole No. 615).

Braithwaite, R. B. *Scientific explanation.* Cambridge: Cambridge University Press, 1953.

Cochran, W. G., & G. M. Cox. *Experimental designs.* New York: Wiley, 1957. Pp. 80–82, 608.

Eiduson, B. T. *Psychiatric Case History Event System: Manual of transcription procedures with lexicons.* Los Angeles: Reiss-Davis Child Study Center, April 1966. (a)

———. Replacing traditional records by event reports. *Hospital and Community Psychiatry*, 1966, 17, 68–71. (b)

* Computing assistance from the Health Sciences Computing Facility, UCLA, sponsored by NIH Grant FR-3, is gratefully acknowledged.

———. *Studies in decision making in psychiatry — Phase I.* Los Angeles: Reiss-Davis Child Study Center, December 1967.

———, S. H. Brooks, & R. L. Motto. A generalized psychiatric information-processing system. *Behavorial Science,* 1966, 11, 133–142.

———, A. Platz, & R. Carmichael. New strategy for psychiatric research, utilizing the Psychiatric Case History Event System. In N. S. Kline & E. Laska (Eds.), *Computers and electronic devices in psychiatry.* New York: Grune & Stratton, 1968. Pp. 45–58.

Eiduson, B. T., & S. Eiduson. Certain behavioral and biochemical parameters during the first 96 hours of life. Paper presented at the meeting of the Society for Research in Child Development, New York, April 1967.

Eiduson, B. T., & I. Lubitz. Certain aspects of infant behavior monitored for the first 96 hours of life. Paper presented at the meeting of the American Orthopsychiatric Association, San Francisco, April 1966.

Eiduson, B. T., A. Platz, & R. Carmichael. Recent developments in a generalized information processing system: The Psychiatric Case History Event System. *Behavorial Science,* 1967, 12, 254–267.

Festinger, L., & D. Katz (Eds.). *Research methods in the behavioral sciences.* New York: Holt, 1953.

Flanagan, J. C. The critical incident technique. *Psychological Bulletin,* 1954, 51, 327–358.

Gower, J. C. A comparison of some methods of cluster analysis. *Biometrics,* 1967, 23, 623–637.

Lingoes, J. C. The multivariate analysis of qualitative data. *Multivariate Behavioral Research,* 1968, 3, 61–94.

Popper, K. R. *The logic of scientific discovery.* New York: Science Editions, 1961.

Winer, B. J. *Statistical principles in experimental design.* New York: McGraw-Hill, 1962. Pp. 281–283.

MAURICE LORR
C. JAMES KLETT

Life History Differentia of Five Acute Psychotic Types

THE present study sought to test, by means of discriminant function analysis, whether a set of computer-derived psychotic types could be distinguished on the basis of certain life history data. Another aim was to examine any between-type differences in order to achieve a better understanding of the types themselves. It seemed plausible to expect that patient subgroups with distinctively different symptom profiles would also differ with respect to life history — on such variables as marital status, schooling, religion, number of prior hospitalizations, and place of residence. If the types evolved could be distinguished on the basis of such data, then their meaningfulness, utility, and validity would be enhanced.

In the initial analysis (Lorr, Klett, & McNair, 1962) six psychotic types with distinctive profiles were isolated within a mixed sample of 556 acute psychotics. These were descriptively labeled Excited, Excited Hostile, Retarded, Intropunitive, Hostile Paranoid, and Disorganized. Ten syndromes of psychotic behavior measured in an interview by the Inpatient Multidimensional Psychiatric Scale (IMPS) provided the descriptive basis for patient comparison. Subsequently, four studies were conducted on large samples of both acute and chronic functional psychotics (Lorr, 1966). Within the acute sample seven equivalent types were found to characterize men as well as women. Analyses of the chronic and long-term patient samples yielded essentially similar subgroups.

Ratings have recently been collected on eleven hundred acute psychotics newly hospitalized in six countries (England, France, Germany, Italy, Japan, and Sweden). The typological analyses revealed five types equivalent to those found among acute American psychotic samples. This report will be concerned mainly with the life history characteristics of this cross-cultural sample (Lorr & Klett, in press).

METHODS OF PROCEDURE

The Sample. The study plan involved two- and three-day meetings with each collaborating university psychiatrist in England, France, Germany, Italy, and Sweden. However, discussions with the Japanese representative in Osaka were entirely by mail. In each case, the aims of the study, the range of patients sought, and the interview requirements were discussed. In addition, several patients were interviewed and rated in order to familiarize each representative with the rating schedule and with the rating process.

Collaborators in each country were asked to interview and to rate a representative sample of two hundred newly hospitalized men and women judged to be functional psychotics. Neurotics, drug addicts, personality disorders, and patients with neurological and/or central nervous system damage were to be excluded. A further requirement was that patients interviewed be either free of drugs or on a minimum drug dosage schedule. Experience and research had shown that tranquilizers reduced or eliminated characteristic symptom profile patterns.

A background data sheet provided information on each patient's age, highest grade completed, religion, and marital status. Other variables recorded were duration of the psychotic episode, number of prior hospitalizations, and place of residence (rural or urban).

The Rating Schedule. The rating schedule, IMPS, was designed to measure ten psychotic syndromes isolated in repeated factor analyses (Lorr & Klett, 1966). Independent ratings by interviewer and observer are completed on each patient immediately following a 30- to 45-minute unstructured interview.

Each syndrome is defined by five to eleven items that measure a unitary pattern of behavior. The ten syndromes are labeled as follows: Excitement, Hostile Belligerence, Paranoid Projection, Grandiosity, Perceptual Distortions (hallucinations), Anxious Depression, Retardation, Disorientation, Motor Disturbances (manneristic postures and movements), and Conceptual Disorganization. These measures have substantial interrater reliability in a wide range of settings. IMPS has also been demonstrated to be sensitive to change resulting from tranquilizers. More extensive data relative to the validity of IMPS has been summarized in the *Manual* (Lorr & Klett, 1966).

Methods of Analysis. A typological analysis has as its aim the identification of subgroups within a heterogeneous sample. The problem is one of sorting score profiles on the basis of similarity into any existing homogeneous and mutually exclusive subgroups. In brief, each patient's ten standardized syndrome scores are fed into the computer and compared with the profiles of all other patients in the sample of one hundred fifty cases that the computer can process. The computer then sorts together "similar" profiles (as judged by an index of resemblance) and identifies any mutually exclusive subgroups to be found (Lorr & Radhakrishnan, 1967). In the analysis of the cross-cultural data, the patient profiles were first separated by sex and then searched for types by country. Five psychotic subgroups were isolated in two or more countries. Members of equivalent types were pooled by sex for the analysis that followed.

A discriminant function analysis was applied to determine whether the five psychotic types could be differentiated on the basis of the life history variables. Since the literature and previous studies with comparable data indicated the presence of sex differences, separate analyses were conducted on the data representing each sex. The canonical variates or dimensions of between-group differences were examined to determine the relative contributions of the variables to the discriminant functions. Finally, the centroids of the subgroups in the reduced discriminant space were computed, plotted, and compared.

Nine life history variables were used in the analysis. Religion and marital status were each coded as two variables: Protestants were coded 1 and all others 0; Catholics were coded 1 and all others 0. Similarly, single persons (never married) were coded 1 and all others 0; those persons currently married were coded 1 and all others 0. The remaining variables were age, years of schooling, duration of psychotic episode, number of prior hospitalizations, and place of residence (rural versus urban).

RESULTS

Sample Characteristics. The age range of the total sample was from 18 to 57. In all countries except Italy, both men and women typically received from 9 to 10 years of schooling; the Italians received from 6 to 7 years of schooling. The percentage of single people (never married) was 63 for the men and 37 for the women. Finally, 46 per cent of the men and 43 per cent of the women had never previously been hospitalized.

The six samples differed in the relative proportion of the various diagnostic classes as defined by the American Psychiatric Association diagnostic manual (1952). Except for Japan and Italy, 40 per cent of the total sample were diagnosed as nonparanoid schizophrenics, 30 per cent as paranoid or paranoid schizophrenics, 22 per cent as depressives, and the remainder as manics. The Italian men and women, on the other hand, were predominantly diagnosed as depressives. The Japanese included a high proportion of nonparanoid schizophrenics and a low proportion of depressives.

The Psychotic Types. In American samples, acute psychotics differentiate into 7 subtypes common to both men and women (Lorr, 1966). Two additional subgroups are unique to the men and two are unique to the women. The affective disorders are represented by an Excited and an Anxious Depressed type. The paranoid patients are allocated to four subgroups called Excited Hostile, Hallucinated, Grandiose, and Hostile. The nonparanoid schizophrenic disorders are represented by a Retarded Motor Disturbed, a Disoriented, and an Anxious Disorganized subgroup. Table 1 presents their mean standard scores.

The mean standard score profiles of the subgroups found in the cross-cultural sample are also presented in Table 1. As in the American sample, the affective disorders are represented by subgroups of Excited and Anxious Depressed. The paranoid disorders separate into Hallucinated and Grandiose. The schizophrenic disorders are represented by a Retarded Motor Disturbed subgroup. These five types are essentially the same for men and women. They are equivalent in mean profile to the comparable five shown for the male American sample. The congruency coefficients between the two sets (Harman, 1960) are all above .95.

The standard scores used in the cross-cultural study were based on the means and dispersions of the overall American samples of men and women (Lorr & Klett, 1966). Thus, the metric used was comparable to that employed in earlier studies.

Members of the Excited type are characterized mainly by elevated scores on excitement. A fair proportion of the type, especially the women, also manifest above-average scores on grandiosity. All other scores average well below the mean. Members of the Anxious Depressed type all manifest above-average anxious intropunitiveness. A few receive mildly elevated scores on retardation. All other syndrome scores are negative.

All members of the Grandiose Paranoid subgroup manifest extremely high scores on grandiose expansiveness. Most members show, in addition, elevated scores on paranoid projection and perceptual distortion (hallucinations). In brief, members exhibit attitudes of self-importance and superiority and report unusual gifts and powers. As may be seen in the table, all other scores are well below the general mean. The Hallucinated Paranoid type includes patients scoring well up above the general

Table 1. Mean Syndrome Scores of Psychotic Types among American and Cross-Cultural Samples of Both Sexes [a]

Psychotic Type	EXC	HOS	PAR	GRN	PCP	ANX	RTD	DIS	MTR	CNP
Male American Sample										
Excited	1.29	−.65	−.80	−.32	−.53	−.68	−.48	−.28	−.03	.47
Excited Hostile	1.42	1.39	.33	.05	−.51	−.75	−.74	−.46	−.29	.34
Hostile Paranoid	−.52	.80	.17	−.42	−.55	−.43	−.55	−.24	−.40	−.61
Hallucinated Paranoid	−.53	.04	1.24	−.23	1.32	−.05	−.24	.22	−.52	−.12
Grandiose Paranoid	.12	−.41	.20	2.02	.51	−.46	−.45	−.14	−.61	−.13
Anxious Depressed	−.46	−.63	−.80	−.54	−.43	1.15	−.45	−.45	−.44	−.62
Retarded Motor Disturbed	−.70	−.83	−.68	−.56	−.55	−.30	1.43	.06	.52	−.26
Disoriented	−.43	−.84	−.93	−.60	−.38	−.88	.87	3.29	.39	.18
Anxious Disorganized	−.50	.10	1.28	−.44	2.20	1.19	1.61	.62	1.18	.48
Female Cross-Cultural Sample										
Excited	1.41	−.21	−.84	−.16	−.55	−.97	−.95	−.46	−.81	−.04
Anxious Depressed	−.61	−.94	−.98	−.53	−.58	1.50	−.28	−.48	−.65	−.78
Grandiose Paranoid	.10	−.33	.75	2.77	.96	−.89	−.73	−.45	−.58	−.29
Hallucinated Paranoid	−.63	−.33	1.20	−.31	1.10	−.82	−.58	−.39	−.66	−.46
Retarded Motor Disturbed	−.87	−.91	−.97	−.50	−.60	−.72	1.38	.11	.24	−.26
Male Cross-Cultural Sample										
Excited	1.75	−.51	−.76	.53	−.54	−.92	−1.01	−.27	−.74	−.04
Anxious Depressed	−.66	−.79	−.91	−.57	−.61	1.26	−.39	−.43	−.67	−.74
Grandiose Paranoid	−.61	−.69	.05	1.81	.24	−.76	−.47	−.40	−.56	−.19
Hallucinated Paranoid	−.62	−.46	.98	−.38	1.27	−.58	−.62	−.30	−.72	−.56
Retarded Motor Disturbed	−.82	−.84	−.72	−.52	−.52	−.83	1.16	.37	.35	−.40

[a] EXC = Excitement; HOS = Hostile Belligerence; PAR = Paranoid Projection; GRN = Grandiosity; PCP = Perceptual Distortion; ANX = Anxious Depression; RTD = Retardation; DIS = Disorientation; MTR = Motor Disturbances; CNP = Conceptual Disorganization.

mean on paranoid projection and perceptual distortion. All other syndrome scores average much below the norm average.

Patients of the type called Retarded Motor Disturbed are slowed in speech and movement, or they may whisper or fail to reply. In addition, they manifest bizarre or manneristic postures and movements, and talk to themselves. Some are also disoriented. The distribution of patients over the five types is surprisingly uniform across sex. Of these 203 men and 215 women classified by computer in one of these five subgroups the percentage breakdown was as follows: (a) 41 per cent of the men and 44 per cent of the women were Anxious Depressed; (b) 11 per cent of both sexes were Retarded Motor Disturbed; (c) 15 per cent of the men and 14 per cent of the women were Excited cases; (d) 25 per cent of the men and 22 per cent of the women were Hallucinated Paranoids; (e) 7 per cent of the men and 9 per cent of the women were classified as Grandiose Paranoids.

Life History Differences. A major goal of the study was to test the equality of the means of the five subgroups with respect to the life history variables. The discriminant function analysis yielded an F of 5.08 (N = 203) for the men, and an F of 4.45 (N = 215) for the women. Both F's are highly significant for five groups and nine variables. The first two latent roots accounted for 81 per cent of the between-group variance of the male scores. In the female sample, the first two latent roots accounted for 78 per cent of the score variance. Since the third and fourth latent roots were relatively small, the interpretation of between-subgroup differences will be based on the first two canonical variates.

The canonical variates, or characteristic vectors, represent the between-group dimensions. When the weights of the variables as shown in Table 2 are inspected, it is seen that the first dimension for the male sample is religion. It is best defined by the Protestant category since Catholi-

Table 2. Normalized Canonical Variates in Cross-Cultural Sample

	Men		Women	
Variable	1	2	1	2
Age	.01	–.01	–.01	–.01
Education	.00	–.05	.04	.05
Residence	–.07	.07	.00	.07
Duration of episode	–.01	–.02	.00	–.03
Previous hospitalizations	.03	–.12	.02	.28
Protestant	–.50	–.22	–.76	.30
Catholic	–.81	–.77	–.51	.06
Single	–.02	–.54	–.35	.05
Married	–.30	–.22	–.22	.90

Table 3. Means and Percentages of Life History Variables Characterizing Five Psychotic Types of Each Sex

Variable	Anxious Depressive	Retarded Motor Dis.	Excited	Hallucinated Paranoid	Grandiose Paranoid	Significance
Five Male Psychotic Types						
Age	39.6	28.9	29.7	31.8	31.6	...**
Years of school	8.1	9.6	11.8	9.4	10.4	...**
Location of residence (coded)	2.7	1.9	1.7	1.8	1.9	...**
Duration of episode (mos.)	4.7	15.9	2.7	6.2	3.9	...**
Number of hospitalizations	.8	1.4	1.6	.7	1.3	
Protestant	61.9%	73.9%	25.8%	16.0%	46.7%	...**
Catholic	31.0%	13.0%	35.5%	34.0%	53.3%	
Single; never married	40.5%	87.0%	54.8%	74.0%	86.7%	...**
Married	48.8%	13.0%	32.3%	20.0%	13.3%	...**
Number in sample	84	23	31	50	15	
Five Female Psychotic Types						
Age	37.7	31.6	41.7	37.1	40.9	
Years of school	8.5	10.1	10.8	9.3	9.5	...**
Location of residence (coded)	2.6	2.1	1.9	2.4	1.8	
Duration of episode (mos.)	3.6	10.8	1.8	12.9	12.1	...**
Number of hospitalizations	1.1	.9	2.3	.6	1.5	...**
Protestant	46.8%	20.8%	29.0%	53.2%	47.4%	...*
Catholic	50.0%	58.3%	25.8%	14.9%	47.4%	...**
Single; never married	26.6%	66.7%	19.4%	31.9%	26.3%	...**
Married	58.5%	25.0%	61.3%	36.2%	52.6%	...**
Number in sample	94	24	31	47	19	

*$p<.05$ **$p<.001$

cism contributes to both variates. The second dimension for the men is marital status, defined primarily by the single (never married) category. For the female subgroups, the first dimension again is religion defined by Protestantism. The second dimension is marital status, but unlike the male sample, it's defined entirely by the married category.

Before turning to the subgroup means on the two dimensions just described, the univariate *F* tests and chi squares reflected in Table 3 will be examined. The Anxious Depressed male subgroup members, compared with the others, are older, have the least education, and are more suburban in residence, more Protestant, and more frequently married. The female members of this type also have the least education, come from suburbs, and are more often married (except for the Excited). Both sexes tend to experience a short psychotic episode. Thus, there is consistency between the sexes on four out of six variables.

The members of the Retarded Motor Disturbed, regardless of sex, are the youngest, the most frequently single, and experience the longest psychotic episodes. The men include the highest proportion of Protestants, whereas the women include the highest proportion of Catholics.

There is also good agreement in the characteristics of the male and female Excited patients. They tend to come from large cities, to have the most education, and to experience the shortest psychotic episodes. Proportionately more report being neither Protestant nor Catholic and thus are irreligious, since the few Jewish patients were not included in the analysis. The women are the most frequently married, and the men are second most frequently married among the subgroups.

Neither the Hallucinated Paranoids nor the Grandiose Paranoids are distinguished from other subgroups via the univariate tests of significance. The discriminant function analysis is comparatively more differentiating.

What is the pattern and kind of intergroup mean differences in terms of the two canonical variates? Plots of the subgroup means (Table 4) on the two dimensions reveal considerable uniformity in the pattern of values

Table 4. Scaled Mean Canonical Scores in Cross-Cultural Sample

	Men		Women	
Subgroup	1	2	1	2
Anxious Depressed	–.39	–.06	–.21	.20
Retarded Motor Disturbed	–.13	–.64	–.22	–.36
Excited	.32	.24	.43	.27
Hallucinated Paranoid	.55	.37	.20	.03
Grandiose Paranoid	–.12	–.38	–.13	.15

for men and women. The Excited and the Hallucinated Paranoids are placed in the upper right-hand quadrant. Both subgroups may be characterized as relatively irreligious, as single in the case of the men, and as married in the case of the women.

The Retarded Motor Disturbed subgroups of both sexes are low in the second dimension, marital status — that is, both are primarily single. Although both are religious, the men are Protestant and the women are Catholic.

The Anxious Depressed subgroups of both sexes are located on the negative side of the first dimension. Both sexes are relatively religious, with the men leaning toward Protestantism. The men are the most likely to be married among the male types, and the women rank second in proportion of married.

The Grandiose Paranoids, in the case of the men, are located between the Anxious Depressed and the Retarded Motor Disturbed. The female Grandiose patients are similar to the Anxious Depressed in their life history characteristics and cannot be distinguished from them.

DISCUSSION

The five distinctive behavioral types are well differentiated by the life history variables. The univariate tests characterized three of the patient subgroups rather well. All subgroups except the Grandiose Paranoid are differentiated by the two discriminant functions. Futhermore, even the pattern of weights on the two canonical variates is consistent across sex.

However, there are a number of issues calling for discussion. The role and importance of religion as a differentiating variable are uncertain. For example, it is not clear why the Retarded Motor Disturbed men are Protestant whereas women of the same type are Catholic. Although the various national groups sampled differ in religion, the two sexes are represented in roughly the same proportions in each country's sample. However, the failure to belong to a religious group does carry valuable information, as in the case of the Excited subgroup.

The importance of marital status in relation to psychopathology is well established. In accordance with expectation, the nonparanoid schizophrenics tend to be unmarried whereas the Anxious Depressed tend to be married. Marital status has uniformly constituted a useful predictor of outcome and duration of illness.

The relative insignificance of socioeconomic factors is of some interest. Education is ordinarily a good index of social class, but here it plays a minor role. The arbitrary and restricted nature of the samples, which were under only limited control of the investigators, may have been responsible. Certainly, they were by no means representative of newly hospitalized cases coming into a country's hospitals. An alternative view is that social class does not play a major role in the behavior disorders.

It should be clear that the findings can carry no causal implications. Religion represents a learned set of attitudes and beliefs. Marital status reflects the individual's personal style of relating to others. The question of why some individuals become depressed, others paranoid, and still others disorganized and schizophrenic cannot be answered by the procedures applied here. The stability of the types across cultures should encourage other investigators to explore this problem.

COMMENTARY

RAMSEY. I'd like to comment on one of your findings that I thought very provocative. This was your finding in your discriminant analysis that 75 to 80 per cent of the variance in your sample of men and women was accounted for by the two largest canonical roots in the analysis. In every discriminant analysis that I have done with psychological variables, I have also found two thirds to three quarters of the variance accounted for by the two largest latent roots. Now, not being a good mathematician, I can't account for this in terms of mathematics. My intuitive feeling is that it wouldn't necessarily drop out that way, yet with psychological variables you keep finding—

LORR. Our measures were not psychological, but rather life history variables.

RAMSEY. Life history variables. All right. Well then, I found it with psychological variables, and you found it with life history variables. It keeps falling out that the majority of the variance is accounted for by the two largest roots. Do you think that this is something that we shall find over and over again because of the basic organization of personality?

LORR. I think, in part, the answer is that in any such analysis, you get a sharp drop in the size of the latent roots. Thus, the first two roots are going to be a large proportion of the total variance extracted. In general, I think this would happen with almost any kind of data, so it isn't too surprising. I agree that in personality questionnaire material the first two principal components typically account for at least 50 per cent of the variance. But I question the generality of your assertion.

MEDNICK. I'm curious to know whether these types are reliable across time. Have you done anything to find out whether people who can be typed as Excited the first week after they come in can also be typed as Excited at the end of six months? or at the end of a year? or on their second admission?

LORR. We do not have data on the second admission and so forth. I can give you this much information: At the Biometrics Laboratory of George Washington University, Rice and Mattson ("Types based on repeated measurement," in Lorr (Ed.), *Explorations in Typing Psychotics*, pp. 151–194) did a study trying to find IMPS types across time. Five or six of their types were equivalent to ours. Patient profiles persisted over time but the profile levels diminished as a result of drug treatment. I examined their data and actually found the average profile of each type, say at the end of two weeks, three weeks, and so on. If you inspected the profile, say of anxious depressed patients, you would find that it decreased in level at successive examinations but the shape of the profile remained the same. In other words, we found that practically every profile, under tranquilizers, remained relatively stable. Now what would happen with placebo patients we do not know. There have been very few studies of profile stability because of the absence of available patients without tranquilizers. In an effort to answer part of your question, Klett and I are now initiating a study. We're collecting data on a thousand newly admitted patients in eight VA hospitals. We're hoping to classify these, and then do a follow-up study three years later. We're planning to have them reassessed whenever they come back to the hospital. Another possible approach would be for some groups to pool their placebo patients and observe any changes in them over time. But for most of our data on patients under drugs, the type does not change. I can say that flatly.

REFERENCES

American Psychiatric Association. *Diagnostic and statistical manual for mental disorders.* Washington, D.C.: Mental Hospital Service, 1952.

Harman, H. H. *Modern factor analysis.* Chicago: University of Chicago Press, 1960.

Jones, L. V., & R. D. Bock. *Multiple discriminant analysis applied to "Ways to Live" ratings of six cultural groups.* Chapel Hill: Psychometric Laboratory, University of North Carolina, 1958.

Lorr, M. (Ed.) *Explorations in typing psychotics.* Oxford: Pergamon Press, 1966.

——— & C. J. Klett. *Inpatient Multidimensional Psychiatric Scale. Manual.* Palo Alto, Calif.: Consulting Psychologists Press, 1966.

———. A cross-cultural comparison of psychotic syndromes. *Journal of Abnormal Psychology*, in press.

——— & D. M. McNair. *Syndromes of psychosis.* Oxford: Pergamon Press, 1962.

Lorr, M., & B. K. Radhakrishnan. A comparison of two methods of cluster analysis. *Educational and Psychological Measurement*, 1967, 27, 47–53.

SOLOMON C. GOLDBERG

Drug Effects and Life History in Schizophrenia

EVER since the phenothiazines were established as being generally efficacious for the reduction of symptoms in schizophrenia, the research program of the Psychopharmacology Research Branch at the National Institute of Mental Health has worked toward discovering the differential activity of these drugs. That is, given that drug-treated patients experience a greater degree of symptom reduction than placebo-treated patients, is there an equal amount of symptom reduction among all schizophrenic symptoms, or are some symptoms affected more than others? Other related research questions are whether certain life history factors are associated with response to treatment and, finally, whether patterns of life history among schizophrenics are associated with patterns of psychopathology.

The results that I shall report are based on two large-scale, multihospital collaborative studies. For purposes of orientation, a schematic outline of the studies is presented below. Essentially, the patients were newly admitted, acutely ill schizophrenics. The treatments in the first study were three phenothiazines and a placebo. In the second study there were three phenothiazines but no placebo. Duration of study treatment was six weeks for the first study and twenty-six weeks for the second. An attempt was made to sample from a broad spectrum of kinds of hospital, including psychiatric units in general hospitals, state mental institutions, and small private and/or university teaching hospitals. The major assessment instruments in both studies were the Inpatient Multidimensional

SCHEMATIC OUTLINE OF THE STUDIES

First Collaborative Study

TREATMENTS: Chlorpromazine, Fluphenazine, Thioridazine, Placebo. 6 weeks' duration.

PATIENTS: 344 schizophrenics, newly admitted, floridly ill, few previous hospitalizations.

HOSPITALS

STATE: Springfield, Md.; Boston; Kentucky; Rochester, N.Y.

RECEIVING: District of Columbia General; Malcolm Bliss, St. Louis

PRIVATE: Institute of Living, Hartford, Conn.; Mercy Douglass, Philadelphia; Payne-Whitney, New York, N.Y.

ASSESSMENTS

1. Psychopathology from interview – e.g., Indifference, Delusions, Hallucinations.
2. Ward behavior by nurse – e.g., Social Participation, Self Care, Irritability.
3. Global ratings of severity of illness and of clinical change.

Second Collaborative Study

TREATMENTS: Acetophenazine, Chlorpromazine, Fluphenazine. 26 weeks' duration; at least 5 weeks in hospital.

PATIENTS: 480 schizophrenics, most newly admitted, floridly ill, any number of previous hospitalizations.

HOSPITALS

STATE: Springfield; Boston; Kentucky; Rochester, N.Y.

RECEIVING: District of Columbia General; Malcolm Bliss

PRIVATE: Institute of Living; Mercy Douglass

ASSESSMENTS

1. Psychopathology from interview – e.g., Indifference, Delusions, Hallucinations.
2. Ward behavior by nurse – e.g., Social Participation, Self Care, Irritability.
3. Global ratings of severity of illness and of clinical change.

Psychiatric Scale and the Ward Behavior Rating Scale as indicators of psychopathological status. In addition, research social workers conducted intensive interviews with the patient's family and on this basis recorded what they hoped were the relevant features of the patient's life history.

In analyzing for differential drug effects, we have found useful the dichotomy of paranoid versus withdrawal schizophrenia originally set forth by Venables and O'Connor (1959b) and listed below. These two groups of symptoms were identified by means of factor analysis in chronic schizophrenic patients.

Paranoid	*Withdrawal*
Hostility	Indifference
Ideas of persecution	Slowed speech
Delusions of grandeur	Disorientation
	Self care
	Confusion
	Hebephrenic symptoms

FIRST COLLABORATIVE STUDY

Symptom Reduction under Placebo. In our first study we noted that under placebo treatment the amount of symptom reduction varied from one symptom to the next, some symptoms showing no change at all. By and large, it was the withdrawal symptoms (Slowed Speech, Hebephrenic Symptoms, Indifference, and Self Care) which did not change at all under placebo, whereas all the paranoid symptoms did show significant reduction (see list of effects below). These results (Goldberg, Klerman, & Cole, 1965) were originally interpreted in terms of Bleuler's "fundamental" and "accessory" symptoms. Over the course of time I have come to think that the paranoid-withdrawal distinction fits the data slightly better. In other words, symptoms of withdrawal showed essentially no reduction except under drug treatment. Moreover, the size of the drug-placebo difference, interpreted as the effect owing to drugs, was greater for the symptoms of withdrawal than for the paranoid symptoms.

EFFECTS OF PLACEBO AND DRUG TREATMENTS
ON SCHIZOPHRENIC SYMPTOMS

"Fundamental?" Symptoms — Improve only on Drug Treatment

Irritability	Self Care
Slowed Speech and Movements	Indifference to Environment
Hebephrenic Symptoms	

"Accessory?" Symptoms — High Improvement on Placebo and No Drug Effect

Feelings of Unreality	Resistiveness
Non-auditory Hallucinations	Guilt
Memory Deficit	Disorientation
Delusions of Grandeur	Pressure of Speech

"Fundamental?" Symptoms — Develop More in Placebo than in Drug Patients Asymptomatic before Treatment

Auditory Hallucinations	Hebephrenic Symptoms
Self Care	Slowed Speech and Movements
Incoherent Speech	Indifference to Environment

Development of Symptoms Originally Not Present. Another question we asked of our data was whether the phenothiazines could avert the development of symptoms which the patient did not have before treatment. Indeed, we did find, among patients who were asymptomatic with respect to given symptoms, that placebo-treated patients significantly developed more of these symptoms than did drug-treated patients. Thus, in addition to being symptom reducers, phenothiazines were shown to be effective in preventing the development of symptoms. For some reason, we did not notice until after the paper (Goldberg, Klerman, & Cole, 1965) was published that the symptoms which were averted under drug treatment were, by and large, the symptoms of withdrawal (Self Care, Slowed Speech,

Hebephrenic Symptoms, Indifference, and Disorientation); none of the paranoid symptoms developed under the placebo condition – only the symptoms of withdrawal.

Putting the pieces together, we can get a fair idea of the dynamics of symptom change over time in the placebo-treated schizophrenic patient. Before treatment, he may manifest either withdrawal symptoms or paranoid symptoms or both. If he starts with symptoms of withdrawal, our data say that the symptoms will not be reduced and, at the same time, that he will not develop paranoid symptoms. In short, this patient will have a stable picture over time (see Fig. 1).

On the other hand, the patient who starts with paranoid symptoms will show a reduction of these over time and, at the same time, will tend to develop symptoms of withdrawal. Obviously, this patient presents a completely different symptom picture from one point in time to the next. Where he was once paranoid, he is now withdrawn. It is interesting to note a parallel to Brill and Glass's (1965) observations that hebephrenic patients earlier in their careers carried other than hebephrenic subdiagnoses.

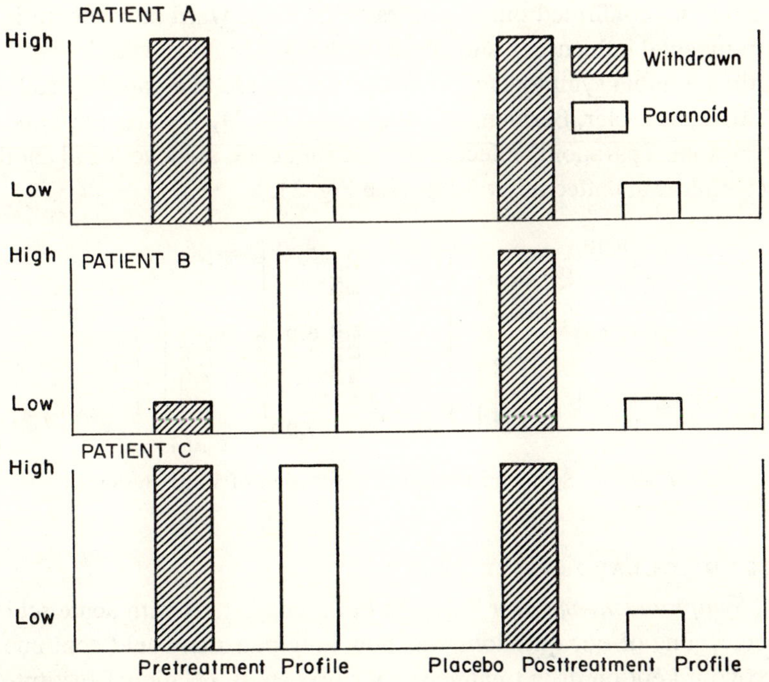

Figure 1. Symptom change over time in the placebo-treated schizophrenic patient.

The final hypothetical patient, who at pretreatment is both paranoid and withdrawn, will maintain his withdrawal but will lose his paranoid symptoms. He, too, looks somewhat different over time.

The evidence seems to indicate that withdrawal is a later stage of the schizophrenic illness, from which there is no spontaneous recovery. In contrast, paranoid symptoms represent a stage from which spontaneous recovery is possible.

Milieu Effects on Symptom Change. In the same study we had some interest in ascertaining the effects of the "atmosphere" of the ward to which the patient was assigned. On the basis of careful surveys of the wards in the study, a number of ward characteristics were identified and could be characterized in terms of the severity of illness of the other patients to whom the subject was exposed. Generally, the results were that subjects assigned to wards whose other patients were more severely ill improved less than did subjects assigned to wards whose other patients were less severely ill. This was a gratifying demonstration of milieu effects in schizophrenia, but the fact that the milieu showed its effects in reducing some symptoms more than others was initially puzzling. We returned to the data and confirmed our hypothesis that since ward atmosphere is an environmental influence, it should affect the symptoms of withdrawal least and the paranoid symptoms most. These results are in a paper by Kellam, Goldberg, Schooler, Berman, and Shmelzer (1967). We thus have one set of symptoms (paranoid) affected by environmental influences and another set (withdrawal) affected by drugs (see Fig. 2).

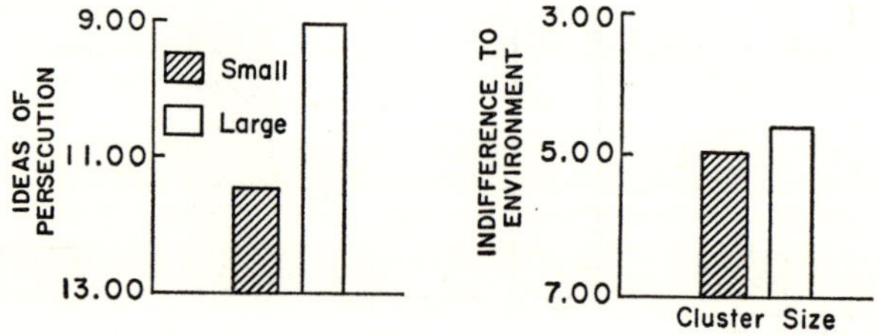

Figure 2. Symptom change as a function of ward cluster size.

SECOND COLLABORATIVE STUDY

Symptom Change over Time. In our second study with acute schizophrenics, one of our questions was how long patients would continue to improve if kept on drug treatment. Our first study (National Institute of Mental Health, 1964), which followed patients for only six weeks, indicated that drug-treated patients were still improving at the end of that time, so we extended the duration of the second study to twenty-six weeks.

We found (Goldberg, Schooler, & Mattsson, 1967) that patients still had not reached a plateau in terms of global improvement by the end of twenty-six weeks (National Institute of Mental Health, 1967) (see Figs. 3 and 4). It was of further interest to examine changes over time

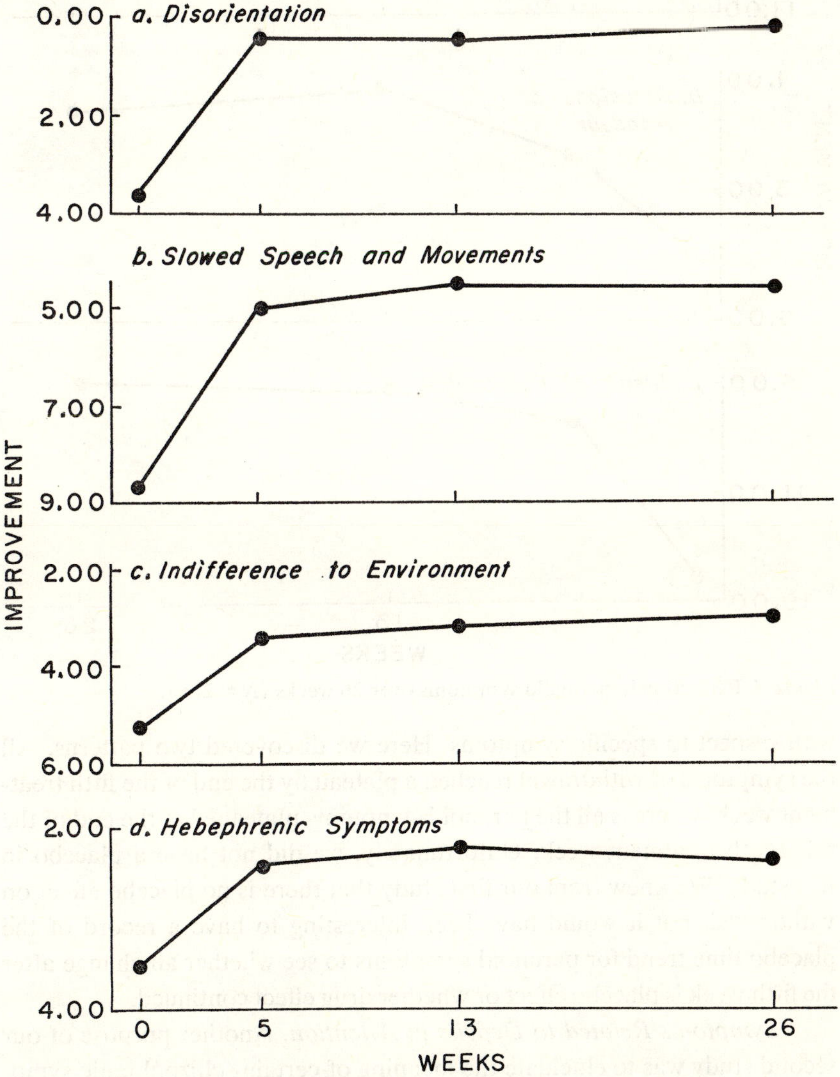

Figure 3. Reduction in symptoms of withdrawal over 26 weeks ($N = 226$).

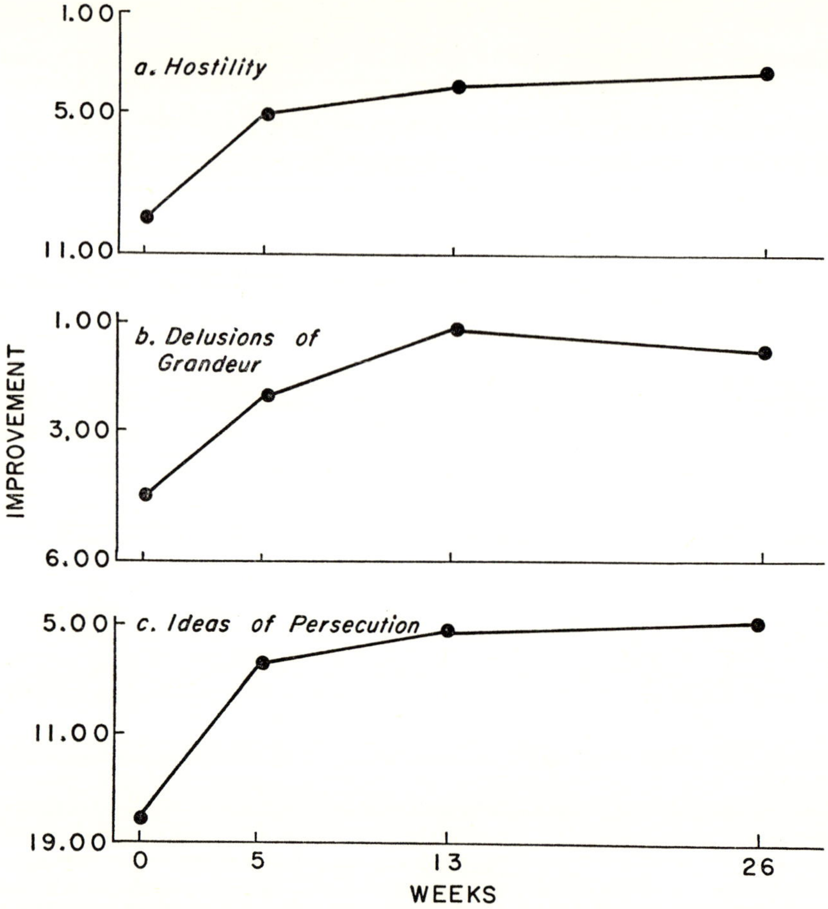

Figure 4. Reduction in paranoid symptoms over 26 weeks ($N = 226$).

with respect to specific symptoms. Here we discovered two patterns. All the symptoms of withdrawal reached a plateau by the end of the fifth treatment week, whereas all the paranoid symptoms plateaued at the end of the thirteenth treatment week. Unfortunately, we did not have a placebo in this study. We knew from our first study that there is no placebo effect on withdrawal, but it would have been interesting to have a record of the placebo time trend for paranoid symptoms to see whether all change after the fifth week is placebo effect or whether drug effect continued.

Symptoms Related to Deficits in Attention. Another purpose of our second study was to elucidate the meaning of certain schizophrenic symptoms by examining their relations with a number of psychological performance tests. One of the tests, reaction time, has been very much in evidence in schizophrenia research. Any number of investigators have found schizophrenics to react far more slowly than normals. In correlating some fourteen measures of reaction time with symptoms, we find (Goldberg, Schooler, & Mattsson, 1968), as indicated in the table below, that reaction time is consistently correlated with withdrawal symptoms and consistently uncorrelated with paranoid symptoms. These results confirm suggestions made in earlier literature by Shakow (1963) and by Venables and O'Connor (1959a).

Thus, we have shown some interesting distinctions between two sets of schizophrenic symptoms, paranoid and withdrawal, in a variety of contexts including (a) symptom reduction under drug and placebo, (b) aversion of symptom development under drug and placebo, (c) symptom reduction produced by ward milieu, and (d) relations with a performance test (reaction time) which is presumably a measure of attention, and (e) differential symptom reduction over time.

How is one to interpret the two kinds of symptoms? Silverman (1967) has provided through perceptual tasks a body of evidence which shows that paranoids are vigilant hyperscanners of the stimulus field, whereas non-paranoids (whom for the moment I equate with withdrawns) tend to narrow and delimit the stimulus field and to modulate the intensity of stimuli. The interpretation for the withdrawn patients is that they *feel* deluged by the number and intensity of environmental stimuli. The

Correlations between Reaction Time and Symptom Severity after Five Weeks on Drug[a] ($N = 354$)

Symptoms	Mean Correlation
Paranoid	
Hostility	−.012
Delusions of grandeur	.032
Persecution	.030
Withdrawal	
Disorientation	.127*
Slowed speech	.184***
Indifference	.271***
Hebephrenic	.108*
Self care	.186***
Confusion	.160**
Auditory hallucinations	.194***

[a] The correlations reported represent the mean correlation of fourteen discrete measures of reaction time; seven means and seven standard deviations.

*$p < .05$. **$p < .01$. ***$p < .001$.

withdrawal is a secondary defensive reaction to the deluge. At the same time, since the withdrawn patient is besieged by too much environment, he should be in an emergency state with respect to autonomic arousal. Evidence to this effect has been provided by Venables and Wing (1962). In other words, beneath the placid, apparently apathetic exterior, is a psyche alertly guarding against the intrusion of more environment. The practical implication of all this is that therapeutic measures aimed at increasing stimulation and arousal in the withdrawn patient are self-defeating.

Do these two kinds of symptoms represent two qualitatively different disorders, or do they represent different stages of the same disorder? The results cited earlier—that patients initially without symptoms of withdrawal developed them in the course of six weeks—would indicate that withdrawal is a later stage of the schizophrenic disorder. Of some pertinence to this point are the results of Goldstein and his associates (1968) at UCLA, who report a modest relation between premorbid competence on the Phillips Scale and the schizophrenic patient's being paranoid or non-paranoid. Since premorbid competence has been shown to be related to age at onset (that is, good premorbids have a later age at onset), this would represent evidence that withdrawal and paranoid symptoms are qualitatively different disorders rather than different stages of the illness.

In the data collected in our first study, although we did not use the Phillips Scale, we did attempt to ascertain the patient's age at the onset of his illness by having the social worker inquire about (a) age at onset of first signs of disturbed behavior of any kind and (b) the patient's age at the first noticeable psychotic episode. In addition to these two items, we also obtained the patient's age on admission to the project. These three items have an average intercorrelation of about .70, so we felt safe in interpreting them as "age at onset of illness." The results were consistent with Goldstein's: the patients with an earlier onset age were low on Hostility, high on Slowed Speech and Movements, low on Ideas of Persecution, and high on Hebephrenic Symptoms. In other words, earlier onsets tend to be associated with what Venables and O'Connor (1959b) have called withdrawal symptoms, whereas later onsets are associated with paranoid symptoms.

Thus, we are faced with controversial evidence on whether schizophrenic withdrawal is "different kind or different stage." However, it is possible that both interpretations are correct. One kind of schizophrenia, characterized by an early onset age, would have withdrawal as a major feature from the very beginning. A second kind would be a later onset schizophrenia, characterized in its early stages by paranoid symptoms and in its later stages by withdrawal. As a matter of fact, Goldstein's chi square results ($\chi^2 = 14.20$, df $= 1$, $p \leqslant .01$; see accompanying tabulation) are quite consistent with this interpretation in that the poor premorbids are invariably non-paranoid, and the good premorbids may be paranoid or non-paranoid. One may assume that the poor premorbids are non-paranoid or withdrawn from the beginning. The good premorbids begin with paranoid symptoms and develop non-paranoid withdrawal symptoms as a later stage of the illness. The good premorbids might manifest paranoid and/or withdrawal symptoms, depending on the stage of their illness in which they were observed.

	Good	*Poor*	*Total*
Paranoid	22	4	26
Non-paranoid .	28	44	72
Total	50	48	98

Aside from chasing down hypothetical notions concerning age at onset and paranoid versus withdrawal symptomatology, which represents a very limited portion of the available data, we decided to do a large-scale, baldly empirical test of the relation in question. Having measured thirty-two life history characteristics on each of some three hundred fifty untreated patients, we computed canonical correlations between these life history characteristics and (a) our fourteen measures of psychopathology obtained by interview and (b) our seven measures of ward behavior obtained from nurses' observations. In both instances, two significant canonical correlations were obtained, the first canonical in each case being extremely significant. No attempt has been made as yet to interpret the canonical weights, nor do we have much appetite for doing so. The fact that the canonical correlations are statistically significant is taken to confirm the hypothesis that patterns of life history are associated with patterns of psychopathology as observed in the interview and on the ward. Since the canonical correlations were significant, we felt that there was license to examine the 672 zero-order correlations within the matrix.

Life history variables that are particularly associated with patterns of psychopathology are Sex, Race, Age at Onset, Rapidity of Onset, Number of Prior Episodes and Hospitalizations, Voluntariness of Patient's Hospitalization, and Aspects of the Patient's Social Class.

With regard to sex differences, we can confirm what generally has been asserted in the clinical folklore, that females show a greater severity of illness than males.

White patients are more severely ill than Negroes on Guilt, Pressure of Speech, Hebephrenic Symptoms, and Memory Deficit; on the other hand, Negroes are more severely ill than whites on Auditory Hallucinations, Poor Social Participation, and Poor Self Care.

Patients with a greater number of prior episodes and hospitalizations seem to be more severely ill than those with fewer prior episodes, except on three factors: they show less Guilt, less Memory Deficit, and, in ward observations, do not appear to be sad.

The patient with the more rapid onset, as might be expected, shows greater severity of psychopathology than the patient with the insidious onset. He is more disoriented, more agitated and tense; he has a greater memory deficit, is more irritable, and shows poorer self care.

The patient who is a voluntary hospitalization shows less severity of symptomatology than the patient who has to be committed, except on the single symptom factor Guilt. That is, the voluntarily hospitalized patient feels guiltier than the patient who had to be committed to the hospital.

With regard to aspects of social class, it appears that lower-class patients are severely ill on Auditory Hallucinations, Non-auditory Hallucinations, Memory Deficit, Social Participation, Agitation and Tension, Ideas of Persecution, Hebephrenic Symptoms, and Self Care. On the other hand, patients of higher social class seem to express more Guilt and show more Attitudinal Apathy.

One point about the effects of prior episodes and hospitalization seems to emerge: the severity of symptomatology seems to increase in succeeding episodes, but feelings of guilt concerning these symptoms seem to decrease. Patients of lower social class also show a greater severity of symptomatology but feel less guilty about it. Finally, non-voluntary patients seem to have the same pattern of greater severity of symptomatology associated with fewer guilt feelings.

Further explorations are obviously needed into the role of guilt and depression in schizophrenia. I might conclude my remarks by offering the speculation that guilt and depression indicate reality testing in that they are reactions to a recognition that one's mentation is unreal.

COMMENTARY

POLLACK. I think that your data and the earlier data presented by the Judge Baker group have something in common which hasn't really been explored too much, though it was discussed by Rosanoff in 1934. He said there were really two etiological factors, that the early onset male schizophrenics do not have an encapsulated paranoid schema. They may have vague ideas of reference that people are against them, but it doesn't have any of the encapsulated paranoid schema, such as the FBI, or anything like that. But all the studies indicate that the delusion system occurs in all schizophrenics. He implied that individuals who are withdrawn, hebephrenic, exhibit poor self care, and are more often male, became that way as a result of an early minimal brain damage. And he felt that the later onset schizophrenic males – the vast majority – and women have a genetic predisposition for some stress relation which he felt would make them more vulnerable to stress; and therefore they would develop more paranoid schema and perhaps have a different type of illness. I think that jibes with your data, as I said, and it perhaps jibes with that of Ricks and his associates.

GARMEZY. I want to comment first on the relationship of voluntary hospitalization to less severe symptoms and more guilt, as compared with that of involuntary hospitalization to more severe symptoms and less guilt. I think that what may be reflected here is the triadic component of symptom formation that Zigler and Phillips have written about. They have demonstrated, I think quite effectively, that withdrawal symptoms and acting out have a hierarchy related to social competence, which differs from symptoms of internalization and turning against the self. What you may have here is a mixed symptom picture, in which the turning against the self represents a higher social competence indicator that, in effect, would be present in people who are voluntary responders in terms of coming into the hospital, and who would have less severe symptoms. The other point relates to the relationship of the nurse's observations on irritability, resistiveness, and poor self care to four factors – prior episode, rapid onset, nonvoluntary admission, and last half of the sibship. Most of those go together fairly well. The disconcerting one, I think, is rapid onset. Rapid onset in general is a more favorable prognostic sign, but irritability and poor self care, if you look at the Phillips Scale section on symptom formation, which no one uses any more, is an accompaniment of poor premorbid status. So that one might expect more prior episodes, and one might expect nonvoluntary admission under that. Rapid onset is a little tricky. The last half of the sibship thing, though, which you specifically asked about, goes with a study in which Rodnick and I found that poor prognosis was accompanied by large sib number in the family and last half of the sibship pattern. We wondered whether, if you come out of the lower class and there is a large family and you're in the last part of the sibship pool, you tend to be even more neglected and more deprived than if you came early in this sequence. That was about the only speculation that we could generate.

GOLDBERG. Well, Carmi Schooler has done a lot of work on this, and I think he finds an interaction between the sex and first half versus last half in chronically hospitalized patients. I think he found that females tend to be in the last half and males in the first half.

RICKS. I'd like to make one very simple suggestion that's consistent with John Berry's data: that these children coming at the end of very large families are born to mothers who are older and are probably not given as much nutritional care, and may simply be damaged biologically. And we find not strong evidence, but certainly a good deal of evidence, for a certain amount of minimal biological damage in those children who end up chronic and who have this kind of pattern.

LORR. I'd like to suggest that possibly there may be a cultural factor. In our American data we clearly found that the patients who were voluntary, who were white, who came from middle and upper social classes were the anxious-depressed—in other words, the guilty—but in Europe we found the less schooled Italians coming in as depressives predominantly. Now how do you explain that?

REFERENCES

Brill, N. C., & J. F. Glass. Hebephrenic schizophrenic reactions. *Archives of General Psychiatry*, 1965, 12, 545–551.

Goldberg, S. C., G. L. Klerman, & J. O. Cole. Changes in schizophrenic psychopathology and ward behavior as a function of phenothiazine treatment. *British Journal of Psychiatry*, 1965, 120–133.

Goldberg, S. C., N. R. Schooler, & N. B. Mattsson. Paranoid and withdrawal symptoms in schizophrenia: Differential symptom reduction over time. *Journal of Nervous and Mental Disease*, 1967, 145, 158–162.

———. Paranoid and withdrawal symptoms in schizophrenia: Relationship to reaction time. *British Journal of Psychiatry*, 1968, 114, 1161–1165.

Goldstein, M. J., J. M. Held, & R. L. Cromwell. Premorbid adjustment and paranoid–non-paranoid status in schizophrenia. Prepublication Report, 1968.

Kellam, S. G., S. C. Goldberg, N. R. Schooler, A. Berman, & J. L. Shmelzer. Ward atmosphere and outcome of treatment of acute schizophrenia. *Journal of Psychiatric Research*, 1967, 5, 145–163.

National Institute of Mental Health, Psychopharmacology Service Center Collaborative Study Group. Phenothiazine treatment in acute schizophrenia. *Archives of General Psychiatry*, 1964, 10, 246–261.

———. Differences in clinical effects of three phenothiazines in acute schizophrenia. *Diseases of the Nervous System*, 1967, 28, 369–383.

Shakow, D. Psychological deficit in schizophrenia. *Behavioral Science*, 1963, 8, 275–305.

Silverman, J. The scanning control mechanism and "cognitive filtering" in paranoid and non-paranoid schizophrenia. *Journal of Consulting Psychology*, 1964, 28, 385–393.

———. Variations in cognitive control and psychophysiological defense in the schizophrenias. *Psychosomatic Medicine*, 1967, 29, 225–251.

Venables, P. H., & N. O'Connor. Reaction times to auditory and visual stimulation in schizophrenic and normal subjects. *Quarterly Journal of Experimental Psychology*, 1959, 11, 175–179. (a)

———. A short scale for rating paranoid schizophrenia. *Journal of Mental Science*, 1959, 105, 815–818. (b)

Venables, P. H., & J. K. Wing. Level of arousal and the subclassification of schizophrenia. *Archives of General Psychiatry*, 1962, 7, 114–119.

STARKE R. HATHAWAY
ELIO MONACHESI
SUSAN SALASIN

A Follow-up Study of MMPI High 8, Schizoid, Children

IN RECENT years psychologists and sociologists have turned their attention to epidemiology as a promising method of study of schizophrenia. This method has frequently been employed to test, implicitly or explicitly, the premise that schizophrenia is associated with unfortunate social outcomes. In testing the premise, however, a methodological error is likely to be committed. For example, when examining a relation between schizophrenia and a possible social outcome, such as school dropout, investigators are likely to determine the percentage of school dropouts in a population of schizophrenics rather than the percentage of schizophrenics in a population of school dropouts. This method reveals that a high proportion of schizophrenics are school dropouts. Left unanswered is the question, At what rate do schizophrenics drop out of school?

Sometimes referred to as an example of retrospective bias, the methodological error may be avoided by putting the horse "schizophrenia" before the cart "social outcome." If, in a sample of schizophrenics, we find that most drop out of school, whereas most normals do not, we can then predict that the schizophrenic is a probable school dropout. When prediction is possible, a rational basis is present for individual counseling and social programing.

What can we say about the life histories of schizophrenics? Examination of previous pertinent epidemiological literature points to a number of adverse social outcomes of schizophrenia. For the purposes of this discussion, the outcomes will be divided into two areas – IQ and school achievement, and social class and occupational status.

Disorders of conceptual thought are a frequently noted symptom of

NOTE: Experimental work reported here was supported by grants from the National Institute of Mental Health and the University of Minnesota Graduate School.

schizophrenia, but until recently little attention has been directed to the relative discrepancy between the intelligence levels of schizophrenic and normal populations. Recent studies, however, appear to demonstrate what may be termed an "underdog phenomenon."

Although some of the findings were later retracted, Lane (1968), Albee, Lane, and others have produced evidences suggesting early defects in abilities in the school records of children who became schizophrenic patients. Albee, Lane, and Reuter (1964) compared the childhood intelligence scores of a control group of children selected from the same grade school class as the later schizophrenics. The total sample was drawn from a low socioeconomic neighborhood. The mean IQ score of the later schizophrenics was significantly below the mean IQ score of the controls. This remained true at the second-, sixth-, and eighth-grade levels.

A later study conducted by Schaffner, Lane, and Albee (1967) demonstrated that adult diagnosed schizophrenics from suburban areas had not had lower mean IQ scores than their classmates, but that they had had lower mean IQ scores than their own siblings at the second-, sixth-, and eighth-grade levels (see also Lane et al., 1964; 1965). Thus, the developing schizophrenics appear to have been intellectual underdogs when compared with their own siblings or, in other instances, with their own classmates.

This relative discrepancy in intellectual ability between pre-schizophrenics and normals, retrospectively identified, suggests a second related area of investigation: a comparison of the later levels of school achievement of schizophrenic and normal populations in terms of number of years of school completed and grade point average, to see if the same underdog phenomenon exists.

Many investigations concerning the social background of schizophrenics have reliably reported that diagnosed schizophrenics tend to cluster in the lower socioeconomic classes. Until recently, however, there did not appear to be consensus on whether this was a matter of accident or design. It now appears that the retrospective bias was responsible for obscuring the nature of the relations under investigation.

Typical of the studies that attributed the lower socioeconomic standing of schizophrenics to the accident of birth is an epidemiological study reported by Hollinshead and Redlich (1958). These investigators demonstrated that the prevalence rates of schizophrenia varied inversely with the social class structure, with an accumulation of schizophrenics found in the lowest social class. They did not demonstrate, however, that this was also true for incidence rates of schizophrenia. Instead of taking a group of diagnosed schizophrenics and investigating their social class background, they looked at the social classes, determined the proportion of schizophrenics in each class, and drew conclusions on that evidence alone. In other words, the cart preceded the horse.

An example of events in their proper order, however, is the work of Goldberg and Morrison (1963) in England. They selected a random sample of diagnosed schizophrenics and, from birth entries in the general registry, determined the father's occupation at the time of the subject's birth.

The results show that although there was an excess of adult schizophrenics in the lowest social class, the social class of their fathers had not differed from expectation. The occupational histories of the schizophrenics also showed that they either had fallen in occupational level before diagnosis, or had never achieved the standard expected from their school performance.

A recent study by Dunham (1965) supports both the techniques and conclusions reached by Goldberg and Morrison: Dunham tested the hypothesis that the incidence of schizophrenia would not vary significantly among the social classes. Predictably, he found a high concentration of schizophrenics in the lowest social class, which caused the rate of schizophrenia for the class to differ significantly from the rates of the upper social classes. This finding of high prevalence, however, led to inquiry into the background of the schizophrenics in order to establish the distribution of incidence.

Again, using the father's social class as the index of social status rather than the patient's, Dunham found that the original social class of the schizophrenic did not differ from expectation, even though the eventual class position of the schizophrenic was indeed at the lowest level. Dunham suggests that the schizophrenic operates at some kind of disadvantage and is more likely to end up in the lowest social class. Apparently, this is a further illustration of the underdog phenomenon.

Note must be taken at this time of a potential circularity in the line of reasoning that we are establishing. However apparent the association between schizophrenia and unfortunate social outcomes may be, nothing can be concluded about the cause and effect relationship between the disease process and social manifestations of it. We are not testing the premise that social failure leads to schizophrenia, nor are we testing the premise that schizophrenia leads to social failure. We are merely observing that research to date indicates that if an individual is potentially schizophrenic, it appears that he operates at some kind of competitive disadvantage in the struggle for education, jobs, and social standing in our society.

It is quite apparent that therapeutic interventions to prevent undesirable social outcomes in low base rate personality disorders, such as schizophrenia, would increase in efficiency in proportion to an increased capacity to identify subjects with a strong probability of developing the disorder. One may, for example, select high probability schizophrenic children by choosing those with schizophrenic family members. Contrastingly, we might hope for a screening test, physiological or psychological, predicated upon responses given by the subjects themselves. Such a test would identify premorbid cases.

For such a psychological test to be possible, we need to presume that there are precursor psychological symptoms that foreshadow the more severe disorder. As noted above, some evidence supports the assumption that there is some kind of predetermining state in the child before he becomes a clinical case of schizophrenia. Also, considerable evidence suggests a genetic defect in schizophrenia. However, we do not now have good evidence for the existence or nature of assumed premorbid psychological symptoms that could be used practically as a screening device to select high risk groups who might benefit from programs of preventative effort.

Another aspect of the problem of general ignorance about significant predictor symptoms concerns us. This is the unknown incidence relationship between assumed premorbid symptoms of schizophrenia and later development of personally or socially disabling outcomes. Is mental illness a rare outcome among a large number of persons who are in some meaningful way premorbidly schizophrenic? Or is there a close relation between early disposition and later symptoms that characterize those persons diagnosed as schizophrenic?

The foregoing lines of thought are not new. A good statement may be found in Meehl (1962), who wrote, among other pertinent points:

> If the interpersonal regime is favorable, and the schizotaxic person also has the good fortune to inherit a low anxiety readiness, physical vigor, general resistance to stress and the like, he will remain a well-compensated "normal" schizotype, never manifesting symptoms of mental disease. He will be like the gout-prone male whose genes determine him to have an elevated blood uric acid titer, but who never develops clinical gout.
>
> Only a subset of schizotypic personalities decompensate into clinical schizophrenia.

In this argument Meehl was establishing the rational groundwork for what he terms *schizotaxia.* Our reference to the point in this paper is independent of whether the precursor of clinical schizophrenia is schizotaxia or some other innate or early acquired determiner. We argue only that our data may be evidential relative to the assumptions, first, that there is a premorbid state (it may be schizotaxia) present in many more persons than those who develop a clinically recognizable schizophrenia and, second, that this premorbid condition does not necessarily operate to handicap the social and personal development of those who do not develop clinical schizophrenia.

Meehl and others have urged making a search for indicators of an assumed premorbid condition. Our point is that available evidence on schizophrenia has not characteristically included follow-up of adjustment outcomes for those persons who show signs of susceptibility to clinical schizophrenia, but who, nevertheless, never develop those disordered cognitive and social behaviors that characterize the schizophrenic patient.

It is too easy to disregard the fact that when we wish to do research on schizophrenia and begin with schizophrenic patients, the data may result from a confusion of two sources. The patients may, as Meehl states it, have decompensated into clinical schizophrenia, and the data may demonstrate some of the influences that caused the decompensation. But, further, the data may be determined more basically by evidences from the predisposing state. The data from the schizophrenic patients, if they could be factored out, would lead to knowledge of what determined the patients' decompensation. If the predisposing data could be purified, they would bear upon the character of the predisposing cause of schizophrenia. Broader knowledge of the predisposing cause of schizophrenia would require study of the negative instances – persons who carry the precursor condition but who never decompensate to become patients – in addition to patients who are positive instances of schizophrenia. Considering this line of thought, Are these negative instances merely normals or are they some special sort for normals? Do they avoid decompensating because they fortunately escape having schizophrenogenic mothers or because of some positive concurrent qualities that compensate for their morbid predisposition?

MMPI normal profiles predict undramatic, good-citizen lives (Golden et al., 1962). Which profiles predict those who achieve in creative and dramatic ways? One could be led to revive the old idea that character traits recognized among mentally ill patients (for example, those with schizophrenia) may be personal and social assets under certain conditions or contingencies. The old statement asserted a direct correlation between mental illness and genius. Many persons without obvious symptoms of mental illness have "abnormal" MMPI profiles. It may be that studying the biographies of these persons would disclose the need for our concept of abnormal personalities to be broadened to include positive normal qualities.

THE BASIC DATA

In 1947, Hathaway and Monachesi began collecting data on a large sample of ninth-grade schoolchildren as a basis for a longitudinal study of the relationship of data routinely available in school records to life outcomes of the same children as adults. The first sample of over four thousand Minneapolis ninth-graders was a prelude to the collection of a larger sample, termed the statewide sample. During the spring of 1954 over eleven thousand more ninth-grade students were tested in 92 public schools and 86 communities of Minnesota. Sampling included a wide selection of urban and rural children, with the final sample approximately 50 per cent rural.

In addition to photographing the routine school records we administered the MMPI to all cases, and teachers were asked for nominations of students likely to get into trouble with the law or to have emotional trouble. The MMPI was repeated on a large sample when the children were in the twelfth grade, and a considerable sample was again tested when they entered college. Besides the grades which were recorded on the school records, there were also records of tests that had been given in the schools, such as intelligence scores and Strong Vocational Interest Blank scores.

Biographical information on the members of samples who could be located with reasonable effort has been collected in an almost continual process from the date of initiation of the studies to about 1965. This information has been obtained chiefly by using field workers in the children's areas of residence and by searching the files of public agencies, including police and institutional records. The statewide sample, from which the present data are drawn, has now been followed to at least age twenty-five. Some data have been obtained on a high percentage of the total sample, but data adequate for analysis, such as that in this study, will be drawn from about 85 per cent of the total statewide sample.

The original and follow-up data are processed for machine use and have been put into card and tape form to permit relatively simple processing of tabular information in the many areas that might be investigated.

A general summary of the results has been published in book form (Hathaway & Monachesi, 1963). The present paper will deal with MMPI high 8 and MMPI normal samples drawn from the statewide sample.

MMPI AND SCHIZOPHRENIA

The Minnesota Multiphasic Personality Inventory (MMPI) was developed as an aid in psychiatric diagnosis. The identification of schizophrenic patients is among the most common diagnostic problems. Work on the MMPI scale related to schizophrenia began early, and Scale 8 (Sc) was a product of more research development than any of the other MMPI scales. Although the scale never reached a very satisfactory level of validity, it has become one of the most important scales in the MMPI profile. The present state of the scale and the diagnostic class are still well stated in a quotation from an earlier paper on schizophrenia and Scale 8 (Welsh & Dahlstrom, 1956):

> Various investigators have found the clinical diagnosis of schizophrenia to be reproduced independently on the same patients by different clinicians in only 30 to 60 percent of the cases. These figures are certainly not too low if less psychotic patients are used for the experiment. The MMPI Sc scale suggests, as do similar scales on other inventories, about the same degree of reproduction of the diagnosis in such clinical groups. There is no accepted way to assert that either the scale or the diagnosis is wrong.

All sorts of other personality tests have been developed to aid in the diagnosis of schizophrenia. None of these has high validity against routine psychiatric diagnostic procedures as a criterion – though, as quoted above, we have little more reason to accept the criterion than to accept the test scores. It would be of great value if we could discover valid, objective symptoms, test items, or scales that would provide a more stable basis for use of the word *schizophrenia.*

MMPI profiles are usually referred to by code. A "high 8" profile is one in which the standard score for Scale 8 is larger than that for any other scale among seven or eight related to classes of mental disorder. Increasingly today, the schizophrenic patient also shows symptoms classically described by the term *paranoid.* For a great many schizophrenic patients, the subtype of schizophrenia is paranoid schizophrenia. In practice, also, many of the diagnostic disagreements among clinicians center about the relative strength of the paranoid and schizophrenic symptom complexes.

The MMPI also includes a scale to identify paranoid trends. This scale, Scale 6, is empirically related to Scale 8. For this reason, also, profiles coded 68 will be included among the high 8 sample, on the assumption that these profiles will identify persons who are similar to the pure high 8. In summary, "high 8," as we define it here, means that the standard score for Scale 8 or Scale 6 was at least as large (*T* score 70) as two standard deviations from the normal mean and, among the eight scales used in the code, Scale 8 or Scale 6 was the most deviant. When Scale 6 was more deviant, Scale 8 was always next in size.

The MMPI was empirically derived from sample groups of patients who had been given the diagnosis schizophrenia. The "high 8" children of our present study had test patterns that have established some similarity to test patterns from adult schizophrenic patients, and one may assert the hypothesis that the children would develop toward the adult syndrome of schizophrenia.

To contribute to the basic description of the clinical and personological meaning of the high 8's, we have data on adjectives used by teachers who described the children of the samples. The descriptions were completely independent of MMPI data, and the adjectives were tabulated out of the recorded teacher descriptions — they were not chosen from a predetermined list.

For the adjectives used often enough so that they could be ranked in frequency, the male high 8's were described most often by: *follower-indifferent*; *unlikable*; *stubborn-hostile*, and *lazy-undependable*. The female high 8's were called *lazy-undependable*, *unlikable*, *erratic-unhappy*, and *peppy-scatterbrained* (Hathaway & Monachesi, 1961).

To obtain a sample of appropriate foils to the high 8 sample, we have chosen all children with profiles that showed no MMPI scale as deviant as *T* score 55. Follow-up data on such normal cases have supported the inference that these children had convincingly low base rates of delinquency or other variations from the social norms of behavior.

For those familiar with the MMPI code system, the MMPI profiles that we are calling high 8 include all profiles of the code classes 8′6... 6′8... or 8′... with omission of Scales 5 and 0. The *F* score was held to less than 22, and the *L* score to less than 11.

For the normals, the code was of the form ′... This signifies no coded high point on any scale among the ten regular scales. The *F* score was less than 16, and the *L* less than 11. No profile was used for either group if there were many questioned items.

There were 2,719 boys with profiles meeting the normal definition and 3,268 girls whose profiles were similarly defined as normal. The cor·

responding samples of high 8 profiles identified 254 boys and 231 girls. These numbers establish incidence rates of about 5.1 per cent and 4.4 per cent among the total samples of boys and girls, respectively.

Our tables never represent all of the cases in the samples since the data necessary for each table will be lacking or inappropriate for a varying proportion of the samples. Usually, the observed numbers could not vary greatly even if the missing cases were quite markedly unlike those listed.

For this paper, we have chosen to analyze some of the data relating ninth-grade MMPI high 8 groups to normals on intelligence, school performance, and socioeconomic status.

PROJECT DATA

The discussion above of previous reports identified social outcomes that have appeared to be associated with schizophrenia. Using the family of origin as the standard or measure for prediction, investigators were cited who have reported that before developing schizophrenia, patients often have had lower IQ's and lower socioeconomic standing than prediction from their original families would indicate. Assuming some degree of

Table 1. Intelligence Levels of High 8's [a]

Intelligence Score (Percentile) [b]	Males			Females		
	o	e	χ^2	o	e	χ^2
1–39	138	69	69	88	60	13
40–68	61	77	3	68	71	0
69–100	53	106	53	69	94	7
Total *N*	252	252		225	225	
Total χ^2			125***			20***

[a] For this and the following tables, the expected numbers (e) for the cells are derived from the "normal" samples. For example, in Table 1, the expected number of low percentile score boys is 69. This proportional value was obtained from (138/252) × 1825, which yields 69. The total number of normal boys for this table was 1,825; the total number of high 8 boys available was 252. Therefore, 69 (e) is the portion of high 8 boys one would expect among the 252 if the high 8's were distributed as are the normals. By contrast, there were 138 high 8 boys observed (o) in the lowest 40 per cent of the intelligence distribution.

The χ^2 weight for this cell is 69, and the total χ^2 for the male portion of the table is 125, which is statistically significant ($p<.001$). Note that the calculation assumes the normals to be the true population; χ^2 is a measure of goodness of fit to them.

[b] See Hathaway and Monachesi (1961), p. 50, for explanation of derivation.

***$p<.001$.

equivalence between schizophrenia and MMPI high 8, the remainder of this paper will be upon support for an analogous relationship of high 8 to social outcome as it develops in the life histories of the cases in the samples.

For a comparison of the intelligence ratings of high 8 children compared with normals, public school test scores from several different intelligence tests had to be equated. We converted these various test scores into percentile scores from the corresponding norm tables and grouped them approximately into high, medium, and low classes using the percentile range of the normals. When the intelligence scores of high 8's and normals are contrasted, the distribution of the samples of high 8 children are strongly skewed positively. There are much higher frequencies in the middle and low intelligence percentile ranges than is true of the distribution of the normals. For both boys and girls, the observed differences are statistically significant and meaningfully large (see Table 1).

Similar positive skewing occurs for the high 8 samples contrasted with the distributions for the normal samples on high school rank (Table 2). Consistently with this low achievement record, both male and female high 8 children were comparatively much more likely to stop their schooling with high school graduation or less as compared with the normal expectations (Table 3).

When the distributions are broken down into low, medium, and high intelligence levels, as in Table 4, the distributions of the high 8's show that their deficient grade levels occur chiefly below the seventieth percentile in intelligence level. This is more significantly true for the girls. Another way of stating this is to say that, with both high 8 and good intelligence, the high 8 children, especially the girls, achieve more nearly at the level of the normals.

The tendency for an interaction among high 8, intelligence, and achievement is further illustrated in Table 5. These data show that children with high 8 and intelligence below the seventieth percentile are less likely to go beyond high school. Again, the data for girls are more definite than those for boys. Stated with emphasis on higher intelligence, it appears that, with high intelligence, high 8 is not much associated with under achievement and this is more true for the girls.

In agreement with some previously published data on schizophrenic case histories (Dunham, 1965), these results seem to indicate that the high 8 condition alone does not predict disabling academic outcomes. It is the high 8 condition linked with low intellectual ability that appears to lead to an academic double jeopardy.

Table 2. High School Rank of the High 8's Who Reached the Twelfth Grade [a]

High School Rank (Percentile)	Males			Females		
	o	e	χ^2	o	e	χ^2
1–39	127	76	34	74	40	29
40–69	39	59	7	46	56	2
70–100	20	50	18	61	85	7
Total *N*	186	186		181	181	
Total χ^2			59***			38***

[a] See Table 1, n. *a*.
***$p<.001$.

Table 3. Schooling Completed by High 8's [a]

Schooling	Males			Females		
	o	e	χ^2	o	e	χ^2
High school only	150	107	17	145	111	10
Beyond high school	77	120	15	63	97	12
Total *N*	227	227		208	208	
Total χ^2			32***			22***

[a] See Table 1, n. *a*.
***$p<.001$.

Table 4. High School Rank Related to Intelligence of Male and Female High 8's [a]

High School Rank (Percentile)	Intelligence Score 1–39%			Intelligence Score 40–68%			Intelligence Score 69–100%		
	o	e	χ^2	o	e	χ^2	o	e	χ^2
Male High 8's									
1–39	85	75	1	31	22	4	11	7	2
40–69	11	18	3	14	19	1	14	14	0
70–100	1	5	3	3	7	2	16	20	1
Total *N*	97	97		48	48		41	41	
Total χ^2			7*			7*			3
Female High 8's									
1–39	50	34	8	20	12	5	3	3	0
40–69	13	22	4	23	23	0	10	12	0
70–100	2	10	6	13	21	3	45	43	0
Total *N*	65	65		56	56		55	55	
Total χ^2			18***			8*			0

[a] See Table 1, n. *a*.
* $p<.05$. *** $p<.001$.

Intrigued by incidence and prevalence rates for schizophrenia in the various socioeconomic levels, we were interested in looking at both the socioeconomic status of the occupations of the fathers of high 8 children and the later socioeconomic status levels of high 8's themselves. Dividing the occupations into three groups — white collar, farmer, and blue collar — we found that the fathers of high 8 boys, *but not* the fathers of high 8 girls, were significantly more often at the blue-collar level (Table 6).

The socioeconomic outcome standing achieved at age twenty-five by

Table 5. Schooling Related to Intelligence of Male and Female High 8's [a]

Schooling	Intelligence Score 1–39% [b]			Intelligence Score 40–68% [b]			Intelligence Score 69–100% [b]		
	o	e	χ^2	o	e	χ^2	o	e	χ^2
			Male High 8's						
High school only	100	86	2	32	27	1	16	13	1
Beyond high school	26	40	5	22	27	1	29	32	0
Total *N*	126	126		54	54		45	45	
Total χ^2			7**			2			1
			Female High 8's						
High school only	71	59	2	46	35	3	26	23	0
Beyond high school	9	21	7	16	27	4	36	39	0
Total *N*	80	80		62	62		62	62	
Total χ^2			9**			8**			0

[a] See Table 1, n. *a*.
[b] See Table 1, n. *b*.
** $p<.01$.

Table 6. Socioeconomic Status of High 8's and Their Fathers [a]

Socioeconomic Status	Male			Female		
	o	e	χ^2	o	e	χ^2
		Father's SES				
Blue collar	129	116	1	103	107	0
Farmer	67	55	3	61	50	2
White collar	52	76	8	57	64	1
Total *N*	248	248		221	221	
Total χ^2			12**			3
		Present SES of High 8's				
Blue collar	101	87	2	78	64	3
Farmer	16	11	2	15	7	9
White collar	71	90	4	56	78	6
Total *N*	188	188		149	149	
Total χ^2			8*			18***

[a] See Table 1, n. *a*.
* $p<.05$. ** $p<.01$. *** $p<.001$.

the male high 8's is also more skewed toward blue-collar status than was that of their fathers, but the differences are moderate. This trend suggests that high 8 boys do seem to originate from families of lower socioeconomic status and to stay lower as they establish their own roles.

Table 6 also shows the outcome distribution of the high 8 girls. Most of these girls were ranked on the socioeconomic status of the worker of the family in which they lived by age twenty-five. Consequently, the data rest heavily on the work level status of their husbands. Although Table 6 showed that the socioeconomic status of the families of these girls was not much different in distribution from the normals, the distribution in Table 6 suggests that in establishing their new families, the high 8 girls did not hold their levels. Like the boys, they tended to lose economic status.

To check the role of intelligence level in the families of origin for the high 8 cases, Table 7 shows the data distributed into three intelligence classes. No significant differences are developed with this analysis. It appears that lower socioeconomic status is more related to the occurrence of high 8 than to lower intelligence.

A third ingredient in the high 8 social equation appeared when the size of community that high 8's lived in as ninth-graders was compared to that into which they later moved. The frequency distributions of the high 8 samples were skewed toward both original and outcome residence on a

Table 7. Father's Socioeconomic Status Related to Intelligence of Male and Female High 8's [a]

	Intelligence Score 1–39% [b]			Intelligence Score 40–68% [b]			Intelligence Score 69–100% [b]		
Socioeconomic Status	o	e	χ^{2c}	o	e	χ^{2c}	o	e	χ^{2c}
			Male High 8's						
Blue collar	73	71	0	29	30	0	27	28	0
Farmer	41	37	0	12	13	0	13	8	3
White collar	24	26	0	19	16	1	11	18	2
Total N	138	138		60	60		51	51	
Total χ^2			1			1			6*
			Female High 8's						
Blue collar	48	47	0	30	34	0	24	28	1
Farmer	25	22	0	16	15	0	16	14	0
White collar	13	19	2	17	16	0	26	24	0
Total N	86	86		63	63		66	66	
Total χ^2			2			1			1

[a] See Table 1, n. *a*.
[b] See Table 1, n. *b*.
[c] Values have been rounded off to the nearest unit.
* $p < .05$.

farm or small town. This tendency was not a function of socioeconomic level or intelligence, since the frequencies of rural and small town residence did vary with socioeconomic level or intelligence.

DISCUSSION

Our data suggests that unfortunate social outcomes are probably associated with the high 8 condition which has a clear positive relationship to low school achievement and low socioeconomic origins and outcomes. But, despite these general data, those high 8's who have high intelligence may also be disadvantaged, though not in any way for which our presently analyzed data provide evidence.

In the introductory discussion, we have suggested the hypothesis that persons who have deviant MMPI profiles but who do not become patients may, under some conditions, actually derive positive value from the deviant condition. In these data, we do not give direct support for the hypothesis, but the fact that the combination of intelligence and high 8 is not predictive of some adverse trends observed with high 8 alone leaves the possibility open. In a later study we shall make available an analysis to develop more evidence on the careers of the intelligent high 8 cases. When we have developed the data further, it may be that high 8, together with some moderator variable such as intelligence, will be established as a contingency that often increases the probability of productive and creative lives.

What can be predicted in summary about those high 8's whose intelligence is not high? Their average life outcomes tend to be worse than normals who seem otherwise to have no better prospects. Not only does the career of the high 8 call to mind the adjectives the teachers applied to them when they were in ninth grade — unlikable, stubborn, indifferent, lazy, and undependable — but if they also have a low ability, they have a greater chance of remaining at the bottom of the social achievement pyramid than disadvantaged normal children without the high 8 characteristic.

In general, we believe the data show that MMPI high 8 children and their careers are suggestively similar to reported data on schizophrenic patients as children and adults. To the degree that this similarity justifies accepting considerable identity between the test-identified children and adult persons diagnosed schizophrenic, research on the consequences and treatment of schizophrenia may be simplified. Experimental groups could be selected at early ages by use of objective personality scales; though many of the high 8's so selected may not actually develop clinical schizophrenia, they are a suitable sample for study of some of the more significant career effects of schizophrenia.

Obviously, this argument does not yet establish a complete identity between the characters of the high 8 children and those of children who later attain a clinical diagnosis of schizophrenia. For one thing, high 8 children are too numerous to permit such an identity. If high 8 is indicative of a premorbid state, it appears that the rate of clinical schizophrenia as an adult outcome cannot be greater than about 20 per cent at the most. Our subjects are not yet old enough to provide data for an estimate. The data, however, are consistent with the hypothesis that high 8 children share a pattern of personal and social psychopathology with those who do later develop schizophrenia.

COMMENTARY

MEDNICK. I'm sorry I'm ignorant about this, but what is the relationship of high 8 patterns and high 68 patterns to IQ among normals?

HATHAWAY. The correlation is very low. I didn't go into it, but there are actually some interesting implications here. For Scale 8 we are studying the positive tail of the distribution. The demonstrated distribution of intelligence for the high 8's is positively skewed. When these variables are even a little related to one another, the upper third selected out by the high 8 is from the attenuated tail of the distribution and the regional correlation is higher.

The correlation between Scale 8 and intelligence is low, though I can't give you the exact correlation now. As one gets more nearly average scores on Scale 8, probably the scale does not correlate with intelligence at all. This is common with certain MMPI scales, particularly those indicating abnormality in one direction only. I believe very firmly that correlation should not be used for many MMPI studies. The MMPI variables do not fit the premises necessary for the use of the correlation formula.

STABENAU. Do you have any data on the clinical status of these individuals at age twenty-five?

HATHAWAY. We have, of course, as much as we could get. The institutional records we have found show that out of some eleven thousand, we have only about thirty to fifty who have been in state mental institutions. Of these, only one is a high 8. I have not mentioned these data because I can make no conclusion at the present about them. We have checked this, and are checking more thoroughly. The more interesting group for that particular study is the Minneapolis sample, the first sample we collected, now thirty-three, an age at which the incidence of schizophrenia should begin to climb. The present data on twenty-five-year-olds are apparently too early. By the way, our incidence of institutionalization data are going to be modified by the changing patterns of institutionalization in the last ten years.

QUESTION. The socioeconomic status of the father appears to be somewhat static. I wonder if you have any data on whether or not the fathers were downwardly mobile, or if there are other studies similar to yours which have taken that into account.

HATHAWAY. We have no direct evidence on that. We took them frozen in place as of the time we collected the data, when the child was in the ninth grade. Some of these fathers are stepfathers, although we hope that we have that straightened out. I'm sure this variable is not very reliable. We know little about the families. Collecting fifteen thousand life histories scattered over the state of Minnesota turned out to be such a huge task that it sometimes amazes me we learned as much as we did, though we are painfully aware of the inadequacy—so much we should have thought of, so many items we should have collected. This is all obvious, and we know so well how much better we could do it if we had the money and freedom needed.

QUESTION. Could you give an indication of the problems you're having in following these people, or what percentage follow-up success you're getting and things like that?

HATHAWAY. Don't tempt me too far, or I'll give you more than you want. Briefly, our first follow-up four years after testing the Minneapolis sample was collected about 1951. This was the one where we should have been able to find the highest percentage. These were Minneapolis cases, and although they were more mobile perhaps than some of the statewide cases, we didn't have to travel so far. We employed fieldworkers who went to the schools, asked where the persons were, obtained class yearbooks, and so on. In that way, we found a majority. The first ones were inexpensive per person, but as we progressed, the price per subject went up. The last cases we found really came hard. In the Minneapolis sample, we achieved 93 per cent follow-up. Follow-up could have been better. It is just a matter of how much you can pay and how much time you can devote.

For the statewide sample, we again had fieldworkers. We tried to employ a county caseworker or a person in the schools, someone who knew all the local people. We had some wonderful agents who kept track of the newspapers, and collected all clippings and local gossip on our cases. We have a number of subjects who killed their fathers and mothers and all sorts of other interesting and notorious events. Some of this documentation is not very scientific. Following the more elusive subjects gets tricky. We have not formally analyzed data about the ones we couldn't follow up. We may make a study of the data we do have on missing cases in the statewide sample now that we've closed the books with the end of our support money. In the Minneapolis sample, the ones we didn't find clearly included more of the deviant cases. If anything is wrong in our reported data, my guess is that the deviant outcome rates are attenuated by the failure to find all of them. More socially adequate people of higher intelligence usually leave their addresses when they move. For a number of interesting reasons, many in our sample didn't leave their addresses, and the postmaster and other sources don't know where they went. Some obvious reasons I leave to your imagination.

The fieldworker's stories about hard-to-find cases were amusing. But it was too expensive to get more. In the statewide sample, we have about 97 per cent with quite a bit of information. This percentage, however, goes up and down, according to the variable.

STRAUSS. I'm interested in what general classes of data you didn't get that you're sorry you missed.

HATHAWAY. Well, the silliest one, perhaps, since we had a faculty member in the Department of Psychology at that time who was interested in sibling order, was the sibling order of our cases. We added that later, as an afterthought. It would be impossible to get all the data I'd like to get. The previous question about whether the fathers have been downwardly mobile is a good example of missing information. We collected what we were able to from the schools, but we didn't see the family at the time of testing. Later on, we often interviewed families, but this was not done systematically.

Then we would have liked fathers and mothers to do Multiphasics. A number of people here are interested in that. In that connection, one of Dr. Reed's studies at the Dight Institute for Human Genetics here has followed up the children of pairs of our original sample who married each other. Propinquity does help determine marriage partners, and being in the same ninth grade apparently helped, for we found a fair number who married each other and had children. Some started early, and there are already a few data for genetic research, since we have Multiphasics of the parents and a student in genetics has followed up by testing some of the first generation. But I'm really overwhelmed when I think of data we could have collected if we had had more foresight and, especially, more money.

One interesting thing that you might expect in the rural-urban sampling of high 8's, which I didn't get into today, is that the high 8's are on the farm — that is, rural — more than is the whole sample. High 8 and rural go together, and if I had prepared the table showing the socioeconomic status of the husbands of high 8 girls, you would see that they went to the farm more than normal.

The data support what sometimes is presented as a prejudicial view toward farmers. Whatever high 8 is, rural children show it a little more frequently than do urban children, and high 8 children tend to move to or to stay on the farm. You know the ecological studies in Chicago which found that the rooming house districts of the city are good places for schizophrenia, and the suburbs are for the manic-depressives. Well, I think we'll find trends in the rural areas similar to those in the rooming house areas.

REFERENCES

Albee, G. W., E. A. Lane, & J. M. Reuter. Childhood intelligence of future schizophrenics and their neighborhood peers. *Journal of Psychology*, 1964, 58, 141–144.

Dunham, H. W. *Community and schizophrenia: An epidemiological analysis.* Detroit, Mich.: Wayne State University Press, 1965.

Goldberg, E. M., & S. L. Morrison. Schizophrenia and social class. *British Journal of Psychiatry*, 1963, 109, 758–780.

Golden, J., N. Mandel, B. C. Glueck, & Z. A. Feder. A summary description of fifty "normal" white males. *American Journal of Psychiatry*, 1962, 119, 48–56.

Hathaway, S. R., & E. D. Monachesi. *An atlas of juvenile MMPI profiles.* Minneapolis: University of Minnesota Press, 1961.

———. *Adolescent personality and behavior: MMPI patterns of normal, delinquent, dropout, and other outcomes.* Minneapolis: University of Minnesota Press, 1963.

Hollinshead, A. B., & F. L. Redlich. *Social class and mental illness.* New York: Wiley, 1958.

Lane, E. A., & G. W. Albee. Early childhood intellectual differences between schizophrenic adults and their siblings. *Journal of Abnormal and Social Psychology*, 1964, 68, 193–195.

———. Childhood intelligence of schizophrenics and siblings. *American Journal of Orthopsychiatry*, 1965, 35, 747–753.

———. On childhood intellectual decline of adult schizophrenics: A reassessment of an earlier study. *Journal of Abnormal Psychology*, 1968, 73, 174–177.

Meehl, P. E. Schizotaxia, schizotypy, schizophrenia. *American Psychologist*, 1962, 17, 832–838.

Schaffner, A., E. A. Lane, & G. W. Albee. Intellectual differences between suburban preschizophrenic children and their siblings. *Journal of Consulting Psychology*, 1967, 31, 326–327.

Welsh, G. S., & W. G. Dahlstrom. *Basic readings on the MMPI in psychology and medicine.* Minneapolis: University of Minnesota Press, 1956.

ELLEN A. LANE
GEORGE W. ALBEE

Intellectual Antecedents of Schizophrenia

BECAUSE both clinical observations and animal laboratory experiments have made it clear that early experiences profoundly affect later behavior (Levine 1962), strenuous research efforts continue to seek childhood behavioral and situational factors that are related to successful and unsuccessful adult adjustment. The many investigatory methods presently used in discovering these factors have been described and criticized by other contributors to this volume (Mednick & McNeil, 1968; Roff, pp. 265–283 below). It is apparent that each approach has some value and many limitations and that under the banner of each can be included good studies and poor studies.

The method of searching for childhood records, which we have used in studying the intellectual development of schizophrenics, can be considered a shortcut to the longitudinal method, without the same demands of fastidious planning and extraordinary patience. The longitudinal method, long successful in the study of child development, has proved less practical for adult psychopathology. With schizophrenia, for example, which affects less than 1 per cent of the general population, it has seemed almost impossible to select large enough random samples of children for significant follow-up studies. Mednick has attempted to overcome the problem by choosing to study a high-risk sample of offspring whose mothers are chronic schizophrenics (Mednick & Schulsinger, 1965; also, pp. 51–89 above). Some evidence suggests, however, that even yearly professional contacts with foster families can have therapeutic side effects on the development of children and the structure of family relationships (Skodak, 1966), so that the possible prophylactic effects of continuing con-

NOTE: The research reported in this paper was supported by Grant M5186 from the National Institute of Mental Health.

tacts may result in a significantly smaller number of schizophrenic breakdowns than anticipated. Such a finding, of course, would itself be worthwhile. Although the searcher of past childhood records is limited to what has been observed or measured in the past and to those records which have not been destroyed, he does not influence subjects' behavior nor can his own biases influence previously recorded measurements.

We wish to illustrate some further advantages and limitations of using the method of studying objective records from the past by describing our research on the intellectual development of schizophrenics.

More than ten years ago we set out to investigate the question of whether children who subsequently became adult schizophrenics differed in school behavior from their classmates. Some of the literature suggested that children who later became schizophrenic adults were generally quiet, shy, and withdrawn. There also was reason to believe that these children would be low in motivation to achieve. It seemed a relatively simple matter to examine school report cards and to compare conduct and effort grades, as well as measures of academic achievement, of pre-schizophrenics and their classmates. To our dismay we learned that in Cleveland report cards from the elementary school level are destroyed long before an individual reaches adulthood. It is obvious that the method of using past records does not allow for the testing of every reasonable hypothesis, at least not from the sources most easily accessible.

While inquiring about these missing report cards at the Cleveland Board of Education, however, we learned that scores on group intelligence tests stretching back to the middle 1930's had been kept intact. The group testing program in the Cleveland schools has continued from its inception to give the same tests to all pupils in regular classes during the same school grades: the Kuhlmann-Anderson Test in second grade, the Cleveland Classification Test in sixth grade, and the Terman-McNemar Test of Mental Ability in eighth grade. In addition, we found that a surprisingly large number of individual Binet tests, beginning in 1920, were available. Here, carefully preserved, were thousands of reports of individual and group intelligence tests for a total population of public school children from which a significant number subsequently became schizophrenic adults.

After obtaining the names and birthdates of adult schizophrenics admitted to state and federal mental hospitals in the Cleveland area, we were able to check at the attendance bureau of the Cleveland Board of Education to determine which schizophrenics had attended Cleveland public schools as children. We were on our way, almost by accident, to studying the early intellectual performance of adult schizophrenics. This phenomenon — the discovery of available information which suggests new studies — has happened to us again and again in this research.

In our first study (Lane & Albee, 1963), we reported that children who subsequently became adult schizophrenics demonstrate a conspicuous and significant average decline of more than 10 IQ points between early childhood (5–8 years) and late childhood (11–14 years). This same pattern of decline in intelligence test scores was found both for schizophrenic adults who had had second- and sixth-grade group tests and for those who had had Binet intelligence tests in both periods of childhood.

The Educational Research Department of the Cleveland Board of Education provided us with a control study which showed that a group of more than eight hundred children who had taken these same two group tests in the second and sixth grades showed a slight increase in IQ over this time, in marked contrast to our group of future schizophrenics. Therefore, when standard scores were used, based on the distribution of scores of the control children, the decline in the pre-schizophrenic group was even more pronounced.

Unfortunately, large numbers do not assure adequate controls. More recently, after we observed that siblings of pre-schizophrenics showed a similar decline in IQ during childhood, we began to have misgivings about our original controls and conclusions. We discovered that a subtle bias in the selection of the eight hundred control subjects, one that seemed unimportant at the time, had led us to an erroneous conclusion. The control group was composed of all those sixth-grade children in the Cleveland schools during a specific year who had previously taken the second-grade test at the same elementary school. A greater preponderance of them, it developed, because of this requirement of stability in residence, came from better socioeconomic neighborhoods or from the more stable families in the lower-class neighborhoods. It was these children who had shown a slight increase in IQ from early to late childhood. Most of the schizophrenics-to-be, in contrast, had attended school in disadvantaged neighborhoods, and they had moved and changed schools frequently within these neighborhoods.

We no longer believe that pre-schizophrenics decline more in IQ than other children with similar social backgrounds. We have recently demonstrated that, with improved control groups, pre-schizophrenics cannot be distinguished from their peers or from their siblings on the basis of a decline in IQ (Lane & Albee, 1968). The fallacy in our original paper illustrates the importance of carefully selected control groups, especially socioeconomic controls, in doing life history research.

Although we were not able to demonstrate a meaningful decline in IQ during childhood, it was obvious to us that the scores we had been collecting for pre-schizophrenics were generally below national averages. We still hoped to discover some differences in intellectual performance between children who later became schizophrenic and other children. In one study we compared the intelligence levels of more than a hundred schizophrenics-to-be with the intelligence levels of childhood peers from their own neighborhoods (Albee, Lane, & Reuter, 1964). Many pre-schizophrenics — a much larger proportion than among normals — who were in special classes for slow learners were not in this study because group tests are given only to children in regular classes. Despite this, we were able to show that children who later became adult schizophrenics scored significantly below the average of other children in their own neighborhood school classes, in second grade, sixth grade, and eighth grade. They were much more frequently in the lowest quarter of their class and much less frequently in the highest quarter of their class than could be expected by chance. We concluded that inferior intellectual performance throughout childhood is characteristic of future schizophrenics even when socioeconomic factors are controlled.

Mednick has raised the question of whether our pre-schizophrenics scored lower than their peers because they were a less mobile group, having remained in the Cleveland area from childhood to adulthood whereas probably a smaller proportion of the peer control group stayed in Cleveland that long (Mednick & McNeil, 1968). The literature cited by Mednick that IQ is positively correlated with mobility is based on rural-urban migration. Further, approximately one third of our subjects were Negro, a group that had almost no migration out of Cleveland during those years. However, his criticism that the control group should have been matched for mobility is well taken, and it was not considered at the time of the study. Whether or not Mednick's criticism is valid, however, this type of error is not tied to the ex-post-facto method, as he suggests, but it can also accompany the longitudinal method when subjects who have moved cannot be located for follow-up study. Another, and perhaps a more valid, criticism of this study would be that our pre-schizophrenic subjects were more, rather than less, mobile as children than the controls, when mobility is defined as multiple address changes within the city (Lane, 1958), and that this type of instability may result in poorer school and intellectual performance.

In either case, we believe that these factors and others were better controlled in a subsequent study which compared the test performance of pre-schizophrenics with that of their own siblings. Although pupils from schools in the same neighborhood were a reasonable socioeconomic control, the pre-schizophrenics might still have come either from the most deprived families or from the intellectually dullest families within those neighborhoods. Unknown cultural or familial factors also could have contributed to making pre-schizophrenics differ from their peers in test performance but not from other members of their own family. We therefore decided to compare the test performance of pre-schizophrenics with that of their own siblings, who had taken the same tests during the same grades at school at approximately the same ages (Lane & Albee, 1965).

This comparison of IQ's obtained on group intelligence tests in second, sixth, and eighth grades for schizophrenics-to-be and for their respective siblings showed that future schizophrenics perform significantly lower than their own siblings on IQ tests throughout childhood. They were, much more frequently than could be expected by chance, the lowest scoring child in the family. Future schizophrenics, whose IQ's were below average, came from families of average intelligence. A control group of children, on the other hand, with matched IQ's and from the same school classes as the future schizophrenics, had siblings whose IQ's were similarly low.

In summarizing this series of studies, we concluded that intellectual deficit is characteristic of children who subsequently develop adult schizophrenic behavior. In brief, (a) these children score, on the average, well below the mean of the population on which the tests were standardized; (b) they score significantly lower than classroom peers from the same neighborhoods on intelligence tests in second, sixth, and eighth grades; and (c) they score significantly lower than their own siblings on the same intelligence tests taken in these same grades.

These findings indicate that intellectual signs of a developing schizophrenic disturbance may be distinguishable during early childhood for persons whose first recognizable onset occurs in adult life. This conclusion contradicts a prevalent notion in classical psychiatry that schizophrenia is a disorder which manifests itself during, or shortly after, puberty either because of endocrinological defects or because of psychosexual conflicts prevalent during this period (Arieti, 1959; Hoerr & Osol, 1956).

Drawing all our subjects from publicly supported mental institutions and from the Cleveland public schools meant that our samples were below average in socioeconomic status. It might be argued that because schizophrenia is much more prevalent in the lowest socioeconomic groups, the use of these Cleveland samples is quite appropriate. But these findings could not be generalized to other social classes.

Therefore, we repeated our Cleveland studies with samples drawn from four large suburban school systems (Schaffner, Albee, & Lane, 1967). Each of these suburbs of Cleveland is composed primarily of white middle- and upper-class families. In addition to public hospital sources, cases were drawn from a large university hospital where a significant number of suburban residents have been hospitalized. One major difficulty we encountered was that the group intelligence tests used in these suburban school systems varied from system to system, and the tests had been changed from time to time over the years, whereas the tests used in the Cleveland system have been strikingly uniform. To permit comparability, all IQ's were converted to standard scores.

We found that our new sample of 114 middle- and upper-class suburban pre-schizophrenics, unlike our Cleveland sample, whose average scores were in the low 90s, had an average IQ of 104 during childhood. Nor did they score significantly lower than their own classroom peers, as did the Cleveland sample. However, these middle- and upper-class children did score significantly below their own siblings at each different childhood age level. This suburban study is an example of the advantage of using siblings as controls, as many contributors to this volume have done. Without the use of sibling controls, suburban pre-schizophrenics with their relatively high IQ scores could not be described as showing intellectual deficit. Yet even bright pre-schizophrenics were detected to be significantly lower in IQ than would be expected in relation to their own siblings, who were even further above national averages.

Intellectual deficit during childhood, as defined in terms of sibling comparisons, can be said to be characteristic of the adult schizophrenic whatever his socioeconomic or familial background. Clearly these findings do not in any way bear on the question of causation. Whether the dullest child in a family is most prone to schizophrenia or whether the child who will be schizophrenic performs the poorest for emotional reasons cannot be ascertained from these data, although we have some evidence from another study (Batman, Albee, & Lane, 1966) that these lowered intelligence test scores are the result of reduced or distorted motivation rather than true intellectual deficit. The method of retrieving past records, in its reliance on what exists, does not supply all of the important related evidence that might be gathered in a planned longitudinal study.

The clinical literature concerned with the effects of schizophrenia on intellectual performance is voluminous but highly contradictory. From Kraepelin's early formulations on, there has been the persistent notion that progressive intellectual deterioration after onset is characteristic of schizophrenia, despite some recent evidence to the contrary (Hamlin & Ward, 1965). Meehl (1962) has spoken of "cognitive slippage" or "associative dyscontrol" as central phenomena. The fact that groups of schizophrenics characteristically score below average on standardized intelligence tests during the psychosis is not adequate evidence of intellectual deterioration. It is well known that low socioeconomic status, lack of motivation, and the negative effects of institutionalization could contribute to these results. Our finding that schizophrenics score significantly lower than control groups during early childhood throws serious doubt on the idea that low scores during the psychosis reflect recent deterioration.

The best way to answer this question of deterioration is to compare premorbid intelligence test results with those taken after the onset of schizophrenia. Although some studies have compared tests during the acute psychosis with army tests at induction shortly before the breakdown, only two studies, with small samples and with contradictory results, found premorbid tests from before adulthood, and these were from adolescence (Fitzherbert, 1955; Rappaport & Webb, 1950). Fortunately, we were able to compare childhood intelligence tests given in elementary school with adult Wechsler-Bellevue tests given routinely upon hospital admission for 112 schizophrenics (Albee, Lane, Corcoran, & Werneke, 1963).

We found that IQ scores on Wechsler-Bellevue tests administered to subjects while psychotic remained at approximately the same level as the earlier IQ scores of the same people on group tests administered during second and sixth grades. Even when hospital scores were compared with the highest childhood Binet (most subjects had had more than one childhood test) for each of 98 subjects, no decline in IQ was found between tests from childhood and tests administered during the psychosis. Although these people score well below average as adults, they had continuously scored low from early childhood, long before their present diagnosis. Without the historical data, the adult performance might have been interpreted erroneously as deterioration accompanying psychosis. We found, in fact, that in many reports based on hospital tests, a psychologist had mistakenly commented that the subject was functioning well below his premorbid level.

Although intelligence tests from shortly after hospitalization showed no deterioration when compared with childhood scores, it was still possible that the deterioration spoken of by Kraepelin and others might appear during the course of hospitalization and even after discharge. We sought to find out what happened to the measured intelligence of subjects, for whom we already had childhood and admissions tests, ten or more years after the first hospital test (Batman, Albee, & Lane, 1966). Some of these subjects were still in the back wards of the hospital, but nearly half had to be located and tested at home. Of 94 subjects, one refused to cooperate, and 15 could not be located. The remaining 78 subjects were each administered the same form of the Wechsler-Bellevue previously used on hospital admission. This study is an example of how follow-up study can be combined with the method of searching for past records which were not originally gathered for research purposes.

When subjects were separated into "those still hospitalized" and "those living at home," a comparison of contemporary scores with hospital admission scores showed that no deterioration was present for the "still hospitalized" group. Even more surprising, a significant *increase* in IQ was shown for *S*s at home. Essentially the same results were obtained when the group was divided into those judged "still schizophrenic" and those judged "no longer schizophrenic," classifications which only partly overlapped with "those hospitalized" and "those not hospitalized." Recovered subjects not only scored significantly above their hospital admissions tests but significantly higher than their own childhood tests, higher than they had ever scored in their lives. The average scores of those judged "still schizophrenic" did not differ from their admission scores or from their childhood scores. The evidence is strong that schizophrenia is not accompanied by progressive deterioration of measured intelligence. Further, the relatively poor performance during both childhood and adulthood does not necessarily reflect basic capacity, because performance can improve significantly with improved circumstances and adjustment in later life.

The use of school records probably provides information on a broader range of hospitalized schizophrenics, both in terms of socioeconomic background and childhood adjustment than does the use of past records from child guidance clinics. To be representative of children who are preschizophrenic, a sample should include the great majority of future schizophrenics from the lower classes who do not receive psychiatric or psychological attention during childhood. Even clinics that offer free services would not have in their caseloads many of our subjects from the lower classes who survived childhood almost entirely by their own devices, without the availability of an adult sufficiently interested to bring them to a clinic.

Other samples may also miss the relatively well-adjusted pre-schizophrenic. Studies that use childhood psychiatric records base their reports almost entirely on schizophrenic adults who were maladjusted children. Some of our subjects did well in school; many were well liked by teachers and peers, and apparently were at least reasonably well adjusted. An excellent, but little publicized, study in the California schools (Bower et al., 1960) found that although high-school-age pre-schizophrenics generally had more emotional disturbance than peers, more than 20 per cent of them were judged normal and more than 20 per cent of a control group were judged pre-schizophrenic by each of three clinical psychologists examining school protocols and transcribed teacher interviews. Using public school records permits the inclusion of this wider range of pre-schizophrenics.

Perhaps, on the other hand, no entirely valid general statements can be made about all the people we call "schizophrenics," with their varied adult behavior patterns and the equally large variation in childhood circumstances and behavior. Some have suggested that two more or less separate patterns of schizophrenic development can be identified: process and reactive. The former is chronic and insidious; the latter, more current, precipitous, and of shorter duration. When we classified our subjects into the categories process and reactive for all those whose hospital records were complete enough for such a rating, it was found that only the process schizophrenics scored clearly below their own siblings during childhood (Heath, Albee, & Lane, 1965). We also found, however, that a much larger proportion of our subjects were classified as process and a much smaller proportion as reactive than other investigators have reported.

In a recent analysis of characteristics of schizophrenics associated with process and reactive ratings, it was found that sex and race were clearly related to this classification (Lane, 1968). Blacks were judged to be process schizophrenics significantly more often than were whites, and male schizophrenics significantly more often than female. Being black increases one's chances of being considered process; being black and male practically assures it. Three possible explanations for these findings should be explored: (a) blacks really tend to be more process schizophrenics than whites, (b) patterns of behavior considered process are more related to differences in normal subcultures in respect to race and sex than to schizophrenia, and (c) white upper-middle-class psychiatrists, whose personal judgments determine the rating, are more prejudiced against blacks and lower-class males than against whites and females.

Many of our schizophrenic sample now have children who attend the Cleveland public schools. Some of these children have taken the same group tests in second, sixth, and eighth grades that their schizophrenic parents had taken as children. Although we are not yet ready to report final results of our two-generation comparisons on intelligence, some of the preliminary findings may be of interest. Incidentally, this study illustrates one of the advantages of the method of past records over the longitudinal approach. Investigators using the longitudinal method of observation, except with animals, have not been able to watch two generations grow up, although this may sometimes be achieved by the efforts of a second generation of investigators. No such extraordinary patience and delay is required in gathering past records.

Although we anticipated children with schizophrenic mothers to fare worse than children with schizophrenic fathers, we have found just the opposite. Children with schizophrenic mothers not only score higher on intelligence tests than children of schizophrenic fathers but also score significantly higher than their own schizophrenic mothers had scored when they were children. Daughters and sons do not seem to differ in this respect. Because of the regression effect, however, we cannot at this time conclude that the higher scores of children of schizophrenic mothers differ from normal regression toward the mean. It will again be necessary to obtain control groups to answer this question.

In order to overcome what could be a serious objection to our anticipated findings — that children of schizophrenics score relatively high because of the better genetic influences of their non-schizophrenic parents — it was necessary to find the childhood intelligence scores of non-schizophrenic spouses of schizophrenics, both having attended the Cleveland public schools as children (Lane, 1967). We found that wives of schizophrenic males scored at approximately the same level of intelligence as had their husbands during childhood, but husbands of schizophrenic women scored significantly lower than their wives. If children of schizophrenics are found to score significantly higher than expected on the basis of their schizophrenic parents' childhood scores, it is not because of the influence of higher intelligence of non-schizophrenic parents. It is interesting, however, that the correlation of the children's second-grade test scores with those of their schizophrenic parents, both mothers and fathers, is approximately 0, whereas a correlation between the scores of these children and those of their non-schizophrenic parents is near the expected .50.

These results add to an expectation that children of schizophrenic parents would not do well on tests. The normal parents are no brighter, and are often much duller, than the schizophrenic parents, who are themselves below average. Further, a certain proportion of these children themselves can be expected to become schizophrenic adults. And finally, many reports in the literature stress the harmful effects of schizophrenic mothers on children.

One explanation for our tentative findings to the contrary, that children of schizophrenics perform unexpectedly well on tests, might be that many of the children in our sample, especially children with schizophrenic mothers, are not being reared at home. These are not the children included in most clinic reports of schizophrenic mother-child relationships. Our results, if validated, should fit in nicely with Waring & Ricks's (1965) findings that chronic schizophrenics frequently come from symbiotic parent-child relationships and that expulsion from the family goes with better prognosis. We are now in the midst of determining the exact life circumstance of each child before, during, and after his or her parent's hospitalization, together with a process-reactive analysis of the schizophrenic made on admission data, to understand more exactly the patterns of IQ's in relation to these variables.

Our studies have been concerned mainly with the intellectual performance of schizophrenics, both in relation to their own performance at different times of life and to the performance of relatives and peers. We have now collected intelligence test scores of schizophrenics from the time they were young children to many years after their first hospitalization, as well as the scores of their spouses, children, and various control groups. We realize that intelligence test performance is a relatively narrow aspect of development, but because we found intelligence tests were available, we studied intellectual differences between schizophrenics and others. Because Fleming was able to locate early records of the emotional status of schizophrenics, she studied emotional differences between schizophrenics and others (Fleming & Ricks, pp. 240–260). Studies like these provide data that will eventually be put together into meaningful patterns. Ex-post-facto studies may not prove cause-and-effect relationships, but they can lead to objective observations about temporal relationships that may later be understood in terms of cause.

As we believe we have demonstrated, this method of doing research stimulates new areas of investigation because records are there. For this reason, we have been led to look into areas other than the intellectual. For example, we were able to find the birth records of fifty-two adult schizophrenics and to compare their birth weights with those of their siblings (Lane & Albee, 1966). The infant who was later a schizophrenic adult was significantly lower in birth weight than the average of his own siblings, even when prematurity and birth order were controlled. These results agree with Pollin et al.'s (1966) findings with identical twins discordant for schizophrenia but not with Pollack et al.'s (1966); at present neither Pollack nor we can explain our different results. Although we do not believe the relation between low birth weight and later schizophrenia is causal, a mother's treatment of her smallest infant, as Stabenau and Pollin (pp. 94–122) have so well described, or a mother's greater emotional stress during a particular pregnancy resulting in her smallest infant, might well be factors worth further investigation.

Because we had available data on the children of schizophrenics, we became interested in the reproductive rates of schizophrenics. In our sample, married schizophrenics produce more children per marriage than the national average – results differing from some genetically oriented studies (such as Goldfarb & Erlenmeyer-Kimling, 1962), probably because of socioeconomic difference in the samples. If child-bearing is an index of heterosexuality, we are well on our way to contradicting the notion that schizophrenics are less heterosexual than the rest of us. A control sample of TB patients from the same county does not differ from schizophrenics in marriage rate or divorce rate. We believe, without all the evidence yet gathered, that they do not differ in child-bearing rate. People who are institutionalized at relatively young ages, who have a condition which carries a social stigma, and who are often hospitalized for long periods of time, all of which are true for both schizophrenics and TB patients, do not marry so often or so early as others, and those who do marry tend to divorce more frequently. These facts can be explained more parsimoniously than in terms of lack of heterosexuality.

These studies are further illustrations of the imperative need for control groups before any generalized conclusions are made that appear at first to be unique to schizophrenia. Schofield and Balian (1959) found that the overlap of common factors in the backgrounds of schizophrenics and normals is much greater than the differences. Moreover, the differences are not always in the directions our biases would have them. In their samples "normals had a greater frequency of poverty and invalidism in their childhood homes, poorer heterosexual adjustment and adequacy of sexual outlet, and a greater incidence of intellectualized, ritualized orientation toward religion." It is not just psychoanalysis, which Roff has justly criticized on this score, which can mistakenly consider circumstances common in normal development as crucial to maldevelopment.

We are also in the midst of investigating our growing suspicion of the accepted finding that schizophrenia is far more prevalent in the lowest socioeconomic group (Hollingshead & Redlich, 1958). We believe that the reported proportions are based on an artifact in the method of measuring social class. Practically all studies of the social class of schizophrenics use educational level, occupation, and place of residence as indices of this variable. Our consistent finding that as early as second grade schizophrenics were performing significantly more poorly on school tests than their own siblings led us to the conviction that they probably do not go so far in school, and do not achieve so high a subsequent occupational rating as their unaffected siblings. This means that in at least two of the three indices of social class the schizophrenic is disadvantaged, and would be rated lower than his siblings. We are now testing this hypothesis with male schizophrenics and their male siblings. To come from a lower social class than one's own siblings may be shown to be the illogical result of the conventional methods of determining social class, producing reports of exaggerated proportions of schizophrenics from the lower classes.

There are still other areas under investigation which we are not yet ready to report on. All are further examples of the fruitfulness of investigating past records that are simply stored away gathering dust. In searching for past records of schizophrenics, we have found available birth certificates, hospital records of birth, juvenile court records, welfare records, social service records of adoption and foster home placement, as well as, of course, school records and mental hospital records. An investigator has a problem in getting the cooperation of every agency he needs, but, once achieved, a gold mine of information awaits his digging.

COMMENTARY

MEDNICK. I was always very intrigued by the Schaffner result that you report in which the future schizophrenic in the upper-middle or middle social classes does not differ from his classmates in IQ.

ALBEE. The future schizophrenic from the suburbs does not differ in intelligence from his peers as measured in school.

MEDNICK. Yet his sibling has a higher IQ, which suggests that the siblings of schizophrenics have a higher than average IQ.

ALBEE. Those in the suburbs, yes.

MEDNICK. I wonder if you'd comment on that. My second question is related to the serious questions I have about the problems of the mobility and migration. Actually, migration is the most serious problem, since migration would be moving out of the county and mobility would be movement within a city or within a county. Dr. Lane suggested that this is not a serious problem, because most of the studies that I referred to in the paper where I criticize this problem refer to rural-urban migration. The 1967 Lansing and Mueller book suggests that even intra- and inter-city mobility would be migration, and certainly they are thinking of intercounty or interstate mobility. This kind of mobility is highly associated with education level and social class. It's hard to know how much of a problem it is, but there's at least a small problem in that the people you've studied were all non-migrant; and it's possible that if you took accountants who are non-migrant, they'd have a lower IQ too. It seemed from Lansing and Mueller's finding that anybody who was not migrant would tend to have a lower IQ.

ALBEE. Well, we're in the midst of trying to think through the questions raised in your paper. I don't know how to account for the first finding which you point out, except that that's the way the data came out. Just to refresh the memories of the rest of you, the suburban children who later became schizophrenic did not differ in intelligence from others in their school classes, but they were significantly lower in IQ than their own siblings – which would suggest, as Dr. Mednick points out, that the siblings of suburban schizophrenics are from an even higher socioeconomic or intellectual group. This again suggests that perhaps we are on the trail of a hypothesis that says it's the treatment of the least intelligent child in the family that is the significant variable, that it's the mother's attitude toward the smallest or least intelligent child, or that this particular child was conceived and carried during an especially stressful period in the mother's life, which then affected the relationship between mother and child. I'm just speculating, but this would be consistent with these kinds of data. So far as the questions about mobility are concerned, we have one study in progress which I hope will elucidate this problem. For the past two years we've been in the process of collecting data on schizophrenics in Hawaii. We had been looking for a long time for a place where there is little out-migration. Happily, we discovered that in the state of Hawaii practically everyone hospitalized goes to the Hawaii State Hospital, and some 85 per cent of the population of the state lives on Oahu, most of them in Honolulu. There is almost no out-migration of the lower classes from Hawaii, since twenty-five hundred miles of ocean are an impenetrable barrier. Thus, I hope that we'll soon have data that will throw some light on this migration question. We are collecting data on the school achievement, and the occupational status of male schizophrenics and their male siblings in Hawaii. Because of the availability of almost total sample data through the school system records, and also because of relatively better chances of getting school completion and occupational information, we hope to be able to answer all these questions on the basis of the sample we're collecting in Hawaii.

MEDNICK. I'd like to mention that we did look at the educational level of individuals hospitalized in Ypsilanti State Hospital who had come from out of state versus those who were born in the state. The ones who had come from out of state had, as a matter of fact, a significantly higher education level.

ALBEE. Well, I think we are building a logical structure that says if future schizophrenics perform poorer on intelligence tests than their own siblings through second-, sixth-, and eighth-grade measures, it seems reasonable to hypothesize that they don't go so far as their siblings in school. They stop their education earlier. Intelligence is a significant variable as related to amount of school completion. Therefore, they would not be qualified for the same level of jobs as their own siblings. One of the chronic frustrating problems involves trying to get accurate information on school achievement, because people don't tell you the truth about this. Informants don't tell you the truth, subjects themselves don't tell you the truth, and if the school records are not clear, as they are not in Cleveland, you really run into a very serious problem in getting this information. Fortunately, in the school system of Honolulu, this information is recorded.

STRAUSS. Have you taken the lowest IQ's in childhood and the highest IQ's of the pre-schizophrenic subjects and noticed any differences in the course of illness or of their future hospitalizations?

ALBEE. We haven't done that.

RICKS. Are you planning to get cross-cultural results in Hawaii?

ALBEE. Yes, we have this information recorded, and we hope to make this kind of cultural comparison. There are many studies possible—for example, on the delusional content of schizophrenics from these various social backgrounds in Hawaii. This can lead to all sorts of further studies. There are lots of other problems there that have not been investigated.

RICKS. I just noticed what may be an interesting consistency, perhaps, or a parallel between some data in your paper and those presented by Dr. Hathaway, despite the obvious differences in your sample and your criteria for picking the sample. And that is that there was a much greater tendency for his high 8 girls, when they got older, to marry men of a lower socioeconomic status or a lower occupation, and you found the difference between the comparison spouses and the husbands of the pre-schizophrenic women.

ALBEE. Yes. We're intrigued by this. Dr. Lane has just published a paper summarizing these data in somewhat more detail, and one can have fun speculating about such questions as how the schizoid or schizophrenic girl is chosen by a man of lower intelligence. Well, you can think of a lot of possible reasons for this, but it is a finding consistent with Dr. Hathaway's paper.

QUESTION. You mention that your finding that the number of children born to married schizophrenics was at variance with the findings of some of the genetic studies. I don't know which ones you're referring to, but I just wanted to mention that the studies started by Dr. Kallman in New York State Psychiatric Institute now being carried on by Dr. Erlenmeyer-Kimling are very similar to this as far as the number of children born to married schizophrenics or the number of children per family. It's in the number of children born to schizophrenics as a whole, if you take married and unmarried, where you find the decrease, and not in the number of children.

ALBEE. Yes, we agree. Of course the fact that schizophrenics, and particularly schizophrenic women, no longer spend so much time in institutions as they did twenty-five years ago means that they're out on the open market, so to speak, during a much more significant part of their lives. This would suggest that they might marry or have the opportunity of conceiving more frequently, and therefore we would see an increase in the number of children as a consequence of this factor.

MEDNICK. I would like to respond further to the points raised by Lane and Albee concerning the influence of migration on their findings. From the census study *Mobility for Metropolitan Areas* and by reference to age-specific rates of migrancy, we can determine that about 63 per cent of the school age population migrates from the standard metropolitan statistical area of Cleveland over a period of twenty-five years. Those who migrate tend to be of higher IQ, social class, and educational level. Since the Lane-Albee schizophrenic samples are almost totally non-migrant, resident hospital patients it is not too surprising that they have a somewhat lower IQ than their more mobile former schoolmates. Many of the higher-IQ future schizophrenics among their former schoolmates probably migrated and thus would have been missed by the resident hospital sampling method. Dr. Lawrence Appleby and I conducted a small exploratory study into this question. In a Michigan state hospital (Ypsilanti) we compared the educational achievement of native, non-migrant Michigan schizophrenics with the educational achievement of schizophrenics who had been born in other states. Whereas 8 per cent of the non-migrant schizophrenics had completed college, 29 per cent of the schizophrenics out of state had completed college. If Lane and Albee could trace the school IQ's of the out-of-state schizophrenics in the Cleveland hospitals, their findings might change. They might also compare their non-migrant schizophrenics with other Cleveland non-migrants.

One more point . . . Lane and Albee "believe that these factors [migrancy] and others were better controlled in a subsequent study which compared the test performance of pre-schizophrenics with that of their own siblings" (p. 193). This implies that by controlling for sibling status they were in some way controlling for migrancy. There is no guarantee that a schizophrenic's sibling will not move. The non-schizophrenic was doubtless more migrant than his completely non-migrant schizophrenic sibling. Sibling status does not control for the effects of migration.

LANE. The mass exodus of middle- and upper-class whites from Cleveland to the suburbs and nearby towns,* did not come from the poorer neighborhoods, schools, and social backgrounds that characterized most of our pre-schizophrenics and their matched controls. Study after study, without regard to place of birth, has shown that schizophrenics are predominantly from the lower classes, as were ours and their controls. If, then, as Mednick states, "Those who migrate tend to be of higher IQ, *social class*, and educational level [italics mine]," such migrants are not typical of the people used as controls in our studies. Movement to the suburbs by Cleveland Negroes, who made up 30 to 40 per cent of our samples, was almost nonexistent until very recently, in contrast to other large Northern cities. Thus, the amount of migration out of the city of Cleveland among the particular control groups used in our studies was probably much lower than Mednick estimates.

Although most of our controls would have done well to have moved to other areas within the city of Cleveland, it is difficult to believe that those who moved out of the city from the poorer neighborhoods were necessarily more intelligent. Some families, for example, who returned to the South (not all subjects or controls were born in Cleveland), may or may not have been bright for their backgrounds, but they probably did not perform better on intelligence tests than their classmates from Cleveland or elsewhere who stayed in Cleveland. Certainly, factors other than intelligence (if intelligence at all) are involved in the psychology of moving from a large city, especially if social class and ethnic backgrounds are controlled. Since neighborhood elementary schools in Cleveland were conspicuously homogeneous in race, religion, ethnic background, and socioeconomic level (which varied most in Negro areas), the argument that mobility influenced our results requires that only the more intelligent persons within each of these social strata later migrated out of Cleveland. Because we used the median class score as the control for each pre-schizophrenic, even if we had eliminated some high scores from each class (on Mednick's thesis that the brightest children from each neighborhood later migrated), we would not have affected the comparisons very much or the conclusions at all. However, this procedure is questionable because findings based on the migration of Southern Negroes to the North do not apply to black and white migration out of Cleveland.

Similar reasoning applies to Mednick's argument that our methods

* Among movers nationwide, some two thirds remain in the same county, and over three fourths of the native-born spend most of their lives in the state of their birth. These rates include data from states with much higher out-migration than Ohio. (M. Speigelman, *Introduction to Demography*. Cambridge, Mass.: Harvard University Press, 1968.)

missed a large number of bright schizophrenics. High rates of mental disorder reported for migrants are not based on the kinds of people that moved from Cleveland to the suburbs, rates for whom may have been extremely low, but, as far as I have seen, are based on the kinds of mobile groups more typically moving into Cleveland: Southern Negroes, Appalachian whites, Puerto Ricans, and American Indians. Furthermore, there is no evidence to negate the hypothesis that even those Clevelanders with presumedly higher than average IQ's, who left the city and became schizophrenic, performed more poorly on childhood tests than their socially equal, mostly suburban-bound, non-schizophrenic peers and siblings; unless, of course, they migrated to Ypsilanti, Michigan. Our study of higher IQ schizophrenics from the suburbs showed that they also performed more poorly than their siblings.

In summary, Mednick has calculated rates of migration for a whole city (which I believe are themselves too high) as representative of smaller areas within the city; he has used high rates of mental disorder found for some migrant minority groups as representative of the people who migrated from Cleveland; and he has indicated that a single factor, childhood intelligence, can distinguish between those within each small neighborhood who later moved out of city limits and those who remained. Although no present demographic study has supported or implied these contentions, it would not be difficult in further research to settle the specific issues of mobility and schizophrenia that Mednick has raised.

REFERENCES

Albee, G. W., E. A. Lane, C. Corcoran, & A. Wernecke. Childhood and intercurrent intellectual performances of adult schizophrenics. *Journal of Consulting Psychology*, 1963, 27, 364–366.

Albee, G. W., E. A. Lane, & J. Reuter. Childhood intelligence of future schizophrenics and neighborhood peers. *Journal of Psychology*, 1964, 58, 141–144.

Arieti, S. (Ed.) *American handbook of psychiatry*. New York: Basic Books, 1959.

Batman, R., G. W. Albee, & E. A. Lane. Intelligence test performance of recovered and chronic schizophrenics. *Proceedings of the 74th annual convention of the American Psychological Association*. Washington, D.C.: APA, 1966.

Bower, E. M., T. A. Shellhammer, J. M. Daily, M. Bower, & D. Blain. High school students who later became schizophrenic. *Bulletin of the California State Department of Education*, 1960, 29 (No. 8).

Fitzherbert, J. Increase in intelligence quotient at onset of schizophrenia: Three adolescent cases. *British Journal of Medical Psychology*, 1955, 28, 191–193.

Goldfarb, C., & L. Erlenmeyer-Kimling. Mating and fertility trends in schizophrenia. In F. J. Kallman (Ed.), *Expanding goals in genetics in psychiatry*. New York: Grune & Stratton, 1962.

Hamlin, R. M., & W. Ward. Aging, hospitalization, and schizophrenic intelligence. *Proceedings of the 73rd annual convention of the American Psychological Association*. Washington, D.C.: APA, 1965. Pp. 221–222.

Heath, E. B., G. W. Albee, & E. A. Lane. Predisorder intelligence of process and reactive schizophrenics and their siblings. *Proceedings of the 73rd annual convention of the American Psychological Association*. Washington, D.C.: APA, 1965. Pp. 223–224.

Hoerr, N., & A. Osol. (Eds.) *Blakiston's new Gould medical dictionary*, 2nd ed. New York: Blakiston Division, McGraw-Hill, 1956.

Hollingshead, A. B., & F. C. Redlich. *Social class and mental illness.* New York: Wiley, 1958.

Lane, E. A. Patterns of change in childhood intelligence tests of psychotic adults. Unpublished Ph.D. thesis, Western Reserve University, 1958.

———. The intelligence of spouses of schizophrenics. *Psychological Record*, 1967, 17, 477–481.

———. The influence of sex and race on process-reactive ratings of schizophrenics. *Journal of Psychology*, 1968, 68, 15–20.

——— & G. W. Albee. Childhood intellectual development of adult schizophrenics. *Journal of Abnormal and Social Psychology*, 1963, 67, 186–189.

———. Childhood intellectual differences between schizophrenic adults and their siblings. *American Journal of Orthopsychiatry*, 1965, 35, 747–753.

———. The comparative birth weights of adult schizophrenics and their siblings. *Journal of Psychology*, 1966, 64, 227–231.

———. On childhood intellectual decline of adult schizophrenics: A reassessment of an earlier study. *Journal of Abnormal Psychology*, 1968, 73, 174–177.

Levine, S. The effects of experience on adult behavior. In A. J. Bachrach (Ed.), *Experimental foundations of clinical psychology*. New York: Basic Books, 1962.

Mednick, S. A., & T. McNeil. Current methodology in research on the etiology of schizophrenia. Serious difficulties which suggest the use of high-risk group method. *Psychological Bulletin*, 1968, 70, 681–693.

Mednick, S. A., & F. Schulsinger. A longitudinal study of children with a high risk for schizophrenia: A preliminary report. In S. G. Vandenberg (Ed.), *Methods and goals in human behavior genetics.* New York: Academic Press, 1965.

Meehl, P. E. Schizotaxia, schizotypy, schizophrenia. *American Psychologist*, 1962, 12, 827–838.

Pollack, M., M. G. Woerner, W. Goodman, & I. M. Greenbert. Childhood development patterns of hospitalized adult schizophrenics and non-schizophrenic patients and their siblings. *American Journal of Orthopsychiatry*, 1966, 36, 510–517.

Pollin, W., J. R. Stabenau, L. Mosher, & J. Jopin. Life history differences in identical twins discordant for schizophrenia. *American Journal of Orthopsychiatry*, 1966, 36, 492–509.

Rappaport, S. R., & W. B. Webb. An attempt to study intellectual deterioration by pre-morbid testing. *Journal of Consulting Psychology*, 1950, 14, 95–98.

Schaffner, A., G. W. Albee, & E. A. Lane. Intellectual differences between suburban preschizophrenics and their siblings. *Journal of Consulting Psychology*, 1967, 31, 326–327.

Schofield, W., & L. Balian. A comparative study of the personal histories of schizophrenic and nonpsychiatric patients. *Journal of Abnormal and Social Psychology*, 1959, 59, 216–225.

Skodak, M. Paper presented at the meeting of the Cleveland Psychological Association, Spring 1966. Original not seen.

Waring, M., & D. F. Ricks. Family patterns of children who became adult schizophrenics. *Journal of Nervous and Mental Disease*, 1965, 140, 351–364.

MAX POLLACK
MARGARET G. WOERNER
DONALD F. KLEIN

A Comparison of Childhood Characteristics of Schizophrenics, Personality Disorders, and Their Siblings

THIS volume attests to the current recognition that the study of developmental patterns relates to the broader problem of the etiology of adult psychiatric syndromes. In our laboratory three hypotheses have guided our research efforts in this area: (a) that adult schizophrenia is not a single disease entity; (b) that developmental variables may be crucial for discriminating among subgroups; (c) that some childhood abnormalities may reflect basic temperamental or cognitive deviancies that do not result solely from malignant environmental influences or child rearing practices. In this we have been influenced by the longitudinal studies of Thomas, Chess, and Birch (1968), who showed that the early temperamental characteristics of children who later developed behavioral disturbances differed significantly from those of their normal sibs.

Our early studies indicated that hospitalized nonchronic schizophrenic patients with histories of severe childhood behavioral abnormality were treated and hospitalized at an earlier age (Belmont, Birch, Klein, & Pollack, 1964), had a poorer response to psychotropic drug treatment (Klein, 1967), made a poorer post-hospital adjustment (Pollack, Levenstein, & Klein, 1968), had lower IQ's, greater perceptual-cognitive impairment (Belmont et al., 1964), and a greater frequency of EEG abnormality (Kennard, Pollack, & Klein, 1966) than those with unremarkable childhood histories.

We then attempted to investigate whether specific variables or patterns of childhood deviance could be identified and related to adult psychiatric status.

NOTE: The study was supported in part by NIMH contract PH 43-66-44, grants MH 12273 and K3MH 19299 (Research Career Development Award, Dr. Pollack).

One important aspect of our research strategy has been the use of two types of comparison groups: First, we have employed siblings as an appropriate non-patient matched comparison group, since they provide better control for factors such as socioeconomic status, home environment, and genetic factors than do unrelated subjects. Second, we have studied, in addition to schizophrenic patients, those with non-schizophrenic diagnoses so as to evaluate whether deviant childhood patterns are specific to schizophrenia or are characteristic of other psychiatric diagnoses as well.

Our first study (Pollack, Woerner, Goodman, & Greenberg, 1966), which we began in 1963, was a pilot project in which we compared childhood characteristics of forty-four young adult psychiatric patients with their closest-in-age siblings. Blind ratings of developmental variables were based on information obtained by a parent questionnaire and interview. Schizophrenic patients, as a group, were rated as significantly more irritable, shy, dependent, and nonaffectionate in childhood than their sibs. They had significantly more conduct problems and neurotic traits, were poorer in school performance, had more difficulties in peer relationships, and were rated poorer on overall childhood adjustment. However, similar differences were found when patients with diagnoses of personality trait disturbance and chronic brain syndrome were compared with their sibs.

Our findings are in essential agreement with the two other studies that have compared childhood personality characteristics in schizophrenic patients and their sibs. Prout and White (1956) studied two aspects of childhood, disappointments (reactions to physical and psychological trauma) and personality, in thirty upper-class hospitalized schizophrenic patients and their "healthy" siblings. The pre-schizophrenic child was described as more sensitive and dependent, less happy and less social than his sib.

Alanen (1966) compared Finnish hospitalized schizophrenics and neurotics with their sibs on developmental, psychological, and psychiatric measures. The schizophrenic index cases were more autistic, seclusive, and dependent on their parents in childhood than were their sibs. Seclusiveness and dependency were also more frequent in the neurotic index cases than in their sibs' histories, but the differences were less marked than for the schizophrenic patients.

All of these sibling studies have depended completely upon retrospective information about childhood characteristics. In our current investigation we have attempted to improve the validity of our variables by incorporating information derived from birth and school records, free of retrospective distortion.

The overall design of the current study, described in detail below, was a comparison of the childhood and adult characteristics of schizophrenic and nonschizophrenic patients and their sibs.

Method

Hillside Hospital is a nonprofit psychiatric hospital with a bed capacity of two hundred one and a patient-professional staff ratio of approximately one to one. Patients, all voluntarily admitted, receive all in-hospital treatment required regardless of ability to pay. Provision is made for relatively long-term in-hospital treatment when necessary; not infrequently this may be more than a year.

SUBJECTS

Consecutive admissions to Hillside Hospital from November 1, 1965, to September 30, 1966, were included in the study if the patients met the following criteria: (a) were between the ages of 15 and 35 inclusive; (b) had a biological sibling between the ages of 13 and 37; (c) had a mother who had reared both the patient and his sibling and was available for interview at the hospital. Negro and Puerto Rican patients were excluded, to reduce social heterogeneity.

Patients. During the eleven-month sampling period, 153 patients met the criteria previously outlined for admission to the study, and of these, 127 were included. The remaining 26 patients were excluded for the following reasons: 8 required medication before the examination period (psychotropic medication would have had a marked influence on psychological test performance and electroencephalograms), the siblings of 7 patients were not available for study, 4 mothers refused to cooperate, and 2 mothers were incompetent reporters. In addition, 5 other patients were excluded from the data analyses: 3 were twins, and in two cases the only sibling was mentally defective.

Siblings. A total of 184 sibs were included. In-person interviews were conducted with 148 of these. Of the 36 sibs not seen, 28 refused to cooperate, 5 lived too far away, and in 3 cases the patient was discharged before the scheduled appointment with his sibs. The 36 sibs who were not seen were nevertheless rated as normal, moderately impaired, or severely impaired on the basis of information obtained from parents and reports from treatment centers. No difference in the distribution of these ratings was found when they were compared with the ratings of the 148 sibs seen directly. In view of this, the 36 sibs have been included in our analyses.

SAMPLE CHARACTERISTICS

Of the 127 patients, 46 were diagnosed as schizophrenic, 68 as personality disorder (most were hysterical, emotionally unstable or passive-aggressive), 7 as psychoneurotic, and 6 as affective disorder. (Details of our diagnostic procedures are described below.) The sex distribution, mean age, socioeconomic status (SES), and education (completed years of schooling) for the schizophrenic and personality disorder groups are presented in Table 1. SES was based on the Hollingshead two-factor index of occupation and education. Because of the large percentage of young subjects who were economically dependent on the family, the SES of the head of the household during the child-rearing period was chosen to represent both the patient and the siblings. The patients in the two major diagnostic groups did not differ significantly in mean age, education, or SES. The sibs of the schizophrenic group were significantly ($p<.05$) better educated than the sibs of the personality disorders.

Table 1. Group Characteristics of Patients and Siblings

Group	*N*	Male	Female	Mean Age	Mean SES[a]	Mean Education
Schizophrenics						
Patients	46	24	22	20.91	3.22	12.52
Siblings	64	33	31	21.52		13.45
Personality disorder						
Patients	68	26	42	20.01	3.03	12.06
Siblings	104	44	60	20.12		11.96

[a] Head of household.

The present psychiatric hospital admission was the first for 59 per cent of the schizophrenic patients and 71 per cent of the personality disorders. The difference was not statistically significant.

	Siblings of Schizophrenic Patients	*Siblings of Personality Disorder Patients*
Normal	58%	52%
Moderately abnormal	25	33
Severely abnormal (including those hospitalized)	17	10
Hospitalized	14	6

Of the 64 sibs of schizophrenic patients, 58 per cent were rated psychiatrically normal, and 8 per cent (5 sibs) were diagnosed schizophrenic. The most frequent diagnosis among the remaining abnormal sibs was personality disorder (25 per cent of the total). Other diagnoses include adjustment reactions, psychoneuroses, and affective disorders. The accompanying tabulation presents the distribution of ratings of severity of disturbance. Of the 11 sibs rated as having a severe disorder, 9 had been hospitalized. These include the 5 sibs diagnosed schizophrenic, in addition to 2 hospitalized with diagnoses of personality disorder, a psychoneurosis, and an affective psychosis.

Of the 104 sibs of patients diagnosed personality disorder, 52 per cent were rated normal, 33 per cent had personality disorders, and only one sib was diagnosed schizophrenic. Other diagnoses include adjustment reactions and affective disorders. Finally, 9 per cent (9 sibs) were categorized as having a severe psychiatric disorder. All but one of these was diagnosed as having a personality disorder, and 4 of the 9 sibs had been hospitalized.

More detailed descriptions of the psychiatric status of the patients and their sibs have been reported previously (Pollack, Woerner, Goldberg, & Klein, 1969).

ADULT EXAMINATIONS

Interviewing and testing of patients was conducted during the fourth week of hospitalization. All psychotropic medication had been withdrawn, and no somatic therapy had been given for the preceding three weeks. Sibs came to the hospital for testing, usually within a week or two of the patient's examination. The following procedures composed the adult examinations for patients and sibs: (a) psychiatric interview conducted jointly by a psychiatrist and a psychologist; (b) WAIS or WISC; (c) MMPI; (d) Perceptual Analytic Rorschach (a test designed to measure thinking disorder, Belmont et al., 1964); and (e) EEG.

The psychologists administering the psychological tests were ignorant of the diagnoses of the subjects; Rorschachs were scored "blind."

Diagnosis. At the end of the psychiatric interview, the psychiatrist and psychologist each independently diagnosed the patient, and at the end of the study, the patients' charts were reviewed by yet another psychiatrist. (Almost all of the patients had been discharged after close to a year's hospital stay; thus the chart contained a great deal of information, including a number of diagnostic interviews.) At a joint conference all three investigators reviewed and compared their diagnoses, and discrepancies were reconciled. The final diagnoses were based on a review of the patient's past history, his research interview, and his course in the hospital. The diagnosis of schizophrenia was made conservatively — that is, all patients diagnosed schizophrenic had unequivocal evidence of a thinking disorder.

The procedure for diagnosing the sibling was similar to that for the patient. Records were obtained concerning any psychiatric treatment. When the sibling had no treatment history, the diagnosis was based on the psychiatric interview. In addition to diagnosis, the two interviewers independently rated each sibling on a six-point scale of severity of disorder. Later, these ratings, together with the treatment histories, were translated into the following three point rating scheme: (a) normal or adequate functioning; free of current psychiatric symptomatology beyond a mild degree, with no history of psychiatric treatment or impairment of functioning which would have warranted treatment; (b) moderately impaired functioning; having current psychiatric disorder *or* a history of psychiatric treatment or impaired functioning; (c) severely impaired; having a history of psychosis or disorder severe enough to have warranted hospitalization, whether or not hospitalization took place.

CHILDHOOD CHARACTERISTICS

Our developmental data were derived from three sources: retrospective reports by the parents, obtained by means of questionnaire and interview; examination of school records, including the confidential reports; hospital obstetrical records and the confidential medical report filed with the New York City birth certificate.

The following is a summary of the types of variables composing our life history data:

Perinatal History. This category includes variables dealing with maternal reproductive history, pregnancy course, labor and delivery, and neonatal condition.

Birth to Two Years. The major categories of variables deal with health, motor and speech development, feeding, sleeping, and temperament.

Two to Five Years. In addition to the above, items covering conduct problems, nervous habits and symptoms, obsessive traits, and fears and worries were included.

Five to Twelve Years. This age period has been the main focus of our attention, and we have attempted to sample a wide range of variables dealing with personality and behavior. In addition to those mentioned above, the categories of items included at this age level are summarized in the list below. The rationale for concentrating on this particular era in development was based on two major considerations: First, information from school records on many variables could be obtained and compared with the retrospective information obtained from parents. Second, this period predates, for almost all of our subjects, the manifest symptoms associated with their current psychiatric illness.

Temperament	Dependence
Interests	Affectionate
Friendships	Mood
Social participation	Emotional responsivity
Isolation	Compliance
Communicative	School behavior
Shyness	Learning problems
Aggressiveness	Academic progress

Thirteen to Sixteen Years. In contrast, this early adolescent period cannot be considered premorbid for many of our patients (and some sibs) since they were beginning to display symptoms of severe psychiatric disturbance. Therefore, in addition to the variables described for the two- to five-year period, we have confined ourselves at this age level to dealing with more global items describing changes in mood, self-reliance, friendships, group participation, eating and sleeping patterns, and interests. In addition, adolescent physical changes and heterosexual interests were also included.

School Records. Elementary and junior high school records on patients and sibs were obtained and information in the following areas was coded "blind": personality and behavioral ratings, interests, attendance, special problems, academic grades, achievement tests (reading and arithmetic), and intelligence tests.

Statistical Analysis. Our intent is to perform a number of different statistical operations. The first will be univariate analyses for each of the variables comparing the patient with his psychiatrically normal sib and the patient with his moderately abnormal sib by major diagnostic group. For the statistically significant variables, analyses by patient diagnostic subgroup will be undertaken. Also, for these significant variables schizophrenic patients can be compared with personality disorder patients. For each of the diagnostic groups, selected childhood variables can be correlated with appropriate adult psychiatric, psychological, and EEG measures. The material also lends itself to multivariate procedures and discriminant function analyses between patients (by diagnostic grouping) and their sibs for childhood and adult characteristics.

PROGRESS OF THE STUDY TO DATE

Analyses of only a few childhood variables have been completed; these indicate that schizophrenic patients differed from their normal sibs with respect to the mothers' reports of the occurrence of fears, worries, and obsessions during early and middle childhood. Personality disorder patients also differed significantly from their normal sibs in childhood; for this group the differences appeared greatest for conduct disturbance variables, but differences were also found for fears and worries. Because these analyses are incomplete, we cannot at this time readily summarize our data. We have sufficient data, however, on intellectual functioning in childhood and at the time of current hospitalization (adolescence and adulthood) to provide a preliminary summary.

Results

Intellectual Differences between Psychiatric Patients and Their Sibs in Childhood and Adulthood. In a series of studies, Lane and Albee (1965) and Schaffner, Lane, and Albee (1967) have shown that adult hospitalized schizophrenics scored significantly lower on IQ tests taken in the second, sixth, and eighth grades than their non-hospitalized sibs. The IQ scores among non-hospitalized sibs of schizophrenic patients correlated positively in the expected range; in contrast, the correlations between the patient-to-be and his sibs were not significant (Lane & Albee, 1965). Furthermore, the scores of these adult patients tested while in hospital were not significantly lower than they had been in childhood (Albee, Lane, Corcoran, & Werneke, 1963).

Several gaps exist in our knowledge of this area which, when filled, will aid in evaluating the significance of intellectual functioning for the etiology and course of schizophrenia. These are: (1) we do not have comparable childhood data for adult hospitalized non-schizophrenic psychiatric groups; (2) we have no comparisons of intellectual functioning between psychiatric patients and their sibs in adulthood; (3) we have little information on the psychiatric status of the comparison sibs other than the fact that they were not hospitalized. We should like to present some data that may elucidate the findings in this area.

Adult IQ of Patients and Normal Sibs. For all of the analyses to be described, we have employed only those patients who had at least one normal sib; only the normal sibs are included. When the patient had more than one normal sib, the one closest in age served as the control. This procedure was followed for the analyses of childhood IQ's as well.

The mean IQ scores for the patients and their sibs are shown in Table 2. Both schizophrenic and personality disorder patients scored within the average range; however, they were significantly inferior to their sibs. The subtest patterns were similar for all four groups, with Verbal Scale scores higher than Performance Scale scores. For both diagnostic groups, patients' scores on vocabulary, digit span, digit symbol, comprehension, picture completion, and object assembly were significantly lower than those of their sibs.

The mean scores of the schizophrenic patients did not differ significantly from those of the personality disorder group on any of the scales or subtests.

Product-moment correlations between IQ scores of patients and their sibs were significant only for the Verbal Scale (.36, $p<.05$, for the schizophrenic group, and .42, $p<.01$, for the personality disorder group). The exclusion of WISC scores did not alter the correlations.

Patient's Age at Onset of Symptomatology and Adult IQ Scores. Patients were subdivided into three groups (childhood, before 13; early adolescence, 13–16; late adolescence and adulthood, after 16), on the basis of their age at the time that serious symptoms related to their current disorder first appeared in their histories. For both diagnostic groups, patients with childhood onset had the lowest mean IQ scores.

Table 3 presents the relation between the age of onset measure and patient-sib IQ differences. Schizophrenic patients with childhood onset

Table 2. Adult IQ Scores of Patients and Normal Siblings

	Full Scale		Verbal Scale		Performance Scale	
Group	Mean	SD	Mean	SD	Mean	SD
Schizophrenics [a]						
Patients	106.6	14.5	112.7	14.1	97.7	14.9
Siblings	114.7	9.9	118.9	10.4	107.0	10.0
Mean difference	−8.1**		−6.2*		−9.3**	
Personality Disorders [b]						
Patients	109.3	14.3	114.1	13.2	101.5	14.7
Siblings	116.0	8.0	119.2	9.2	109.2	8.9
Mean difference	−6.7**		−5.1*		−7.7**	

[a] $N=27$. [b] $N=33$. * $p<.05$. ** $p<.01$.

Table 3. IQ Scores Grouped by Patient's Age at Onset of Psychiatric Disorder

Age at Onset	No. of Patient-Sib Pairs	Patient Mean IQ	Sib Mean IQ	Mean Difference
	Schizophrenics			
Childhood	9			
Full		99.4	115.3	−15.9*
Verbal		108.3	119.7	−11.4
Performance		87.8	107.4	−19.6*
Early adolescent	8			
Full		110.4	114.5	−4.1
Verbal		114.2	118.1	−3.9
Performance		103.5	107.2	−3.7
Late adolescent and adult	10			
Full		110.1	114.3	−4.2
Verbal		115.3	118.7	−3.4
Performance		101.9	106.4	−4.5
	Personality Disorders			
Childhood	13			
Full		103.2	116.3	−13.1**
Verbal		108.4	120.0	−11.6**
Performance		96.5	109.4	−12.9*
Early adolescent	11			
Full		112.3	118.9	−6.6**
Verbal		117.2	120.9	−3.7
Performance		104.1	113.6	−9.5**
Late adolescent and adult	9			
Full		114.2	111.9	2.3
Verbal		118.7	115.9	2.8
Performance		105.6	104.9	0.7

*$p < .05$ one-tailed t test. **$p < .025$ one-tailed t test.

had significantly lower Performance and Full Scale IQ scores than their sibs, whereas those with early adolescent or late adolescent and adult onset did not differ from their sibs on any of the IQ measures. Personality disorder patients with childhood onset had significantly lower scores than their sibs on all three IQ measures; those with early adolescent onset were lower than their sibs on Performance and Full Scale IQ; and those with late adolescent and adult onset did not differ from their sibs.

CHILDHOOD INTELLIGENCE TESTS

Although the school record data have not yet been completely processed, we have made some analyses so that we could present a preview of findings on the childhood IQ's of our patients and their normal sibs.

For these analyses we culled from the records those group tests which were most frequently given to our subjects within particular grade levels. The testing program in the New York City schools has not been so systematic as we should have wished; however, we were able to obtain reasonable samples on the following group tests:

a. Pintner-Cunningham Primary Test (kindergarten–second grade, K–2 Pintner): 94 per cent were given in the first grade; a small number given in kindergarten (3 per cent) and second grade (3 per cent) have been included.

b. Otis Quick Scoring Mental Abilities Test (third–fifth grade, 3–5 Otis): primarily given in third grade (82 per cent); a small number given in the fourth (12 per cent) and fifth grades (6 per cent) have been included.

c. Otis Quick Scoring Mental Abilities Test (sixth–eighth grade, 6–8 Otis): primarily given in sixth grade (76 per cent); a small number given in the seventh (12 per cent) and eighth grades (12 per cent) have been included.

d. Pintner Intermediate Test (sixth–eighth grade, 6–8 Pintner): primarily given in eighth grade (66 per cent); 24 per cent were given in the sixth and 10 per cent in the seventh grade.

Because different tests have been used at the various grade levels, and the scores may not be directly comparable, we have refrained from making longitudinal comparisons of scores for the same subjects across tests. Instead, we have compared patients' and siblings' scores on each test separately, and have employed correlational techniques for longitudinal comparisons.

Diagnostic Group Differences. Table 4 presents the mean scores on

Table 4. Childhood IQ's of Schizophrenic and Personality Disorder Patients

Group	K–2 Pintner	3–5 Otis	6–8 Otis	6–8 Pintner
Schizophrenic patients				
N	18	17	17	10
Mean IQ	104.3	105.4	112.4	113.3
SD	16.3	16.9	14.5	22.7
Personality disorder patients				
N	15	16	17	12
Mean IQ	100.7	104.7	109.5	121.6
SD	14.5	10.7	13.7	22.8
t	0.64	0.13	0.59	0.81

Table 5. Patient-Sibling IQ Differences in Childhood

Subject	K–2 Pintner	3–5 Otis	6–8 Otis
Schizophrenic			
Patient			
Mean	104.4	105.5	113.4
SD	16.4	17.1	15.2
Normal sibling			
Mean	114.5	114.6	114.9
SD	16.0	10.6	13.1
Patient-sibling difference	−10.1	−9.1	−1.5
p	<.05	N.S.	N.S.
Number of pairs	15	14	11
Personality Disorder			
Patient			
Mean	101.9	108.7	105.6
SD	15.1	7.1	17.4
Normal			
Mean	123.0	122.9	122.2
SD	15.1	13.2	16.5
Patient-sibling difference	−21.1	−14.2	−16.6
p	<.005	<.005	<.05
Number of pairs	13	10	8

each test for the schizophrenic and personality disorder patients. Since not all patients had scores for each test, the samples vary somewhat from one comparison to another. It can be seen, however, that there is no indication of a significant difference in mean IQ score between schizophrenic patients and personality disorder patients on any of the childhood tests. These findings parallel our findings for current adult individual IQ tests reported in the preceding section (Table 2).

Patient-Sibling Differences. Table 5 presents the patient-sib IQ comparisons for each childhood test. The 6–8 Pintner was excluded because too few matched pairs were available. For each childhood test we used only those pairs from the total sample for which we had scores for both the patient and his closest-in-age normal sib.*

The table indicates that patients scored lower than their sibs on each childhood test. The difference is significant for the K–2 Pintner; it is of about the same magnitude, but falls just short of statistical significance on the 3–5 Otis. The patient-sib differences on the 6–8 Otis do not approach

* As a check on the representativeness of these partial samples, we also computed the mean Full Scale adult IQ's for the same pairs that were compared on the childhood tests. For each of the partial samples, the finding reported in the previous section for the total sample was confirmed — that is, patients scored significantly lower than their normal sibs on adult Full Scale IQ. The adult means for patients and sibs in the partial samples were very close to those for the total sample.

statistical significance. Further discussion of longitudinal trends must await further analyses, but it should be pointed out that nothing in our data indicates a decline in intellectual performance at any point during the elementary school years.

For the personality disorder group, Table 5 indicates that patients scored significantly lower than their sibs on all three childhood IQ tests. Thus, these findings indicate that the inferiority of patients compared with their own normal sibs on tests of intellectual ability is not unique to schizophrenics, but is equally characteristic of patients with diagnoses of personality disorder.

INTER-TEST CORRELATIONS

Table 6 presents the intercorrelations between the four childhood tests and the adult IQ for each diagnostic group. Again, because not all subjects had all of the tests, the number varies from one comparison to another. For the schizophrenic group all comparisons resulted in statistically significant correlations between tests for both the patients and their normal sibs. Correlations between childhood and adult tests tend to increase with the higher grade levels, as might be expected. For the personality disorder group, the pattern is similar to that for the schizophrenic group with the exception of one nonsignificant correlation between the K–2 Pintner and the adult test for sibs. Thus, for both patient and sib groups, the data indicate that the subjects tend to maintain the same relative position on these varying tests across the longitudinal span.

Discussion

Our findings support the studies of Lane and Albee (1965) and Schaffner et al. (1967) indicating that children who later became schizophrenic scored significantly lower than did their non-hospitalized sibs on group IQ tests in the elementary grades. Our mean scores are virtually identical with those found in their suburban sample. However, since the results for the personality disorder patients parallel those for the schizophrenics, interpretation of the relationship between childhood intellectual deficiency and adult schizophrenia must be tempered with the realization that similar patterns exist for other psychiatric syndromes. Thus, the significance of intellectual impairment in childhood as a clue to the etiology of a specific syndrome such as schizophrenia must be questioned.

One hypothesis which might explain our results and those of Lane,

Table 6. Correlations between IQ Tests for Patients and Their Normal Siblings

Test	K–2 Pintner	3–5 Otis	6–8 Otis	6–8 Pintner
		Schizophrenic [a]		
K–2 Pintner				
Patient	. . .			
Sibling	. . .			
3–5 Otis				
Patient	.79***	. . .		
Sibling	.79***	. . .		
6–8 Otis				
Patient	.56**	.73***	. . .	
Sibling	.73***	.67***	. . .	
6–8 Pintner				
Patient	.77***	.76***	.97***	. . .
Sibling	.82***	.88***	.90***	. . .
Adult				
Patient	.52**	.75***	.64***	.81***
Sibling	.65***	.68***	.73***	.82***
		Personality Disorder [b]		
K–2 Pintner				
Patient	. . .			
Sibling	. . .			
3–5 Otis				
Patient	.55***	. . .		
Sibling	.48*	. . .		
6–8 Otis				
Patient	.69***	.82***	. . .	
Sibling	.45*	.66*	. . .	
6–8 Pintner				
Patient	.54***	.78***	.91***	. . .
Sibling	.81***	.79***	.53***	. . .
Adult				
Patient	.50*	.75***	.72***	.77***
Sibling	.32	.54*	.83***	.62*

[a] Number of pairs differs for each comparison. The range is from 7 to 24 pairs.

[b] Number of pairs differs for each comparison. The range is from 8 to 34 pairs.

* $p<.05$. ** $p<.025$. *** $p<.01$.

Albee, and their associates is that those patients, regardless of adult diagnosis, who scored significantly lower than their siblings in childhood, may have had a congenital abnormality associated with brain dysfunction (i.e., "early minimal brain damage syndrome"). In one study, Lane and Albee (1963) reported that about 40 per cent of their adult schizophrenics had been in special classes for dull or retarded children in grade school. The average late-childhood Stanford-Binet IQ for their *total* sample was 69.7; for the subsample attending these special classes it may well have been considerably lower. The combination of low IQ and behavior disorder in childhood is frequently associated with an "early minimal brain damage syndrome" (Pollack, 1967).

It is our hope that the study of life history factors in various diagnostic groups, and in different clinical settings may clarify some of the varying etiological hypotheses which have emerged on the basis of studies restricted to particular samples.

COMMENTARY

ALBEE. I'm fascinated to see the comparability of many of your findings with some of those that Dr. Lane and I reported. But I'd like to ask about, or comment on two points. First, this minimal brain damage question. We have, as Dr. Lane reported, one study that suggests that IQ goes up very significantly after the individual recovers clinically from his schizophrenia. In fact, ten years after their first hospitalization, those people who are out and/or those people who are recovered or symptom-free score significantly higher than even their highest childhood IQ. I suggest that this fact might contradict the notion of minimal brain damage. The second comment is that one of our doctoral students did a fairly large scale study of neurotic children, and this was very carefully defined, from a Cleveland child guidance clinic, comparing their IQ's with their siblings'. These were neurotic children, and he found no significant difference in IQ between the neurotic child and his siblings, both of them currently in school.

POLLACK. Well, the latter work is consistent with the findings of Rutter and of Wolf.* Rutter found that the only clinical group of children that had subnormal IQ's were the so-called childhood schizophrenics. (The term is, I think, a misnomer, since almost all show evidence of minimal brain damage.) Neurotic children did not have lower IQ's than their sibs. Now I have no way of judging which kinds of adult schizophrenics showed higher IQ's with clinical improvement. I have no doubt that the pattern exists, as I have no doubt there is a deteriorating group of schizophrenics who show a decline in intelligence. I've seen enough of those cases to believe that that's true, regardless of institutionalization and regardless of the effects of medication or electroconvulsive therapy. I think the drop in IQ parallels an endogenous deteriorative phenomenon characteristic of a certain group of schizophrenics. In a previous follow-up study, the low IQ patients that we rated as early minimal brain damage had very poor outcomes. Even when they were not in hospital, they were not working and their social participation was poor.

GOLDBERG. To some extent, George Albee asked the question I was

* M. Rutter. Intelligence and childhood psychiatric disorder. *British Journal of Social and Clinical Psychology*, 1964, 3, 120. M. G. Wolf. Effects of emotional disturbance in childhood on intelligence. *American Journal of Orthopsychiatry*, 1965, 35, 906.

going to, and to some extent you answered it. I wanted to mention that in our own work the closest thing that we had to an intelligence test was the similarities test. Under drug treatment there was significant improvement, and though I didn't break down the cases into various types here to see which improved or which possibly deteriorated, there was definite test score improvement over time. Now what I don't know is what their real pre-episodic level was on the similarities test. But with regard to your own comparisons, I wonder if there was the opportunity to measure intelligence level after recovery or possibly in remission, and then compare with siblings to see whether they are at the same level as siblings, higher, or lower.

POLLACK. Well, we have two types of data. First of all, we have a subsample of the present study, about forty cases, for whom we can compare Wechsler IQ scores from a previous testing during adolescence — that is, at the time of their first clinical contact — with their scores at the time of current hospitalization. Their IQ's did not go down over this period of time — if anything, the mean IQ's of this group went up. The second finding we have is our drug work. We compared patients who were medicated with chlorpromazine and those given placebo. On placebo, regardless of clinical outcome (most did poorly), there was about an 8-point gain in IQ over a five-week period. Now, with chlorpromazine, even though there was greater clinical improvement than in the placebo group, there's a diminution in the IQ scores (not on the verbal ones) on the so-called concentration subtests, digit span, digit symbol, and arithmetic.

STABENAU. I'd like to pursue the minimal brain damage issue. I want to ask about the Performance–Verbal IQ differences. I noticed a great difference between the Performance and Verbal Scores. Was that not significant?

POLLACK. It's about the same for the siblings as it is for the patients.

STABENAU. Well, is there any difference for the patient group, between Performance and Verbal IQ's? But I'm thinking along the lines of Churchill's work with twins, where the verbal IQ was lower for the lower-weight-at-birth twins, the more immature twins. Might this be a higher risk group for chronicity or a more process type of schizophrenia? In our twins, the incidence of documented asphyxia, cyanosis, and the like appeared significantly more often in the index twins. And in the same twins, when examined as adults, there was a significantly greater number of soft signs. Now we're not certain whether this is an effect of drugs, institutionalization, and somatic treatment or not.

POLLACK. First of all, we don't find soft signs only in the schizophrenic patients. We have analyzed our data and find the frequency of a history of soft signs to be approximately the same for the personality disorders as for the schizophrenics. But as you know, John Churchill* found that the lower-weight-at-birth twin had the lower school-age IQ. Now I don't think we're going to find any Performance-Verbal differences for the

* J. A. Churchill. The relationship between intelligence and birth weight in twins. *Neurology*, 1965, 15, 341.

patient-sibling comparison. The only thing I can tell you is that one of our assistants surveyed the WAIS IQ's of the whole hospital population for one year and selected the patients who had more than a 25-point discrepancy (it was always, by the way, in the direction of higher Verbal rather than Performance scores). And then we did some fancy work. We selected two control groups from the original sample. One matched the discrepancy group for mean Verbal IQ; the second matched the discrepancy group for mean Performance IQ. The discrepancy group had a significantly higher incidence of males and EEG slowing than was found in the two control groups. When compared with the group equated for Verbal IQ, the discrepancy group did not differ significantly on any verbal subtest. When compared with the group equated for Performance IQ, the discrepancy group was significantly lower on the object assembly subtest.

DENT. I just want to be sure I understand those subgroups. In your findings Drs. Albee and Lane, it's the process group that shows this intellectual deficit, and process group is defined largely in terms of symptoms, if I am right, rather than in terms of premorbid functions?

ALBEE. Yes, symptoms on admission.

DENT. And in yours, Dr. Pollack, was it age at onset of schizophrenia?

POLLACK. No, it was age of onset of behavioral problems.

DENT. Was that the early onset subgroups that showed the intellectual deficit in schizophrenia?

POLLACK. Both for personality disorders and schizophrenia. As a matter of fact, it held better for the personality disorders. For the personality disorders, those with childhood and early adolescent onset differed from their sibs, whereas for the schizophrenics, those with early adolescent onset of behavior problems did not differ from their sibs in IQ. In other words, those who had late adolescent or adult onset, whose first behavioral problems occurred after the age of seventeen, did not differ from their normal sibs in IQ, whether they were personality disorders or schizophrenics.

REFERENCES

Alanen, Y. O. The family in the pathogenesis of schizophrenic and neurotic disorders. *Acta Psychiatrica Scandinavica Supplementum*, 1966, 189, 42.

Albee, G. W., E. A. Lane, C. Corcoran, & A. Werneke. Childhood and intercurrent intellectual performance of adult schizophrenics. *Journal of Consulting Psychology*, 1963, 27, 364–366.

Belmont, I., H. G. Birch, D. F. Klein, & M. Pollack. Perceptual evidence of CNS dysfunction in schizophrenia. *Archives of General Psychiatry*, 1964, 10, 395–408.

Kennard, M. A., M. Pollack, D. F. Klein. The EEG qualities in a group of young adult hospitalized psychiatric patients. In J. Wortis (Ed.), *Recent advances in biological psychiatry*. New York: Plenum Press, 1966. Pp. 277–282.

Klein, D. F. Importance of psychiatric diagnosis in prediction of clinical drug effects. *Archives of General Psychiatry*, 1967, 16, 118–126.

Lane, E. A., & G. W. Albee. Childhood intellectual development of adult schizophrenics. *Journal of Abnormal and Social Psychology*, 1963, 67, 186–189.

———. Childhood intellectual differences between schizophrenic adults and their siblings. *American Journal of Orthopsychiatry*, 1965, 35, 747–753.

Pollack, M. Early "minimal brain damage" and the development of severe psychopathology in adolescence. *American Journal of Orthopsychiatry*, 1967, 37, 213–214 (abstract).

———, S. Levenstein, & D. F. Klein. A three-year post-hospital follow-up of adolescent and adult schizophrenics. *American Journal of Orthopsychiatry*, 1968, 38, 94–109.

Pollack, M., M. G. Woerner, P. Goldberg, & D. F. Klein. Psychopathology and gender concordance in the siblings of schizophrenic and nonschizophrenic psychiatric patients. *Archives of General Psychiatry*, in press.

Pollack, M., M. G. Woerner, W. Goodman, & I. M. Greenberg. Childhood development patterns of hospitalized adult schizophrenic and nonschizophrenic patients and their siblings. *American Journal of Orthopsychiatry*, 1966, 36, 510–517.

Prout, C. T., & M. A. White. The schizophrenic's sibling. *Journal of Nervous and Mental Diseases*, 1956, 123, 162–170.

Schaffner, A., E. A. Lane, & G. W. Albee. Intellectual differences between suburban preschizophrenic children and their siblings. *Journal of Consulting Psychology*, 1967, 31, 326–327.

Thomas, A., S. Chess, & H. G. Birch. *Temperament and behavior disorders in children*. New York: New York University Press, 1968.

LEE N. ROBINS

Antecedents of Character Disorder

THE study reported in my book *Deviant Children Grown Up* (Robins, 1966) was a stepping-stone to the study in which my associates and I are now engaged. In the first study we took records from the St. Louis Municipal Child Guidance Clinic, which was started by the Commonwealth Fund about eight months after the Fund started the Judge Baker Center (see Ricks & Berry, pp. 31–48). We studied a consecutive group of 524 children seen at the St. Louis Clinic between 1924 and 1929 to learn what kinds of problems they had as adults. They had a median age of 43 at the time we located them. Instead of going to hospital records and finding only the schizophrenics who happened to be or to have been in that particular hospital, we tried to interview everybody personally and to find a wide variety of information about them. For the whole group, we found a 5 per cent incidence of schizophrenia – about five times the expected rate (Robins, 1966, pp. 239–244).

However, our emphasis in the first study was not on schizophrenia but on the sociopathic personality, which some doctors find a troublesome diagnosis. People so diagnosed have trouble in getting along in all kinds of situations, but they have no thought disturbances. We found that the psychiatrists in the study used a hierarchy of diagnosis: if a subject had thought disorders with or without antisocial behavior, he was called schizophrenic; if he exhibited widespread antisocial behavior in the absence of thought disorders, he was called a sociopathic personality. Neurotic symptoms, however, did not disqualify him as a sociopath. The sociopathic personalities were people in many kinds of trouble – multiple divorces, multiple arrests, unemployed. If they got into the service despite their criminal record, they performed very poorly. They were usually financially dependent on agencies or relatives, and many of them had been in psychi-

NOTE: This research was supported by National Institute of Mental Health Grants No. MH-05804 and MH-07126, and by U.S.P.H.S. Special Fellowship 36,598.

atric hospitals – not because they volunteered or felt ill, but because they got into trouble in prison or in the army or something of that sort.

There are three main findings from the first study. The first is that our subjects' antisocial behavior in childhood was a very powerful predictor of poor adult outcomes, a much better predictor than other symptoms. The second is that social class, which has always been thought to be correlated with antisocial patterns in adulthood, was a poor predictor. In fact, it did not predict adult problems when the child's level of antisocial behavior was taken into account. The only thing it predicted independently of the child's antisocial behavior was educational level and job level, which, obviously, are closely connected. But social class did not predict the *quality* of performance on the job, only the job level – that is, it did not predict chronic unemployment, absenteeism, getting fired from jobs for being drunk, and so on. The third finding is that for children who were only mildly antisocial, having an antisocial father greatly increased the risk of the subject's antisocial behavior as an adult. Having an antisocial father did not increase the risk for severely antisocial children, who had a poor prognosis whether their father was antisocial or not, nor did it make very conforming children antisocial adults. But if the child was mildly antisocial and had an antisocial father, chances of a poor outcome were greatly increased.

A group of control children was selected from public school records for comparison with the clinic group. The not very rigid criteria for the control group were: they could not have gone to the St. Louis Municipal Child Guidance Clinic; they could not have repeated a full year of elementary school; they did not have any notations of truancy in their records; and they had not been transferred to a correctional institution while in elementary school (though they could have been in high school). Despite the fact that they were matched with the clinic patients for economic background (we picked them from the neighborhoods in which the clinic children lived, mostly slums), by the time they were adults, 60 per cent of them had moved to the suburbs; they had good jobs; many or almost all of them had graduated from high school, and some, not a great many, had gone to college; they were stable citizens; they had no more divorces than the national average. They had no more difficulties of any kind than did Terman's gifted children, who are a selected group. They obviously did not have jobs ranking so high as Terman's children did, but they had no more divorces, no more hospitalization, and no more crime, although they had been brought up in the city slums.

The adult success of our control subjects made me think that not having repeated a full year of elementary school and not being noted as truant must be powerful predictors of adult conformity. And I began planning to test some of the hypotheses growing out of the first study in a new study using only schoolchildren as subjects. Why did I want to do this? Well, when you work with a clinic population you worry about why they got there — that is, Are they a normal sample of deviant children or did the judge, when the child came before him, decide that "this child is really a little peculiar and I'm going to send *this* truant to the clinic and not that truant"? Perhaps some clue to which the judge reacted was predicting outcome rather than deviant behavior in itself.

STUDY II

Thus, I was interested in following a sample of normal schoolchildren. But the problem with a normal sample, when studying something as rare in our society as getting hospitalized, is that you have to study a large sample to get enough cases with problems. I decided to study Negro boys, because it was obvious that the Negro population has more trouble with jobs, more arrests, and as the Maryland registry has shown, more psychiatric hospitalization than the white population. Negroes appeared to be a group in which I could study predictors of adult problems in a normal population selected from school records. This promised the best of both worlds — that is, there would be no preselection of cases, since the boys chosen were in school whether or not they had initial pathologies and they had not been treated so far as I knew; but at the same time, I should still obtain a sample in which adult problems were common. The value of good school records has already been pointed out. Perhaps the best thing about them is that they are prospective records which somebody else has gathered for a total sample of children.

My associates and I decided to use boys for several reasons: (a) After they grow up, they are much more likely than women to show certain kinds of adult psychiatric and social pathology, particularly crime, alcoholism, and drug addiction. (b) Their adult social status is a reflection of their *own* achievement, rather than their spouse's. (c) They're much easier to find for interview since they don't change their names, and they collect more records by registering for the draft, appearing in credit corporation ratings, driver's license rosters, and so forth. We decided to study only children with IQ's of 85 or higher, which was the median IQ for the St. Louis school population of Negro boys, because we were interested in the predictive value of school failure when it did not result from mental retardation. We wanted to be sure that these were boys who *could* have passed regularly in elementary school if they had attended and behaved themselves in school. We took only children born in St. Louis – we suspected that children from rural backgrounds might have trouble in school because they were not acculturated to city life, and of course the Negro children who were not born in St. Louis were mostly southern farm children.

We took only children born between 1930 and 1934 so that all would be approximately the same age at follow-up. The follow-up study deals with three periods of time: before intake, the interval between intake and follow-up, and "the present." Even "the present" is an *interval*, not a moment in time, since most of the things we're interested in involve adjustments over time. In other words, to determine current job adjustment, one finds out how many times a man has been fired over the last few years; whether or not he's working *today* is a much less valuable piece of information. Ideally, the lengths of each of the three intervals should be the same for each subject, but unfortunately, this is seldom the case in follow-up studies. In the study reported by Ricks and Berry (pp. 31–48), for instance, which investigated all children who had ever been seen in the Judge Baker Center, some of the subjects are now much older than others, with many more years at risk of being hospitalized than others. For schizophrenia, the differences in current age are not too serious a problem because schizophrenia is a young person's illness. But if one studies diseases or behaviors that occur late in life, such as suicide, it becomes a very serious problem.

For these reasons, we selected subjects approximately the same age. Originally, we had hoped to include only children born in 1931, but we needed a five-year period to get enough people for the design. Since we wanted them all to have the same interval between intake and follow-up, we interviewed them all within a one-year period, between 1965 and 1966. By means of these two techniques, the time intervals remained fairly constant throughout the sample. We also insisted that our subjects should have been St. Louis residents at some time since 1959, so that they might all have been exposed to a common job market, a common police force, a common hospital system, and so forth. Thus, differences found would be differences in behavior, not differences in the risk of getting arrested in one area as compared with another. It might have been easier, since we wanted people who had lived in St. Louis, to have started with an area sample of adults and then to have looked for their school records. However, such a design has certain flaws: If a man is in a jail or a hospital or if he has died, he does not fall into a sample of everybody living in a given neighborhood. If he has moved out of town or into the suburbs, you also would lose him. On the other hand, if the base is a childhood sample, *everybody* must be accounted for.

Selecting a Sample. We decided to use the very simplest measures from school records because this had worked so well with our control sample in the previous study (Robins, 1966). And we decided to look for variables in school records that we thought would be related to the hypotheses developed from the other study. For the first variable, juvenile antisocial behavior, several clues could be used: We could simply count absences, since days attended were recorded on every school record. We could see whether a child had repeated a grade or not because the grade to which he was assigned in any particular quarter was always recorded. We could see if he had been transferred to a special class, an ungraded room, or a correctional institution. We also found notations of being expelled from school, but these were very rare and when they occurred, in almost every case the child had been absent so much that one would suspect he had been truant. Our second variable was socioeconomic status. To measure this, we had the occupation of the guardian listed on the school records. The third variable — the hardest to find a measure of — was whether or not there was an antisocial father. The only means that we could think of for determining this was to see whether or not the father's name appeared as the guardian. If the name of the guardian was male, and if the last name was the same as the boy's, we assumed it was his father. In all other cases we assumed that it was not — if the guardian's name changed, if there was a female name, if the last name was different from the boy's, or if the boy's name was changed, we assumed that there was a broken home. We decided to use evidence of a broken home as a measure of antisocial fathers because we had found in our earlier study that desertion is a particularly good criterion for antisocial behavior in the father. It occurs along with arrests, excessive drinking, failure to work, and so forth in white fathers. We were gambling that most of the absent fathers would be cases of desertion. This was not always the case, of course, and the fact that we didn't find the father's absence to be more highly related to outcome may be because our measure is crude.

What we wanted to do was to collect a sample that would wipe out the correlations among these three variables — juvenile antisocial behavior, socioeconomic status, and father's absence. Such a special sample was necessary because exploring the effects of three variables in a random sample of Negro boys would have required a very large sample, so that even when controlling on two variables simultaneously we would have enough cases to test the effect of the third variable statistically.

Before choosing the sample, we studied the entire population of boys born in 1931 who attended the St. Louis public schools in order to find out what part of the school population met our criteria. By studying the total population of boys for one year, we found out what the median IQ was, how many came from the South, and so on. We found out, for instance, that of children who met the IQ criterion, only a quarter did not have a father's name on the record. And we found that obtaining enough children whose guardians had high status would be a problem. In 1937, when these children entered school, job opportunities for Negroes were extremely poor. We found 75 per cent of the population in the lowest job categories, either unemployed or on WPA or domestics, janitors, or laborers. Only 25 per cent had a better job and only 5 per cent of the population had a white-collar job. This survey of the 1931 population showed us that if we had investigated the effect of guardian's occupation in a random sample, we would have needed a tremendous sample to get enough cases in the higher occupation ranges to allow statistical tests.

We then dichotomized the three variables, school problems, guardian's occupation, and father's presence, and took all possible permutations of them, giving us eight groups. We wanted 30 boys for each group, a total sample of 240. Furthermore, the IQ distribution within each of the eight groups was to be the same. Each of the four groups with high occupations was to have the same proportion of white-collar occupational levels; each of the four low occupation groups was to have the same proportion unemployed. School problems had to be equally severe in each school problem group. As a result we set up quotas for occupations, absences, IQ scores, and so forth, producing a rather elaborate design. We then picked from school records the 240 boys who best fulfilled the quotas and began to hunt for them. If we found that one had left town before 1959 or had died before 1959, we took the next best case. Absence from St. Louis before 1959 was accepted only if a relative said the subject had left town before 1959 or he himself wrote us (on our self-addressed postcard) saying he had last lived in St. Louis before 1959. Death certificates were obtained for those who died, to be sure the death was before 1959. At the beginning, we had a pool of 930 cases that met our criteria. In order to get the final sample, we looked for 322 men. Before 1959, 12 had died, and 75 had moved away. The final sample consisted of 235 instead of 240 subjects, because there was one group we could never fill: that with father absent, high occupation, and no school problems; we had to settle for 25 boys in this group instead of the intended 30.

The elementary school records were on microfilms. Although race was not recorded, the schools were segregated at the time, and consequently, we could tell from the name of the school if the child was Negro. We photographed records for all eligible boys to allow us to pick the sample in our own office. We also got the boys' high school records, and ran our three variables against high school graduation for all boys born in 1931 to find the best breaking points at which to dichotomize the variables. We assumed that breaking points maximizing our ability to predict high school graduation would also maximize our ability to predict adult job success. For school problems, the breaking points best related to high school graduation were being held back as much as two quarters and being absent more than 20 per cent of the time in five or more quarters. For socioeconomic status, the best breaking point was white collar versus non–white collar, but unfortunately, there were too few white-collar families to allow us to use this breaking point. Therefore, we divided the socioeconomic variable arbitrarily at a Duncan Socioeconomic Index score of 10 or less versus 11 or more.

Having chosen a sample, we began searching for the target group of all those subjects still living in St. Louis in 1959. Of the total original group, we lost just under one third from migration and death before 1959. We located 98 per cent of those still residing in Missouri in 1959, and to our great surprise, because we had been warned that we had to have Negro interviewers (whom we could not find), we interviewed 95 per cent of the sample. (The refusal rate of only 1 per cent, I believe, resulted from the fact that we offered to pay the subjects for their time. We were able to locate 98 per cent largely because we looked at so many records that sooner or later a recent address was sure to turn up. Obviously, we tried the telephone book and city directory first. If the boys had transferred to another school system, we got transcripts. We also obtained records from police; prisons; city, state, and federal probation and parole; city and state welfare; public housing; voting registration lists; five hospitals; three clinics; two credit bureaus; the Missouri State Employment Service; the Federal Bureau of Narcotics; the armed services; and the VA.

We interviewed those subjects who had left town *since* 1959 by sending people to see them. (They had most frequently gone to California, and medical students are very eager to go there to interview.) We wrote to men both in and out of the city, telling them that we were interested in boys who had gone to St. Louis schools before integration to see how their outcome would compare with children going to school now. This introduction was devised to make all subjects feel they were part of the same group. One handicap in the earlier study (Robins, 1966) had been that we could not avoid telling subjects whether they were controls or patients. In the current study, we did not want subjects to identify themselves as having been selected as children with or without school problems because such identification might cause them to alter their histories accordingly. Our explanation, though incomplete, did make sense in the context of the interview—we were interested in occupation, what had happened to them, and what their school experience had been like. In our letter, we offered to pay the subjects $7.50 when we came out to interview them, but if they would come in, we would pay them $10.00 "to cover transportation costs." We thought that the differential, being considerably greater than bus fare, would increase the number of volunteers for office interviews. Apparently it did, since 50 per cent volunteered to be interviewed in the office. If a subject had not telephoned within about three days after the letter was sent, we went to see him. We did not tell him in the letter exactly what time we would come because we did not want him to arrange to be out.

About the same time we were setting up interviews, another group at Washington University was studying people living in the neighborhood surrounding a Negro housing project. The population was very similar to ours, but the interviewers were having a hard time getting cooperation. The three important differences between their method and ours probably were: Our sample received a letter which made them think this was a legitimate enterprise. The payment made a big difference. But our biggest advantage perhaps was that we had a name—we were looking for a particular person, rather than ringing doorbells. Consequently, a potential subject did not say, "Why don't you get someone else?" Having a particular person to see made the interviewers feel much better, too.

We have not yet completed the analysis, but we already have a few interesting findings (King, Murphy, Robins, & Darvish, 1969; Robins, 1968; Robins, Darvish, & Murphy, in press; Robins & Hill, 1966; Robins, Jones, & Murphy, 1966; Robins & Murphy, 1967; Robins, Murphy, & Breckenridge, 1968).

I think the validity of the interview is very high. We have run a validity check on drug use (see table on p. 235). Of the subjects, 31 had a public record of trouble with narcotics, and 26 of the 31 told us in the interview that they have taken drugs. Of those who did not tell us, two had been arrested as sellers, and there was no evidence in the records that they had ever taken drugs themselves. One had been arrested for suspicion of narcotics possession and immediately released because there was no evidence. One was a peculiar character who wanted to get out of the army and told the medical officer, "I am an alcoholic, I take drugs, I am a homosexual. Please let me out." He did get out, but subsequently he was hospitalized, asked about drug use, and denied it, so I think he was telling the truth to us rather than to the army. The last one was a suicidal and alcoholic man whose uncle brought him into the hospital and said, "He's been acting so peculiar I think maybe he's on drugs"; that was the only evidence for his using drugs. So even the five who have a drug record, yet told us that they had not taken anything, may well have been telling us the truth.

An important discovery of the study is that we could not have dispensed with the interviews. Interviews are hard to get, and initially we hoped to get reasonably good estimates of adult adjustment by using records alone. It turned out that this is impossible. *Information* on record might be adequate to assess adult adjustment, but too many records are missed without interviews to direct you where to look. Clerks in agencies are sometimes careless in looking through file drawers for men with common names, and even we ourselves made mistakes in files we were allowed to check. We missed about 15 per cent of our high school graduates on the initial record check. When we did not find a record for those who claimed high school attendance or graduation, we rechecked — to find that the record was out of place, that the man had transferred to another school, or that there was an error in our identification data. Only one man claimed high school graduation who probably did not graduate (he claimed graduation at an age when he was still a sophomore). And we probably would have lost around 20 per cent of the army records if we had not asked in the interview whether the subject had been in the service. With additional information — dates of service, the branch, and occasionally a new middle name — we found many more army records. One important reason we missed them the first time is that many subjects quit school and joined the army between the ages of 15 and 17 by falsifying their birth dates; consequently, when we sent their real birth dates for a record search, the clerk did not identify them.

Elementary School Records and Later Outcome for Negro Boys

Outcome Variables	School Performance			Occupation of Guardian		Presence of Father			
								Boys Without School Problems	
	Truancy [a] *and* Failure [b]	Truancy [a] *or* Failure [b]	Neither	Very Low [c]	All Others	Father Absent	Father Present [d]	Father Absent	Father Present [d]
Delinquent before age 15	25%	20%	9%	19%	12%	14%	17%	13%	15%
First delinquent at age 15 or 16 (of those not delinquent earlier)	9	18	15	18	15	18	14	14	16
Non-entry into high school....	27	6	1	11	5	11	6	2	0
High school dropout..........	78	42	32	40	46	52	35	40	27
Any drug use	57	45	50	48	51	50	49	55	47
Heroin addiction	11	4	13	10	10	10	10	15	10
Any record of alcohol problem.	32	17	15	15	22	22	17	16	13
Designated alcoholic (or medical complications)	14	4	2	4	6	5	5	2	2
In prison at follow-up	11	2	2	2	6	5	4	3	4
Dead at follow-up	11	4	1	3	6	5	4	0	2
By homicide	5	1	0	1	2	2	1	0	0

[a] Truancy defined as absent more than 20 per cent of the time in five or more quarters (out of thirty-two).
[b] Academic failure defined as repeating two or more quarters or being placed in an ungraded room.
[c] Duncan Socioeconomic Index of 10 or less (unemployed, domestic, laborer).
[d] Only one guardian listed, whose name is male and last name is same as boy's.

RESULTS

Elementary school performance was, as we expected, an excellent predictor of outcome. It predicted every variable that we have looked at so far with two exceptions: it does not predict drug use, and it does not predict delinquency in boys who are first delinquent after their fifteenth birthday, though it *is* a good predictor of becoming delinquent before fifteen. Interestingly enough, these two variables, drug use and late initial delinquency, are inter-related. We found that the drug users were boys whose performance in elementary school was indistinguishable from other boys', but who became delinquent in high school before they began using drugs, and most of whom became high school dropouts. Relatively few of the delinquent boys who never *entered* high school became drug users; apparently the high school was the site of exposure to drugs. Another finding is that the earlier a boy was exposed to drugs, the greater his risk of addiction.

We have also studied death rates and causes of death for the whole group (326) we looked for, including people who died or left town before 1959 and four men temporarily substituted for men we thought might be ineligible but who turned out to be eligible. I was struck by the fact that being dead at follow-up and being in prison at follow-up (about age 33) could be predicted by the same variables. The same percentage of boys had died as were located in prison. There is an overlap of two cases – two boys died in prison. Both being in prison and being dead were unrelated to occupation of the guardian and to the father's presence or absence during elementary school, but a combination of truancy and failure in elementary school was strongly related to both outcomes. We sent for death certificates of those who died, and were shocked to find that of the fourteen boys who had died, five had died by homicide. Four of the five homicides occurred among boys who had been both truant and failing in elementary school. It seems that the high rate of school problems among Negroes may be one explanation for the high Negro death rate: 11 per cent of the boys who were both truant and held back at school were dead at follow-up, and 5 per cent of them were dead by homicide. That means that of this highly troubled group one out of twenty had been killed in the eighteen years since they got out of elementary school.

The death rate for whites born the same years and alive at age fifteen is something like 33/1000 during the next eighteen years (i.e., by age 33). Our Negro boys had a rate of 49/1000, somewhat high as compared with the white rate. But for Negro boys who were *neither held back nor truant*, the death rate was only 13/1000, which is less than half the white rate during the same ages. Obviously then, there is a very striking relation between elementary school performance and risk of death for Negro boys. And the predictors of a risk of death closely resemble predictors of a risk of imprisonment.

The group with truancy and failures in elementary school also more often had some agency record indicating an alcohol problem. Of this truancy and failure group, 32 per cent have been arrested for drunkenness, admitted to a hospital for alcoholism, complained about by the wife to the welfare worker, and so forth. Among those who have a record indicating not merely some drinking problem but rather full-blown alcoholism, again the pattern is very similar to the imprisonment and death pattern, highly related to school performance but to neither childhood socioeconomic status nor father's presence.

Another finding showing the importance of truancy is that truancy was as powerful a deterrent to high school graduation as was low IQ. In our analysis of the total group of boys born in 1931 and attending St. Louis schools, we found that boys could graduate from high school with IQ's in the low 70's if they attended regularly – about 38 per cent of those with IQ's of 70–79 graduated from high school. Among boys with IQ's above 105 who were highly truant in elementary school, about 30 per cent graduated. Thus, as far as high school graduation went, it was as bad to be truant as to have a low IQ.

Our measure of antisocial behavior in the father, if it does measure that, did not work out as anticipated. There is no indication that for boys with mild school problems, those without a father in the home (according to records) had any more of the adult difficulties we have studied than had those with a father in the home. I don't know whether this is because antisocial fathers do not play the same role for Negro boys that they do for whites or whether our measure is so poor that we are not finding the true relationship. In the interview we asked questions about the father's behavior, and after further analysis we shall know whether behavior problems in the father are reflected in his absence on school records, and if not, whether his behavior problems do predict outcome for mildly antisocial Negro boys as they did for whites.

On the basis of these findings, I have begun to feel that attendance during elementary school is a very powerful predictor of adult adjustment. At present we have only a correlation. We do not know whether, if we could increase attendance, boys would lead better adult lives, but no one has seriously tried yet to see what effect improved attendance in elementary school might have. This experiment should be tried with very young children. One of the startling things to me was that of all the boys who ever became seriously truant in elementary school, 82 per cent were already excessively absent in the first or second grade. Truancy began very, very young. I think our past concentration on improving adult chances by trying to do something for high school dropouts is directed at the wrong age group. Excessive absence begins as a phenomenon of the very young. It continues into high school, but it certainly does not start there.

COMMENTARY

QUESTION. What is the relationship between the student's absence and illness?

ROBINS. Illness plays some part. This is why we set a rather high criterion for absences (20 per cent of the days in five or more quarters). We found no difference between children with no absence and children out 20 per cent of the days in no more than one quarter. But when this much absence occurs in two quarters, chances for graduation begin to drop, and the big dividing point was this much absence in more than four quarters.

RICKS. In a study of character disorders based on the case histories of the Judge Baker Guidance Center, it was found that the degree of antisocial behavior is predictive of a character disorder adult diagnosis. It was also found that acting out behavior by the father did not seem to be related to adult character disorder in his offspring. We got findings similar to your results, just using the case history records.

ROBINS. I think that the reason our very simple measures — how many days do you go to school, and do you go on to the next grade — work so well is that they're measuring two things — are you conforming to rules and are you achieving anything. Most of life asks the same things of you. If you can do both of those things, you get along.

QUESTION. Is there a separation of your two groups of failure and truancy, and failure and sticking it out?

ROBINS. Yes, we've got all the possible combinations.

QUESTION. Does it make any difference whether they stay or go into truancy?

ROBINS. If they are failing but not truant, or if they are truant but not failing, they do better than if they're both truant and failing.

QUESTION. Do they do better if they're failing and truanting than if they're failing and staying?

ROBINS. No. Either alone is worse than nothing, but both together are very bad. This is for the outcomes we've mentioned so far. There are still other measures of outcome to be examined.

FLEMING. I wonder what the lack of findings on the father is related to. Is it a cultural characteristic of lower-class Negro homes?

ROBINS. Peterson and DeBord's study (1966) from Vanderbilt on school achievement shows that whether the official status of the home is broken or not broken is not a predictor of school achievement, but that a more subtle look at the home is predictive. The important thing, according to their findings, is the way parental roles are filled by whoever fills them. Good grandparents may be just as good as good parents.

REFERENCES

King, L. J., G. E. Murphy, L. N. Robins, & H. Darvish. Alcohol abuse: A crucial factor in the social problems of Negro men. *American Journal of Psychiatry*, 1969, 125, 12.

Peterson, A., & L. DeBord. Educational supportiveness of the home and academic performance of disadvantaged boys. *Institute on Mental Retardation and Intellectual Development Behavior Science Monograph* (George Peabody College for Teachers, Nashville, Tenn.), 1966, No. 3, 162 pp.

Robins, L. N. *Deviant children grown up: A psychiatric and sociological study of sociopathic personality*. Baltimore: Williams & Wilkins, 1966.

———. Negro homicide victims — who will they be? *Trans-action*, June 1968, 5 (No. 7), 15–19.

———, H. Darvish, & G. E. Murphy. The long-term outcome for adolescent drug users: A follow-up study of 76 users and 146 non-users. In J. Zubin and A. Freedman (Eds.), *Psychopathology of adolescence*. New York: Grune & Stratton, in press.

Robins, L. N., & S. Y. Hill. Assessing the contributions of family structure, class and peer groups to juvenile delinquency. *Journal of Criminal Law, Criminology and Police Science*, 1966, 57, 325–334. Reprinted in D. Glaser, *Crime in the city*. New York: Harper, in press.

Robins, L. N., R. S. Jones, & G. E. Murphy. School milieu and school problems of Negro boys. *Social Problems*, 1966, 13, 428–436.

Robins, L. N., & G. E. Murphy. Drug use in a normal population of young Negro men. *American Journal of Public Health*, 1967, 57, 1580–1596.

——— & M. B. Breckenridge. Drinking behavior of young urban Negro men. *Quarterly Journal of Studies on Alcohol*, 1968, 29 (No. 3), 657–684.

PATRICIA FLEMING
DAVID F. RICKS

Emotions of Children before Schizophrenia and before Character Disorder

THIS chapter presents findings on the emotional experiences of preschizophrenic youngsters, as studied through case materials, particularly therapists' notes. In style and method, the current work is similar to that of Ricks and Berry (pp. 31–48); it parallels earlier reports of the Judge Baker Schizophrenia Research Project (Gardner, 1967a; 1967b; Nameche, Waring, & Ricks, 1964; Ricks & Nameche, 1966; Waring, 1966; Waring & Ricks, 1965). These studies isolated antecedents of schizophrenia in the areas of family relationships, parental psychopathology, and early childhood symptom patterns. Following a logical sequence from the early project reports, a closer look at the available case materials was taken in an effort to determine the effect of pathological home environments, parental personalities, and current life experiences upon the child himself, his feelings, and his relationships with the world around him. Appraising subjective experiences of youngsters was possible because the Judge Baker Guidance Center has made it a rule to collect extensive psychotherapy notes, in which the child's own perspective and "own story" is consistently recorded. Other information in the Clinic's files was also used when it added data about the child's feelings.

Theoretical support for the present study is found in the writings of Arieti (1955), Sullivan (1962), and Laing (1960). These gifted clinicians, working with observations gained in intensive psychotherapy with schizophrenic adults, have stressed the long-term interpersonal process of personality maladjustment in their patients' life histories. The early warpings began, for most, in intense relatedness with parents which created unmanageable anxieties and interfered with the child's developing a sense

NOTE: This research was supported by Grant MH 10-466 from the National Institute of Mental Health, and by grants from the Scottish Rite Committee for Research in Schizophrenia.

of his own identity and autonomy. The closed in, locked nature of these bonds ranged in quality from marked overdependency to bizarre symbiotic relationships. Poor social contact, initiated within the home setting, was augmented during school years by the youngster's inability to relate effectively with peers. He was thereby kept from securing the remedial effects of friendships and from achieving a sense of self.

From adult psychotic patients' reports, clinicians have gained an impression of early years marked by insecurity and uncertainty; anxiety was ever present and increasingly incapacitating. From childhood on, life was a series of defeats and failures, with few counterbalancing moments of pride and mastery. Withdrawal, both physical and emotional, became the primary mode of defense against unendurable interpersonal anxieties. But the isolated individual felt even more alone, helpless, vulnerable to the demands and intrusions of others, and unable to cope effectively on his own. Efforts to make sense out of his dismal situation in life led to unusual interpretations and helped create feelings of unreality. The psychological vacuum that came from isolation was filled, in part, by compensatory fantasies and magical hopes which the individual was fearful of testing out in any real sense. This, in turn, increased already present feelings of bodily detachment, for the person who tries to live apart from others and "in his head" has little sense of the wholeness and realness of his total being. While finding some safety in his inner world, he is never fully guarded against the awareness that his adjustment is different from others' – peculiar and unsatisfying. Yet he feels incapable of involving himself more fully in a world which presents the chronic threat of annihilation through relatedness. Over the long term, this untenable position and inner turmoil may drive many to seek protection and refuge in hospitalization and "craziness." Autobiographical accounts by persons who have undergone mental disturbance describe this process of hoped-for escape in madness (Alvarez, 1961; Green, 1964; Kaplan, 1964). The hospital and the sick role hold a promise of safety for the patient which the world outside could never offer.

The road to recovery seems to lie in the direction of confronting once more the intolerable emotions which first led to psychotic disorganization. Since this road back to a more stable, healthy adjustment is painful for all and impossible for many, one hopes that alertness to the presence of such intolerable emotions would lead to early identification of vulnerable youngsters who have a high risk for schizophrenia. It may then be possible, through effective intervention, to deflect the ongoing process of personality deterioration into less seriously incapacitating developmental lines.

The present study explored the emotional experiences of children and adolescents, most of whom were not considered psychotic at the time of contact with the Guidance Center, but who were hospitalized for schizophrenia during their adult years. The research report is divided into two sections; the first part discusses comparisons of pre-schizophrenics and control subjects; the second part extends the investigation to additional groups of pre-schizophrenics and controls, with the inclusion of character disordered subjects. Following the general conclusions of these two related studies, initial findings of replications and extensions of this line of work will be presented. Finally, some implications for psychotherapeutic approaches to such precariously integrated youngsters will be discussed.

Study I

A study by Fleming (1966) on pre-schizophrenic emotional experiences was the first systematic research into an area that had previously been described only in a clinical or literary fashion. Autobiographical reports and theoretical formulations provide relevant hypotheses about pre-psychotic emotional experiences, but the data from which they are derived are subject to adult biases, psychotic distortions, and the faultiness of retrospection. Therefore, these hypotheses must be tested on data gathered in childhood and adolescence, well before hospitalization for schizophrenia.

On the basis of clinical and autobiographical reports of how adult schizophrenics felt during earlier years, we predicted that certain sets of intolerable emotions would differentiate those youngsters who were eventually hospitalized for schizophrenia (the "pre-schizophrenics") from those who achieved a nonpsychotic, socially adequate adjustment in adult life (the "controls").

Hypotheses. Specifically, it was hypothesized that in childhood or adolescence, more pre-schizophrenics than controls experience: (a) feelings of *anxiety*; (b) feelings of *vulnerability* in the areas of identity formation and interpersonal relationships; (c) feelings of *unreality*; (d) feelings of an *uncanny*, mystical, or extraordinarily religious nature; and (e) feelings of *isolation and alienation.*

Method. To provide a systematic method for abstracting case records and to facilitate coding and computer analysis, a Personal Feelings Inventory (PFI) was assembled, containing 81 items suggested by published accounts of prepsychotic experiences, available mood scales, and current research on emotions. Items were grouped into the five major areas specified by the hypotheses: anxiety, 15 items; vulnerability, 25; unreality, 15; uncanniness, 3; and isolation and alienation, 23.

Without knowledge of the eventual adult outcome, the investigator read the total clinic record, made extensive notes, and scored the PFI. An independent judge, evaluating a subset of records, showed 79 to 100 per cent agreement on the presence or absence of specific emotional experiences.

Subjects. Preliminary study of the case materials not included in the study sample indicated that records of youngsters seen by one therapist for a minimum of five or more sessions contained sufficient information for judging the main emotions reported by the child. Three groups of records, categorized by adult outcome, were assembled (see Table 1). *

Table 1. Adult Diagnosis, Age When Seen at Judge Baker Guidance Center, Median Age at Hospitalization, and Median Years Hospitalized for Subjects and Comparison Group

Adult Diagnosis	N	Median Age When Seen	Median Age Hospitalized	Median Years Hospitalized
Chronic schizophrenic (in hospital)	24	13	19.5	11
Released schizophrenic (returned to community)	25	13	19.5	2
Socially adequate control	25	13		

RESULTS

The results will be presented in terms of the specific hypotheses, each of which concerned a different area of emotional experience. Table 2 represents the general group differences between the schizophrenic and control groups for each of the five areas studied.† The general hypothesis that early emotional experiences are related to subsequent hospitalization for

* For a further description of the criteria for inclusion in the various diagnostic groups and the demographic variables used for equating the groups, the reader is referred to the chapter by Ricks and Berry (pp. 31–48).

† General group differences were assessed by summing chi-square values for individual items within each area of emotional experience. It was recognized that this procedure inflated the obtained probabilities because the specific items within each area were not strictly independent. However, the clinical judgments were made with considerable effort at independence; moreover, the items themselves dealt with different behavorial or affective components, and, finally, the obtained probabilities are far beyond minimal levels of significance. Therefore, the obtained results appear to reflect meaningful differences between the pre-schizophrenic and control groups.

Table 2. Chi Square for Differences in Frequencies of Experienced Emotions between (a) the Combined Schizophrenic Groups (SX) and the Socially Adequate Control Group (SA), (b) the Chronic Schizophrenics (CSx) and the SA Controls, and (c) the Released Schizophrenics (RSx) and the SA Controls in Study I

Emotion	*df*	Group Differences		
		SX>SA	CSx>SA	RSx>SA
Anxiety	15	35.46***	30.20**	23.63
Vulnerability	23	66.36****	63.12****	37.33
Unreality	15	60.20****	72.24****	34.21***
Uncanniness	3	NA	NA	NA
Isolation and alienation. . .	23	87.73****	91.24****	36.91*

* $p<.05$. ** $p<.02$. *** $p<.005$. **** $p<.001$.

schizophrenia was supported. Differences were most marked for the areas isolation, vulnerability, and unreality. Significant differences were also obtained for feelings of anxiety, but the groups did not differ on uncanniness.

Table 3 indicates the specific items which contributed most to the overall differences between the groups in each area studied.

Within the area of *anxiety*, significant differences between the groups were in the predicted direction, with more pre-schizophrenics than controls experiencing various aspects of anxiety. *Very nervous*, *apprehensive*, and *highly sensitive* were terms often used to describe the pre-schizophrenics. Nearly three quarters showed speech difficulties associated with anxiety, such as stuttering and blocking. Verbal and motoric hyperactivity were noted in the records of over half of the pre-schizophrenics; they were given to incessant chattering and moving about, outbursts of erratic behavior, and preoccupation with meaningless activities, such as drumming on tabletops. For the controls, anxiety was present, but it more often seemed to be confined to specific stress situations, such as school or beginning to date. Also, the degree to which nervousness prevented successful social experiences was mild for the control group, in contrast to the ever-present, heightened anxiety experienced by the pre-schizophrenics.

Feelings of *vulnerability* in the areas of identity formation and interpersonal relationships (Table 3) were marked for the pre-schizophrenics and infrequent for the control group. About 90 per cent of the pre-schizophrenics felt helplessly inadequate and defenseless in a world seen as hostile, rejecting, and unfair. Lacking basic security about themselves as human beings, they showed difficulties in achieving sound and appropriate sexual identification. These youngsters, especially the children who were

Table 3. Percentage of Subjects in Chronic Schizophrenic (CSx), Released Schizophrenic (RSx), and Socially Adequate Control (SA) Groups Experiencing Particular Types of Anxiety, Vulnerability, Unreality, and Isolation and Alienation in Study I

Item	CSx	RSx	SA
Anxiety			
15. Nervousness, agitation, trembling, jumpiness; overreaction to noises.[abc]	73	76	36
21. Speech disturbances or difficulties associated with anxiety; stuttering, stammering, hesitation, blocking in speech, rise in voice.[ab]	79	72	46
22. Feels driven to activity, pathological need to be active, to work off tension.[abc]	58	60	24
Vulnerability			
31. Sense of continuity, or personal identity, of oneself over time, distinction from others, separateness, uniqueness.[ab]	29	56	72
38. Vulnerability, defenselessness; unprotected in a world that seems no good, hostile, unfair; feels deserted, betrayed.[a]	88	88	60
45. Loss of self-control, not knowing when or how to stop; press of sudden urges, impulses, or thoughts racing without control.[abc]	62	60	28
46. Overwhelmed by *intense* emotional states, unaccompanied by reason, flood of emotions.[abc]	62	48	12
51. Feelings of aimlessness, random, meaningless activity; pressured compliance with the demands of others.[abc]	70	76	32
54. Feels that other people can read his thoughts or see through him; experiences "ideas of reference."[abc]	46	40	8
Unreality			
58. Sense of personal integration or wholeness, healthiness, feels real, warm, very much alive.[ab]	37	52	72
59. Good contact with reality.[abc]	46	76	100
60. Unreality, unfamiliarity of own experiences; inconsistency, discontinuity, lack of sameness.[abc]	52	35	8
61. Senses blurred or disfunctional so that things look, feel, taste wrong or different; perception disturbed in quality or intensity.[abc]	42	40	8
65. Feelings of a delirious nature — illusions, visions, hallucinations, delusions.[ab]	46	24	8
67. Feelings of self-estrangement, detachment, depersonalization, dissociation, sense of being incomplete, unreal, dead.[abc]	42	48	12
68. Feelings of disintegration, personal dissolution, internal fragmentation; inner disorganization felt in physical, mental, or emotional terms.[ab]	46	28	8
72. Experiences self (thoughts, feelings, actions) as crazy.[b]	62	24	20
Isolation and Alienation			
19. Feelings of friendliness, sociable, outgoing; wants to have friends, to be with them; wants to please others; openness, acceptance of others.[abc]	26	64	92

Table 3 – Continued

Item	CSx	RSx	SA
25. Feelings of acceptance, of being liked, wanted, approved of, cared for by others; has a friend; feelings of being valued, important, worthwhile to another person.[abc]	13	36	68
32. Feelings of being turned inward, timid, withdrawn; self-protective apathy and indifference; solitary, insulated, isolated.[ab]	83	72	52
33. Desire to withdraw from others; avoids people and wants to crawl into self; tries to hide feelings, uses unresponsiveness, evasiveness.[ab]	92	72	56
36. Feels apart from others, like a stranger, outsider, onlooker; cut off from everyday life; friendless and forlorn.[abc]	96	84	48
37. Feels less developed than other children, not keeping up with his class, age group, group of friends.[ab]..........	96	92	56
38. Feels insignificant, unimportant to others, feelings of being looked upon as small or of no account.[ac].........	83	92	64

[a] Significant difference ($p < .05$): all schizophrenics from socially adequate controls.

[b] Significant difference ($p < .05$): chronic schizophrenics from socially adequate controls.

[c] Significant difference ($p < .05$): released schizophrenics from socially adequate controls.

later chronic, defensively identified themselves with relatives, groups, historical persons, and even animals. These identifications continued past the age when they might be appropriate, and they served more to compensate for lack of real relationships than to enhance identifications with real persons and development of integrated personalities.

Many of the pre-schizophrenics evidenced identity loss – they indicated that their own behavior (e.g., stealing, running away, and sexual acting out) was unexplainable, even to themselves. It was as if someone they did not even know was doing the things that brought them to the Guidance Center. Feeling confused, unprotected, and deserted, they were unable to rely upon those closest to them for much needed support. Yet they had little in the way of inner resources to fall back upon in times of stress. Capacities for initiative, organization, and perseverance were poorly developed. These youngsters needed too much to rely on outside cues for direction and limits, and several reported feelings of "drifting through life." Stabenau and Pollin (pp. 94–122) report that youngsters who become schizophrenic are slow in developing the biological maturity required for organized perseverance.

Youngsters in the control group did not show this marked impoverishment of self. In sharp contrast, nearly three quarters of them had achieved, by childhood or adolescence, some sense of personal identity and continuity. They showed more understanding of themselves and took more responsibility for their actions and feelings. They were better able to turn to others for help and to share themselves with another person without pathological fears of loss of identity. To varying degrees, they had some real sense of functioning as people whose thoughts and feelings emanated from within themselves. Neurotic concern about loss of self-control was noted for about a quarter of the control group, but few of them reported being overwhelmed by their feelings.

Four times as many pre-schizophrenics as controls were described as given to periods in which they were "dazed," "trance-like," and "completely absorbed" by their feelings. This experience of being overwhelmed by a particular emotional state, be it, for example, fear, helplessness, or loneliness, was noted primarily within the chronic group. For example, one boy was so completely terrified by thunderstorms that at the first sign of ominous weather, he would hide in the corner and shake with dread. His sense of total vulnerability was devastating at these times.

Along with an inability to manage inner stresses, some pre-schizophrenics felt defenseless against intrusions from the outside. Almost half of this group felt that they were exposed emotionally and that nothing was private or personal in their lives. Some were certain that others could know them better than they knew themselves, without their having said anything directly. One girl who became a chronic schizophrenic reported that she would never confide in her mother, fearing that if she did, she would lose the experience as her own. In the control group, two girls were said to be having difficulties in finding a compromise between sharing everything with their mothers and desires for complete privacy. However, the problem of felt emotional exposure was not a major source of concern for the control group as a whole.

In the area of *unreality* (Table 3), most of the pre-schizophrenics lacked a secure sense of being alive, healthy, real, and whole. Preoccupation with body functions, abnormalities, and injuries were noted, as were marked passivity, odd gesturing, and assumption of unusual roles with others. As youngsters, some of those who were later chronic schizophrenics spent inordinate amounts of time in front of mirrors trying out ways of looking different or just staring at themselves. Several were described as robot-like in their approach to others, with stiff gait and averted gaze. Their strong inhibitions apparently did not allow them the freedom needed to participate in everyday activities and so develop more healthy awareness of their own intactness, capacities, and limitations. In contrast, children in the control group were much more often described as showing responsiveness and healthy vitality in their approaches to others. They seemed to experience satisfying involvement in the world around them. Active in school, jobs, sports, and social groups, they were becoming increasingly aware of themselves, their bodies, and their emotional investment in others.

Although all of the controls were judged as being in good contact with reality, over half of the chronic and a quarter of the released schizophrenic groups had impaired reality testing. Several pre-schizophrenics reported that their sense of taste was strange or changing. They showed food fads and phobias. Many became upset and suspicious when a new or different food was presented, and a few openly feared poisoning by relatives and preferred to eat apart from the family. Some children who were later chronic schizophrenics became disoriented in familiar places, and there were occasional reports of failure to recognize their own relatives. In contrast, only two cases of "hazy" perception and "poor" hearing were reported in the control group, and these complaints did not have the pathological tinge noted in the records of pre-schizophrenics. For example, one boy who eventually became a chronic schizophrenic believed that his mind was "slower than most people's"; he reported that his body and brain were gradually becoming weaker, and that he was, at times, in imminent danger of death. He was certain that masturbation led to insanity and felt that some unexplainable thing was wrong with him which would prevent him from growing up.

Over 60 per cent of the chronic group experienced feelings of being crazy. They felt strange or abnormal and thought, accurately, that their ideas and feelings were unlike those of other people. One girl feared she was becoming psychotic because she "used to understand things easily and now everything seems so confused." Another was sure that her increasing shyness was a definite indication of being crazy. Only a quarter of the released schizophrenics experienced concern with actually being crazy. Moreover, these youngsters had not accepted their present mental distress without reservation, whereas the chronics apparently felt "fated" to be insane. Only a few of the controls were concerned with the normality of their feelings and actions, and these individuals benefited from frank discussion and reassurance with their family or therapist.

Feelings of *isolation* and *alienation* (Table 3) differentiated the pre-schizophrenics and control group more strikingly than any other area of emotional experience. The pre-schizophrenics' records showed long-standing histories of difficulty in establishing or maintaining peer relationships. Several mothers and a few fathers were overprotective and possessive. Extremely threatened whenever the child sought emotional relationships outside the immediate family unit, these parents did not encourage the child's efforts toward establishing contact with others. In some cases, they actively discouraged or punished the child for attempts to make friends. As a result, many pre-schizophrenics were locked into prolonged symbiotic ties to their mothers or fathers. Although some reportedly related well to other adults, few were able to form meaningful relationships with peers.

Felt unacceptability was a major problem for the pre-schizophrenics; they often said they were ignored by others or called names such as *queer*, *sissy*, and *odd one*. Many of those who felt rejected by peers also felt unwanted in their own homes. They were unable to discuss with their parents or siblings their difficulties in making friends, and they found little family support for their efforts to relate to others.

On the other hand, most of the controls were described as friendly, sociable, popular, or well-liked. They had several friends or special pals with whom they shared interests and activities. These youngsters, quite unlike the pre-schizophrenics, showed a basic openness toward others and active participation in the world around them. Also, they seemed better able to verbalize any felt anxieties about social contacts, and their families and therapists helped with these problems. Although a few in the control group were described as shy and sensitive, peer groups seemed to have accepted these individuals more readily than they did the pre-schizophrenics, and children in the control group, in general, did not experience overwhelming feelings of alienation.

Unable to cope with the stresses of human relationships, nearly all the pre-schizophrenics tried to remove themselves emotionally, and often physically, from contact with others. They resisted efforts to engage them in peer or family activities. The chronic group could not elaborate upon the feelings beneath their urges to withdraw; they seemed to sense that the only way to escape the pain of relatedness was to avoid others and to isolate themselves. The released group seemed to link their desires to withdraw to concrete situations and particular feelings. When angry with family members, some of these youngsters would retreat to their own rooms. Others left school rather than face competition, and a few wanted to "run away" from it all. For the control group, withdrawal was generally episodic and short-lived. It was an expression of underlying aggression or resentment for some, but these youngsters could be relatively easily persuaded to join group activities. For them, withdrawal did not become a primary mode of defense, as it did for the pre-schizophrenics.

Many of the pre-schizophrenics, particularly those in the chronic group, seemed never to have had any satisfactory emotional relationships with anybody. They felt "cut off" and in their few group relationships they were often described as the peripheral members, the hangers-on, and the onlookers. Feelings of social inferiority and inadequacy were intense for the pre-schizophrenics. They were devastated by doubt and shame about themselves in comparison with others. Many pre-schizophrenics felt less developed mentally, physically, or emotionally than other children their own age and found their only companions in younger groups. Some felt that they were not valued by anybody they knew and that others' treatment of them as insignificant was justified. In general, the control youngsters were better able to achieve a sense of importance in some areas of their lives and were not preoccupied with such intense feelings of insignificance. They also experienced occasional moments of pride and mastery (in school, sports, social activities, etc.) — a source of gratification generally unavailable to the pre-schizophrenics.

Feelings of mystical intuition, cosmic influence, or extraordinary religiousness (termed *uncanniness* in the present study) were experienced very infrequently by the pre-schizophrenics and hardly at all by the controls. Probably these particular feelings, so often described by adults as preceding the psychotic break, represent a last-ditch effort to stave off impending psychosis and to make sense out of chaotic feelings. That few of the pre-schizophrenics experienced such feelings attests to the probability that despite their extreme emotional states, most of these youngsters were not yet on the brink of psychotic episodes at the time they were seen at the Guidance Center. Most, in fact, were not hospitalized until six or seven years afterwards.

Roff (1963) found that pre-schizophrenic youngsters are reported by teachers to have poor peer relationships. The findings in this study indicate that pre-schizophrenic children feel isolated and alone, and that they can report such feelings to interested adults. The subjective data in this study are the internal counterpart of objective data reported by Roff.

Study II

In Study I, we found the Personal Feelings Inventory to be an effective tool for differentiating pre-schizophrenics on the basis of feelings reported during therapy sessions. We then wanted to know which feelings might be generally pre-pathological and which might be related to specific personality disorders in adult life. For example, since anxiety and isolation have also been described as characteristic of delinquents, we anticipated that these emotional experiences would be found in a group of character disorder subjects, but to a less incapacitating degree than in the early lives of pre-schizophrenics. In addition, we believed that feelings of unreality would be found mainly in the pre-schizophrenic sample and hardly, if at all, among the character disorder group. Inclusion of the additional disturbed group tested the discriminating ability of the PFI. It was anticipated that the results in certain areas would reflect a continuum of adjustment from pre-schizophrenic to character disorder to socially adequate controls. Such findings could help in building developmental models for the different types of personality disorganization.

Hypotheses. Study II was exploratory in nature, and no specific hypotheses were formulated with regard to the three diagnostic groups (schizophrenic, character disorder, control). We were interested in discovering what sets of feelings described the early emotional experiences of the character disorder group and how these subjects resembled or differed from the pre-schizophrenics and controls.

Method. No changes were made in the PFI data schedule or in the method of reading, analyzing, and scoring each case record. Again, the investigator remained blind to adult outcome until the scoring of the records was completed.

Subjects. The second study included no additional chronic schizophrenics, 12 new released schizophrenics, 25 character disorders, and 15 new socially adequate controls.

The first step in analyzing the data of Study II was to be sure that the new schizophrenics and control subjects were like the previous sample, not only in terms of the demographic variables, but also in terms of their early emotional experiences. Happily, this was the case. In none of the five areas of emotional experiences were significant differences found between the two sets of released schizophrenics. Only for Isolation was there a significant difference ($p<.05$) for the control subjects, with the second

Adult Diagnostic Group	*N*
Chronic schizophrenics	24
Released schizophrenics	37
Character disorders	25
Socially adequate controls	40
Total	126

sample showing even more signs of healthy sociability than the first. At this point, we combined our two samples (see tabulation on preceding page).

RESULTS

The general results are presented in Table 4. Compared with the controls, the pre-schizophrenic group experienced significantly more disturbed feelings in each area studied except uncanniness. The direction and quality of these differences support the results of the original research and indicate that objective study of subjective experience can identify relevant emotional antecedents of schizophrenia.

Table 4. Chi Squares for Differences in Frequencies of Experienced Emotions between (a) the Released Schizophrenic Group (RSx) and the Socially Adequate Control Group (SA), (b) the RSx and the Character Disorder (CD) Group and the CS and the SA Control Group in Study II

Emotion	*df*	Group Differences		
		RSx>SA	RSx>CD	CD>SA
Anxiety	15	38.50**	NS	27.56*
Vulnerability	25	66.26**	NS	NS
Unreality	15	75.56**	46.13**	NS
Uncanniness	3	NS	NS	NS
Isolation and alienation	23	82.17**	NS	103.36**

* $p<.05$. ** $p<.01$.

Supporting the notion that character disorder subjects experience anxiety and feel alienated, Table 4 shows that these two areas are the only ones in which there are significant differences between the character disorder and control groups. However, character disorder subjects do not show the marked vulnerability or the feelings of unreality noted for pre-schizophrenics, and in these areas, they are not significantly different from the controls. These results suggest that though children in the character disorder group do experience anxiety and isolation, their feelings are not complicated by the basic lack of security regarding one's own identity or by the disturbing sense of unreality which the pre-schizophrenics have to contend with even in their early years. Free from these concerns, the character disorders may be able to seek resolutions of their disruptive feelings through action in the environment rather than through inner transformations of personality.

Anxiety. The pre-schizophrenics were rated as more disturbed than the controls on all anxiety items, the summed difference across the fifteen items being significant at the .01 level. Similarly, differences between the character disorder group and the controls were significant ($p<.05$), and the difference on each item was in the expected direction. When the two pathological samples were compared, the pre-schizophrenics were rated as more anxious than the character disorder group on twelve of the fifteen items, with significant differences obtained for hyperexcitability, generalized body tension, and physical symptoms related to anxiety. On three items, however, the character disorder group was judged as being more anxious. Of particular interest is the breakdown for the item which reads "Evidence that the child feels driven to activity, pathological need to be active to work off tension": 30 per cent of the controls, 48 per cent of the released schizophrenics, 58 per cent of the chronic schizophrenics, and 72 per cent of the character disorders experienced such a press for activity. It appears that the character disorder group had learned, even in early years, to convert internal stress into action-oriented expressions, as seen in their hyperactivity. The pre-schizophrenics, feeling generally much more anxious and nervous than the other two groups, did not have as ready a mode available to them for releasing felt inner tension. Several were explosively active at times, in tantrums or shows of rebellion, but their activity usually failed to relieve tension effectively.

Vulnerability. Feelings of vulnerability in the areas of identity formation and interpersonal relationships were marked for the pre-schizophrenics and infrequent for the control group, with overall differences being significant at the .01 level. Over 80 per cent of the pre-schizophrenics felt unsafe in the world and unable to cope by themselves; many lacked a sense of personal identity, continuity, and distinction from others. Over half the group experienced loss of self-control over impulses or thoughts, and sensed that they were being overwhelmed by intense feelings. In sharp contrast, most of the controls had achieved some sense of self, and their lives had more gratification, meaning, and direction. They felt they could act on their own initiative, were involved in their feelings and activities, and had ample scope to live in their own ways.

The overall difference between the character disorder group and the controls was not significant, but more youngsters in the character group were judged to be having difficulty on twenty-one of the twenty-five vulnerability items. Significantly more were afraid of thinking about or expressing their own feelings, and more of them were given to periods of intense emotions. However, they showed less inhibition and restraint of their own impulses, were less impatient with themselves, and were more intolerant of others than were the controls. Thus, the character disorder group appeared to share with the released schizophrenics certain feelings of helplessness and defenselessness. But this sense of vulnerability was not so devastating, since the character disorder group also had feelings of personal identity and strength similar to those found mainly among the control group. In fact, they were significantly less vulnerable to the demands and intrusions of others, and were more able to be assertive and ask for what they wanted, than either the pre-schizophrenics or the controls.

Unreality. Differences in feelings of unreality, between the released schizophrenics and both the character disorder and control groups, were in the predicted direction. Disturbances in sensory acuity, reality contact, and orientation were noted for the released schizophrenics, but the proportion in this group experiencing such feelings was considerably less than that in the chronic group. For example, although 52 per cent of the released group were judged to have a "sense of personal integration, wholeness, healthiness, feels real, warm, very much alive," only 37 per cent of the chronics were so rated. These percentages are significantly less than both the character disorder group and the controls (over 80 per cent). The character disorder group was quite similar to the controls in their freedom from feelings of unreality, with the notable exception of one item: 52 per cent of the character disorder group were rated as "experiencing his own fantasies as more real than the world outside" (released schizophrenics, 57 per cent; chronic schizophrenics, 96 per cent) whereas nearly two thirds of the controls were judged as not experiencing such a feeling. In general, however, the character disorder group shared with the controls a healthy sense of personal integration and good reality contact.

Isolation and Alienation. As in the report of Study I, the most striking differences between the pathological groups and the controls were in the area of isolation and alienation. Apparently all youngsters who lack a sense of positive affiliation are headed for personality disturbance of one sort or another in later years. In some ways, the character disorder group resembled the pre-schizophrenics in terms of feelings of isolation. Children in both groups characteristically did not experience trust and confidence in another person; both felt unable to communicate their feelings to someone; and both felt that no one understood them. However, the pre-schizophrenics, especially the released group, maintain a potential openness to others, a desire to reach out and communicate, which is greater than that of the character disorder group. For example, 85 per cent of the controls experience a general friendliness toward and acceptance of other people, but such feelings were found for only 57 per cent of the released schizophrenic group and for less than 45 per cent of the character disorder group. Feelings of being accepted by someone else were present for significantly more controls (70 per cent) than character disorders (28 per cent), released schizophrenics (32 per cent), or chronic schizophrenics (12 per ccnt).

The character disorder group seemed to want to have little to do with others. Besides a general attitude of unfriendliness, the majority (60 per cent) showed *no* desire to touch or be physically close to others in an active sense or to be passively held (62 per cent). Their sources for interpersonal comfort were limited; they felt apart from others, but this sense of alienation stemmed largely from their own desire for minimal contact. Withdrawal for them seemed to be self-initiated. On the other hand, the pre-schizophrenics showed a poignant awareness of human relatedness and their own inadequacies in this area. They wanted to have a friend, to be understood, held, cared for by another, but they felt rejected by peers, and their withdrawal seemed to be *reactive*, stemming from their inability to establish and maintain human relationships.

Discussion

The general hypothesis that childhood and adolescent emotional experiences are related to subsequent adult disturbances was supported by the findings of these two studies. The major conclusion to be drawn is that more pre-schizophrenics than controls experience disruptive emotions in childhood and adolescence — particularly feelings of anxiety, vulnerability, unreality, and isolation. Character disorder subjects also differ from controls in ways consistent with their adult disorders, being in some ways even more isolated and opposed to human contact than the pre-schizophrenic group. Since these feelings were identified in the reports of children and adolescents before the development of adult psychotic reactions, and since they clearly differentiate groups who are only much later differentiated by psychiatric diagnoses, it seems reasonable to infer that these childhood and adolescent experiences are relevant to the development of schizophrenia and of character disorder.

The present study parallels earlier work of the Judge Baker Schizophrenia Research Project in showing that important antecedents of schizophrenia can be found through careful investigation of the early life histories of persons who were later hospitalized for schizophrenia.

It appears that the individual's feelings are as meaningful indicators of future mental hospitalization as are overt signs of neurological or behavioral disorder in the child, or of pathology in his parents, home environment, or community. We can find antecedents of schizophrenia in the events and situations of the child's early years, but predictions can be strengthened if we also consider the ways in which he interprets them and responds. A passive, lethargic child may respond pathologically to a psychotic mother, whereas a more active, assertive youngster might develop peer relationships supporting feelings of positive identity and independence.

It should not be thought that the youngsters who were seen at the Guidance Center for personality problems in childhood and adolescence and later achieved a socially adequate adjustment never experienced feelings similar to those of the pre-schizophrenics. Most of the control group did not have such feelings, but a few did. For these few, however, the feelings were generally more circumscribed, less intense, and less incapacitating than were those of the pre-schizophrenics. Some of the controls infrequently, in moments of stress, fatigue, or desperation, felt the way most of the pre-schizophrenics did chronically in most areas of living. Moreover, the individuals in the control group experienced the balancing effect of pride and mastery, as well as gratifying interpersonal relationships that the pre-schizophrenics, as a group, lacked.

Nor should the presence of any one anxiety-related symptom be taken as prognostic of schizophrenia, without investigating the depth and pervasiveness of the other types of feelings the person can report. In this research stuttering was noticed in some of the very anxious youngsters who later became schizophrenic. But Roff's (1956) study, focusing on stuttering specifically, across the whole range of children in whom it occurred, found that it did not have significance for a poor prognosis.

These findings echo Searles's (1960) contention that the mature personality experiences a wide range of emotions, not excluding those of psychotic quality or intensity but including much more. Because he can fit extreme feelings into a more balanced context, the mature person is not overwhelmed or devastated by his emotions, as is the pre-schizophrenic. Thus, the mere presence of emotional experiences or feelings similar to those noted for the schizophrenic group or the character disorder group, per se, should not lead one to conclude prematurely that the individual is likely to suffer severe personality maladjustment. One would need to know a good deal more about the pervasiveness of such feelings, the individual's preoccupation with such emotions, and his ability to cope with disturbing affect.

It appeared that the controls had, in childhood and adolescence, "something" which the pre-schizophrenics lacked. On the basis of the other studies in the Schizophrenia Research Project, it might be conjectured that the difference stemmed from genetic, neurological, or environmental factors. One might also hypothesize that the "something" the control youngsters had was their capacity to involve themselves with others and to profit from opportunities for living in a self-enhancing, rather than a self-defeating manner. The clinical impression gained from the records of the control group suggested that areas of strength, health, mastery, and positive feelings should be studied more fully in further investigations.

Replication Studies. Two ongoing studies will be reported briefly. Both support the findings in the first two studies and indicate generality beyond the confines of the clinic population on which they are based.

In the first of these studies, Rhoda Geller (1969) used the PFI to judge the experiences reported by thirty childhood schizophrenics and thirty childhood character disorder patients at the Psychiatric Institute of the Columbia Medical Center. The cases were judged blind, with all data indicating diagnoses removed from the record. The results indicate that the schizophrenic children feel more anxious, more vulnerable, more isolated, and less sure of the reality of their experience, as compared with the character disorder group. These findings are in the same directions as those just discussed, but the groups are more sharply differentiated. One difference between the two sets of results, which is consistent with the fact that Geller's subjects were already diagnosed schizophrenic whereas those studied by Fleming were not diagnosed schizophrenic until later, was Geller's finding that her schizophrenic patients had uncanny experiences and mystical feelings more often than the character disordered patients. It appears, on the basis of Geller's findings, that feelings of anxiety, vulnerability, and so forth will characterize groups who are already diagnosed schizophrenic even more than those who are pre-schizophrenic. The difference between groups also seems open to replication in contexts such as the mental hospital as well as in a child guidance clinic population.

A second study, by Suzanne Ross (1969), investigated whether the results of our Studies I and II would hold if one judged the presence or absence of feelings from direct interviews rather than from therapy records. Ross interviewed thirty-six schizophrenic adolescents and compared the interviews with those gathered with thirty-six normal adolescents. The interviews were structured around the feelings the subjects experienced, and around the solutions they had reached to the adolescent tasks listed by Gardner (1959): modification of unconscious concepts of parental figures, assumption of internalized standards of morality, identification with sex role and body rootedness, and the making of choices in regard to educational and vocational futures. Scoring of the interviews, which were recorded, was done by skilled psychologists who were not informed about the diagnosis of the child or where the interview had taken place. The solutions to adolescent tasks were found to be much more developed in the normal group, as expected, and reactions to failure in achieving solutions were found to be related to the kinds of anxiety, vulnerability, isolation, and feelings of unreality that had been found by Fleming and confirmed by Geller. Since Fleming's research had suggested that normal adolescents differed from pre-schizophrenics in the possession of strengths as well as in the absence of pathology, this study investigated, also, whether systematic recording of strengths differentiated the groups as well as systematic recording of pathological symptoms and disturbed emotions. The answer, to our surprise, proved to be negative. Items that tapped pathology differentiated schizophrenic from normal youngsters far better than those that tapped strength. Disturbed experiences were infrequent in the normal sample (in spite of contrary impressions of those of us who have adolescents in our homes, classes, or consulting rooms), and experiences of strengths were frequent enough in the schizophrenic group to lose some differentiating power. These results support those clinicians who argue that even in schizophrenic youngsters there are considerable islands of strength and adequacy on which one can count when offering help.

Implications for Treatment. These studies indicate that early intense, painful emotional experiences are indicators of future personality disorganization. They also indicate that feelings, ephemeral as they may be, are valid research data. This conclusion is not new. Wilson's (1963) review of animal studies in behavior pathology concluded that emotional responses, not keyed to the contingencies of the environment and cumulating because spontaneous escape activity was inhibited, led to behavioral disintegration. Surveying both animal and human studies, he concluded (pp. 69–70):

> Taking the studies as a group, two significant features stand out in all cases of behavior pathology. On the one hand, the foundation for pathology is laid by a progressive state of emotional arousal that finally reaches disastrous proportions. Acute anxiety is the common denominator of these studies, and at

early stages it is expressed in autonomic fluctuations, in panic reactions, and in behavioral disorganization . . . the indispensable feature of pathology is the state of anxiety . . .

The results in the studies reported here also indicate that emotional states of extreme intensity and chronic duration precede and predict psychopathology, but they question the central position of anxiety. Preliminary factor analysis of some of the data indicates that the central differentiating factor in the schizophrenic group, and probably also in the pre-schizophrenic, is the feeling of vulnerability, with anxiety, uncertainty, and isolation as secondary elaborations on this feeling. People who become schizophrenic can apparently be identified early by their striking sense of helplessness and inability to cope effectively on their own. A similar analysis in the character disorder group, on the other hand, suggests that isolation/alienation from others is the primary factor, with feelings of vulnerability, anxiety, and drivenness secondary elaborations on this theme.

Initial contact with disturbed youngsters might increase in usefulness if clinicians can be alert to the emotional experiences that characterize each group. Central points of focus might well be the child's feelings of vulnerability or strength, his closeness to others or alienation from them, and the presence or absence of feelings of security, integrity, and identity. If a child speaks of having no friends at all, of being anxious or frightened most of the time, if he is uncertain about himself in most areas of living, and if he is unsure of the reality of his everyday sensory experiences, he might well be regarded as being in a high-risk group for adult schizophrenia, and his state might be seen as justifying major efforts toward early intervention and help.

Interest in disruptive feelings, however, should not lead intervention into the discovery of psychopathology for psychopathology's sake, nor into the typical therapeutic methods for dealing with neurotic difficulties — that is, uncovering of painful vulnerabilities and anxieties. If the child cannot cope with his feelings, then nothing could be more devastating than simply uncovering them and stripping from him whatever ways of avoidance he has worked out.

Investigation of the methods used by the most effective therapists, using the criterion of the adult outcomes of children seen by them in childhood or adolescence, suggests that these effective therapists shared certain characteristics, not the least important of which was their ability to keep extremely fragile and withdrawn children interested in therapy and eager for help. They did this through establishing warmly supportive, actively interested approaches to the child, and through the use of every resource available in the child himself, his family, and his community. They supported the autonomy and value of the child, often to the point of directly intervening with the parents in regard to specific things the parents had been doing (such as threatening that masturbation would make a boy go crazy), or in recommending and helping arrange temporary or permanent separation of parents and child (Waring, 1966). This may involve a great deal of support for a parent who has been clinging to the child. The warmth of the most helpful therapists and their active interest in the children with whom they work make them anchors to reality for children uncertain about trusting themselves or others, and they are thus able to discuss with the children such issues as whether others can read their thoughts, whether they are going crazy, why they shake, and other issues that frightened children need to work out with a supportive person. The best therapists seemed not at all averse to giving advice and actively promoting the capacity of the child to cope with difficult situations. They worked with the child toward solution of immediate problems and, by their own example of realistic effectiveness, built up a conception of how problems could be approached and solved.

To a very marked extent, the early stages of schizophrenia are still fluid, conflicted, and painful. Intervention seems to be effective if it can offer the child supports he has been missing, and so help him to be active and spontaneous enough to realize himself—that is, make himself real. The therapist who increases feelings of anxiety, vulnerability, unreality, and isolated alienation, without helping the child do anything about them, may precipitate a psychosis. The therapist, or the whole helping institution, that helps the child develop enough strength and confidence to face these feelings slowly, at a pace that permits mastery, may deflect, or even reverse, the years-long process of going mad.

COMMENTARY

MEDNICK. Did you look for neurotics, and how many did you find?

FLEMING. No. We didn't have them in our sample.

MEDNICK. Do you think you could get them?

RICKS. The only way you could get neurotics for this kind of sample design would be to take hospitalized neurotics, since we're looking only for people who have some kind of hospital diagnosis in adult life. And that would not be a very representative sample of neurotics. We haven't tried to do anything like getting clinical practitioners in the Massachusetts area to scan our lists and find the cases and so on; I don't feel that hospital data is the best data in the world, but it is preferable to what would be available if we tried to go out and find the records of individual practitioners.

LORR. I wonder what kind of character problems these were. You mentioned them being impulsive. Is there any corresponding APA diagnostic group? What kind of problems specifically and concretely brought them to a hospital? It's unusual to have a hospital with character disorders unless they're alcoholics.

FLEMING. I'm not too familiar with the follow-up on the specific diagnosis. My group of character disorders are the portion of Dr. Berry's sample that stayed in therapy over five sessions with one therapist. He reports that most of them have a psychopathic personality diagnosis. Since he did it, I didn't go back and check it.

RICKS. The biggest group are those who act out by fighting, stealing, troublesome activity. There's a smaller subsample that might in a long-term study be differentiated whose primary form of acting out is deviant sexuality.

LORR. What have they done to be hospitalized? This is what is so surprising. Were they sent by the court, or what?

RICKS. Many of them are quite young. It might well be that in later years they might pick up a more severe diagnosis, and the hospital was just being kindly.

FLEMING. One striking thing reading the records blind – we made our own guesses about what we thought the person was. It's pretty easy once you get used to the data scheduling to read the things in your own way. If you use your own feelings as a guide, you can pick out pre-schizophrenics pretty well. I was about 77 per cent accurate at this. The character disorder group, by and large, do not express feelings very much, even in therapy in adolescence and childhood, and their record has a blandness, so I was better than chance guessing them too. But it was by the absence of feelings that I picked them, not by the presence of many bad feelings, as was true for the pre-schizophrenics.

MEDNICK. I wonder if you would repeat what you said about the anxiety findings. I thought I recalled you saying that between the recovered schizophrenics and the character disorders there were some differences within the anxiety scale, but across the entire scale you found no differences. Could you go into some detail on that?

FLEMING. Across the whole group, the released schizophrenics are more anxious. But on three of the fifteen items the character disorder groups are more anxious than the schizophrenics. This finding in the opposite direction brings down the chi-square value to less than significance. Only one item, that says they're driven to activity, reaches significance for the character disorders and really pulls the thing down. On twelve items the schizophrenics were more anxious – on fears and worries, and things like that.

QUESTION. I noticed that you talked about what might be considered,

I suppose, as the mirror image of thought disorder, which is the defensive aspect of escape into fantasy and so forth. At least it seems to me that that may be the other side of the thought disorder coin. Did you notice any confusion or evidence of thinking disorder in the records of some of these pre-schizophrenics and others, or was there any kind of differentiation among the later patients?

FLEMING. That area is included in the data schedule in my dissertation. I'm reporting here only those areas where we hypothesized directional differences between the pre-schizophrenic group and the control group. We didn't predict the character disorder group. We included cognitive differences, and specific feelings about mother, father, therapist, siblings, and things like that. A preliminary look at the pre-schizophrenic and the control group shows that there was no difference in the items, overall. There were fifteen items on cognitive disruption, on which there was slightly more confusion in the pre-schizophrenics — slightly more obsessive thought, but not reaching significance.

QUESTION. Somewhere about two thirds of the way through, did I understand that it is feelings of vulnerability that you see as the core of the problem? Is there any way to measure this behaviorally or is there a preventive therapeutic intervention? How do you pick these kids out? Is it the absence of friends, or do you have any ideas about what might be done?

FLEMING. These are children who have very little sense of their own autonomy from others — overly dependent children. I can't list all twenty-five items in that area of the PFI, but these children are very fearful of trying out anything new, they don't know anything about themselves. They won't become active in sports because they really are afraid of finding out they can't play baseball — and they don't want another failure. They won't join a girl scout group because they're afraid they won't sew right, or cook right, or do anything like that, and they don't want to know, even in early years, that there's one more thing they can't do. You get a sense that all these kids know is their own failures, and they don't want to find out anything new. This includes riding bikes — any athletic activity . . . you can pick it up on a number of subtle things. I have copies of the data schedule. Each item reads, "Evidence that the child experiences . . ."

LORR. Well, this is your judgment though.

FLEMING. That's right. It's my judgment. And we ran reliabilities on both the original data schedule research and this research, and they were very good.

RICKS. I will say that although the reliabilities were very high, the cases are hard to judge. You have to read forty hours of therapy notes and try to compensate in your own mind for what kind of therapist this is, and what he tends to say about people, and then you make a judgment. I was always surprised that people had high reliability. One interesting thing about therapists, though — at least at the Judge Baker Guidance Center, where we worked — is that they do keep quite adequate notes on feelings.

What was very frustrating was that they wouldn't say what was going on in school or in the kids' everyday lives outside. But if the kid said he felt bad or felt good, or he was upset, or anything like this, the therapists tended to put that in their notes, and there is a tradition at this clinic of having very detailed long notes, which helps.

QUESTION. Is it possible that the absence of more discrimination on thought disorder was partly a product of that kind of orientation on the part of the therapist?

RICKS. Well, let me propose the other alternative, that the thought disorder is not nearly so obvious at this point; that the feelings really differentiate, and the thought disorder, which might differentiate in later years in the hospital *if* the hospital is bad enough, doesn't differentiate yet. I think Mednick has argued quite convincingly that an awful lot of what we call schizophrenia is caused by hospitalization, and the sensory deprivation and social deprivation of hospitalization. You don't see these things yet in our cases.

REFERENCES

Alvarez, W. C. *Minds that came back.* New York: Lippincott, 1961.

Arieti, S. *Interpretation of schizophrenia.* New York: Robert Brunner, 1955.

Fleming, P. Emotional antecedents of schizophrenia: Inner experiences of children and adolescents who were later hospitalized for schizophrenia. Ph.D. thesis, Teachers College, Columbia University, 1966.

Gardner, G. E. Psychiatric problems in adolescence. In S. Arieti (Ed.), *American handbook of psychiatry.* New York: Basic Books, 1959.

Gardner, G. G. The relationship between childhood neurotic symptomatology and later schizophrenia in males and females. *Journal of Nervous and Mental Diseases,* 1967, 144, 97–100. (a)

———. Role of maternal psychopathology in male and female schizophrenics. *Journal of Consulting Psychology,* 1967, 31, 411–413. (b)

Geller, R. L. Subjective experience of schizophrenia: Reported emotional experiences of schizophrenic children. Ph.D. thesis, Teachers College, Columbia University, 1969.

Green, H. *I never promised you a rose garden.* New York: Holt, 1964.

Hays, W. C. *Statistics for psychologists.* New York: Holt, 1963.

Kaplan, B. (Ed.) *The inner world of mental illness.* New York: Harper, 1964.

Kraepelin, E. *Dementia praecox.* Chicago: Medical Book Co., 1919.

Laing, R. D. *The divided self.* Chicago: Quadrangle Books, 1960.

Landis, C. *Varieties of psychopathological experience.* New York: Holt, 1964.

Nameche, G. F., M. Waring, & D. F. Ricks. Early indicators of outcome in schizophrenia. *Journal of Nervous and Mental Diseases,* 1964, 139, 232–240.

Ricks, D. F., & G. F. Nameche. Symbiosis, sacrifice, and schizophrenia. *Mental Hygiene,* 1966, 50, 541–551.

Roff, M. Childhood social interactions and young adult psychosis. *Journal of Clinical Psychology,* 1963, 19, 152–157.

Ross, S. Reported emotional experiences of disturbed and non-disturbed adolescents. Ph.D. thesis, Teachers College, Columbia University, 1969.

Searles, H. F. *The nonhuman environment in normal development and in schizophrenia.* New York: International Universities Press, 1960.

Sullivan, H. S. *Schizophrenia as a human process.* New York: Norton, 1962.

Waring, M. Averting hospitalization for adult schizophrenia: A search for ameliorative factors. *Journal of the National Association of Social Workers,* 1966, 2 (No. 4), 34–42.

——— & D. F. Ricks. Family patterns of children who became adult schizophrenics. *Journal of Nervous and Mental Diseases,* 1965, 140, 351–364.

Wilson, R. S. On behavior pathology. In D. S. Holmes (Ed.), *Reviews of research in behavior pathology.* New York: Wiley, 1968.

MERRILL ROFF

Some Life History Factors in Relation to Various Types of Adult Maladjustment

MOST of the other papers in this volume have dealt with a single adult disorder, and the authors have been intimately acquainted with the particular maladjustments under consideration. In contrast, the program to be discussed here deals with the whole range of adult maladjustments and their antecedents. I am primarily an individual differences psychologist and statistician, not a clinical psychologist. I have been working with a large sample of child guidance clinic cases and with a second large sample of juvenile delinquents (non-clinic), and comparing this earlier information with outcome information for the young adult period obtained from the military services and related agencies. Adult criterion information has been obtained on more than eleven thousand cases up to this time. I am thus dealing with adult outcome groups of all the kinds which occur frequently enough to make it worthwhile studying them, and am not specializing in schizophrenia, psychoneurosis, character disorders, "psychosomatic" reactions, and so forth. Data have been collected, though as yet only partially analyzed, to provide some information about the childhood antecedents of the whole adult range of maladjustments. This gives a generalist, rather than a specialist approach, and there are both advantages and disadvantages to such a position.

To start with the disadvantages, it requires a constant attempt to keep abreast of a literature larger than one person can possibly digest. In the psychotic area, for example, in one major handbook on schizophrenia (Bellak, 1958) the bibliography alone occupied 250 pages. That was published ten years ago when the publication rate was substantially less than it is now. (Fortunately, it seems from our data that the term *schizo-*

NOTE: The work reported here was supported in part by U.S. Army Medical Research and Development Command Contract No. DA-49-007-MD-2015.

phrenia is almost co-extensive with the term *psychosis*, at least in the young adult period. The number of persons diagnosed manic-depressive or psychotic depressive among the young adult males of our total sample is negligibly small, so that coverage of the literature on schizophrenia is, in effect, coverage of the literature on functional psychoses.)

One of the problems concerning which the literature is either ambiguous or flatly contradictory is the status of the classical subtypes of schizophrenia. Some authors consider these very meaningful, whereas others consider them obsolete or worthless. In a recent book on psychopharmacology, for example, Lehmann (1965) points out that the different classical subtypes seem to respond somewhat differently to pharmacotherapy, so that there the distinction is considered definitely meaningful. Those who emphasize the process versus reactive types of schizophrenia tend to disregard the classical subtypes; one paper suggests that "schizophrenic persons, instead of being categorized into a unitary diagnosis, can be described as varying in their degree of pathology according to the degree of social maturity attained before their breakdown" (Kantor & Winder, 1961). The papers in this volume also seem to show some disagreement on this matter.

The solution of these terminological problems is not our primary concern. My associates and I simply work with the diagnoses shown in the records, made by a large variety of different psychiatrists. The fact that our adult diagnoses have been made by many persons, though perhaps resulting in a loss in purity of experimental design, has the advantage that the adult diagnoses are not dependent on the biases of any one individual.

A major advantage of the multiple outcome approach, and it is enough to make this whole line of work worthwhile, is that it is possible to find out whether or not some factor which appears to be clearly predictive of one bad outcome is specific to that outcome, is actually more important as an antecedent of some other maladjustment, or is common to several maladjustments or to bad outcomes in general.

This series of studies started with the main child guidance clinics in Minneapolis and St. Paul. In going through the clinic files initially, we had accepted only those male cases with enough of a case history to make it worthwhile following up the individuals. This eliminated cases, of which most clinics have a certain number, who had been referred only for mental test to find whether or not they were retarded. It also excluded cases where the mother was interviewed and then the case aborted. In addition to the clinic groups, we studied a control sample contemporary with them which was randomly drawn from the files of the Minneapolis public schools.

Criterion information came in two stages. The first of these was acceptance or rejection (or permanent deferment) by the Selective Service System; the second was the actual record of military service. Third-stage criterion information, from VA records, has been obtained for the earlier Minnesota cases. This has not yet been secured for cases from other states.

The group first studied was a World War II sample (Roff, 1956). The number of permanent deferments for the control group was only 6 per cent; it was less for the problem groups. The proportion rejected for behavioral reasons was, not surprisingly, greater for the problem group than for the control group, more or less across the board. When we look at the outcomes in service, we find that 90 per cent of the control group remained in service until demobilized. For the problem groups (for which information was presented separately by age of the groups) around 75 per cent, or three out of four, remained in service until demobilized (Roff, 1956).

If we were obsessed with hypothesis testing, we could point out that the hypothesis that the problem group did not come out so well as the control sample was indeed tenable, and we could, as is commonly done, draw the conclusion that former child guidance clinic cases do not get along so well in young adult life as does a random sample of the general population. I should prefer to emphasize that three out of four of the former clinic patients seemed to get along about as well as other people, and that rejection of a former clinic patient for that reason alone would cost three more or less satisfactory persons for every unsatisfactory one who was excluded. We obviously need to do much better than this before making extensive use of this particular variable in selection.

Work was subsequently extended to other parts of the country. Experience with clinics in several major cities has indicated that there are those whose cases are on the average more serious than those of the Minnesota clinics; in these other clinics the proportion subsequently unsatisfactory is substantially greater. It is also possible to find clinics which drew from the more prosperous part of their communities, so that the average education of their patients was above that of the community as a whole, and the adult problems of the former child guidance clinic cases were correspondingly mild.

We have had quite a bit of experience with inter-clinic variability. When I first began studying these cases, there was little interest in this problem. Eiduson, Ramsey-Klee, and associates (Eiduson, Johnson, & Rottenberg, 1966; Eiduson & Ramsey-Klee, pp. 127–143) have provided much information for clinics in the Los Angeles area. I have not done so much formal work with this as can be done, and have not written up some of the things that have been done. However, this experience gives a background for evaluating work reported with samples from different clinics, which is privately very useful.

Our procedure of starting with a general child population and following it to all possible outcomes gives a total picture which is not commonly available. In civilian life, the poor outcomes could eventually show up in a court or penal institution, as patients of a psychiatrist, as outpatients in a clinic of some kind, as patients in a mental hospital, or as in the case of some psychosomatic disorders, as cases of doctors with no psychiatric orientation at all. In the military services, the medical or psychiatric discharge cases are of interest to medical personnel whereas the disciplinary-administrative discharges are primarily of interest to nonmedical personnel, and these are not combined. Only through a life history follow-up can a comprehensive count of all these different outcomes be made.

In the first research report of this project (Roff, 1956), detailed tallies of outcome in service for the Minnesota clinic group and the control group were presented along with highly condensed descriptions indicating the behavior exhibited at the adult level by individuals referred to by any one diagnostic term. I shall not take time to review the detailed outcome picture, since that has been published and is available on request.

Other groups for which follow-up information was published in this same report included a special sample consisting of a group who had been classified as mentally retarded during the grade school period and placed in special classes within the school system. Of these, about one in ten was rejected because of mental deficiency, and about the same proportion of those who entered service were given mental deficiency discharges. Apart from these, the overall picture was similar to that for the general clinic group, although less satisfactory than that for the control group. They were rejected for psychoneuroses and for bad conduct at about the same rate as the clinic group. In service, attrition was greater than for the control sample, but not markedly different from those in the problem groups. Psychiatric discharges were primarily for psychoneurosis and anxiety state, but the total number of these was less than 9 per cent. The relatively low number of bad conduct discharges (2 per cent) suggests that they did not tend to become serious disciplinary offenders. Altogether, 70 per cent of those in service remained there until demobilized, although their average rank was less than that of the control group.

Another special group consisted of a sample of 228 individuals who as children had been classed as moderate or severe stutterers. This group was included to see what kind of adult psychiatric histories they would have, apart from the stuttering. There were 8 rejections, or less than 4 per cent of the sample, explicitly for stuttering. These could have occurred because their stuttering was so severe, or because some psychiatrist thought that stuttering was an indication of nervous instability. The 10 physical rejections included 4 for spastic paralysis; this is a greater proportion than occurred in other samples. The service outcome of the stuttering group is as good as that of the control group. Not one was discharged because of stuttering, although the records indicate that some individuals still stuttered. A history of stuttering was not adverse in terms of adjustment in military service. Stuttering appears as a specific habit difficulty, rather than an indicator of some more widespread psychopathology.

Two other samples were mentioned in this first report. The first of these, the sibling group, consisted of the brothers of all the problem cases for a certain time span in one particular city. The general result obtained from the sibling study was that, taking both Selective Service and military service information into consideration, they come out just about halfway between the problem group and the control group in the proportion of unsatisfactory cases. Various outcome patterns appeared in different families. In a great many cases two or more brothers came out satisfactorily. In other cases, one of the adult family members would be unsatisfactory, but it was not always the original index case.

One of the most interesting findings was that a family which produced a boy with some kind of unsatisfactory adult outcome would be at least slightly more likely than the average to have some other unsatisfactory adult outcome in male siblings. There was a slightly greater tendency for the brother of a neurotic male to exhibit conduct problems, and vice versa.

Another item of interest was the relative infrequency of the same behavior difficulty in siblings. There was no family in which more than one brother had a psychoneurotic outcome. This might be due to the fact that "neurotogenic" mothers (whether this be interpreted hereditarily or environmentally) would avoid having large families. Or it might be that anyone who had a large family would be unable to give each of them the attention that might make them all neurotic. On the other hand, it was possible, though not common, for a whole set of brothers to turn out seriously delinquent.

There was one most unusual family with four brothers of whom three became schizophrenic; for the fourth, no information was available. Their mother was hospitalized as manic-depressive when the index patient was about five years old, and the brothers were placed in an orphanage, where they remained. With a set of such intensely unfavorable childhood circumstances, it is obviously possible only to speculate concerning the outcome if either the heredity or the life histories had been markedly different.

My interest in intra-family resemblances and differences has been strong and long-standing (Roff, 1950), and these results seemed very interesting, but they were not reported pending the obtaining of cases from additional clinics. We now have the index cases for a comprehensive sibling study over all the clinics, but the criterion information for the brothers has not yet been obtained. Some indications of what might be expected from such a study will be presented below.

Before leaving this first report, it may be noted that the life history approach may result in the splitting of two or more maladjustments which are commonly grouped together on a cross-sectional basis. Asthma and peptic ulcer are two of the most prominent "psychosomatic" reactions. However, from a life history approach these are quite different. This was obvious when some of the first child cases with adult diagnoses in these two areas were examined. Asthma tended to have been present from childhood. Studies of parent-child interactions where asthma is involved are thus commonly dealing with a situation in which the difficulty is already present, and thus potentially influencing the parents' treatment of the child. On the other hand, the peak age for ulcers has not yet been reached in the twenties, and they are less frequent in our young adults than they would be in an older sample. In the pre-ulcer cases, there is almost never any suggestion at all of a childhood ulcer, and whatever the parents may be, or may not be, doing to the child is not influenced by their realization that they have a sick child on their hands. It thus seemed undesirable to group these two together in studying the childhood case histories, and as it happens, we have not yet made intensive studies of either. It should be recognized in reading studies of parental behavior and asthma that the asthma was usually already there early in life.

Once we had obtained a large number of adult outcomes, a preliminary study was made during the summer of 1953 (Roff, 1956) to see to what extent experienced clinical psychologists could predict good or poor outcome on a global basis, using the entire case history. For a group of 209 cases, about 40 per cent of the total, it was predicted that the outcome would be as good as that of the general population. Of these, only 15 per cent were unsatisfactory by our criteria. At the other end, 66 cases were judged to have the poorest likelihood of satisfactory adjustment in service. Of these, 70 per cent were in fact unsatisfactory. One rater picked a small group of 13 cases and predicted that these would be trouble-free. They all were. This study showed that there was some predictability in the data, but it did not indicate what the decisive information was for those making the predictions. An attempt at a more analytic approach seemed an obvious next step.

At this stage we had a very substantial amount of fascinating information, recorded partly during childhood and partly during the young adult life of the same individuals. The way in which we proceeded has been described in another chapter (see pp. 10–29). Briefly, we engaged in intensive pick-and-shovel work, digging out items of information in various categories to see if they seemed promising for extensive exploitation. The general logic used was similar to that of the statistical procedure of sequential analysis, in which enough cases were studied to indicate, usually, that a lead was not a very fruitful one. To fit our data, an ad hoc grouping of adult maladjustments was made, as follows:

Group 1: Psychotic. In our data psychotics were almost without exception schizophrenics. Since there were, however, a few diagnosed as psychotic only, we used the more general term to refer to them, thus effectively removing the study from the consideration of that substantial group of people interested in schizophrenia. The number diagnosed as manic-depressive was negligible — this was a permissible diagnosis in this setting, but it was simply not used with this population of young adult males.

Group 2: Psychoneurotic. Here we used the standard set of subdivisions in the diagnostic manual. Diagnoses of anxiety state or reaction were more common than all the others combined. Based on the childhood case histories, it seems very possible that the rare conversion reaction cases may not belong with the other psychoneurotics at all. Their backgrounds are more similar to those of the bad conduct cases than to those with anxiety.

Group 3: Personality Disorders. Our criterion information here includes psychiatric diagnosis and detailed records of disciplinary offenses. The largest single group of unsatisfactory individuals consists of those who exhibited severe bad conduct. Many of these cases were seen and diagnosed by psychiatrists as antisocial reactions, emotionally unstable personality, sociopathic personality, and so forth. In many cases, the descriptions of behavior are more concrete and detailed than the psychiatric diagnostic term itself. It is thus in some ways more satisfactory to treat these bad conduct cases in terms of the behavior exhibited rather than in terms of the diagnostic label.

Three other types of behavior in this general area occur with sufficient frequency to make it desirable to include them as separate subgroups — (3b) *schizoid personality*, (3c) *sexual deviation*, and (3d) *personality disorder without severe bad conduct*. The most frequent diagnosis in the last category is passive-aggressive personality (passive-dependent type, passive-aggressive type, or aggressive type.) We have a sample of childhood cases for these partly analyzed.

The first group studied were the psychoneurotics (Roff, 1957; 1959). We narrowed our activities down to the group with psychoneurotic outcomes, and compared these with a group judged to have had good outcomes. The sample studied consisted of 208 persons who all had dealt during childhood or adolescence with a child guidance clinic. Half of these, the psychoneurotic group, had been medically diagnosed as having difficulty of a psychoneurotic kind (anxiety reaction or state, dissociative reaction, conversion reaction or conversion hysteria, phobic reaction, obsessive-compulsive reaction, depressive reaction, other) leading either to medical discharge or, in a small minority of cases, to hospitalization or outpatient treatment followed by a return to duty. The other half, also former child guidance clinic patients, who served as a control group, were a "good" group selected as having reached and kept a grade of at least sergeant or equivalent, without a history of disciplinary or mental health trouble at any point following entrance into service. The two groups were matched in pre-service IQ from information contained in their original case histories.

As possible predictors we had information about the mother, the father, siblings, health and nervous habits, social adjustment outside the family (particularly in the school setting), school performance, psychological test results, and psychiatric evaluations. To study these separately, information on a topic was abstracted from the case, so that a reader making a prediction based, for example, on school performance, would not be influenced by his knowledge of the characteristics of the mother.

One problem of interest was the predictive significance of different kinds of comments by psychiatrists, recorded in the child cases. (In our first two clinics, definite pronouncements were found in only a minority of cases.) An example of a definitely unfavorable comment is: "His problems are so set and of such long standing that he cannot control himself and his feelings. At no time has he been accessible to real psychotherapy." An example of a clearly favorable comment is: "Mother always seems to be much relieved when I tell her that he is a very fine boy and is in no danger whatsoever of getting into any serious mental or social difficulty."

Three different kinds of psychiatric comments were located which did not clearly point in one direction or the other. One type of these may be called "contingent predictions"; in them, a hope is expressed that if some presently adverse factors in the situation change somewhat, an improvement might be expected. For example, "If he could be separated from his present bad home situation, he might get along all right." A second kind of predictively unhelpful comment is a statement of what the boy was considered to be adjusting to, sometimes in terms of a "psychodynamic" interpretation, sometimes in a recapitulation of factors in the home or elsewhere which seemed contributory to the problem. For example, "His temper outbursts are reactions to frustrations which probably have been developed in the home." The third type of these comments is the "relative" comment. One form this may take is a statement that the individual is "improved," without indicating that he is in good condition. Also, "He is making as good an adjustment as could be expected."

When statements of these three types were disregarded, there were 35 where the psychiatric comment could be classified as definitely favorable or unfavorable. For the Minnesota clinics only (Roff, 1959) these can be broken down as follows: clearly unfavorable comment with unfavorable outcome, 19 cases; clearly unfavorable comment with favorable outcome, 5 cases; clearly favorable comment with favorable outcome, 11 cases; there were no cases with favorable comment and unfavorable outcome.

Work with additional clinics has indicated that there is a difference both in the readiness to make comments and in the long-time predictive accuracy from one clinic to another. This has not been analyzed in detail.

We developed a set of ground rules for working with abstracted information, some of which have subsequently been modified. It was found desirable in abstracting a particular bit of information to retain the relationship to the subject of the person who provided the information (teacher, mother, and so forth). Similarly, it seemed helpful to preserve the chronology, so that we knew when a particular statement was made. For various reasons, one of which was that it seemed to work, we concentrated most intensively on information concerning the peer relationships during boys' childhood. We developed, as a result of much trial and error, a guidelist for information to be evaluated as positive, neutral, and negative in appraising peer group adjustment. We found that some rather subtle distinctions seemed to work, and this finding was one factor in keeping us from what could have been a superficial coding of the material.

An illustration of this is the category "misbehavior in the classroom." In itself, this did not work well. Further study indicated that the critical thing seemed to be not the mere fact of the misbehavior, but the reported reaction to it of the other children. If the other children regarded it admiringly, it was a favorable sign. If they took a neutral attitude, its significance was neutral. If they said, in effect, "Shut up and sit down," its weighting was negative. It was thus found possible to get useful information from an item which had originally given unpromising results. Sometimes extra effort spent on coding qualitative materials will pay for itself by yielding valid information which would have been missed if the coding had been more casually done.

With the assistance of a list of behaviors to be evaluated as positive or negative, graduate student readers who were blind as to outcome and worked only with the abstracts made evaluations of good or poor peer adjustment, with a judgment of "uncertain" permitted when necessary. It was found that youngsters who antagonized their associates to an unusual degree tended to manifest psychoneurosis in military service some years later.

The work described up to this point was carried out under the sponsorship of the Air Force School of Aviation Medicine, with Dr. S. B. Sells as the project monitor. At about this time, co-sponsorship by the National Institute of Mental Health began. Soon after that, Dr. Sells left the Air Force, and the service sponsorship was shifted from the Air Force to the Army Medical Research and Development Command. The chief project monitors have been Dr. Philip Sperling and Lt. Col. James Hedlund. With NIMH funds, it was possible to expand operations to clinics located in many of the main cities in the eastern half of the country. Some follow-up information was eventually obtained for a total of 11,283 cases.

This large a number of cases meant that we could find a prepsychotic sample large enough to permit us to divide it into those cases twelve years of age and below when first seen at a clinic, and the teen-age cases, who tended to be approaching more definitely the structure of their adult difficulties (Roff, 1963; 1965; Roff, Mink, & Hinrichs, 1966). We found that the prepsychotic cases first seen during the grade school period, almost all pre-schizophrenic, were not the "too good," shrinking violet type, but were seen by their teachers and peers as a more or less actively unpleasant group of youngsters. This group, like the neurotics, had poor peer relations – this also held for childhood social interactions and young adult bad conduct, whether this be labeled delinquency, sociopathic or psychopathic personality, character disorder, or something else (Roff, 1961).

It has thus been very interesting to me that other contributors to this volume have discussed youngsters with poor peer relations who later showed poor adult outcome. Mednick (pp. 51–89) describes twenty children of schizophrenic mothers who themselves became mentally ill adults, and compared them with twenty other individuals, also with schizophrenic mothers, who seem to be getting along all right as adults. The well group was matched with the patient group at about the age of fifteen, for sex, age, education, social class, childhood rearing conditions, and "*exactly the same level of adjustment rating by the psychiatrist*" (my italics). When various information about these two sets of individuals was examined in detail, it was found that the children in Mednick's sick group showed characteristics similar to those of our disliked youngsters, as described by teachers. They were "more disturbing to the class," "evidenced more disturbance in class than did the well subjects," and "tended to get upset more easily." This school difference occurred in spite of the careful matching on the variables listed above; without such rigorous matching, the difference could be expected to be even greater.

It was also interesting to find from Hathaway et al.'s paper (pp. 171–185) that when ninth-grade boys and girls with high scores on the schizophrenia scale of the MMPI were described by teachers, the term *unlikable* was among the top two or three adjectives applied to both sexes.

A further indication of cross-population robustness on this point is given by Fleming and Ricks (p. 248), who found that "Feelings of *isolation* and *alienation* (Table 3) differentiated the pre-schizophrenics and control group more strikingly than any other area of emotional experience. The pre-schizophrenics' records showed long-standing histories of difficulty in establishing or maintaining peer relationships." That is to say, those with very poor peer relations described subjective feelings of isolation and alienation which were apparently a not too inaccurate reflection of their objectively observable peer relations.

Later work with the child guidance cases has dealt with two additional outcome groups, adult schizoid personalities (Roff, 1965; Roff, Mink, & Hinrichs, 1966) and adult homosexuals (Roff, 1966). A substantial amount of qualitative information about individual cases in both these groups has been presented in the order of the age at which the individuals were first seen at the clinic. It is not possible to infer accurately from the present status of a fifteen-year-old what he was like at the age of seven or eight. Particularly in the pre-schizoid personality cases, it appears that earlier retrospective studies have failed to penetrate accurately through the adolescent period. In the *Diagnostic and Statistical Manual, Mental Disorders* (American Psychiatric Association, 1952), the statement is made in the description of "schizoid personality" that "as children, they are usually quiet, shy, obedient, sensitive, and retiring." Our information strongly contradicts this. At around the ages of seven or eight, pre-schizoid children might engage in vigorous acting out, whereas at the age of fourteen or fifteen, they might appear somewhat quiet and withdrawn. Sometimes retrospective information turns out to be accurate, and sometimes it does not; until we have actual follow-up information, it is not possible to evaluate it.

Both the schizoid personality cases and the homosexual cases also showed patterns of early peer rejection. The fact that this single predictor cuts across all these later difficulties does not mean that there can be no differentiation on this variable between different outcome groups. Many clinicians have seemed interested only in the differentiation among different kinds of poor outcomes, and are relatively indifferent to a discrimination between good outcomes and poor outcomes in general. This latter seems to me the primary task, and I have been fortunate that my sponsors have shared this point of view.

Since there is a very real communication problem with people who are not familiar with case materials, we have published a case book, *Developmental Abnormal Psychology* (Roff et al., 1966). Graduate students, particularly in the earlier stages of their careers, sometimes get the impression that there is this theory, that theory, and the other theory, without having any basis to choose among them. This book provides a substantial amount of factual material on the childhood antecedents of adult maladjustments, which will give students and others a basis for evaluating the claims of various theories.

In addition to the follow-up of child guidance clinic cases, a series of reports has been published on the young adult outcome of juvenile delinquents. The sample of these now consists of around five thousand cases, located in two states in different parts of the country, for whom adult criterion information has been obtained. The most useful single finding from this series of studies is that the most important predictor of later outcome seems to be the disposition that was made of the case by the general juvenile court–probation office procedures. There were clear and replicable differences among delinquents who were never confined, those who were sent to a county training school, and those who were sent to the state training school. The state training school delinquents were unsatisfactory in the service in well over half the cases. This means that in comparison with a mild delinquency group, not more than 10 per cent of whom would get in trouble, serious consideration should be given to the military rejection of this group with the lowest positive yield. The first three of these reports have been combined and published in a chapter in a book (Roff, 1969).

Following the indications we obtained of the importance of early peer relationships as predictors of later good and poor adjustment, a new project was initiated to make a more intensive study of peer adjustment. This was a five-year contract with the U.S. Office of Education in partnership with Dr. S. B. Sells of Texas Christian University (Sells & Roff, 1967).

Peer nominations of "like most" and "like least" were obtained on mark-sense cards for a sample of almost forty thousand third- through sixth-grade children, about half in Minnesota and half in Texas. It was possible to process the mark-sense cards through a reproducer and a computer so that raw and standard peer scores for the large sample could be obtained in a short period of time. In addition to peer scores, a structured interview was conducted with each Minnesota teacher to obtain detailed qualitative information about a group selected from the larger sample. The interviews followed an outline which included questions about appearance, behavior, school performance, family characteristics, and qualitative information about peer interactions.

The mimeographed final report of this project is being reworked into a book, which will be available before too long. One of the most interesting sets of findings was obtained in the follow-up of these cases for early delinquency, which has been published separately (Roff & Sells, 1968). At the upper and middle socioeconomic levels, delinquents tend to be those with personality difficulties that are reflected in their rejection by other boys. Almost no high-choice boys from the upper levels were delinquent. On the other hand, in the lowest socioeconomic octile, delinquency occurred with about equal frequency among the most-rejected and best-liked boys. The qualitative material from the teacher interviews contributed greatly to making this result comprehensible. For example, at the lowest socioeconomic level, teachers indicated by their comments that the well-liked boys tended to be well-adjusted in the school setting, whether or not they happened to be delinquent outside the school. They were, at the grade school ages, simply not in rebellion against that so-called middle-class institution, the school, although they might show some delinquent behavior now and then, particularly in other settings.

Although in the early days of this project we did a substantial amount of work on the analysis of family characteristics, differentiating later psychoneurotics from later normals and later psychoneurotics from later bad conduct cases, when we began collecting cases on a national basis we deferred this work until we had data collected for our very much enlarged sample. We are still planning analyses of this family information. This awaits the collection of criterion data for all the brothers.

The analysis of family characteristics has now become an active field of work, and I should like to review some of the recent studies, including some of those by contributors to this volume. As indicated in my discussion above of our sibling study, there is considerable non-specificity in the relations between parental characteristics and child outcome. This is parallel to our peer group findings, where individuals with a variety of adult outcomes show below-average peer group adjustments during childhood. This does not preclude the finding of some differences in the peer group adjustments of individuals with different adult outcomes, but it suggests that, in general, the differences must be viewed against a background of general unsatisfactoriness in early peer relationships.

I have for a long time been interested in the similarities and differences in different members of the same families, and have published a review (Roff, 1950) of a wide range of materials, "Intra-Family Resemblances in Personality Characteristics." This was written with an attempt at total avoidance of the heredity-environment problem, in the belief that an unbiased delineation of the network of relationships would be of value. It is still a live paper, but the treatment of "low incidence maladjustments" was relatively meager compared to what we can do now. Without attempting a completely comprehensive coverage, I shall point out where current work seems to be leading us.

One illustration of the non-specificity of family characteristics in relation to outcome is given in a paper by Kantor and Winder (1961). In reporting a retrospective study of the backgrounds of schizophrenics, they made an intensive survey of the literature concerning the life histories of schizophrenics. As they observed, "This literature suggests that in the backgrounds of schizophrenics, certain events have occurred with unusual frequency and intensity. Examples are a severely neurotic parent, a psychotic parent, excessive emotional turmoil within the family, early death of the mother, the child degraded and devalued, symbiotic over-protection, severe marital discord, severe physical punishment of the child, father dominated and ineffectual, and mother domineering and cold." No one of these is in any way specific to schizophrenia. Every one of them can also be found with a greater than chance frequency in the histories of children showing almost any kind of adult maladjustment.

At about the same time, Rosenthal (1959) observed: "Other kinds of psychiatric disturbances occurred with high frequency in the families of both concordant and discordant pairs. These included mental deficiency, alcoholism, psychopathy, neuroses such as anxious-phobic states and reactive depression, and personality problems such as diffidence, excessive worrying, etc."

Eiduson and her associates (1966) commented as follows: "One of the striking findings is the extremely high incidence of psychopathology among some families. In 18 of the 50 families, there were 7 alcoholics among parents or grandparents, 1 addict, 9 instances of mental illness serious enough to demand hospitalization, 5 suicidal attempts, 2 murder sentences and 2 retardates."

A recent study – "Short-Term Improvement in Schizophrenia" (National Institute of Mental Health, 1968) – sent me by Dr. Goldberg, which is credited to their Collaborative Study Group, points out: "Some form of emotional disturbance or clear-cut psychiatric illness was recognized by the research social workers during the series of interviews in nearly half of the patients' parents. The most frequent disturbances in the parents of male patients were of neurotic type, while the female patients tended to have neurotic mothers and alcoholic fathers. About one-fifth of the male patients, and about one-third of the female patients had psychotic mothers. More mothers than fathers had a recognized history of psychosis."

Lidz, Fleck, and Alanen (1963) report that of the twenty-four siblings of seventeen schizophrenic patients, only five or six were making "a reasonably adequate adjustment." Three were schizophrenic; six or seven were severe psychopathic personalities; and eight or nine were neurotic, acting out, or had psychosomatic ailments.

Myers and Roberts (1959, pp. 74–75) reached the following conclusions: "Nearly two-thirds of the schizophrenic patients had parents who, according to the judgments of our research team psychiatrists, displayed psychopathology at the descriptive clinical level, such as mood disorder, severe neurotic symptoms, alcoholism, and psychotic illness. Both parents were unstable in 20% of the cases, the father alone in 32%, and the mother alone in 12%. These figures represented the minimal amount of disturbance, including only those manifestations of internal difficulties obvious in surface behavior. . . .

". . . Their [the parents'] psychopathological symptomatology did not seem to be transmitted directly to the patients, either genetically or through socialization. For example, we found no distinctive personality traits or neurotic patterns among the parents; few could be classified as schizophrenics; nor did the patients' symptomatology correspond directly with their parents'. Rather, the parents' personality problems contributed to the distorted interpersonal relations within the family and the unstable home environment in which the patients were reared."

A very important new approach to the family influence problem has been made by Stabenau, Pollin and their associates (see pp. 94–122). My comments here are taken from an earlier paper of theirs (Pollin, Stabenau, Mosher, & Tupin, 1966). They have been studying identical twins who are discordant for schizophrenia. Without going into their work in detail, we are interested here in the diagnoses made of the non-schizophrenic identical twin, in the eleven pairs reported.

Of the eleven cases, only one was characterized as showing no evidence of psychopathology. On the other hand, types of deviation seemed markedly restricted when compared with other studies. The non-schizophrenic twins were characteristically described as either obsessive-compulsive, depressive, or passive-dependent. These terms, alone or in combination, were applied to nine of the other ten cases. The tenth one, whose schizophrenic sibling was diagnosed as borderline, was described as having no gross psychopathology but some imprecision and vagueness, like the schizophrenic twin, and some hysterical features. The significance of this homogenization is not entirely clear.

Waring and Ricks (1965), in a study of family patterns of children who became adult schizophrenics, analyzed the descriptions of the mothers given in child guidance clinic case histories. Twenty of the schizophrenics were classed as chronic, and thirty were classed as released. A control group was employed which consisted of child guidance cases who escaped mental hospitalization, matched with the schizophrenics on age, sex, IQ, presenting symptomatology, social class, ethnic background, and era seen at the Judge Baker Guidance Center. These were not otherwise selected as having had good outcomes. Their most consistent finding differentiating the three groups was the frequency of psychotic and near-psychotic disabilities among both parents of the chronic group. (This is a simple gross family resemblance (Roff, 1950).) Among the released schizophrenics they found that almost half the mothers were either depressed or compulsive women. This is interesting in comparison with the results from Pollin and Stabenau's research discussed above. The small group of compulsive mothers were considered by them to be similar to the traditional "schizophrenogenic" mother. A sample of the terms social workers used to describe these mothers included the following: tense, driving, severe, reserved, cold, unemotional, demanding, dominant, perfectionistic, unresponsive, earnest, determined, aggressive, coldly threatening, and having to control. But contrary to the implications of the "schizophrenogenic" hypothesis, children of these mothers were most frequent in the control group and least frequent in the chronic. The control group in this study was closely matched to the schizophrenic group, and hence included many schizoid and other disturbed persons. There is, then, no implication here that the compulsive women raised healthy children. However, this finding does indicate that schizophrenia is not the necessary, or even the most likely, outcome of a childhood lived with such a mother.

One study is available of a group of individuals who had been separated soon after birth from their schizophrenic mothers, reared in foster homes, and studied as adults. Heston (1966) studied a group of 45 individuals, about two thirds male, who were born between 1915 and 1945 to schizophrenic mothers confined in an Oregon state psychiatric hospital. According to him, all of the children were discharged from the state hospital within three days of birth, either to the care of relatives or to foundling homes. Only those children were included who had had no contact with their natural mothers and never lived with *maternal* relatives. About half the group went to the *paternal* relatives, who would have known all about the mother's hospitalization; the other half lived in foundling homes up to as long as five years, until placement. There is no way of knowing whether or not the foster parents of these knew that the child had a psychotic mother. If they did, this could have had some influence on their behavior. If they did not, some potentially important information was being kept from them.

Heston had a control group selected from the records of the same foundling homes and matched for sex, type of eventual placement (adoptive, foster family, or institutional), and length of time in the foundling home. These controls came out somewhat better than the experimental group. Our primary interest here is the exact outcomes for the adopted children of the schizophrenic mothers. Out of forty-seven of these, five were schizophrenic, four were mentally defective, nine were sociopathic personalities, and thirteen had neurotic disorders. The mean IQ of the experimental group was 94, that of the control group was about 10 points higher. This indicates the non-specificity and variety of outcomes in a group of children who had schizophrenic mothers and were raised by other persons.

Although, as mentioned, five out of the forty-seven children of schizophrenic mothers became schizophrenic, none of the controls did so. The author concludes (p. 823): "The results of this study support a genetic etiology of schizophrenia. Schizophrenia was found only in the offspring of schizophrenic mothers. . . . Furthermore, about one-half of the Experimental group exhibited major psycho-social disability. The bulk of these persons had disorders other than schizophrenia, which were nearly as malignant in effect as schizophrenia itself."

In weighing this conclusion, it is necessary to consider possible environmental differences between the families who adopted the children of schizophrenic mothers and the families who adopted children without such heredity. One of my own samples (Roff, 1956) contained some children who were born to mothers in mental hospitals and then placed, usually directly from the hospital, at the age of six or eight months or so. Since it was not possible to appraise the effect of their backgrounds being known to the foster parents, and possibly to themselves, and since we did not have enough information about the way they were brought up to know whether their having had a psychotic mother influenced the way they were treated by their foster parents, this was not pursued further. A rationale for a certain suspension of judgment here is contained in the cautionary statement of the National Academy of Sciences (1967, p. 893) on the problem of possible genetic differences between races in this country: "In the absence of some now-unforeseen way of equalizing all aspects of the environment, answers to this question can hardly be more than reasonable guesses." We do not know that there were no differences in the families of the experimental and control children. We can feel certain that the two groups were not randomly selected from the same pool. In such a situation, it seems best to be cautious about interpreting the results.

It would be possible to list more studies of this kind, and to carry them back in history to the period when people frequently talked about a "hereditary taint," which was quite non-specific in its effects. There is substantial agreement on the general facts here by people at all points of the continuum from extreme hereditarians to extreme environmentalists. However, the details of the picture are not at all clear, and we need a firm picture of what we are trying to explain before we attempt to explain it. This is an active field in which people are getting interesting and, I believe, increasingly accurate results, but we have a great deal to learn. It is very possible that attempts to force explanations, either genetic or environmental, on these data are premature.

It will be very interesting to see what the next ten years will bring. We should have a greater clarification here of the relations between parental characteristics and the outcomes in offspring by that time.

COMMENTARY

QUESTION. You were probably unduly harsh in your criticism of the Heston study; the ongoing study in Copenhagen by Kety and others pretty much substantiates what Heston found with a larger sample. In Copenhagen, they have better controls, inasmuch as because of all the registration systems in Denmark they were able to look at all children adopted in the greater Copenhagen area, and at the biological parents and the foster parents of all adopted children. They can also get a group of adopted children who, when they grew up, became schizophrenic, and a group of adopted children who, when they grew up, were normal. They matched these groups for relevant background variables, then looked at the biological parents. They found more schizophrenia than in any of the other groups, but they also found schizophrenia in some of the biological parents of the adopted who were normal when they grew up. In general, there was a confirmation of the Heston finding, and that study will be published in the book edited by Kety and Rosenthal.

ROFF. Part of what I was talking about was that some of you people concentrate on the schizophrenia only, without paying any attention to all the other maladjustments.

QUESTION. Well, I think that has changed too; what you have to do is constantly keep in mind the base rate for all these various other disorders. What we're talking about here is the relative incidence of schizophrenia in the children of schizophrenic mothers who have had no contact with them, compared with the base rate of about 0.85 per cent. When you start to talk about the amount of neurosis and character disorder that you see in the offspring of these mothers, although that may compose the bulk of disorders in the offspring, the base rate for neuroses and character disorders is so much greater than for schizophrenia that the contrast becomes much less marked, inasmuch as you have character disorders and neuroses in the offspring of the other group.

ROFF. But the contrast is still very marked between the children of schizophrenic mothers and the control group on all these other things. They all showed a difference. Mentally retarded four to nothing, for example. Just like the schizophrenics. As far as base rates are concerned, I have never been able to find satisfactory base rate information for neuroses, and the base rate of 0.85 per cent was obtained from a New York sample which was not necessarily representative of the country as a whole.

QUESTION. Yes. I don't understand the mentally retarded one myself.

ROFF. I'm not trying to explain this. I'm just raising the question and pointing out that we ought to look at all the outcomes, rather than just the schizophrenics.

STABENAU. I'd like to make some comments about the same two studies. In the Heston study, all of the mothers were psychotic at the time of the birth of the child who was placed in a foster home. One thing about this study is that we don't know the character of the families who reared these children, as you pointed out. Now in the Rosenthal-Kety study, I believe only about 16 per cent of the mothers were psychotic before the birth; the remainder became psychotic after the placement, which is an important control. In this study you can come up with the same kind of criticism — that you do not know the nature or the character of the home that these children were placed in — and if there is some consistent bias in placement, either in the Heston study or in this study, one would need to know about this. If there isn't, then it's a very striking finding. To cite the cases in the Kety study, three index cases, that is of biologically schizophrenic parents, were diagnosed as schizophrenic, and I believe several others were borderlines, whereas there was only one borderline in the foster placement, non-biologically disturbed parents. That's quite a striking difference.

ROFF. You understand, my position is not anti-heredity or anti-environment, it's just trying to get the whole record in, which I think we need to do.

POLLACK. I'm particularly interested in your finding of gender concordance among male juvenile disorders or personality disorders among the brothers. Another possible hypothesis is this: What I've done is a series of studies of siblings of childhood disorders, and they more often are male, just as the index case is male, in all the childhood disorders such as stuttering. But not only that, they come from families in which there are more males, even though the other males are not abnormal.

ROFF. I noticed with great interest your finding that a brother and a brother might have one outcome and a brother and a sister might have a different outcome.

POLLACK. Right. In fact, we had five antisocial cases, and they all had sisters who were all normal. I'm not saying that there aren't female patterns. Childs at Johns Hopkins has the idea that there are some mothers who produce male incompatible children, because of differences in chromosomes. In other words, they may have pregnancy complications almost specific to the male, and this would leave the male offspring of these kinds of mothers with a handicap that wouldn't affect the female, and then there may be an environmental interaction pattern.

ROFF. I think it's very clear from our whole discussion of the last two days that we have an extremely complex situation, and I'm just trying to get all these other things thrown into the same hopper, which haven't always been there.

RICKS. I like the term that Merrill Roff introduced – robust results. I think when you see Hathaway, Pollack, Roff, and Fleming with different samples, different methods, different areas, reaching some similar conclusions, there's something robust about the material, there's something that shows through no matter what you do with it. I think it's also clear that when the methods of study become most exact, it's easiest to get the best confirmatory results; I was most struck by Pollack's confirmation of Lane and Albee's work. Working with very similar samples of suburban kids, you get very good measurement and clear confirmation. In spite of the clear confirmation and the robust results, I don't think we have more than a good start yet – but we do have that.

REFERENCES

American Psychiatric Association. *Diagnostic and statistical manual, mental disorders.* Washington, D.C.: Author, 1952.

Bellak, L. *Schizophrenia: A review of the syndrome.* New York: Logos Press, 1958.

Eiduson, B. T., T. Johnson, & D. Rottenberg. Comparative studies of learning problems seen in five child clinics. *American Journal of Orthopsychiatry,* 1966, 36, 829–839.

Heston, L. L. Psychiatric disorders in foster home reared children of schizophrenic mothers. *British Journal of Psychiatry,* 1966, 112, 819–825.

Kantor, R. E., & C. L. Winder. Schizophrenia: Correlates of life history. *Journal of Nervous and Mental Disease,* 1961, 132, 221–225.

Lehmann, H. E. Drug treatment of schizophrenia. In N. S. Kline & H. E. Lehmann (Eds.), *Psychopharmacology.* Boston: Little Brown, 1965.

Lidz, L., S. Fleck, Y. O. Alanen, & A. Cornelison. Schizophrenia patients and their siblings. *Psychiatry,* 1963, 26, 1–18.

Myers, J. K., & B. H. Roberts. *Family and class dynamics in mental illness.* New York: Wiley, 1959.

National Academy of Sciences. Racial studies: Academy state positions on call for new research. *Science,* 1967, 158, 892–893.

National Institute of Mental Health. Psychopharmacology Research Branch, Collaborative Study Group. Short-term improvement in schizophrenia: The contribution of background factors. *American Journal of Psychiatry,* 124 (1968), 900–909.

Pollin, W., J. R. Stabenau, L. Mosher, & J. Tupin. Life history differences in identical twins discordant for schizophrenia. *American Journal of Psychology*, 1966, 36, 492–508.

Roff, M. Intra-family resemblances in personality characteristics. *Journal of Psychology*, 1950, 30, 199–227.

———. Preservice personality problems and subsequent adjustment to military service: Gross outcome in relation to military service. Rep. No. 55-138. School of Aviation Medicine, USAF, 1956.

———. Preservice personality problems and subsequent adjustment to military service: The prediction of psychoneurotic reactions. Rep. No. 57-136. School of Aviation Medicine, USAF, 1957.

———. Preservice personality problems and subsequent adjustment to military service: A replication of "The prediction of psychoneurotic reactions." Rep. No. 58-151. School of Aviation Medicine, USAF, 1959.

———. The relation between certain preservice factors and psychoneurosis during military duty. *U.S. Armed Forces Medical Journal*, 1960, 11, 152–160.

———. Childhood social interactions and young adult bad conduct. *Journal of Abnormal and Social Psychology*, 1961, 63, 333–337.

———. The service-related experience of a sample of juvenile delinquents. Report No. 61-1, January 1961, *U.S. Army Medical Research and Development Command*, Contract No. DA-49-007-MD-2015.

———. Some multivariate criterion problems in the adjustment area. Symposium on Research and Teaching Methods in Multivariate Experimental Design, ONR Account No. 71-23-40, pp. 41–45, March 1962.

———. Childhood social interactions and young adult psychosis. *Journal of Clinical Psychology*, 1963, 19, 152–157.

———. The service-related experience of a sample of juvenile delinquents. II. A replication on a larger sample in another state. Report No. 63-2, December 1963, *U.S. Army Medical Research and Development Command*, Contract No. DA-49-007-MD-2015.

———. The service-related experience of a sample of juvenile delinquents. III. The predictive significance of juvenile confinement. Report No. 64-3, March 1964, *U.S. Army Medical Research and Development Command*, Contract No. DA-49-007-MD-2015.

———. Some developmental aspects of schizoid personality. Report No. 65-4, March 1965, *U.S. Army Medical Research and Development Command*, Contract No. DA-49-007-MD-2015.

———. Some childhood and adolescent characteristics of adult homosexuals. Report No. 66-5, May 1966, *U.S. Army Medical Research and Development Command*, Contract No. DA-49-007-MD-2015.

———. The service-related experience of a sample of juvenile delinquents. IV. Results with a second Minnesota sample. Report No. 67-6, March 1967, *U.S. Army Medical Research and Development Command*, Contract No. DA-49-007-MD-2015.

———. The service-related experience of a sample of juvenile delinquents. V. The relation between education, number of juvenile apprehensions, and outcome in service. Report No. 68-7, May 1968, *U.S. Army Medical Research and Development Command*, Contract No. DA-49-007-MD-2015.

———. Juvenile delinquency and military service. In R. W. Little (Ed.), *Selective service and American society*. New York: Russell Sage, 1969.

———. The service-related experience of a sample of juvenile delinquents. VI. The predictive value of education in a second delinquent sample and in a normal control group. Report No. 69-8, April 1969, *U.S. Army Medical Research and Development Command*, Contract No. DA-49-007-MD-2015.

Roff, M., W. Mink, & G. Hinrichs. *Developmental abnormal psychology*. New York: Holt, 1966.

Roff, M., & S. B. Sells. Juvenile delinquency in relation to peer acceptance-rejection and socio-economic status. *Psychology in the Schools*, 1968, 5, 3–18.

——— & M. Golden. *Peer relations and personality*. San Francisco: Chandler, in press.

Rosenthal, D. Some factors associated with concordance and discordance with respect to schizophrenia in monozygotic twins. *Journal of Nervous and Mental Disease*, 1959, 129, 1–10.

Sells, S. B., & M. Roff. Family influence as reflected in peer acceptance-rejection resemblance of siblings as compared with random sets of school children. *Psychology in the Schools*, 1965, 2, 133–137.

———. Peer acceptance-rejection and personality development. Final report of a five-year research program, including studies of the origins of acceptance-rejection, effects on early delinquency and school dropout, and developmental dynamics. U.S. Office of Education, January 1967.

Waring, M., & D. F. Ricks. Family patterns of children who became adult schizophrenics. *Journal of Nervous and Mental Disease*, 1965, 40, 351–364.

DAVID F. RICKS

Life History Research in Psychopathology: Retrospect and Prospect

A CHAPTER labeled *conclusions* would provide a comfortable sense of closure at this point. But no one can offer conclusions in a field as open, diverse, and full of new developments as life history research. Instead, I shall look back over the studies reported in this volume and the discussions that grew out of them, and try to assess where we have been, where we stand now, and where we are going.

When the great Gregory Pincus was asked what he saw in the future on the basis of his early experiments on human reproduction, he answered, "I can't tell, but there are no big steps, there are all little steps. We have to follow processes systematically. The big questions are: why does an egg start to develop, and why does it continue to develop?" The big questions for life history research in psychopathology are, paraphrasing Dr. Pincus, Why does schizophrenia (or depression, or character disorder, or alcoholism, or neurosis) start to develop, and why does it continue to develop? We also have to follow processes systematically, over the whole period of development.

The preceding papers exemplify some of the best current approaches to these big questions. As a participant observer in life history research, prone to worrying about research designs and strategies, I find these research methods fascinating. But the primary value of these studies to the public that pays for them, or to the clinicians and teachers entrusted with helpful intervention into the lives of high-risk children, lies in their results and the clues these offer to helpful treatment. As we look for the point at which a disorder starts to develop, and as we study the influences under which it continues to develop or is arrested, it becomes apparent that research can suggest times and methods for effective prevention and intervention. Since researchers still function as guests in the clinical house, I should like to indicate that we are paying our board and room before I go on to comment on how we are doing it.

CLUES TO INTERVENTION

In the United States today there are over 40,000,000 people under the age of nineteen. If we make a rough estimate of 1 per cent incidence, we can predict that about 400,000 of these young people will one day be hospitalized and diagnosed schizophrenic, and that those whose life trajectories will include repeated difficulty with the law, more or less chronic alcoholism, or neurotic misery and ineffectiveness will be even larger. If we can find ways to recognize people with high risks for various kinds of adult disorder, to reach them early, and to identify areas of special weakness or strength, we may be able to provide inventive clinicians, public health specialists, and teachers with the information they need to intervene effectively.

We know, for instance, that many educational and other environmental influences can raise the kind of intellectual competence measured by IQ scores. Hathaway, Lane, and Pollack* all reported in this volume that low IQ scores, relative to one's contemporaries, classmates, or siblings, seem to be one consistent antecedent of psychotic disorder. In Hathaway's report, and in that of Robins, we see confirmation for Lane's guess that this lower intellectual competence might be related to motivational and personality factors. One of the places to look for children with a high risk for psychosis, then, is in the public schools, among those children who test low on IQ and on achievement, and who are regarded by their teachers as indifferent, unlikable, stubborn, lazy, undependable, erratic, unhappy, or scatterbrained. (These additional criteria are necessary because most children with relatively low IQ's do not become psychotic.) It seems reasonable to assume that clinicians and teachers could already, with methods now available — such as early sensory stimulation, psychomotor training, reading skills instruction, and therapeutic tutoring — raise the intellectual competence (and even teacher and peer appeal) of such students. Such help might well make it possible for them to work out life patterns in which their potential for disorder remained permanently latent.

Whether one comes to the issue of early identification from genetic and early observational data, as Stabenau and Mednick did here, or from prepsychotic test data, as Hathaway did, one reaches the conclusion that some people carry within themselves measurably greater potential for psy-

* For the sake of brevity in this summary, I shall refer to the persons who reported these various studies and not to the full research team. Most of these large, long-term studies are, of course, the work of many people. References to materials other than the chapters in this book are listed at the end of this chapter.

chotic breakdown than do others. But that potential need not necessarily be actualized. Looking at all of the work reported here, we might speculate that psychosis ordinarily requires, for its production, (a) some early genetic, prenatal, or birth defect, resulting in an organism with heightened irritability and sensitivity, (b) low intellectual and social competence, and (c) inability to find routes into socially acceptable and personally satisfying alternatives to madness, such as low-pressure lives in rural surroundings not likely to overstimulate a hyperreactive nervous system or make demands that are too heavy for low competence to bear. Contrary to popular opinions and to much of the current folklore of clinical practice which locate the disorder wholly within the person or within his family, this conception of psychological disorder would suggest that it usually takes both inner weakness and outer rejection, both inner incompetence and outer demand, summating more or less consistently through two or three decades, to produce the eventual breakdown that leads to mental hospitalization. A theme justifying hope that runs through these papers, it seems to me, is an awareness that no one is doomed at birth to schizophrenia, or character disorder, or any other kind of adult maladjustment. Although vulnerability can be established at conception, in the uterus, or at birth, it is not likely to determine adult disorder without long-continued social compliance from the family of the child and from the surrounding community. The majority of biologically vulnerable children probably reach an equilibrium somewhere in the gray area between psychological health and hospitalizable disorder.

When should intervention take place? On the basis of Mednick's report, and research by other students of the genetics of psychopathology, it would seem that the first point for effective intervention is before conception. Some prospective parents might be counseled that their offspring will have a high risk for psychological disorders, and so might choose not to have children (or not to marry at all, as many schizoid and schizophrenic men do now). But even parents with a presumably heavy genetic burden are still most likely to produce children who will not be psychotic. Genetic counseling might help those who want to have children, even when they know the problems they may face, to maximize their children's life chances by using every community resource available to supplement their own child-rearing efforts. Later intervention can also take place in the schools, and in the community.

Fleming's research indicated that the child who is prone to schizophrenia can describe his own inner sense of vulnerability, anxiety, alienation from others, and uncertainty about the reality of his experiences and his own sanity. Schizophrenia usually does not take on relatively permanent forms until adolescence. Ross (1969) indicates that the sense of vulnerability may be based on inability to solve the developmental tasks of adolescence. Psychotherapists, residential treatment centers, or other helping persons or agencies interested in guiding healthy trips through adolescence might, even at this late date, help high-risk young people out of their anxious, vulnerable, increasingly untenable ways of life by helping them solve developmental tasks. The crucial facts seem to be that development of disorder is a long-term process, and that it can possibly be deflected anywhere along the route. A good summary statement on the schizophrenic life history is provided by Stabenau: "differences in early biological maturity relate to differences in competence, which in turn appear related to the development of schizophrenic symptomatology." As Goldberg showed, it is possible to modify even those aspects of schizophrenia that seem most basic and most biological, by drug treatments. Future attempts to prevent schizophrenia will certainly use biological interventions that decrease vulnerability to stress, as well as methods that promote competence or lower environmental stimulation and pressures.

LIFE HISTORY RESEARCH METHODS

To the researcher the most interesting parts of the preceding papers may be the methods that different investigators have developed for seeking out the beginning of psychopathology and systematically following developmental processes. Although this book is not a handbook on life history research methods, it does provide observations of how scientists go about recognizing real problems and working out methods for solving them. Often, as in the work of Robins, and almost elegantly in the work reported by Lane, this involves a series of investigations in which each successive step is suggested by the results of previous work and its critique by the scientific community. The sophisticated use of control groups in Lane's work, and in that of Robins, Pollack, and Mednick, is likely to excite any researcher. It may be worthwhile to point out some other special features in these studies.

Most readers have probably noticed the degree to which life history research is methodologically open and flexible. Contributors to this volume include genetically oriented psychologists, statisticians and psychometric investigators, psychiatrists, psychopharmacologists, experimental psychologists, sociologists, and clinical psychologists. Each uses primarily the language, the perspectives, and the tools of his particular trade. But there is substantial agreement upon where and how to look for the origins of psychopathology. In Roff's terminology, the data of life histories have enough *robustness* to make themselves apparent across a variety of populations, investigated with many different methods. Another reason the volume reaches convergence might be the interdisciplinary nature of the investigators themselves. Mednick, a clinically trained experimental psychologist, sounds like a sociologist in some discussions, whereas in others he comes at the data with the questions and approaches of a geneticist. Pollack, a psychologist, is investigating neurological as well as familial data.

Notice, also, that something has happened to the scale of the research reported here. Lorr collected sets of 556, 1,100, and 1,000 schizophrenics, in six countries. Roff has follow-up data on 11,283 cases for whom he also has child guidance clinic data. Hathaway has an unusually thorough and comprehensive follow-up of 15,000 children for whom he has early MMPI tests and teacher ratings. Goldberg's studies are large-scale, multi-hospital efforts. Mednick appears to have mobilized much of Denmark. These samples offer considerable opportunities for selection of appropriate controls for any given comparison, and hence for neatly refined judgments. In much of this work it is possible to move beyond the gross comparisons typical in older research—that is, between "schizophrenics" and "normals"—and to compare sets of people who have a particular adult disorder with several sets of people who have other disorders. This kind of work is absolutely necessary if we are to be specific about the antecedents of particular disorders, and if we are to distinguish between such specific antecedents and others such as low IQ and peer rejection that seem to be general antecedents of psychopathology. Clinical research workers often assume that the subtle matters with which they are concerned can be comprehended only through intensive investigation of small samples. A better case can be made for the proposition that complex, subtle issues require multidimensional study of large samples. Large study populations can also provide for observation and coding samples of people who are broadly representative of a given country, social class, or whatever; when the samples are not representative, comparison with public information such as census and migration data can provide an estimate of the degree of distortion involved. Problems remain, and the investigators are well aware of them, but the population base for this work is much superior to that of most published psychopathology research. Starting from a large base, one can specify several characteristics he wants to look at in combination in special samples and still have sets of people to study. Even when he can't find them, a new discovery may be in the making: A few years ago cancer researchers, starting with an original sample of 250,000 men, looked for a group (a) over 60, (b) who had smoked since adolescence, and (c) didn't have lung cancer, in order to see if some naturally occurring element might be found that would account for the absence of lung cancer deaths. Very few such men could be found, and this led to the discovery that the "prevention element" was death from heart disease. These large samples offer the opportunity for comparable discoveries—and in part seem already to have shown them. Hathaway's suggestion of migration to low-stress occupations and areas as an alternative to schizophrenia is one example of a possible major discovery.

The scale of the research means that most of these studies have been team efforts, carried out over long periods of time by several investigators. One of the unsolved issues in this research, in fact, is how to organize such efforts so that they will be institutionalized, continuing beyond the research career, or even life span, of any one investigator. My own belief in this respect is that state and national psychiatric data banks should be set up, probably on computer models such as that reported by Ramsey, with long-term funding as free as possible from the fluctuating research grant system of finance. We know that the payoff of traditional longitudinal studies has generally been geometrically increased by every additional year of data collection. That is also likely to be the case in the studies reported here. It is also unfortunate that the present set of papers contains no research reports by people directly involved in just those agencies that have the best opportunity to institutionalize life history research—the public school systems, publicly supported community clinics, and state departments of mental health.

Since much attention has been focused recently on experimenter effects in psychiatric, psychological, and sociological research, it should be noted that most of the data on which the research reports are based are non-reactive, not open to the influence of the researcher. Typically, the data have been gathered by people other than the researcher, for purposes connected with functions of a school, clinic, or state. Although some reviewers have argued against the utility of such data, the weight of the evidence is in its favor. It is made up of facts as real and hard as research with human beings ever gets to handle. Practical people are accustomed to making important decisions on the basis of such data as early IQ, school achievement, ability to get along with one's peers, and so on.

Because these hard data are readily available, in a variety of settings and in relation to many diverse populations, the conclusions of any one study can be confirmed or rejected by others. A life history strategy of research thus meets one of the main canons of scientific method: openness to replication and correction. I have already mentioned some of the main indications of population robustness in the results of life history studies. Others will be mentioned below. At times, our sets of data allow us to proceed like anthropologists using accumulated files on various cultures, each of which has been observed by a person whose approach and biases are known. To quote Stabenau again, "Since the twins studied lived during a time span covering nearly a century, and the reports issued from investigators of clearly hereditary to clearly environmental bias, we feel with some confidence that these data are not primarily artifactual in nature, but do represent underlying early premorbid characteristics for schizophrenic twins" (p. 103). Having multiple observers can serve as a check on bias, both in the observers and in the experimenter.

The studies have used both laboratory and naturalistic methods. Some studies, such as those reported by Stabenau and by Mednick, have moved freely between the environment and the laboratory, in the best tradition of ethological research. And like the ethologists, who found surprising regularity and predictability when they studied the organism in his own environment over the course of his life, the investigators represented in this volume have found order and predictability in areas that previously seemed open only to literary description or clinical speculation. The crucial difference between these studies and those that depend on retrospective methods is the use of data actually recorded in infancy, in childhood, in adolescence, and in adulthood, so that predictions are made from data put into the record at the time the predictor events were taking place to data recorded at the time the outcome was occurring. At times these studies have used retrospective information, but they have done so with full awareness that this is a short-cut method of data collection offering only a first approximation to concurrent data.

All research people are skeptical by training, and many might still ask whether research done on people *in vivo* can ever escape the fact that the schools, clinics, or courts in which the records originated must have influenced the results obtained, usually to unknown degrees. This must be frankly admitted, and the comparative study of clinics or schools is still far less developed than we should wish. As systematic data on different clinics are gathered, it will be possible to study them regarding adult outcomes of comparable groups of children in whose lives they have intervened. The adult outcomes of groups seen by different individual therapists can also be studied, and if some seem to be particularly adept at deflecting life trajectories away from schizophrenia, crime, or other poor outcomes, we can examine their attitudes and methods as possible clues for the next generation of therapists. But this work is only starting, and much remains to be done.

The gaps and idiosyncrasies in clinical records also raise problems for life history research, problems only partly solved by large samples since the types of data missing in early records are clearly related to adult outcomes. The Judge Baker research team owes an immense debt of gratitude to Healy, Bronner, and others who established at the Guidance Center a tradition of systematic record keeping and comprehensive coverage of the child's history in the context of his family and community. But children on the road toward character disorder do not always report much about feelings, and children on the road toward schizophrenia may not regularly say much about school, friends, or community life. One answer to the problems of missing data is feedback from life history research to the people who generate records, so that successive generations of teachers and clinicians will report more systematically on early characteristics shown to be related to adult outcomes. Mednick's procedures, for example, might well be adopted as part of the diagnostic methods of currently operating child guidance clinics.

Roff's research strategy indicates a solution to a related problem, protection of the privacy and anonymity of specific patients and therapists. Often the most convincing information we can offer on a given issue is a set of detailed case histories. Patient, therapist, and clinic anonymity can be protected if we have data from large numbers of clinics, scattered across the country. So far only Roff has managed the Herculean task of gathering such a set of records.

Lorr's extensive research, together with other studies directed toward systematizing diagnostic terminology and practices, promises to provide more definite criterion data for predictive studies than any now available. Carefully specified, reliable adult criterion data will allow the current modest validities of early predictors to increase, probably quite strongly. Since this work is highly technical in method, if not in outcome, clinical researchers had best plan to make themselves expert in understanding multivariate techniques, even when these are not involved in their own research.

Any human life, seen in context, is enormously complex. When large numbers of human lives are studied with some devotion to the ideal of keeping their actual complexity in mind, vast arrays of data are generated. All life history researchers have grappled with the problem of too much data, and so far in addition to simply wading in and immersing themselves in the data, they seem to have found three main answers: select by theory, reduce the data to a few underlying dimensions by factor analysis, or put it all into coded form and store it in a suitable computer system. Mednick's work is the best example of systematic data collection to test, refine, and modify a coherent theory. Lorr's work offers a model of data reduction through factor analysis. And Ramsey describes the most ambitious current research on case history data storage and retrieval. Although there is no inherent reason that all three methods cannot be used together, we have yet to see what might result if this were tried. Factor analysis, or some simpler method of cluster analysis, promises to be helpful in bringing order to domains like early emotional experience, early symptom syndromes, and the relation of these to external influences. Since age, for example, can be treated as one variable among others, one can correlate such variables as depth of depression, frequency of aggressive acts, or degree of withdrawal with age, and in a factor analysis check to see whether age is or is not related to their changes. When Beck (1967) correlated age with depth of depression, for example, he found no evidence for the commonly held view that depression increases with age in psychiatric populations. This result, in turn, lends weight to Berry's demonstration of low self-esteem in many adolescents headed toward disturbance. The ways in which depression is expressed may change with age, though this has not been demonstrated, but it is well to be alert to signs of depression in young people as well as in old.

FOLLOW BACK OR FOLLOW UP?

There is one remaining question of research strategy, in many ways the most difficult of all. Where should we start an investigation, with a group of children who may have a vast range of adult outcomes, or with a group of adults, homogeneous as to adult outcome, who may have had a vast range of different childhood backgrounds and experiences? It is important to answer this question in terms of the advantages and disadvantages of both methods, for the two strategies approach their materials differently, serve slightly different ends, and answer somewhat different questions.

Take a sample problem.* Suppose we are interested in investigating the relationship between truancy and alcoholism. We can either begin with a population of adult alcoholics and search early school records to find the proportion of truants, or we can begin with a large population of truants and follow them into adulthood to discover what proportion has been diagnosed as alcoholic in military or civilian life. The two methods will give quite different proportions: Robins (1966) found 11 per cent of a sample of truants to be alcoholic in adult life, but for a sample of adult alcoholics Robins, Murphy, and Breckenridge (1967) found a 77 per cent rate of truancy in school records.

The difference in frequencies is not surprising. The two methods both ask for evidence of a relationship between early data and late, but they ask different questions about the relationship. The strategy of beginning with adults asks, What proportion of alcoholics truanted as children? The answer is that about three quarters of them did. It therefore makes sense to consider truancy as one of the frequent antecedents of alcoholism, perhaps related to alcoholism in ways important enough to be studied. The strategy that begins with a population of children asks, What proportion of truants are likely to become alcoholic? The answer is that only about a tenth of them are, and therefore it makes sense to look for other outcomes from truancy, such as sociopathic personalities, schizophrenia, and healthily rebellious young reformers, along with alcoholics.

The follow-back strategy is preferable if the investigator is interested in the characteristics of alcoholics, some of whom were truants; the follow-up strategy is preferable if his concern is with truants, some of whom will become alcoholics.

Beyond these obvious points, there are certain ways in which the two research strategies may be valuable for specific purposes. If the researcher is concerned with a wide variety of possible antecedents of some disorder, and if he has no strongly preferred hypotheses, then the strategy of beginning with an adult psychopathological population and looking for antecedents in their school, clinic, or court records will allow him to eliminate a great many possibilities quickly and so to narrow the field to the few

* This example, and the stimulus to this discussion, comes from Kohlberg, LaCross, and Ricks' (1969) paper on the prediction of adult psychopathology from childhood data. Their evaluation of follow-up and follow-back methods, however, differed slightly from that reached here.

most likely forerunners of the disorder. Many of the possible antecedents will simply not occur in the research population, or will occur with such low frequencies that they can hardly be considered as related to the adult outcome being considered. Beginning with the adult psychopathological sample, then, will ordinarily be the best way to get rid of wrong ideas. For example, Waring (1966) searched the Judge Baker study cases for various traumatic events commonly considered to cause psychopathology, and found no more in the pre-schizophrenic group than in comparison children who grew up to more adequate adult lives. These findings suggest that dramatic environmental "traumas" are less likely to be antecedents of serious disorder than are everyday long-term influences within the child himself and in his relationships with the people around him. A follow-back method is also likely to open up new possibilities that the researcher has not anticipated. No existing clinical theory, except for Szasz's unpopular argument that most conversion reactions are fakery, would have predicted that "bad conduct" and conversion reactions would occur in the same group, as Roff found, but his results are confirmed by Berry's finding of many hysterical symptoms in boys later diagnosed character disorders, a group that overlaps with Roff's bad conduct service group. This finding, which runs counter to a traditional contrast between neurosis and character disorder that dates back at least to Freud, indicates the value of beginning with adult diagnostic groups and keeping an open mind as their early characteristics are being investigated. The method also has the economic advantage of locating large samples of specific adult outcomes. Comparisons can then be made between the early characteristics and environments of large numbers of schizophrenics, character disorders, alcoholics, and so on, allowing description of both general antecedents of psychopathology and the characteristics specific to the early histories of each group. Since this method begins with adults, it is possible to follow out the course of the adult disorder long enough to differentiate between antecedents of chronicity and recovery and to do reliability studies on various hospital diagnoses, within the lifetime of one investigator.

The alternative design, beginning with a specific group and following it into adult life, also has several advantages, some of which have been described by Hathaway and by Mednick. In general, these are comparable to using a rifle rather than a shotgun in some kinds of hunting. If Mednick is wrong about the relevance of stress reactions, for example, or about the importance of genetic predisposition in predicting schizophrenia, his clear miss offers only the cold comfort of negative success — that is, of showing as decisively as one can at this point that some important ideas are wrong. If he is right, on the other hand, his control over the whole experimental procedure, and the specificity and relevance of his long-term observations will make his data far more convincing than that gathered from the usual records available to an adult-anchored research strategy.

Although both approaches face formidable problems of data collection, the follow-up strategy has generally resulted in more representative designs and more clear-cut methods. The problem of migration and loss of population is dealt with by making the follow-up as complete as possible, attempting to account for all possible outcomes of all people in the sample. These data provide our most reliable prevalence and incidence estimates. Of the 15,000 children seen at the Judge Baker Guidance Center and now adult, only about 1 per cent were found to be diagnosed schizophrenic by a check of the hospitalization records of the state of Massachusetts. How many were missed? In her more complete follow-up of 524 children seen in a comparable clinic in St. Louis, Robins found an incidence of schizophrenia closer to 5 per cent. So one would have to conclude that the Judge Baker sample is a very select group of schizophrenic adults who managed to be hospitalized in Massachusetts, and it is possible that three or four times as many children have been hospitalized outside that state, or privately, and given the same diagnosis. Also, some of Robins most interesting findings relate to early homicides and accidental deaths, outcomes which by their very nature exclude themselves from most adult records. Since migration and sampling problems are so crucial for both follow-up and follow-back study, the best solution seems to be to locate both types in areas of low migration, such as Hawaii, preferably with superb social record systems such as that in Denmark.

The complete follow-up method, though it can ensure a sample representative of any given agency, cannot easily compensate for bias present in the original population. Many private hospitals, child guidance clinics, and court populations are extremely biased to begin with, and research with such populations must take this bias into account. When the method begins with large public school populations, particularly in the early grades, there is less possibility of bias. Probably the best current sample for such a study is the perinatal project population of 50,000 children on whom birth data are available, although, as Roff points out, these children were obstetrics patients of university hospitals, a group that may already be unrepresentative of the large numbers of mothers in America who are poorly fed and inadequately cared for during the course of carrying and bearing their children. We have a great deal of evidence that the mothers on whom we should focus concern are those very women, many of whom are quite disturbed themselves and others of whom are too poor or too frightened to obtain care at expensive and imposing university centers.

To the degree that a complete follow-up is obtained, the two research strategies overlap, and if the follow-up covers all cases, it is possible to approach the data from either end. It is possible to overemphasize the differences between the two methods, and the generally good agreement shown between the results of both types of strategy argues for the utility of both. Both Roff and Hathaway developed a variable (peer rejection, High 8 MMPI) in work with adult-anchored designs, then applied the variable in a prospective study. This may be the optimal strategy to follow.

The conventional wisdom of research design has taught, ever since the primitive times when most of us were in graduate school, that causal inferences can be made only on the basis of experimenter-manipulated variables. To make causal inferences on the basis of mere measures of association, or of correlation, has been considered grossly inappropriate. This point of view is egocentric, and it would deny the possibility of causal inference in nonexperimental fields such as economics, astronomy, and most of genetics, which clearly do deal with causes, but it is still accepted by most psychologists. If we accept it, we must conclude that we can make no causal statements on the basis of merely observed life history data. But fortunately for life history research, current discussions of philosophy of science and of research design put experimental and observational data more on a par so far as causal inference is concerned. Neither method can ever prove causality beyond all reasonable doubt, but suitably designed life history studies can now be considered to investigate causes, and not just correlates, of adult disorder (Blalock, 1964; Campbell, 1963; Yee & Gage, 1968). This fits with the sense of most life history students that we are investigating materials basic to psychopathological outcomes, not mere epiphenomena. With refinement of both predictor data and outcome criteria, life history research will be able to (a) establish precise numerical indices for the homogeneity of both the predictive syndromes and the outcome syndromes, (b) discover what kinds of groupings result in the lowest error scores, and (c) show the extent to which these groupings improve prediction beyond the levels gained with individual symptoms, feelings, community pressures, test scores, or a priori syndromes as predictors.

THE NEXT STEPS

Extrapolating from these papers, we can see that it is fruitful to study the genetic antecedents of disorder and their method of operation in the individual psychopathological life history. But we must also refine and extend twin studies in order to tease out the specific effects of genetic predisposition from other influences toward disorder. The current problem is not to decide whether there are genetic factors in psychological disorders, but to estimate their weights and study their influences on different patterns of development.

Birth data, including the nutritional and health history of the mother, seem crucial to testing the ideas advanced by Stabenau, and in other work by Lane and Albee (1966) regarding the possibility of early biological impairment in the high-risk youngster.

The characteristics of the parents, their relationship with each other, and the kind of environment they create for the growing child need investigation. The research reported here gives little support to either the critical traumatic incident theory of adult disorder or to the idea of critical periods. An important exception to this latter point, however, is the possibility that an episode of depression or family crisis might establish special vulnerability during the early life of the child who is later more disturbed than his siblings. This possibility might be checked by finding a sample of mothers in postpartum depressions and comparing the developmental courses of their children with those born to the same women when they weathered childbirth more serenely. There are also important studies to be done on the ages at which different syndromes "crystallize" into relatively permanent disorders.

Research seems to confirm Healy's clinical intuition that it is always worthwhile to learn the child's own story as well as finding out what parents, teachers, and probation officers have to say about him. The child's feelings about himself and his world, sensitively listened to and recorded by helping people he has reason to trust, appear to be not only reasonably powerful predictors of adult psychopathology, but also convincing explanations of why disorders develop.

The strong and consistent findings with IQ data and with academic achievement make some of these reports, as Robins commented, songs in praise of school records. Given the clear relevance to adult outcome of ability to achieve and to conform (which school records note quite consistently), much more work will be done with this readily available source of childhood information. These data have already exploded the long standing myth of schizophrenic deterioration before hospitalization, a result that indicts the social and stimulus poverty of institutional life for deterioration observed within the hospital. In combination with data on personality and motivation, these data promise to show readily apparent and demonstrably valid early indicators of adult maladjustment.

Peer relationships are also readily studied, appeal to common sense, and consistently predict adult psychopathology. Roff's finding that peer relationships must be taken into account in using school misbehavior—outcome depends on what the other children do about it—suggests that studies of other areas should try to take into account the presence of this powerful and pervasive influence. The counterpart of poor peer relationships is the inner sense of isolation and alienation, which Fleming showed to be a strong predictor of psychopathology.

Data with Scales 8 and 6 of the MMPI indicate that these, by themselves, do not predict schizophrenia, if we mean by that some combination of hospitalization and hospital diagnosis. However, they do something far more important. They locate vulnerable children, and in combination with IQ and social data, indicate that several alternative ways of living with vulnerability can be worked out. Apparently bright young people, especially bright young girls, can "carry" schizotaxic characteristics without becoming schizophrenic, although vulnerability takes its toll in impaired performance in the competitive job and marriage markets. These findings suggest that suitably planned and focused school and vocational guidance might play a major role in preventing schizoid vulnerability from progressing into schizophrenia. This sort of research should appeal to school systems equipped to offer such services. Research might make a demonstration of a rate of schizophrenic "fatalities" below the base rates in groups of children picked for being High 8, low in peer standing, low in IQ, and expressing feelings of vulnerability, anxiety, and isolation. Like the lowering of pilot deaths by adequate selection and training in World War II, such a procedure would have enormous impact on the next generation of work with high-risk groups.

The tests most often used in clinical diagnosis of schizophrenia, such as the Rorschach and TAT, are not represented in the studies reported here. Whether this is because these tests have too low reliability and validity, as some believe, or whether adequately administered and scored projectives will prove helpful in life history research, as I believe, their present status in this research is certainly no basis for more than clinical faith.

Whereas mere enumeration of "traumatic events" seems to have little use in predicting adult outcomes, studies of the ways in which these change relationships between the high-risk child and his surroundings promise to be productive. Mednick suggests that the longer a high-risk child is with his disturbed parent, the greater the possibility of apathy, chronic disorder, and apparent "process" schizophrenic characteristics. On the other hand, children separated from their disturbed parent were more acute, "reactive," and given to the production of mixed sets of behavioral and affective symptoms along with their withdrawal. This result suggests that the difference between the two groups might be differing degrees of pathology in parents who could continue to care for their children and in those who could not. But since even obviously psychotic parents sometimes continue to cling to their children, and healthier parents sometimes see value in residential treatment, this is not a very systematic variable. Research by the Judge Baker group (Ricks & Nameche, 1966) suggests that the crucial difference is that continued association with bewildering and contradictory parents leads to feelings of impotence and apathy, whereas separation tends to stabilize the child in a somewhat less regressed mixture of protest and despair suggestive of the "loss complex" Rochlin (1965) found in depressed people.

It is instructive to contrast the differentiated descriptions of developing psychopathology in these studies and in the few published life histories of disturbed people (Roff, Mink, & Hinrichs, 1966) with the barrenness of developmental data of most hospital-based research. The history of the disorder is not a history of the person, and it is abundantly clear that schizophrenia does not begin with the first hallucination nor character disorder with the first devious manipulation. The "onset" of psychotic symptoms, which usually begins the central narrative of mental hospital reports, is not the first indicator of disorder. Some of the traditional psychiatric distinctions, such as that between organic and functional disorders, seem simplistic when one looks at them in relation to more adequate data. In several of these reports there are indications that organic conditions such as a hyperreactive nervous system or organically based intellectual incompetence can play a strong role in the genesis of such "functional" disorders as schizophrenia. The myth of "acute" disorders, which emerge suddenly in reaction to a particular environmental stress, can hardly survive the clear demonstration that adult disorders have systematically observable long-term precursors. The most pernicious myth, it seems to me, is that modern form of the doctrine of infant damnation that claims every adult schizophrenic was really schizophrenic from birth, but managed to compensate for his schizophrenia until the time he broke down. I do not think any serious geneticist believes this, but many clinicians do, and one often hears that a person who is beginning to show some oddities of behavior is "decompensating." This idea offers an easy rationalization for therapists who make their patients worse rather than better, an effect that has been cogently demonstrated (Bergin, 1967), but it is far too pessimistic about the chances of vulnerable children who may encounter more helpful therapists, teachers, or employers. Adult disorders are developed in relation to a family and a community that fails to stop them, not encapsulated in the personality during infancy, to spring out full blown in reaction to some adult trauma.

A MODEL FOR SCHIZOPHRENIC DEVELOPMENT

If pre-schizophrenic children do not somehow harbor a life-determining bad seed from infancy on, and are not necessarily shut in, but even at times actively unpleasant, rebellious, or difficult (like the rest of us), then we have to develop evolutionary models for schizophrenia. A skeleton sort of model can be sketched out on the basis of these papers and some extrapolations from them (see p. 305). Of course, no one model can summarize all schizophrenic histories. As Berry indicated, there are different routes into schizophrenia, depending on such things as degree of biological deficit, ways in which the parents and the school react to the child's shyness or hyperactivity, how low the IQ and other types of competence are, and so on. It is also frequent, as Roff pointed out, for a child to manifest one syndrome in early childhood and a contrasting one later. Perhaps the most frequent change begins with early attempts to work off chronic hyperarousal by restless overactivity and ends with attempts to escape arousal by avoiding people and work. In these early stages the behavior that is called withdrawal has little in common with the apathy that is seen later, but is instead, as Goldberg said, "alertly guarding against the intrusion of more environment." Another change, most frequent in adolescence, is an exaggerated swing from extreme dependency and symbiotic closeness to a parent into a violent rebellion and defiance, sometimes homicidal or suicidal in its intensity.

The possible sources of vulnerability, and the child's experiences and symptoms, suggest potentially helpful methods of intervention at each stage of development. The values of some of these, such as foster home or residential school placement, and drug treatments to control anxiety, have

Possible Sources of Vulnerability, Early Characteristics, and Potentially Helpful Methods of Intervention in Pre-schizophrenia

Age and Life Stage	Possible Sources of Vulnerability	Relationships, Experiences, Symptoms	Potentially Helpful Methods of Intervention
Before birth	genetic factors poor maternal health poor maternal nutrition attempts to abort		genetic counseling adequate prenatal care
0–2, infancy	birth damage postpartum depression early illness leaving permanent damage restriction and under-stimulation	overly dependent slow in developing speech poor coordination shy	adequate obstetrical care adequate pediatric care treatment for mother's depression early stimulation & training
3–6, early childhood	low IQ low social competence hyperreactive nervous system influence of disturbed family	shy, sensitive, irritable poor peer relationships speech problems awkward and rigid hyperactive	speech therapy physical training nursery school training in socialization
7–12, late childhood	low IQ low social competence poor school achievement disturbed family	shy poor peer relationships teachers report: indifferent, unlikable, stubborn, unhappy, lazy, scatterbrained	tutoring in speech, reading play therapy therapeutic camps & schools family therapy foster home or residential school placement
13–18, adolescence	sexual maturation in self and peers failures in adolescent developmental tasks	poor peer relationships withdrawal, tantrums, defiance feelings reported: vulnerability, anxiety, alienation, unreality some psychotic-like symptoms begin	reality oriented psychotherapy tutoring in school subjects vocational guidance into low-pressure jobs and areas foster home or residential school placement
19–25, early adulthood	failure in young adult social and vocational development	withdrawal despair apathy psychotic syndromes apparent but often not stabilized	drug treatment to minimize anxiety psychotherapy vocational guidance into low-stress areas & jobs institutional care vocational and social rehabilitation

been at least partly demonstrated in life history research. Others, such as vocational guidance into low-stress areas and jobs, are suggested by research results. Some of the methods are useful in modifying or preventing specific disorders, such as reading disabilities or unclear speech, and these changes clearly increase the competence of the child to deal with his environment. Since anything that increases competence may decrease the probability of a schizophrenic outcome, it seems a plausible hunch that these methods also may help prevent schizophrenia.

The model presented here ends with the development of the symptoms leading to hospitalization and the diagnosis of schizophrenia. The progressive changes in schizophrenic symptoms go on during hospitalization as well, as Goldberg showed; some young people who come to the hospital in states of grandiose expansive protest, or in schizo-affective states in which despair is marked, often show spontaneous recovery, and others slip off into apathetic withdrawal, a relatively steady state from which the chances of spontaneous recovery are much reduced. The most extensive available review of the literature on affective factors in schizophrenia (Zubin, Sutton, Salzinger, Salzinger, Burdock, & Peretz, 1961) found that in 159 studies in which the relation of affect to prognosis was reported, the presence of any overtly expressed affect, regardless of its quality or direction, generally related to better outcomes.

The complexity of this model for schizophrenic development, with genetic, biological, familial, school, and community factors all involved in the production of the disorder, suggests that there is not likely to be any dramatic new development that will suddenly indicate one "cure" for schizophrenia. Progress is likely to take the form, on the other hand, of a series of partly effective attempts to intervene in the long process of schizophrenic development, each "little step" of which will chip away at the 1 per cent incidence figure. If increased use of genetic counseling, contraceptive methods that avert botched abortions, improved maternal nutrition and care for children at birth, remedial education, psychotherapy, and vocational guidance reduce the figure to .5 per cent incidence over the next generation the change may appear small, but it will mean approximately 200,000 fewer hopeless lives in mental hospitals. Toward this goal these studies have much to contribute.

REFERENCES

Beck, A. T. *Depression.* New York: Harper, 1967.

Bergin, A. Some implications of psychotherapy research for therapeutic practice. *International Journal of Psychiatry*, 1967, 3, 136–150.

Blalock, H. M., Jr. *Causal inferences in nonexperimental research.* Chapel Hill: University of North Carolina Press, 1964.

Campbell, D. T. From description to experimentation: Interpreting trends as quasi-experiments. In C. W. Harris (Ed.), *Problems in measuring change.* Madison: University of Wisconsin Press, 1963.

Kohlberg, L., J. LaCross, & D. F. Ricks. The predictability of adult mental health from childhood behavior as shown by life history research. In B. Wolman (Ed.), *Manual of child psychopathology.* New York: McGraw-Hill, 1970.

Lane, E. A., & G. W. Albee. Comparative birth weights of schizophrenics and their siblings. *Journal of Psychology,* 1966, 64, 227–231.

Ricks, D. F., and G. Nameche. Symbiosis, sacrifice, and schizophrenia. *Mental Hygiene,* 1966, 4, 541–551.

Robins, L. N. *Deviant children grown up: A psychiatric and sociological study of sociopathic personality.* Baltimore: Williams & Wilkins, 1966.

———, G. E. Murphy, & M. B. Breckenridge. Drinking behavior of young urban Negro men. *Quarterly Journal of Studies on Alcohol,* 1968, 29 (No. 3), 657–684.

Rochlin, G. *Griefs and discontents: The forces of change.* Boston: Little, Brown, 1965.

Roff, M., W. Mink, & G. Hinrichs. *Developmental abnormal psychology.* New York: Holt, 1966.

Ross, S. Reported emotional experiences of disturbed and nondisturbed adolescents. Ph.D. thesis, Teachers College, Columbia University, 1969.

Waring, M. Averting hospitalization for adult schizophrenia: A search for ameliorative factors. *Social Work,* 1966, 2 (No. 4), 34–42.

Yee, A. H., & N. L. Gage. Techniques for estimating the source and direction of change in panel data. *Psychological Bulletin,* 1968, 70 (No. 2), 115–126.

Zubin, J., S. Sutton, K. Salzinger, S. Salzinger, E. Burdock, & D. Peretz. A biometric approach to prognosis in schizophrenia. In P. E. Hoch & J. Zubin (Eds.), *Comparative epidemiology of the mental disorders.* New York: Grune & Stratton, 1961.

LIST OF CONTRIBUTORS AND PARTICIPANTS

List of Contributors and Participants

George W. Albee, Ph.D., Psychology Department, Case Western Reserve University, Cleveland, Ohio 44106

John C. Berry, Ph.D., Napa State Hospital, Imola, California 94558

James K. Dent, Ph.D., Research Psychologist, Adult Psychiatry Branch, National Institute of Mental Health, 9000 Rockville Pike, Bethesda, Maryland 20014

Bernice T. Eiduson, Ph.D., Reiss-Davis Child Study Center, 9760 West Pico Boulevard, Los Angeles, California 90035

Patricia Fleming, Ph.D., Counseling Center, Queens College, Flushing, New York 11367

Norman Garmezy, Ph.D., Department of Psychology, University of Minnesota, Minneapolis, Minnesota 55455

Solomon C. Goldberg, Ph.D., Assistant Chief, Clinical Studies Section, Psychopharmacology Research Branch, National Institute of Mental Health, 5454 Wisconsin Avenue, Chevy Chase, Maryland 20203

Starke R. Hathaway, Ph.D., Director, Division of Clinical Psychology, Department of Psychiatry and Neurology, University of Minnesota, Minneapolis, Minnesota 55455

Donald F. Klein, M.D., Director, Research Department, Hillside Hospital, Glen Oaks, New York 11004

C. James Klett, Ph.D., Chief, Central Neuro-Psychiatric Research Laboratory, Veterans Administration Hospital, Perry Point, Maryland 21902

Ellen A. Lane, Ph.D., Department of Psychology, Case Western Reserve University, Cleveland, Ohio 44106

Maurice Lorr, Ph.D., Department of Psychology, The Catholic University of America, Washington, D.C. 20017

Sarnoff A. Mednick, Ph.D., New School for Social Research, 66 West 12th Street, New York, New York 10011

Elio D. Monachesi, Ph.D., Chairman, Department of Sociology, University of Minnesota, Minneapolis, Minnesota 55455

Max Pollack, Ph.D., Senior Research Associate, Hillside Hospital, Glen Oaks, New York 11004, and Department of Psychology, Queens College, Flushing, New York 11367

William Pollin, M.D., Chief, Section on Twin and Sibling Studies, National Institute of Mental Health, Bethesda, Maryland 20014

Diane M. Ramsey-Klee, Ph.D., Reiss-Davis Child Study Center, 9760 West Pico Boulevard, Los Angeles, California 90035

David F. Ricks, Ph.D., Department of Psychology, Teachers College, Columbia University, New York, New York 10027

Lee N. Robins, Ph.D., Department of Psychiatry, Washington University School of Medicine, St. Louis, Missouri 63110

Merrill Roff, Ph.D., Institute of Child Development, University of Minnesota, Minneapolis, Minnesota 55455

Susan Salasin, Research Fellow, Division of Clinical Psychology, Department of Psychiatry and Neurology, University of Minnesota, Minneapolis, Minnesota 55455

Fini Schulsinger, M.D., Psychological Institute and Department of Psychiatry, Kommunehospitalet, Copenhagen, Denmark

James R. Stabenau, M.D., Chairman, Department of Psychiatry, University of Connecticut School of Medicine, Hartford, Connecticut 06105

John Strauss, Ph.D., Chief, Psychiatric Assessment Section, National Institute of Mental Health, 9000 Rockville Pike, Bethesda, Maryland 20014

Robert D. Wirt, Ph.D., Director, Clinical Psychology Training Program, University of Minnesota, Minneapolis, Minnesota 55455

Margaret G. Woerner, Ph.D., Research Associate, Hillside Hospital, Glen Oaks, New York 11004

INDEX

Index